their own separate wallpaper, colors, and program settings. As long as you're on the network, your user profiles will be available, so you can have your own familiar desktop greet you no matter what machine you log onto. The default behavior of Windows 95, however, does not use profiles. In this video, you'll learn how to tell Windows 95 to use them.

• System Resources Monitoring— `Sysres.avi`

System resources have been a problem since Windows 3.0. They're *less* of a problem under Windows 95, but they can still cause you troubles. System resources are a small area of memory that Windows uses to keep track of all of the programs and program components currently running on your system. In this video, you'll see how to monitor system resources and you'll gain some insight into how you can run out of resources even when you're not running any programs.

• Network Neighborhood Secrets— `Netnav.avi`

If you're connected to a network, Windows 95 makes viewing and using network resources simpler than ever. This video shows you how to use the Network Neighborhood to browse a workgroup, and then go on to browse your entire enterprise network. You also learn how to designate which workgroup and domain your system is a part of.

• A Guided Tour of the Network Applet— `Netctrl.avi`

If you've viewed the previous videos on networking, then you have noticed how important the Network applet in the Control Panel is to defining and controlling networking under Windows 95. In this video, you'll take a guided tour of this applet, showing you every aspect of this extremely important—and often confusing—part of Windows 95.

• The Registry Editor Revealed!— `Regedtex.avi`

You're not a true Windows 95 expert until you're comfortable with the Registry Editor. This video provides an example of using the Registry Editor by demonstrating the *undocumented* way to change the name of the Recycle Bin.

Utilities from AllMicro on the Enclosed CD

The enclosed CD also contains special tryout versions of two useful utility programs from AllMicro:

• Skylight™

Skylight is a troubleshooting utility that allows you to uncover the mystery of how Windows is using your computer's resources. Skylight runs transparently as a Windows 3.1 application, and displays accurate real-time information about your system's memory usage. The program's built-in editor lets you easily edit WIN.INI, SYSTEM.INI, CONFIG.SYS, and AUTOEXEC.BAT.

• AllMicro AntiVirus™

AllMicro AntiVirus offers the most complete solution for the detection and elimination of thousands of computer viruses. Provides vital security by protecting your computer from all known viruses and alerting you to any new viruses entering the system. AllMicro AntiVirus verifies the security of your boot sector, partition table, LAN drives, and files—even if compressed. As an added protection, this program provides a heuristic program that, when activated, searches for behavior patterns that indicate the presence of potential viruses that might otherwise be undetectable.

The Expert Guide™
to Windows® 95

MARK MINASI

with Patrick Campbell and Christa Anderson

SYBEX • *San Francisco • Paris • Düsseldorf • Soest*

ACQUISITIONS MANAGER: Kristine Plachy
DEVELOPMENTAL EDITOR: John Read
EDITOR: Doug Robert
TECHNICAL EDITORS: Denise Martineau, Jon Gourdine
BOOK DESIGNER: Suzanne Albertson
TECHNICAL ARTISTS: Elizabeth Creegan, Catalin Dulfu
DESKTOP PUBLISHER: Dave Bryant at London Road Design
PRODUCTION COORDINATOR: Kimberley Askew-Qasem
INDEXER: Ted Laux
COVER DESIGNER: Ingalls + Associates
COVER PHOTOGRAPHER: Mark Johann
CD: Dan Tauber

SYBEX is a registered trademark of SYBEX Inc.

TRADEMARKS: SYBEX has attempted throughout this book to distinguish proprietary trademarks from descriptive terms by following the capitalization style used by the manufacturer.

Every effort has been made to supply complete and accurate information. However, SYBEX assumes no responsibility for its use, nor for any infringement of the intellectual property rights of third parties which would result from such use.

Library of Congress Card Number: 95-72703

ISBN: 0-7821-1519-5

Manufactured in the United States of America

20 19 18 17 16 15 14 13 12 11

This is dedicated to my wife, Darcee. Usually authors dedicate books to their wives "for all the patience she's shown while I wrote this," but I'm dedicating this to her because I'm crazy about her.

Acknowledgments

AS with most of my books, this Sybex book grew out of one of my company's technical seminars. As with so many of our successful seminars, much of the credit must be given to our sponsor, Jess Sieple, owner of Alexander Hamilton Institute, the marketing firm that handles many of our seminars.

The pace of software change—notice I didn't say "innovation"—has made it harder to turn out books like this one in a timely fashion. Once, I could do it myself, but *this* book couldn't have been done in the time that it was without my co-authors, Patrick Campbell and Christa Anderson. You see Patrick's work in the chapters on Novell and Remote Access; Christa wrote the Registry, Failure Recovery, and DOS Programs chapters. Having said that, however, I of course assume responsibility for any errors in the book. The MMCO research assistants Holliday Ridge and Leslie McMurrer provided invaluable assistance in editing and proofreading—very little gets past them! I thank them both for their essential role in creating this book and in helping to make it as error-free as possible. Thanks also to my management team of Donna Cook, Ceen Dowell, and Patrick Campbell, for shielding me from the outside baloney while I wrote this.

I would be amiss if I were to forget to mention IBM for their VoiceType Dictation Adapter for Windows. I was afflicted with carpal tunnel syndrome (the "black lung" of writers, I suppose!) while putting this together under tight deadlines. Though the version I have was not designed for Windows 95, it worked fine under Windows for Workgroups, and allowed me to write chapters 1, 2, 3, and 5 while my wrists were healing. Get those 95 drivers written, guys—my wrists are getting sore again!

Sybex's Master of the Written Word, the one and only Gary Masters, was the man who commissioned this book, and without his leadership this and many other useful tomes might never have seen the light of day. Our editor Doug Robert brought keen insights to the process, and clarity to the most confusing topics, and for that I give my thanks. If it weren't for Kristine Plachy, we'd still be waiting for the betas; thanks, Kristine. And darn, but do I miss Rudolph Langer! This was one of the last books that Dr. Langer approved before leukemia stole him from us. Wherever you are, Rudy, I'm sure you're getting some great books ready for the rest of us when we join you, if we're that lucky. There are no doubt other people who were part of putting this book together, and to those whom I have left out here, I apologize.

CONTENTS AT A GLANCE

TABLE OF CONTENTS

INTRODUCTION

WELCOME to *The Expert Guide to Windows 95*! Before we start discussing VxD's, Plug and Play, the Registry, and whether to use the Microsoft NetWare Client or the Novell NetWare Client, let me take a couple of pages and explain how this book is different from other Windows 95 books, and what's in it.

The massive pre-marketing of Windows 95 led book publishers to stoke the literary engines and churn out Windows 95 books by the dumpster-full, even before the product was available. What's this book got that others don't?

Well, most Windows books fall into one of two categories. The first kind, of which this book is most certainly not a member, are the "click and drag" books, the books that teach you how to use Windows 95; they introduce you to the GUI, discuss whether to use My Computer or Explorer, mention that there's a thing called the Registry, and offer a cook's tour of the Control Panel. The second kind is the "tips and tricks," "power user," or "secrets" kind of Windows 95 book. These books tell you that right-clicking the Inbox in 4/4 time while holding down the Alt key and whistling "The Bridge Over the River Kwai" will present a hidden 10-minute video of Bill Gates expounding on the virtues of good dental health.

Secrets are terrific things; it's fun to know them (particularly when your friends and coworkers don't), but, to me, a "secret" is just an example of incomplete documentation on Microsoft's part. I've spent 13 years as a PC support person and technical teacher, and as far as I'm concerned, the greatest secrets are the answers to the questions, "How does Windows 95 *really* work, and how can I *keep* it working?"

That's what this book is all about. Over the past six years, Sybex and other computer publishers have been kind enough to publish ten of my books,

books which are usually modifications of the course books that I use for my technical seminars. If you've ever picked up *The Complete PC Upgrade and Maintenance Guide, Mastering Windows NT Server*, or *Troubleshooting Windows*, for example, then you know what to expect: I'll explain how something works, and how sometimes it *doesn't*, and from there it's usually simple to see how to fix it. That's the basic approach of *this* book as well, with one more part added: *examples*. Nothing frustrates me more than reading something technical that lacks examples. Sadly, that describes most of the technical Windows 95 literature, so I've tried to include as many examples as possible.

Basically two kinds of people will find this book useful: PC support people and power users. When I say "PC support people," I mean anyone who has to solve a Windows problem—like "my PCMCIA card isn't recognized," "the Network Neighborhood folder is empty," or "I need to disable a system policy." It could be a person at home using Windows 95 to keep his checkbook, or it could be someone working on her company's Help Desk. As to power users, well, you know who you are.

Overview of the Contents

The book starts with a technical overview of Windows 95. In Chapter 1 you'll learn a bit about how the GUI works, discover that Windows 95 is not all that terribly great a leap from Windows for Workgroups 3.11, and find out if Windows 95 or Windows NT is the right 32-bit operating system platform for you.

Chapter 2 discusses the structure of Windows 95 with a look "under the hood" to find components with names like GDI, VMM32, and Configuration Manager. You'll need this understanding of the parts of Windows so you'll know where to go to fix problems. After all, if you didn't understand the parts of your car, you might pop the hood when trying to fix a flat tire.

Chapter 3 looks at setting up Windows 95. Sure, it's a simple matter to shove the CD into the drive and type *setup*, but this chapter looks beyond that, and provides some help for those who must install and reinstall Windows 95 on a number of machines. The secret to simplifying Windows installations is to write a Windows "installation batch file," which you'll learn to do in this chapter.

One of the newest and most important concepts for PC support people is the Registry. In Chapter 4, my co-author Christa Anderson adapted a chapter from our NT book (NT has a Registry as well) to explain what the Windows 95 Registry is, how you'd work with it, what you can do with it, and when *not* to do anything with it.

Chapter 5 begins a string of chapters about networking with Windows 95. This large chapter is an introduction to networking under Windows 95. You'll learn about protocols, network binding interfaces, client software, browsers, and the like here. It's the starting point for Chapters 6 through 8.

Chapter 6 is for the folks out there trying to make Microsoft's desktop operating system (Windows 95) work with Novell's network operating system (NetWare). You have a choice under Windows 95 about how to access a Novell server. You can either use programs written by Novell or some written by Microsoft. Choosing which to use isn't simple, and my co-author Patrick Campbell leads you through the pieces of NetWare connectivity in this chapter.

Patrick then returns in Chapter 7 with lots of information about Dial-Up Networking, the essential part of Windows 95 that makes remote networking possible. Dial-Up Networking has a bunch of nice features that aren't documented very well by Microsoft, and Patrick attempts to fill in the gaps.

Chapter 8 shows you how to leverage your network in order to use it as a PC support tool. You'll learn how to simplify Windows 95 installations by using your network, for starters. Then you'll see how to use User Profiles to allow your favorite desktop settings to follow you around the network. Profiles are even useful if you *don't* have a network, as they make it possible for you to share a computer with other users while keeping your desktop settings separate from theirs.

In Chapter 9, Christa discusses how to handle Windows 95 crashes. As Windows 95 is almost an "all-in-one" operating system, some kinds of failures are simple PC boot failures. The causes of boot failures are the same no matter what operating system you're running, so she's taken a discussion of disk failure recovery from one of my previous books and expanded it to include specifics of Windows 95, then added new sections on the Windows debugging switches and BOOTLOG.TXT, an invaluable diagnostic tool.

Now that DOS is dead, you'll have to install all of your new hardware under Windows 95. Even though Windows 95 is meant to relieve you of ever needing to deal with the arcane details, it can't do it for every piece of hardware out there, so chances are that someone you work for is going to ask you for the details anyway. It can get a little tricky; not only must you know the Control Panel, you have to understand IRQs, DMAs, I/O addresses, and so on. Chapter 10 takes you through the process, including a discussion of Plug and Play, the centerpiece of Windows 95's hardware support. What's that, you say? You don't have a Plug and Play computer? Well, if you have Windows 95, then think again—you *do* have a Plug and Play computer. It's all in Chapter 10.

Chapters 11 and 12 look at those two most important peripherals, disks and printers. You'll learn how to install new ones, diagnose problems on existing ones, and how to rev up their performance a bit.

Finally, in Chapter 13, Christa shows you how to run existing DOS programs on Windows 95. Wondering what all those settings are in the property sheets for your DOS programs? You can find out here.

That's what you'll find in this book. If you found something that you liked, or something that you didn't like, or if you think that we should have covered something in more detail, then drop me a line. You can find me at mark@www.mmco.com. Thanks for reading, and I hope this book makes your life as a Windows "techie" easier!

Typesetting Conventions

When you're talking about a new operating system, with new ways of naming files and new ways of envisioning user input and command prompts, you have to keep clear when you're talking about the new way and not the old way. In this book my editors have tried to enforce some consistency on these things to help reduce the confusion inherent in the process.

Here are a few of the conventions used to differentiate between the types of elements you'll run into in this book:

- DOS-style filenames (which follow an eight-dot-three convention) are usually shown in a special filename typeface, all uppercase.

  Example: `SYSTEM.DAT`

- Long filenames, now available with Windows 95 and any 32-bit application, are shown in the same special filename typeface, with upper/lowercase distinctions as maintained by the program or author.

  Example: `Steering Committee's version of 96 facilities budget.DOC`

- Directory and folder names are also shown in the filename typeface (and usually lowercase).

  Example: `C:\windows\mmco\windows95 book\ch01`

- File contents (for example, entries in the `WIN.INI` file), are shown in regular text, not in a special font.

  Example: "In the [UserInfo] section, the device= and timercount= lines are optimized for a single-server configuration."

- Resources that you have *named* (for purposes of sharing them over a network or making them available to other users) are usually shown in regular text, though in certain situations they're styled as italic to avoid ambiguity.

  Example: "Make your printer available over the network as *HP2 next to watercooler.*"

- Menu commands and options, and options in dialog boxes, are usually regular text, but have been styled as italic whenever it might not be clear that the words you're seeing are part of the option, not part of my instruction to you.

  Example: "Double-click on the Print option on the File menu, or the Properties setting in the Display dialog box" shows option names that are perfectly clear, but "Click on *Update user data while polling*" makes it obvious that I'm not expecting you to wait until *you're* polling to click on the option.

- Text or values you are expected to type into a dialog box or file are shown as boldface.

  Examples: "Enter **2** for the number of copies"; "Change f:\123R3 to **\\server\ted\123R3**"

CHAPTER

1

Windows 95 Overview

WHAT can Windows 95 do for you and your company? Is it worth upgrading? If you've already bought 95, what benefits does it offer over competing operating systems?

In this chapter, I'll touch on many things you'll learn about later in the book. It's not my intention in this chapter to explain any of these concepts in great detail; rather, this is something of a teaser showing you some of what you'll see later.

GUI Improvements

The most visible part of 95 is its *GUI*, its Graphical User Interface. It is an improvement over the older Windows GUI in a number of ways:

- The desktop paradigm is greatly improved over previous versions of Windows.

- Folders that hold things, including other folders, allow a deeply nested storage and management structure.

- Shortcuts make getting to things easier (although they *are* somewhat inferior to the object-oriented shadows found in OS/2).

- The Taskbar makes everything just a few clicks away, and this makes it harder to get confused about what's loaded and what isn't.

- There are many more places to hide things in 95, so the Find option is useful.

- The autorun option on CD-ROMs makes software installation from a CD-ROM easier.

I know that you're probably somewhat familiar with these things, so I'll only examine them briefly.

The Desktop

Like many GUIs, Windows uses a desktop metaphor—your monitor's screen represents an imaginary desktop cluttered with folders, items, and objects like printers or modems. Personally, I've always found the whole desktop idea kind of silly, inasmuch as I can't imagine working in an office with a 14-inch desktop. I spend a lot more time shuffling things around on my tiny computer desktop than I ever did on my real-world desktop. That said, however, the desktop metaphor works in many ways, perhaps most important of which is that you can customize your desktop's colors, fonts, and the things sitting on the desktop. What I'd really like is a six foot by three foot backlit LCD panel about 7000 pixels × 2500 pixels—you know, a *real* desktop. One of these days, I guess…

It's undeniable that the 95 desktop makes a lot more sense than the 3.x desktop did. It's easier to keep things in order and there are more places to put things. Where Windows 3.x required that you fiddle with the Control Panel and the Print Manager to control your printers, for example, 95 only requires that you open the Printers folder and open whichever printer you wish to control.

Multiple Nested Folders

The Windows 3.x and OS/2 1.x user interfaces relied upon a Program Manager to let people choose applications. You could place related applications into *groups*, which were represented as folders in a file cabinet. Unlike folders in a file cabinet, however, you couldn't put a group inside a group.

Windows 95's user interface does away with the Program Manager Instead, Windows creates a directory called `C:\windows\desktop` to which the GUI programs on the screen link. Anything copied t `C:\windows\desktop` shows up on the user's screen and is represente as a small picture called an *icon*. Double-clicking on an icon *opens* that icon. To open an icon means:

- If it refers to a program—that is, if the icon represents a binary program file like the familiar .EXE files—then Windows starts the program.

- If the icon refers to a data file, then Windows looks to see which program is associated with that kind of data file. Then it launches the program and feeds it the data file. (Unfortunately, this association is still only built upon extensions, a pretty simple and dumb way of telling the operating system, or OS, what program to use to start up a file. Perhaps when Cairo arrives, they'll fix that.)

- If the icon refers to a directory on a storage device, then Windows opens up a window displaying the contents of the directory.

Even the disk drive itself is represented (in My Computer) as a series of folders. For those who are interested, the apps you can start straight from the Taskbar are located in C:\windows\start menu. There is a folder called \windows\start menu\programs, which holds folders corresponding to the old Windows 3.x groups. For example, if you upgraded your old Windows implementation or you installed old Windows 3.x applications on a 95 desktop, then you'll have groups. Suppose you've got a group called Lotus Applications, which contains an icon to start up Ami Pro 3.0, and one to start up Freelance for Windows; suppose also you've got a folder called Microsoft Apps, which contains an icon to start up Microsoft Excel 5.0. You'd then have a \windows\start menu\programs directory containing:

- A directory called Lotus Applications, containing a file called Ami Pro 3.0.lnk (note that files can have names longer than eight characters under Windows 95!) and another file called Freelance for Windows.lnk, where the .lnk files are *shortcuts*, something we'll get to in a minute.

- Another directory called Microsoft Apps, containing Microsoft Excel 5.0.lnk.

This is a terrific strength, but it's got a weakness, which you'll see in the next point.

Shortcuts

Suppose you've got (as I do) a directory that you use frequently, but it's four levels down in the directory structure. Whenever you want to get to it, you've got to open My Computer, open up the C: drive, open the first level of the directory structure, ...and so on. What I'd really like is for the directory to be right on my desktop where I can get to it with a click or two, but I don't want to actually move the whole directory.

Similarly, consider commonly used programs. If my word processor sits in C:\amipro, then I don't want to have to open up the C: drive every time I want to start Ami. I *would*, however, like to have Ami on my desktop without moving all of the program there.

In both cases, I'm looking for a Windows *shortcut*. They've had them in the Macintosh world for years and called them *aliases*; OS/2 users have had them for years and called them *shadows*. Basically, a shortcut is just an icon that's a direct path to some other location on disk (even on some other disk, as you'll learn in the "Wired 95" chapter).

NOTE The failure of shortcuts is that opening up their properties gives you the properties of the *shortcut*, not the properties of the original object. The object-oriented version of Windows, which will appear in 1997 or 1998, may remove that limitation.

The Taskbar

Previously, Windows always had a Task List, a simple text list of which programs were active. Now there's the *Taskbar*, which not only lets you see what programs are running, but allows you to launch new ones.

The value of the Taskbar is that it gives you an at-a-glance look at all the loaded programs. Now, when one window obscures another, you don't have to wonder whether it's loaded; instead, just look at the Taskbar. You can not only see what's loaded, you can go to that program with just a click.

Powerful Search Engine Built In

The Windows desktop paradigm essentially takes your disk structure and makes it into your desktop. It's not a *terrible* paradigm (you know what they say about paradigms: "shift happens"), but it *does* imply that there are now many more places to lose a program or a data file. This is why the Find option is nice. You just specify what you're looking for and where to look for it, and the search goes on in the background while you continue to work. You can even tell it to look for particular strings of text. I *do* wish that the Find option were attached to every window instead of just the Taskbar, but it's still a nice feature.

Autorun CD-ROMs

Software vendors can now design an *autorun* CD-ROM, a CD that starts up a program as soon as you insert the disc in the CD-ROM. For example, the Windows 95 disc that I'm working with now has this file called AUTORUN.INF in its root directory:

```
[autorun]
OPEN=AUTORUN\AUTORUN.EXE
ICON=AUTORUN\WIN95CD.ICO
```

Those two lines tell 95 to run AUTORUN.EXE whenever the disc is inserted in the CD-ROM drive. The ICON= line just specifies the icon to use when displaying the CD in the Explorer view.

By the way, if you want to *disable* this feature, all you need to do is open the Control Panel, double-click on System, and choose the Device Manager tab. Then examine the properties of the CD-ROM object and uncheck *Auto-insert notification*.

Document-centric Model

One of the basic parts of Windows 95's design is the notion that users should work with documents, not applications. Each program registers with Windows in the Windows *Registry* what kinds of files the program can create or work with. This is part of how Windows knows how to open a document when you double-click it.

For example, I use Lotus Ami Pro. Prior to Windows 95, I'd create a new Ami document by starting up Ami, then clicking on File ➤ New. Under Windows 95, I just click the File and New menu items from any folder, and I get the option to create many different types of new documents, with Ami Pro as one possible type.

Of course, the basic effect of clicking the document is that Windows starts up Ami Pro; this makes me wonder what the difference is between this new document-centric and the old application-centric model. In any case, document-centricity means that Windows programs are moving away from the MDI approach, where a single Windows program might have one main (or *parent*) window and a bunch of smaller *child* windows within it (a notion Microsoft pushed hard in 3.x), to a program model where you would edit four different documents with four different copies of the word processor. This is something that Microsoft said was a really bad idea in 3.x, but now thinks is a really good idea in Windows 95. *Plus ça change* and all that.... (Actually, yet another example of how things don't change is the fact that it's *still* a pain to use characters outside of the American English set; for the life of me, I couldn't get the previous French fragment to print the lowercase cedilla on my printer. But explaining that would bring up Unicode, a discussion for another day.)

New Support Tools

Windows 95 wasn't just built with ease of use for users in mind. It's also got some good news for PC support people: new support tools. (There's also some bad news, of course: in particular, 95's greater complexity.) Some of those tools include:

- The Network Monitor Agent
- The emergency restore utility
- The configuration backup utility
- The System Policy Editor
- The network batch setup utility

- Remote registry support
- BOOTLOG.TXT

The Network Monitor Agent

With the Network Monitor Agent, you can take the Windows 95 System Monitor and the Network Watcher and extend them across the network to look at other people's workstations. It's also the client part of the Server Management System (SMS), if you use that.

Network Batch Setup Utility

Setting up Windows 3.x over a network required some real rocket science. Windows 95 has programs that will automate two very important parts of network setup: creating the shared directory on the server (NET-SETUP.EXE) and creating the batch files to simplify setup (BATCH.EXE).

Why would anyone care about these two features? Well, Windows 95 is big—it's easy for your Windows directories to reach 60MB. That may be too great a hard disk burden for many companies to inflict on a user's workstation, so some firms prefer to put most of the Windows files on a shared directory on the server. Then they do a network setup on Windows 95, and 95's setup program puts a small subset of its files on each user's workstation. That way, users aren't losing tens of megabytes by installing Windows. NETSETUP.EXE does the groundwork to make network setups possible.

Once it's time to install Windows 95, you have lots and lots of questions to answer. Walking around to dozens of machines clicking the same buttons over and over again gets old fast; this is why you'll like BATCH.EXE. There has always been a way to set up Windows with a response file, a file that pre-answers all the setup questions. It's just been a pain in the neck to actually sit down and figure out how to write one. BATCH.EXE solves that problem by supplying a bunch of dialog boxes and fill-in-the-blanks forms; these in turn generate the .INF files necessary for an unattended installation of Windows 95.

The Emergency Restore Utility (ERU)

Unlike older, simpler operating systems, Windows 95 doesn't all live in one place, and neither does one of your configurations. Backing up a Windows 95 configuration is a bit more complex than backing up CONFIG.SYS and AUTOEXEC.BAT. That's why Windows 95 comes with the Emergency Restore Utility, or ERU. The ERU is a simple little program that just backs up all the important parts of your Windows configuration. On a smaller scale, there is a program called CFGBACK.EXE that allows you to retain up to eight Registries in backup sets.

The System Policy Editor

Through the years, support folks have wished to place bounds on the things that users can do to their individual systems. These desires didn't come out of any fascist need for control, but rather the need to provide a set of safeguards allowing users to work productively in an environment without having to worry about accidentally doing something dangerous that might cost them time or perhaps their work.

With the System Policy Editor, you can restrict the features that can be installed on a Windows 95 workstation and what kinds of changes users can make to big things (like redirectors) and small things (like wallpaper). The System Policy Editor is an extremely important tool for user support, and you'll learn how to use it in greater detail in Chapter 7.

Remote Registry Support

Most of Windows 95's configuration information no longer lives in .INI files, although those .INI files still exist (mainly for compatibility with older Windows apps). I'll discuss the Registry in a few pages, but for now just understand that it contains most of 95's setup and runtime configuration information. What's really interesting about 95's Registry is that, with the addition of a simple service, an administrator can remotely modify the Registries of other machines *over the network*. What that means is that you can examine, diagnose, and repair many network problems without ever leaving your chair.

BOOTLOG.TXT

What a difference a file makes; while earlier versions of Windows would create a BOOTLOG.TXT, it was a poorly organized file of only marginal use. Windows 95's BOOTLOG, in contrast, is better-organized and more likely to be a source of useful information to the Windows troubleshooter.

Improved Networking

A lot of what you just read concerned 95's ability to let you control things over the network. That brings up an important point: 95 and networks are much better friends than were 3.x and networks.

If you were a support person for an operating system before 1995, there was the chance that you might have lived your life and done your job without knowing anything about networks—but if you're a Windows 95 support person, then that's not even remotely possible.

32-Bit Redirector and Drivers

One of the biggest pains about networking in the DOS/Windows days was dealing with huge network drivers and protocol stacks. But under Windows 95, the network drivers, the transport stacks, and the redirectors are all native-mode 32-bit code, meaning that they *don't* live in your machine's bottom 640K. That means that networking capabilities are available to any DOS programs that you run, but those DOS programs don't pay the memory price for network capabilities.

NOTE Windows 95's network drivers are even *hot swappable*. This means that if you start up your computer without a network card in place but insert one while you're working in 95, then the network drivers and other software all load *without requiring a reboot.*

The 32-bit drivers should also be faster than the drivers you've seen in previous versions of Windows or DOS, unless you've been working with Windows for Workgroups. In that case, you won't see much of a difference, as Workgroups always used 32-bit drivers.

Simpler Redirector Interface

Windows 95 now makes it easier to understand what network programs you're loading and what programs you need.

Previous versions of Windows made adjusting your network rather difficult. The Control Panel handled some networking functions, but others were in the Windows Setup program. Under Windows 95, all of networking sits in the Control Panel.

If you imagine networking from a layered perspective, then Windows 95's networking system will make a lot of sense. Windows separates networking into three parts: the board driver, the transport protocol, and the redirector (or, as it is more and more commonly said, the client software).

Novell Redirector Built In

Many of us—67 percent of us, in fact—use Novell software. However, until Windows 95, making Windows and Novell work together has been as much fun as pulling teeth without Novocain. Microsoft has made this integration much easier because Windows 95 includes a complete Novell redirector. Although Microsoft and Novell are not the best of friends, the built-in network support in Windows 95 is far superior to what we *haven't* seen in previous versions of Windows. Windows 95 even gives you the option to use either the Novell-written redirector or a Novell-compatible redirector written by Microsoft.

The version of the NetWare client from Microsoft that ships in the Windows 95 box does not support NetWare 4.x's Novell Directory Services (NDS), but Microsoft has released a revised version of the client software which *is* NDS-aware. You can find it on Microsoft's Web site, www .microsoft.com.

Remote Registry Control and Network-Based Boots

You have probably read of the importance of the Registry in Windows 95. Even more important, in many ways, is the fact that you can store a user's Registry on a network server rather than on the user's workstation computer. This means that centrally controlling registration from a network under Windows 95 will be much simpler than it ever was with Windows 3.1. Additionally, Windows 95 offers a way to install itself on a user's workstation so that most of Windows 95 will live on the server, rather than the user's workstation; this means a tremendous savings in disk space. Of course, this was possible under earlier versions of Windows, but the fact that Windows 95 is an all-in-one operating system makes the network note auction somewhat more impressive.

These features are actually not connected; it is possible to install Windows 95 so it sits mainly on a server, but it is also possible to install 95 on a workstation but edit that workstation's Registry via the network anyway.

Better Kernel

Besides the new GUI, perhaps the most important driving force behind the creation of Windows 95 was the pressing need for a new system architecture. The Windows 3.x architecture was designed to run on 286-based computers. It probably seemed like a good idea at the time, but the corporate world's quick acceptance of 386-based computers soon shone a bright and unattractive light on Microsoft's architecture decisions.

With Windows 95, Microsoft was able to wipe the slate clean and redress many of the shortcomings of the earlier Windows merchants. Windows 95 makes full use of the 386, 486, and Pentium processors in a way that older Windows never could; that's what people mean when they say that Windows 95 is 32-bit.

Superior Multitasking

Most modern operating systems support some kind of multitasking, and Windows 3.x was no exception. Windows 3.x used a form of multitasking, also found in the Macintosh computers, called *cooperative* multitasking. This kind of multitasking is called cooperative because in order for multitasking to work at all, it relies upon the computer's applications to behave cooperatively with each other. If just one application chooses to not cooperate, then the other applications and the operating system can't do anything about it; the system is entirely at the mercy of the uncooperative application.

In contrast, Windows 95 uses a more powerful multitasking method, commonly known as *preemptive multitasking*. With preemptive multitasking, Windows 95 can force an application that is using a lot of CPU time to wait for a brief period and yield CPU time to another CPU-starved application. Related to that feature is the *asynchronous input queue* feature, which was how Windows 3.x handles queued-up mouse clicks. At some point, you have probably seen the hourglass and have waited for it to disappear before Windows would accept your mouse clicks. That was an example of the cooperative nature of Windows 3.x; until one application yielded the mouse, no other applications could receive mouse clicks. Under Windows 95, it is possible for one application to be busy, and yet you can enter mouse clicks to other applications. In fact, there is a new cursor that sometimes appears instead of the hourglass: the launch pointer. The launch pointer indicates that even though Windows 95 is busy with one application, Windows 95 can still pass mouse clicks and keystrokes to other applications.

Now, to hear Microsoft tell the story, Windows 95 will solve all the input queue problems; they say you'll never have to wait again. Unfortunately, that isn't true. It is still possible for an old Windows 3.x program to stop the entire system. For example, my electronic mail program sometimes decides to slap the hourglass up on the screen; when it does that, nothing else happens under Windows 95. When I asked a Microsoft employee about this, he agreed that, yes, it still was possible for an old Windows 3.x program to lock up Windows 95. When I indicated that I had thought that Windows 95 would help this problem, he responded that it was "just a temporary problem, until you upgrade to a Windows 95 version of your electronic mail program."

NOTE   As a matter of fact, the preceding is an observation that can be made in general about Windows 95: To get the most out of Windows 95—and for that matter in order to get many of the features of Windows 95—you must be operating only with applications designed for Windows 95. Just one non-Windows 95 application is sufficient to mess up the entire operating system on your PC.

Access to More Memory

As I mentioned before, one of Windows 3.x's big problems was that it was built for the 286 processor; the 286 processor can only access 16MB of memory, and so Windows 3.x had a problem even trying to use memory above 16MB. In contrast, Windows 95 is built around the 32-bit 386 architecture; that architecture includes a 32-bit memory model, and, as two to the thirty-second power is slightly over 4 billion, Windows 95 can access up to 4GB of memory. (Now, once the 1GB SIMMs become available, we will finally have an operating system that can use them....)

Actually, every Windows 95 program works with a mythical 2GB workspace. That may sound like a lot, but it really isn't. For those of you who are wondering, that doesn't mean that Windows 95 needs 2GB to get started. One of the interesting things about Windows 95 (to me, at least) is that it really only needs as much memory as earlier versions of Windows did; for example, if you work with Windows 3.x now, and you like the way it runs on 4MB, then you will be perfectly happy with Windows 95's performance on that same 4MB system. (That happy person, however, would not be me; I recommend an absolute minimum of 8MB RAM.)

Of course, like Windows 3.x, Windows 95 includes a virtual memory system which allows you to promise more memory than you actually have. For example, if you had an 8MB machine and wanted to run 12MB of programs, then you most likely would not receive an Out of memory error message. Instead, your system would use some of your unused disk space to fill in as memory, making up the difference between your true 8MB and the 12MB that your programs need. In that sense, Windows 95 is similar to the older version of Windows—but that is also where the two differ. As you will see in Chapter 11, Windows 95 uses a completely different approach to allocating and maintaining virtual memory.

More Resources

And speaking of memory, one of the oldest Windows problems has been that of resources. It was not uncommon to find that you had plenty of free memory under Windows 3.x but were unable to run any more programs. What kept you from running those programs? Simple: something called *system resources*. You see, Windows needs small scratchpad spaces to keep track of what is on your Windows screen and of what Windows is managing. Those scratchpad areas are called system resources. There's nothing wrong with the idea of resources, but under earlier versions of Windows, the total amount of space set aside for resources was far too small. The result? You might have plenty of RAM, but not enough resources, and so you'd often see Out of Memory errors, despite having plenty of memory.

Why were resources so very scarce under Windows 3.x? Well, remember that Windows 3.x was based on the 286 technology, which was a 16-bit technology. Two raised to the sixteenth power is 64K, so system resources were held to 64K. Given this explanation of the limits based on 286 technology, you would assume that system resources under Windows 95 would be 32-bit, or 4GB in size.

Well, that's almost true, but for purposes of backward compatibility, Windows 95 continues to retain some 64K-sized resource areas. As a result, it is still *possible* to run out of resources under Windows 95—it's just a little harder than before. Nevertheless, the frustrating fact is that resources are still a way of life under Windows 95; that is why you may find that using some of Windows 95's more advanced features, such as OLE 2.0, may be only a pipe dream. It's hard to say whether this will really be the case;

presently, there aren't enough 32-bit applications around to allow for real, honest-to-God testing.

No Speed Loss

I mentioned this a page or two ago, but it's worth re-emphasizing: Windows 95 really does get as much done in 4MB of RAM as Windows or Windows for Workgroups did. As a matter of fact, in some specialized instances, it can do a better job. That's not to say, however, that you shouldn't be looking to buy more RAM when you upgrade to Windows 95. While I recommend 8MB minimum, 16MB is much more useful, and even then, if you're buying a new machine, make sure that it lets you upgrade your RAM to 64MB or more—you may want it soon enough.

Better Protection Model

All Intel processors since the 286 have supported a memory protection model. This model makes it possible for two programs to run in the same computer without stepping on each other. This protection system is built upon a four-level privilege model; the purpose of those four privilege levels was to simplify the assignment of memory control to different programs in the computer. For example, we obviously want the kernel to know more about the system than an application does.

Windows 3.x, however, was not built with the protection model in mind—in fact, Windows 3.x ignored the protection model altogether. That led to a host of problems, including the infamous and dreaded GP fault.

Windows 95 is much better suited to the Intel protection model and exploits this feature much better than did Windows 3.x. This means that you can more easily ferret out troublesome programs under Windows 95 than under Windows 3.x.

New File System

One of the most frustrating things about designing the new version of Windows probably wasn't the problem of how to build a brand new operating system—more likely, it was the need to preserve backward compatibility with the *features*, or as we better know them, the *weaknesses* of old versions of Windows. Perhaps one of the most frustrating weaknesses was the file system. Known as the File Allocation Table, or FAT system, it was originally defined as a means of keeping track of data on floppy diskettes. Among other things, the FAT file system had the requirement that no file name could be more than eight characters long, with the option of a 3-character file extension.

Windows 95's design team must have wanted very badly to throw away the FAT altogether and build a new file system. But eliminating the FAT would also have eliminated any hope that Windows 95 would have for winning over the marketplace, inasmuch as the FAT file system is integral to many existing DOS and Windows 3.x applications.

Windows 95 solves the problem of backward compatibility in an ingenious way: The designers of Windows 95 managed to retain compatibility with eight-dot-three while at the same time allowing for filenames under Windows 95 to be up to 256 characters long. This is managed, without loss of backward compatibility, with a neat trick. When Windows 95 saves a file name whose length is greater than eight characters, Windows 95 simply stores two separate directory entries. One of these directory entries is the long filename, encoded in a way that DOS or old Windows would never see it or look for it; thus, this kept any problems from arising in the first place. Then Windows 95 creates a special filename that fits within the DOS eight-dot-three filename constraint, truncating the name using a simple algorithm. For example, a file named `Letter to my boss.doc` would be saved as `LETTER~1.DOC`. These short filenames are unique, but, unfortunately they are not very clear. This implies that using files with long names under an old DOS or Windows program will take a little getting used to; however, the compromise seems to be a good one.

Compatibility with NT Applications

Perhaps Windows 95's best feature is what I think of as its "self-destruct" feature. Windows 95 has some basic architectural flaws that probably cannot be designed away. That will be true no matter whether it's Windows 96, 97, 98, or 2099. The only way to build a robust, reliable, powerful operating system is to cut the cord with some of the older DOS and Windows applications and build a whole new operating system from the ground up. Now, that isn't practical today; there are too many of those old DOS and Windows applications on the market. Introducing an operating system that did not support these apps would be, as I mentioned about the file system, simply suicidal. But in just five short years, from 1989 to 1994, people put aside DOS programs and adopted Windows programs. Over the next few years, people will similarly adopt Windows 95 programs and put aside their old Windows 3.x programs. Once the market has reached a critical level—let's say 80 percent of applications are Windows 95 applications—then an interesting thing will happen.

You see, Windows 95 programs aren't *really* Windows 95 programs—that is to say, there's no such thing as a Windows 95 development system. Rather, there is a system called Win32 which describes the Windows 95 development system. It also happens to be the Windows NT development system, so you can really say that Windows 95 programs are Windows *NT* programs, at least for business applications.

More Complete DOS Support

Now, I just got through telling you that in a few years DOS and old Windows programs will be unimportant, but we're not there yet. In fact, one of the lingering and nagging problems about Windows 3.x was that it could not run every DOS program. In particular, Windows had problems with game programs (for which, of course, we hard-working business people have no need) and memory-hungry DOS programs, ones requiring more than, say, 550K of free conventional memory (for which we hard-working business people *do* have a great need).

Windows 95 can run a much wider array of DOS programs than the older Windows ever could. The first way that it accomplishes that is in its new and improved virtual machine model. If Windows 95 deems it necessary, it can actually reboot your system to a minimal configuration, allowing the DOS program to control the system as much as it could want to. In this case, however, Windows 95 would stop running in the background. Thus, for many of us this is not a terribly useful feature, but it's better than not being able to run the DOS program at all.

Perhaps more interesting is the memory question. Under Windows—or rather, I should say, under Windows *and* DOS—there was a heavy memory hit for supporting networks, SCSI devices, and indeed Windows itself. Only by the application of some memory manager black magic could a DOS session get more than 480K of memory. If you've never done it, try this out: open up a DOS session under Windows 95 and type **mem**. Without doing any memory management at all, I'd be surprised if you didn't end up with at least 550K of free memory—and there are still tricks that you can do to squeeze out even more RAM!

That's not to say, however, that Windows 95 will run all DOS programs and provide one hundred percent backward compatibility. In particular, you may find that Windows 95 will not support device drivers for some older hardware. It might not be a bad idea to contact your hardware vendors (assuming, of course, that they still exist) and find out whether or not their hardware is Windows 95-compatible. (Unfortunately, some vendors will simply use that as an excuse to sell you some new hardware.)

What's NOT New: VxD's, VFAT, VCACHE

Microsoft would have you believe that Windows 95 is all-new and completely different from previous versions of Windows. Certainly, much of Windows 95 *is* different, but more of Windows 95 is older stuff.

Virtual Machine Managers Aren't New

Windows 386, announced in 1988, introduced a virtual machine manager—and a look at Microsoft's device driver development kit for Windows 95 shows that *some of the original Windows 386 code is still there!*

Windows 3.0 introduced the idea of the 386 enhanced mode. This mode replaced the old system BIOS and device drivers with 32-bit protected-mode device drivers. If you still have Windows 3 around, just look in the SYSTEM.INI file under the [386enh] section and you'll see remains of device drivers like device = vmd. In this case, VmD means virtual mouse driver; there is also a VkD, a virtual keyboard driver. Look further, and you will see many of these virtual drivers. There are so many of them with similar names—virtual "something" driver—that they were given a generic name: VxD's. Those VxD's have not disappeared in Windows 95; in fact, they are a basic architectural element.

You can think of VxD's in this way. You know how much trouble TSR's or device drivers have given you under DOS? Well, VxD's will be as much trouble under Windows 95. They'll be a blessing and a curse. If someone says that something is impossible under Windows 95, then some clever programmer may think, "But not if I wrote the right VxD..."

The 32-Bit File System Isn't New

As I have mentioned before, one of the best features of Windows 95 is its "32-bitness"; part of that feature is a set of 32-bit drivers for accessing the hard disk. Of course, DOS used a 16-bit disk driver, but what did Windows 3.x use? Well, it depended on which version you used. Windows for Workgroups had a neat 32-bit file system which is basically the one included in Windows 95. (During the beta test process of Windows 95, the program was called *Chicago*; since I live in Washington, D.C., I called Windows for Workgroups *Cincinnati* as it's halfway to Chicago.)

There are two parts to the 32-bit file system: the virtual FAT (VFAT) and the virtual cache (VCACHE). Those two parts of Windows 95 are lifted almost entirely from Windows for Workgroups.

Now, you may be recalling a different 32-bit part of Windows, and recalling it with chagrin—32-bit *disk access*. That was a feature of Windows 3.x, and it was one that I never recommended that people use, as it just wasn't reliable. But the years have gone by, and Microsoft seems to have worked out the bugs from the 32-bit disk system, so I can now recommend it in good faith.

Lots of 32-Bit Is Really 16-Bit

And the ubiquitous 32-bitness of 95 isn't really accurate. Many of the 32-bit calls to Kernel, GDI, or User just get 16 zeros subtracted from the front of them and then get passed on to the 16-bit Kernel, GDI, or User; this process is called *thunking*. There are lots of thunks in Windows 95.

There's a good reason for that. First of all, the 16-bit code is already working and well-understood. Second, 32-bit code will be larger than 16-bit code, meaning Windows 95 would require more RAM to run if it truly was 32-bit. And, finally, there are a *lot* of function calls that don't benefit from 32-bitness: the time of day can fit very nicely into 16 bits, for example.

And incidentally, even 32-bit code isn't new; it was possible to run many Win32 programs under Windows for Workgroups with a tool called Win32S.

But DOS Is Gone, Right?

And if you still doubt whether there's old code remaining in Windows 95, try pressing Shift+F5 when booting; the resulting C:\> will no doubt look somewhat familiar.

You may recall that DOS 6 introduced a disk compression utility called DoubleSpace. Other (and better) disk compression utilities existed at the time, but one interesting thing about DoubleSpace was that DOS loaded it without requiring a device= statement in CONFIG.SYS; this is called the *preload* feature. It just means that certain device drivers are implicit.

Windows 95 boots just like that. Where MS-DOS was based on two programs named IO.SYS and MSDOS.SYS, Windows 95 uses a single program called IO.SYS, and that program preloads not only the disk compression routines, but also HIMEM.SYS (the memory manager), IFSHLP.SYS (the redirector), SETVER.EXE, and WIN.COM. So DOS is still there, all right.

Is This Bad?

Does this deceit spell bad news for 95? No, not really. It's just sad that Microsoft has spent so much ink and air time explaining that 95 contains all new, rewritten-from-the-ground-up code when it's not true. Windows 95 is 95 percent marketing, and 5 percent new technology. But, you know, there's another word for new code—*untested* code. Personally, I don't mind that much of 95 has been around since '88. But, as they say, the acorn doesn't fall far from the tree, meaning that there are things that 95 will probably never do as well as a freshly built system would. Hey, did somebody mention NT?

Basically, Windows 95 is just Windows for Workgroups with a new user interface and a centralized device manager with Plug and Play support.

Which Is Better for You, NT or Windows 95?

It can be confusing when you consider that Microsoft offers two PC-based, 32-bit operating systems: Windows 95 and Windows NT. Which one will work best for you?

Well, in the long run, Windows NT is more powerful. It has a rock-solid memory protection system, a no-nonsense multitasking system that even my electronic mail program can't lock up, a C2-compliant security system, and all in all, it's an industrial-strength operating system. Of course, there are some down-sides to Windows NT; that's why Microsoft sells Windows 95. Windows 95 is superior to Windows NT insofar as:

- 95 requires less memory.
- 95 runs faster on a given machine.

- 95 supports a wider array of drivers.

- 95 runs more applications than Windows NT.

- 95 costs less than NT.

The major argument against NT and in favor of 95 is the fact that NT really requires 16MB of RAM to operate minimally well, and Windows 95 can provide the same level of usefulness with just 8MB of RAM. Someday the price of RAM will fall—that day has certainly been long enough in coming—but for now the difference in price between an 8MB workstation and a 16MB workstation is significant. In a practical sense, then, the price of NT is hundreds of dollars higher than it would be if memory were cheaper. Additionally, the software price of NT is higher; where 95 costs around one hundred dollars, NT workstation costs over three hundred dollars. I hope Microsoft changes that pricing policy, but that's up to them.

Memory is not the only difference between 95 and NT on any given machine. Speed is also important. For example, I am writing this on a 75 MHz laptop computer that sometimes runs Windows 95 and sometimes runs Windows NT. When running 95, the laptop usually seems faster than when running NT. However, one reason 95 seems faster than NT is that 95 takes less time to load a program than NT does. When you're actually *running* the program, however, 95 may not be that much faster than NT. The fact that 95 starts programs faster certainly makes it *seem* faster, however.

Although 32-bit apps will often run faster under NT than under 95, 16-bit applications will run more slowly, because NT must monitor 16-bit applications closely. Existing Windows 3.x apps will run much more quickly under Windows 95. Of course, when they crash under 95, they can crash the whole system, something they would *not* do under NT. That's part of the NT/95 tradeoff.

Another important difference between Windows 95 and NT is the availability of device drivers for each. When I teach NT classes or work in NT, I am sometimes frustrated by the fact that there are many pieces of hardware for which I simply cannot get an NT device driver. This has not been a problem for Windows 95—it seems that most hardware out there has 95 drivers either in the box or coming really soon. In contrast, when I ask hardware vendors when they will have the NT drivers done, they tend to hesitate, not wanting *exactly* to tell me to take a long walk off a short pier, but you can tell they are *thinking* about it. However, it's getting better in one major area: network drivers. Windows 95 uses the NDIS 3.1 network driver specification, which, thankfully, is also the network driver specification for NT Version 3.51. That means that any time a vendor creates a network driver for Windows 95, the vendor automatically has a network driver for Windows NT Version 3.51. Now, you might think that the next step would be to unify *all* of the drivers—like hard disk adapters, video boards, etc.—but, unfortunately, that won't be so easy. The built-in secure nature of Windows NT means that merging the NT and 95 driver specification may happen one day, but not this year.

The very same Windows NT security model that makes it hard to unify device drivers is also the reason that Windows 95 runs more old applications than does Windows NT. Any DOS or Windows application that attempts to directly access hardware is rebuffed by NT.

In fact, *no* application under NT—whether it be a DOS application, an old Windows application, or even an NT application—can directly access the hardware, and that's all there is to it. Now, usually this is not a problem, as NT uses the now familiar virtual device drivers to act as stand-ins for the actual hardware. Whenever a device or Windows program requires access to a piece of hardware, NT just lets the virtual device driver fool the DOS application into thinking that it's accessing the actual hardware, and the DOS application is happy.

Unfortunately, that means that the NT designers have to create a virtual device driver for each and every possible piece of hardware. Of course, that's not too terribly hard when you're talking about common hardware: mice, keyboards, displays, and so on. But there is a class of important-but-unusual hardware that isn't prevalent enough to warrant writing a virtual device driver: take fax boards as an example.

Fax applications are perhaps NT's biggest pain. There is no problem with running a fax application designed for NT, but unfortunately there aren't too many available. There *are*, however, lots of them for Windows 3.x, and people want to run those applications under NT. However, NT doesn't like those applications to directly access the hardware, and so it does not allow them to run—thus providing a major incompatibility problem for NT and old Windows applications.

In contrast, Windows 95 has no such qualms. As it's not built with security in mind, it can run just about anything you throw at it. And, at the moment, there are so many DOS and Windows applications around that NT's inability to run a few DOS and Windows applications will hamper its acceptance in the marketplace—at least until a full suite of Win32 applications appears and renders this spotty backward compatibility less important.

Right now, there aren't as many Windows NT applications, mainly because Windows NT has largely assumed a position in the marketplace of a server operating system in a client-server world. Therefore, the most common kinds of applications for NT are big server applications, like database engines; people aren't stumbling all over themselves to write word processors for Windows NT. That *isn't* true for Windows 95; you can be sure that by the time this book is available that there will be bushels of word processors, spreadsheets, electronic mail programs, and the like for Windows 95. And, as I mentioned earlier, since any Windows 95 program is also a Windows NT program, this means that Windows NT will simultaneously find itself with a rich array of compatible applications.

Once people learn how powerful and robust Windows NT is, I think that down the road they will not choose Windows 96, 97, or 98, etc., but instead choose NT 96, 97, or 98, etc.—but that's in the future.

So, in sum, is NT better for you than 95? I think the answer is probably, "Yes, but not yet." NT will beat 95 when:

- Memory prices drop.
- Lots of 95 apps appear (which are NT apps).
- NT gets 95's GUI.
- NT's price drops.
- More NT device drivers appear.

My call on a time for that? Sometime in 1997.

CHAPTER

2

Under the Hood—
An Overview of
Windows 95 Architecture

IN some ways, Windows 95 is an improvement upon old Windows 3.x. But you'd be surprised how much of the creaky old Windows 3.x is in 95—and that will make your support and use of Windows 95 harder.

Much of Windows 95, however is an improvement over previous Windows. In this chapter, you'll learn about the good, the bad, and the ugly in Windows 95.

The Parts of an Operating System

Like all operating systems, Windows 95 has one, and only one, major job: to make your applications and hardware work together. You have purchased applications and hardware, and you want the applications to be able to use that hardware to get your job done. Simply put, all operating systems look something like Figure 2.1.

Let's zoom in on those pieces of a generic operating system before looking specifically at Windows 95.

Applications

As I said before, the main reason for having an operating system—or, for that matter, having any computer at all—is to run the applications that let you get your job done. But applications do not and *cannot* directly access hardware in the computer. (Well, actually, in many systems, the applications *do* access the hardware—but it causes a host of problems, and,

Pieces of an operating
system

```
┌─────────────────────────────────────────────┐
│  ┌───────────────────────────────────────┐   │
│  │ Application(s)                         │   │
│  └───────────────────────────────────────┘   │
│  ┌───────────────────────────────────────┐   │
│  │ Application Program Interface:         │   │
│  │ The set of commands that an            │   │
│  │ application can issue to an OS,        │   │
│  │ like "make file" or "read kbd"         │   │
│  └───────────────────────────────────────┘   │
│  ┌───────────────────────────────────────┐   │
│  │ Kernel:                                │   │
│  │ The overall manager of the             │   │
│  │ system.  Keeps track of multi-         │   │
│  │ tasking, memory management,            │   │
│  │ device allocation                      │   │
│  └───────────────────────────────────────┘   │
│  ┌───────────────────────────────────────┐   │
│  │ Device drivers:                        │   │
│  │ Programs that let the kernel take      │   │
│  │ a generic request, like "read mouse,"  │   │
│  │ and make it specific to a particular   │   │
│  │ piece of hardware                      │   │
│  └───────────────────────────────────────┘   │
│  ┌───────────────────────────────────────┐   │
│  │ Hardware                               │   │
│  └───────────────────────────────────────┘   │
└─────────────────────────────────────────────┘
```

truthfully, that's why we're working with Windows 95 to begin with.) If an application wants to do something like open a file, read a keystroke typed on the keyboard, or put a dialog box up on the screen, then the application does not actually do those things itself; instead, it passes that work to the operating system.

Why doesn't the application do these things? It's really a matter of control, convenience, and division of work.

Control

Control is a concern because most pieces of hardware can only accommodate the request of one piece of software at a time. For example, if three programs all simultaneously say to the disk, "What is the next free disk cluster?" then the disk subsystem could potentially give the same cluster number to all three programs; the result is that all three programs try to write their data to that same cluster. Control is also a concern with modern multitasking operating systems, because as multiple programs run, they all wish to put data on the screen, and to read mouse positions, button clicks, and keystrokes. That's not the problem. The problem lies in how to route the input to the appropriate application. After all, some applications are in the foreground and some are in the background, and no input is intended for every open program.

Convenience

Convenience is of importance because Microsoft, and for that matter *all* operating system designers, want to make writing programs for Windows 95 simple and fast for applications designers. One of the benefits of an operating system should be that it can avoid reinventing the wheel. For example, consider common dialog boxes. Prior to Windows 3.0, designers had to build their own File ➤ Open dialog boxes. You can see this in any older (pre-1992) Windows app; just click File, click Open, and look at the dialog box that results. Try it with six programs and you'll get six different dialog boxes. This is bad for two reasons. First, it makes life difficult for users trying to learn a number of new Windows programs—the things that they learn from the first Windows program do not help them in understanding subsequent Windows programs. And, second, it means that every Windows application designer must waste time reinventing the same old dialog boxes that every other Windows application designer must also reinvent. With Windows 3.1, Microsoft included a set of common dialog boxes, thereby turning a little Microsoft time into a lot of saved developer time. That's an example of the convenience part of an operating system.

Go back far enough in computer history, and you can see that more and more of the problems over which application programmers worried have been subsumed into the operating system. Back in the first days that I programmed a computer, I couldn't just say to the operating system, "get me the next keystroke." Instead, I had to write a routine in my application program that knew how to interrogate the keyboard for keystrokes. Thankfully, that's all over now—that kind of operation is generally considered to be the responsibility of the operating system rather than the application.

Division of Work

The third reason, division of work, is related to the convenience issue. Software nowadays can be so complex (using mice, high resolution graphics screens, huge mass storage devices, and networks, to name a few things) that if every applications designer had to master network programming, diskette driver programming, mouse interface, etc., then only a few very well-funded applications would ever get to market. By dividing an operating system into several pieces, it becomes possible to build and maintain a reasonably priced system.

API's

Anyway, once we believe that an operating system will be of value, the next question is, "How can an application use this operating system?" The operating system lives in one part of the computer's memory and applications live in another part, just as management in a large company works in a different part of the building from the factory workers. It is possible for a factory worker to communicate with a member of management, but usually not by just walking up to the executive suite and banging on the boss's door. Instead, there is usually some kind of well-defined interface—perhaps, in this case, a receptionist.

In the same way, an application that calls upon the operating system by simply emerging into the middle of the operating system can cause problems and the system can crash. That's why applications must access the operating system through well-defined interfaces, called *Application Program Interfaces*, or API's. An API is the published set of legal things that an operating system can do for an application—again, examples would include opening a file, reading a keystroke, or ending a program. Of course, as these are computers, there are i's to be dotted and t's to be crossed; for example, one operating system might open a file with the command `DOSOPENFILE` and another might open a file with the `MAKEFILE` command. Those two commands do the same thing, but they do it in different operating systems, in much the same way that you express the idea "hello" in so many different ways in every language. Windows NT, OS/2, and basic Windows 3.x all used different API's, and so developers have always had to decide on which API to focus their efforts. Because of the size of the Windows market, most vendors work first in the Windows market, then move from there, porting their applications from Windows to some other operating system.

This proliferation of API's, which, as you'd expect, has caused some operating systems to be application-rich while others are application-poor, has merged in Windows 95 and Windows NT into an API called the *Win32 API*. This is extremely important because it means that, as I mentioned in the last chapter, every time someone writes a Windows 95 application, Windows NT will automatically have a new application available for it.

N O T E In addition to the Win32 API, Windows 95 includes older API's of earlier operating systems. As you'd expect, that includes DOS and Windows 3.x.

The Kernel

The heart of the operating system is generally called the *kernel*, a term borrowed from the UNIX world. The kernel is the manager of the entire system. The kernel knows which program is using what memory, which program is currently in the foreground and which programs are in the background, which threads have higher priority than other threads, which programs are printing at the moment, and so on. Here, I am using the term kernel loosely; a little later, you will see that in the Windows world the kernel has several pieces—or, perhaps, I should say lieutenants.

Device Drivers

The kernel doesn't actually *control* anything, except in an indirect way. For example, the kernel never actually asks keyboard hardware whether it has a keystroke ready to be received. The reason why the kernel doesn't do that is that the software to access a keyboard can vary from one type of keyboard to another. Actually, keyboards aren't such a good example, as they are *all* pretty much compatible with one another; video boards or LAN boards are another story.

Once upon a time, operating systems were pretty much built to support only the two or three most popular pieces of hardware in any given hardware category; that wasn't much of a problem, as there often weren't more than two or three brands of a given hardware to begin with. But, as the variety and number of LAN boards, printers, and the like multiplied, it became impossible to include support for every possible piece of hardware in an operating systems kernel—at least, to do that *and* keep the kernel size under .5GB.

So, about twenty years ago, programmers began designing operating systems that had the programs which controlled hardware segregated out into separate smaller pieces of software called *device drivers*. The benefit of device drivers is obvious; for one thing, they can be updated to increase features and remove bugs without having to change the entire operating system. For another, when a new piece of hardware appears, then supporting that hardware is quite easy. All the hardware vendor must do is write a device driver for this new piece of hardware and include it with the hardware; when the user installs the device driver on the operating system, then the operating system immediately recognizes the new hardware.

Of course, that's the *good* side of the story; sadly, there is also a bad side. Suppose you were the hardware vendor creating some new printer, LAN board, or whatever; where would you place your programmer's time? You know that it takes time to write a device driver, and time is money. Will it necessarily pay you to create that Windows NT driver when you could be spending that programmer's time working on an OS/2 driver—an operating system with more users at the moment? As you'd expect, the bottom line is that vendors write the DOS and Windows 95 drivers first, as those are the largest market. OS/2 or Windows NT drivers are the poor stepchildren, and as a result they may not get support quickly—or ever.

Parts of Windows 95

Windows 95's structure parallels the structure of a generic operating system, but with pieces added on. You can see this in Figure 2.2.

FIGURE 2.2

Windows 95's structure

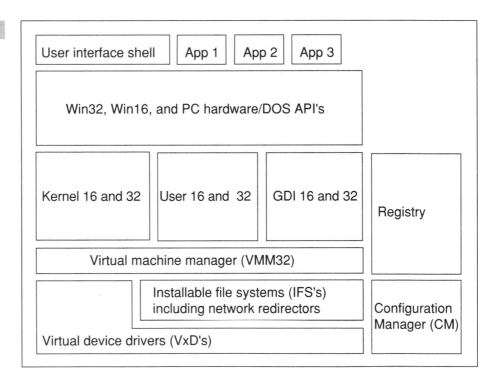

The rest of this chapter explains these pieces and how they fit together.

API's under Windows 95

Okay, that's the overview of how operating systems are put together; now let's look at the specifics of Windows 95. Since API's were at the top of the list, let's look there first.

When Windows was first introduced in 1984, it had a wide variety of possible API calls. When Windows 3.0 appeared, Microsoft added even more calls and adapted Windows to the 286 processor architecture. As the 286 processor was 16-bit, so were the commands that a program could issue to the old Windows operating system; that set of possible commands was called the Win16 API. As you read earlier, Windows 95 has a newer API called Win32. Now, for a developer building a completely new application, Win32 is a good choice; it's more powerful, and in many ways it's easier to code for than was Win16. But there are thousands of older, yet perfectly good, Windows programs around, and if Windows 95 didn't support them then people wouldn't buy Windows 95. That's why Windows 95 includes both the new Win32 API *and* the older Win16 API. That way, it can support older and newer programs simultaneously. And that's not all; don't forget the importance of DOS programs—Windows 95 hasn't. Windows 95 includes a DOS-compatible API, and in fact it appears in some ways better than the API that ships with regular old DOS, as it supports multitasking (and the DOS API does not).

Of all of the operating systems out there, DOS is clearly the hardest one to support, paradoxically because it isn't really an operating system. Although DOS does the things that operating systems are supposed to do—provide low-level services and make the division of labor possible—for historical reasons, programmers do not use the DOS API. Instead, they write their programs to go directly to DOS's device drivers or even to the hardware itself. We'll talk more about this in a later discussion of VxD's, virtual device drivers. (And, by the way, if you're thinking that it's impressive that Windows 95 includes API's for older versions of Windows and DOS, as well as for Windows 95 itself, then take a look at OS/2; it contains API's for older Windows, DOS, older OS/2 versions, *and* modern OS/2 versions. It's kind of the Swiss Army knife of operating systems.) You might say that the true DOS API is a multitasking emulator for the original DOS API, the BIOS, and typical PC hardware.

Kernel Modules

Much of Windows is the "back office" of Windows, so to speak; the job of many parts of Windows is to support drivers and not, directly, applications. Windows programs themselves interact with six main modules I call the kernel modules:

- Kernel16
- Kernel32
- GDI16
- GDI32
- User16
- User32

Kernel16 and 32

As you read a few pages back, the kernel's job is to manage the system and to keep track of who is using what memory, who's using the printer, who has priority, and so on.

The kernel did not make its debut with Windows 95; it has, in fact, existed in Windows for the last few versions. However, as the previous version of Windows was defined for 286 processors, it would only support 16-bit instructions; that's why we refer to the older version of Windows as being 16-bit. One of the big selling features of Windows 95 is the fact that it is built for the 386 and later processors and so it can be 32-bit. For that reason, the kernel was redesigned to use the full power of 32 bits. In order to support older Windows programs, Windows 95 contains both the older kernel (which is referred to as Kernel16), as well as the new kernel, which, as you have probably guessed, is called Kernel32. This will be a pattern that you will see in many Windows components, as Microsoft was forced to retain many 16-bit pieces in Windows 95 in order to assure good backward compatibility.

GDI (Graphical Device Interface)

Like all good managers, the kernel doesn't do all of its work; it farms some of the work out to one of its helper programs called the Graphical Device Interface, or GDI. Like the kernel, GDI existed back in earlier versions of Windows, and so there is a GDI16 and a GDI32.

As you'd imagine from its name, GDI specializes in graphical things. Whenever you put a bitmap on the screen, your request is funneled through GDI. GDI has areas of control that include:

- Bitmaps
- Color
- Cursors
- Icons
- Fonts
- Graphical objects (lines, rectangles, curves, and the like)

GDI is the part of Windows that is activated whenever you try to change the color of a Windows component: a window, a button, or whatever. GDI also worries about fonts; if you have many fonts, then you stress GDI. The more advanced nature of the Windows 95 GUI (as compared to the older Windows GUI) means that GDI has a lot more to do than in previous versions of Windows; that's one reason why it's a good thing that GDI is now 32-bit. You'll see in a later section that GDI must keep track of every color, cursor, icon, etc., and so it needs a place to store information about all of these things. Those storage places are called system resources. They will turn out to be a problem area—but we'll talk about them later.

User16 and 32

Much of the business of running Windows lies in the user interaction with those windows—clicking buttons, selecting menu items, dragging icons, choosing from list boxes, and so on. Those things are all handled by a module called User. As before, older Windows used a 16-bit version of User and more recent Windows uses a 32-bit version.

Now and then, you will see an error message which indicates that the module User32 or User16 has failed; when that happens, you often get a choice to cancel, continue, or perhaps close a window. If you stop and think about it, this is kind of a contradiction in terms—here, Windows has told you that User (the part of Windows that handles button clicks) has failed, and would you please push a button to choose what to do next? I think of this as a kind of remote-control time bomb with the buttons representing the activation switches. You will not see *many* User failures, but they do occur sometimes. When they do, the best thing is to just shut down the PC and restart it.

Virtual Machine Manager (VMM32) and VxD's

While it's not considered part of the Windows kernel, there is a very important part of Windows that helps perform the functions of the kernel (as I defined it in my generic description of an operating system). This part is called the virtual machine manager, or VMM32.

The Virtual Machine Manager

As I've already told you, one of the tasks for the people designing Windows 95 was to design an operating system that could support DOS programs, particularly since they are badly behaved programs. Each DOS program is something of a spoiled child, meaning that it wants every piece of hardware for itself—DOS programs just plain don't know how to share. If a DOS program sees COM1, a serial port, then there's a good chance that it will claim that serial port for its own, even if it doesn't need it. The same thing holds true for memory—most DOS programs start out by swallowing up every byte of memory on a system. DOS programs sit on the keyboard, watching it every instant to see if you've pressed a key—and then they assume that the keystroke is for them. Obviously, DOS programs weren't born to multitask.

To get around this problem, most operating systems that multitask DOS programs—a list that includes OS/2, NT, and 95—take your PC and break it up into multiple virtual PCs, or, to use the correct term, *virtual machines*. Logically enough, the program that manages all of these virtual machines is called the *virtual machine manager*. Virtual machine managers all exploit a terrific feature of the 386 processor (and of all the processors that came to market after it in the Intel family) called *page mapping*.

The trick works something like this. Suppose you have a computer with 16MB of memory: DOS only sees 1MB of memory. That 1MB of memory, however, must be the *first* megabyte of memory—and this is where page mapping gets interesting. With page mapping, a processor can take a hunk of memory—say, the memory from the 3MB address to the 4MB address—and sort of "carve it out" of the rest of the processor's memory. Then the processor takes this 1MB of memory and says to the DOS program, "Here is your PC; it only has 1MB of memory. Trust me." Then, when the DOS program tries to access an address in this 1MB—for example, address 7000—then the page mapping feature of the processor just says, "Oh, when that program says seven thousand, I should add 3MB to that." Thus, the memory request is transparently converted into its actual physical memory address.

Managing Virtual Memory

The program that manages all of this memory juggling is, as you've probably figured out by now, the VMM32. It not only manages virtual machines, it also keeps track of virtual memory. Virtual memory gives an operating system the ability to promise more memory to its applications than it actually has; in operating system lingo, that's called *overcommitting* memory. So, for example, if your computer has 16MB of RAM, but you want to run 40MB of programs, you can—for a price.

The virtual machine manager lets you overcommit memory because it uses disk space on your computer as if it were memory. When you try to load programs beyond the actual RAM of your system, the virtual machine manager takes a look around and says, "Let's see... Which memory has programs in it, but hasn't been used in a while?"

Memory on a 386 or later computer is partitioned into 4K-sized pieces called *pages*. The part of the virtual machine manager that worries about memory—it's called (no big surprise) the *virtual memory manager*—has no real concept of programs and memory, but rather of *pages* and memory. It knows both how many pages it has committed to the various programs in the system and which ones are actually sitting in RAM and which are, well, merely promises.

For example, you might have loaded Excel a few hours ago, but haven't done anything with it for a while. The memory manager would know that nothing's touched a whole pile of pages in memory (the Excel pages) for a while, so the virtual memory manager would then take those pages and move them from RAM to disk, in a kind of staging area for virtual memory called the *paging file*. That, in turn, would free up some physical RAM, allowing you to load a new program; except for a bit of excessive disk activity, there's a good chance that you'd never even know what's going on.

If you later decide to come back to Excel, then Windows would try to access Excel's memory space. When the processor tries to execute some code in a page of memory owned by Excel, it finds that the page is not actually in RAM; this generates an hardware error condition called a *page fault*. (Just in case it wasn't clear, programs can't execute from disk—they have to be in memory to run.) The page fault wakes up the virtual memory manager, which then must make room to reload the Excel memory image. Now, it's probably still the case that there isn't enough room for all of your programs in memory, so the virtual memory manager must again figure out which programs are monopolizing memory that they're not using.

NOTE Virtual memory and virtual machine management was once a feature only found in expensive operating systems; it's a measure of how much times have changed that you see it in as basic an OS as Windows.

Virtual Device Drivers (VxD's)

While the ability to map and page memory quickly, easily, and efficiently is one of the important foundation pieces in providing a multitasking DOS environment, it's not the whole story. Not only do DOS programs steal memory at will, they also grab whatever other hardware they see, to the detriment of other programs. To explain that, I'm going to have to get a little technical here, but bear with me for just a moment. The key to understanding what stealing hardware means is something called *input/ output addresses*.

Input/output addresses, or I/O addresses, are the way that a program communicates with a piece of hardware, like a keyboard, video board, LAN board, or whatever. They're similar to memory addresses, except that memory addresses only access memory and I/O addresses access all kinds of hardware. For example, an application that wishes to communicate with the keyboard does it by listening at I/O address 60; that's the standard I/O address for the keyboard. You can read further on I/O addresses in Chapter 10.

Now, as I've already said, DOS programs are a real pain in that they like to cling to the keyboard (I/O address 60) and snatch any activity before any other application (you know, like the operating system) gets it. So any virtual machine manager worth its salt will need some kind of way to keep all of those DOS applications from taking over the hardware. Fortunately, there is such a way: a virtual device driver or, in the Windows 95 world, a *VxD*.

A virtual device driver is a program that the processor kind of thumbtacks to an I/O address. To continue the keyboard example, a keyboard virtual driver would be nailed to I/O address 60. Then when a program attempted to directly access I/O address 60, the virtual keyboard driver would spring into action, behaving very much like the original piece of hardware.

A virtual keyboard driver is fairly easy to imagine: when a DOS program addresses it, saying "Hey, keyboard, are there any keystrokes for me?" then the virtual keyboard driver looks around and says, "Hmmm... is this DOS program in the foreground?" If the DOS program *is* in the foreground, then the virtual keyboard driver just passes along whatever's in the keyboard to the DOS program. If, on the other hand, the virtual keyboard driver sees that the DOS program is in the background, then, by definition, there are no keystrokes for the DOS program. (After all, how do you type into a program in the background—by walking behind the computer and typing?) In that case, the virtual keyboard driver, still masquerading as the keyboard, simply tells the DOS program, "No, there's nothing for you right now."

You can see the VxD that controls each piece of hardware by looking at the Device Manager in the Control Panel. For example, my System device manager tells me that my mouse is using two drivers, one named `lmouse.vxd`, and another named `lmouse.drv`. You can also see which drivers load and in what order by examining a file called `BOOTLOG.TXT`, but you must start up Windows differently than usual to see it. When you see the "Starting Windows 95..." message, press F8. You will then be given a menu of boot options, one of which is to boot and create a `BOOTLOG.TXT`.

Registry

If you worked with previous versions of Windows, then you are no doubt familiar with the `.INI` files. These files contain basic setup information and configuration data for Windows 95. They are in some ways an improvement over the old Windows 3.x approach, but they have their own problems, as you'll find when you read the next chapter. Additionally, there are pieces of information that are generated internally or *dynamically* by Windows 95; for example, every time your system starts up, it creates a map of what hardware is inside it. That is, of course, a dynamic piece of data in that it can change from usage to usage. You can't modify this; however, you might find great use for this information in troubleshooting a nasty Windows problem. You will learn more about this in the upcoming chapter on Windows hardware troubleshooting (Chapter 10). In any case, the Registry is as fundamental a part of Windows as the kernel, GDI, or the user interface manager.

IFS

There must be a way for an operating system to access storage devices. For example, in the DOS operating system, all storage devices have a similar name: a letter of the alphabet followed by a colon. Additionally, data must be organized on a storage device in a particular way. Since the days of DOS, data has been organized in a way originally designed for maintaining files on a floppy diskette (this is the famous, or perhaps infamous, FAT file system). However, if I were to ask you, "Where is the program that controls the FAT file system under DOS?" you wouldn't be able to tell me—that's because there *isn't* such a place in DOS. The FAT file system is so basic and so integral to DOS that there isn't any one place in DOS that implements the FAT.

However, with new operating systems, there is a need for more powerful and more flexible file systems. For example, the FAT file system doesn't work well on networks or on CD-ROMs; as a result, it has been difficult to implement CD-ROMs and LANs under DOS. The answer is *not*, however, to try to build a single file system that can be all things to all applications. Instead, it makes better sense to try to build an open architecture for file systems, a sort of plug-and-play capability that would allow the user to easily install CD-ROMs, LANs, optical drives, large hard drives, or whatever. After all, the lesson of the last ten years must certainly be that there is no way to design an architecture that will work as well now as in the future, since the future just isn't easy to predict.

For example, consider a case of well-executed forward thinking— the DOS device driver. The first modern version of DOS first appeared in 1983 with the introduction of DOS version 2. At the time, the designers of DOS knew well that they could not look into the future and know what hardware would be common, so they decided to leave a back door in DOS—device drivers. At the time, no machine had a CD-ROM, a local area network, or even a mouse—things that virtually every PC has these days. Without the device driver, none of those things could have been supported by DOS, and, as a result, they probably never would have taken hold in the marketplace. Device drivers made it possible for the vendors of these new pieces of hardware to introduce this hardware to DOS. Once a device driver was written for DOS, then DOS could, in many cases, simply treat the new device as just another disk with a name composed of a letter and a colon; of course, that wasn't true for everything—the mouse is an obvious example—but it was a very good model for more than ten years. My point is that we need something like this for file systems. Something like that *has* appeared, in the form of the *Installable File System* (IFS).

Actually, the IFS isn't new. It first appeared in 1989 with OS/2 version 1.2, an operating system that offered an alternative to the FAT file system in its HPFS, the High Performance File System. As implemented in Windows 95, the IFS is a sort of software socket into which can be plugged file systems like the familiar old FAT file system, network file redirectors, and CD-ROM file systems. The best news to most of us will be that file names can now be hundreds of characters long. What other benefits will IFS bring? At this writing, I cannot imagine all of the uses to which the IFS will be put; but I *can* guarantee somebody will figure out a clever use of IFS that I can't predict.

Configuration Manager

The emergence of Plug and Play technology as part of Windows 95 means that Windows 95 will treat your computer differently than have other operating systems. You see, in order for an operating system to work, it obviously must know what kind of hardware you have in your computer— and there's the rub.

How do we tell an operating system what hardware is sitting in its PC? Well, there's the obvious approach (and the one that has been used most often): Introduce a static list of hardware and drivers and require the user to reconfigure the operating system every time a new piece of hardware is added to the system. This is familiar to any veteran of operating system support. It's something that you've had to do to support DOS, Windows in its earlier incarnations, OS/2, and NT. Plug and Play, however changes that story in a number of ways.

Think about what you have to do when you add a new board to a typical computer. I can't speak for *your* experience, but mine works something like this: First, I remove the board from its box, then I root around looking for its documentation. On those occasions when the documentation is actually present, and on those rarer occasions when the documentation is accurate, I settle down to flipping DIP switches and moving jumpers to fit my new board into my PC without causing any interrupt conflicts or the like. Then, once I've run a test on the board to make sure that the board is working properly, I fire up the Setup program on my operating system; here I tell it that my new hardware—video display, SCSI adapter, or whatever—is now present, and, perhaps, also to tell it that an old piece of hardware is no longer present. And I'd *better* do this or I typically find that my operating system won't work anymore.

With Windows 95 and Plug and Play, things work very differently. First of all, there are no jumpers or switches. Plug and Play compatible hardware is completely software-configurable. Now, this may not sound very exciting in the late '90s because software-configurable boards appeared years ago in the PS/2 days. Since then, we've seen software-configurable EISA boards and even ISA boards. So what's the big deal with Plug and Play?

Well, the big deal is that Plug and Play does both the hardware installation and the software installation, and it does it automatically—or, at least as automatically as is possible. With Plug and Play computers, every board gets configured every single time you turn your computer on, believe it or not. Every time you start up your machine, new interrupts are assigned to all of your adapter cards so that they don't conflict with each other. Then, the configuration information that results is passed to Windows, which, in turn, passes that information to your hardware drivers—the VxD's.

The mastermind behind this whole operation is a new piece of software called the *Configuration Manager*. It is not only an integral part of Windows, it is also part of the system BIOS of a Plug and Play-compatible system. There's a catch, though: for full Plug and Play compatibility you'll need to buy new PCs, expansion boards, and a whole new operating system. Well, at least you have the new operating system...

What about those of us without Plug and Play hardware? Is the Configuration Manager still useful? The answer is yes, definitely. The Configuration Manager is quite useful in that it is incredibly smart about detecting hardware settings on a variety of boards—so good, in fact that there's a rumor around that the Microsoft NT developers first install Windows 95 on a machine to find out what's in the machine, and then use that information when configuring Windows NT. (Of course, this *could* just be apocryphal...) Seriously, while it is impossible for a piece of software to completely detect hardware in a non-Plug and Play system, the Windows Configuration Manager does the best job of it that I've ever seen; this will no doubt raise the minimum standard of excellence for hardware detection software in the diagnostic and operating system software business.

NOTE

You will interact with the Configuration Manager mainly through the Control Panel, in the Device Manager. You'll learn more about Configuration Manager and Device Manager in Chapter 10.

System Resources under Windows 95

Starting to learn to work with Windows—either an older version or the most recent—can actually be a bit of fun. Of course, learning anything new can be frustrating and time-consuming; but, once you get it—that is, once you really understand the working-with-Windows paradigm—then you start to actually feel like there is something new and better that you can get done with this new operating system. So you start putting it through its paces, loading a bunch of programs, doing OLE... And that's when you start to find the limitations.

That's the frustrating part.

For example, anyone who has worked with Windows 3.x has come across an Out of Memory error. It displays a strange error message, saying something like "You do not have enough free memory. Close a few applications and try again." So you close a whole bunch of applications, but you *still* can't run your program. You take a quick look at the amount of free memory and see that there are perhaps tens of megabytes of memory free, yet you keep getting this annoying Out of Memory error message.

Well, Windows experts will by now know what caused this problem: system resources. Remember the Windows components named GDI and User? They have many things to keep track of. GDI must remember the name and location of every bitmap on the screen, as well as any colors of any objects on the screen, usage of cursors, icons, fonts, etc. User must keep track of every possible menu selection on each active program, as well as the location of every window on the screen, the location and state of every button on the screen, and so on. These two Windows subsystems must have a place to set aside that information, a sort of scratchpad location for keeping this information. Those scratchpad locations are called *system resources*.

Under Windows 3.x, the basic architecture was, as you know, 16-bit. That led to some important limitations, and one of the most important was in system resources. The number 2 raised to the 16th power is 64K, and that's where the trouble began. You see, GDI only had one of these 64K memory areas for recording all of its information, and, unfortunately, it was fairly easy for a heavy-duty Windows user to exceed that 64K. This led to the odd situation whereby it was possible that a user could have megabytes of free memory space—yet the user would be unable to run a program because GDI didn't have enough space to keep track of that program's cursors, colors, bitmaps, etc. (the program's system resources).

Now, when Microsoft announced Windows 95, many of us were quite happy to hear that it would be 32-bit in nature. As 2 raised to the 32nd power is over 4 billion, that would imply that system resources would no longer be a constraint. That's only partially true, unfortunately: old 16-bit programs and 32-bit OLE programs can still chew up resources.

As old programs (the 16-bit ones) aren't trained to go look for the new, bigger 32-bit heap, they keep going to the 16-bit areas. Now some of the heap space that they used to burn up they burned up indirectly: by asking GDI to do something, they caused GDI to put some data in its heap. Now, when that happens under Windows 95, GDI will usually put the data in the larger 32-bit heap. *The result:* There's more space left for the legacy apps. But it is a finite space, and so it's still possible to fill up the heaps with 16-bit applications. (When in doubt, it's always easiest to blame those legacy application developers.)

Even 32-bit applications end up putting a little information in the heap. 32-bit apps are built up out of sub-applications called *threads*, which are built either with or without message queues. The threads that need message queues are the ones that do OLE. According to Matt Pietrek in an article in *PC Magazine* ("Stability and Capacity," September 26, 1995), every eight threads with message queues used up one percent of User's heap. Depending on how OLE is implemented in your application, you may need one thread for each linkage. That means that you couldn't run more than a few hundred linkages without running out of resources, even if you're running 32-bit applications. Again, the bottom line is that it's still possible to run out of resources under Windows 95.

It may be cold comfort, but it's easier to monitor system resources under Windows 95 than it was with Windows 3.x. One of the optional applications that you can load with Windows 95 is the Resource Meter, your system resource monitor, which you see in Figure 2.3.

FIGURE 2.3

System resource
monitor

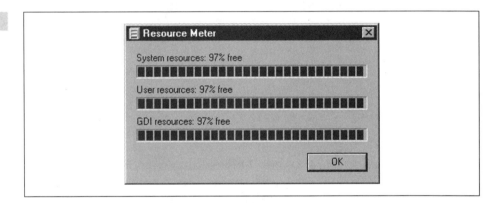

Since I've beaten up on Microsoft for keeping the 16-bit stuff around, it's only fair that I point out that the sample Resource Meter that you see in the previous figure shows a reading for my system after I opened several important applications. Under Windows 3.x, opening Ami Pro was enough to drive the resources down to 80 percent, but under Windows 95, Ami only brings resources down to 94 percent; this is quite an improvement, and not merely a cosmetic one. I have several very large documents that simply could not be worked on using Windows 3.x; I would invariably run out of resource space when trying to edit those documents. So far, that has not been the case with Windows 95.

That said, I should point out that it is still possible to run out of resources with Windows 95—it's just a bit harder. It *is* a bit frustrating, however, to see Microsoft demonstrate Windows 95 and show off how wonderful it is on resources by opening up 25 copies of their Excel spreadsheets. Understand that this is a somewhat bogus demonstration, as Excel is a so-called multiply instanced application. What that means is that when you load your first copy of Excel, then it takes up memory, resources, etc. When you start a second copy of Excel, however, it does not load a completely new copy of Excel; instead, the first copy of Excel is just augmented with a few new data areas. As a result, it is quite easy to load many copies of a single application (this multiply instanced type of application is quite common) and not see a great resource hit. To see how impressive Windows 95 can potentially be, try opening 25 *different* applications rather than 25 copies of the same application. (Of course, Microsoft doesn't do that in public demonstrations...)

What should you do about potential resource bottlenecks? Well, I'll offer the same advice to you that I offered under Windows 3.x: Use the Resource Meter to keep track of which programs are the real resource hounds. Then you can opt to avoid those applications, to contact the program authors, and to tell them to trim their applications a bit. And *please* be sure to keep an eye on the Resource Meter before you start doing any fancy OLE stuff. (If you're *really* stuck, then go to Windows NT.)

System Vulnerabilities

In a perfect world, an operating system would be no more than a toolbox of prebuilt software routines, routines to do the donkey work of programming: "put the word Hello on the screen," "draw a circle," "get the employee ID numbers of every employee born between 1965 and 1975," and so on. Applications programs would be aware of each other and could transfer data among themselves in an orderly, well-organized fashion. Unfortunately, the real world doesn't work that way. The frenetic pace of software technology advances has shortened software development cycles, making it just about impossible to ship a useful piece of software that's both *on time* and *bug free*.

So most vendors opt for on time.

That means that nobody trusts the operating system code, nobody trusts the device drivers, and nobody trusts the apps. When a piece of code crashes, we want to know which piece of code it was and who's to blame. Ideally, we'd also like to restrict the damage—a flakey application shouldn't be able to crash the whole operating system.

Memory Management under Windows 95

That's where protection models and memory management come in. You've already read a bit about memory management when you read about system resources; let's look further into how Windows 95 manages its memory.

It's possible on an x86 processor to designate privilege levels for computer code. Some programs can be designated ring 0, and that's the highest privilege level. Others are rings 1, 2, or 3, in decreasing importance. Ring 0 programs can protect memory in that they can allocate spaces of memory to particular programs and detect when another program tries to invade that space; such an invasion is called a General Protection Fault, or GPF. Ring 1 programs can also allocate memory, but only so long as they don't override a command of ring 0 programs; ring 2's can't override ring 1's, and so on.

Windows 95 uses only two rings: The virtual machine manager and its VxD's are ring 0, and everything else is ring 3, including Kernel, GDI, and User. The salient points of how Windows 95 manages and protects memory are as follows:

- The VMM32 and VxD's are protected in ring 0. (If they're buggy, however, nothing can stand against them, as they can write to any piece of memory, anywhere. And don't forget that some of your VxD's are just pieces of software that came with one of your pieces of hardware, which means that software written by some third-party hardware vendor becomes part of the central operating system— Where's your guarantee that they were all well-written?)

- The Kernel, GDI, User, and other system DLLs have their own memory space; they're ring 3, which means (read on) they're usually safe from Win32 apps.

- The Win32 programs—the Windows 95 applications—all have their own separate address spaces, and can't see out of it. Buggy Win32 programs will usually crash only themselves.

- On the other hand, Win16 programs must live in the same memory space as the Kernel, GDI, and the like, making the operating system vulnerable to bugs in Windows 3.x applications. Once again, the dirty little secret of Windows 95 is that you need Windows 95 applications to get the benefits of Windows 95.

While on the subject of Windows architecture, it is important to point out a very important weakness in the architecture of Windows 95, especially as concerns DOS programs. As you recall, each DOS program gets its own virtual machine, which is essentially a PC. As I said before, this whole idea of virtual machines is essential to the success of Windows (or, for that matter, any operating system), mostly because DOS programs are all hogs in the way they use memory and hardware on the computer.

Although I did not mention it, there is another very good reason for virtual machines: They protect one program from the bugs of another program. Here's what I mean. Suppose you are running two DOS programs, perhaps WordPerfect version 5.1 and some free DOS-based game. If the DOS-based game does something stupid and decides to crash, what happens to your Windows programs and the DOS WordPerfect program?

In a well-designed operating system, like Windows NT or OS/2, any program that dies just dies, and the operating system cleans up after it; that's all there is to it. The creators of Windows 95 decided to make a design decision that, on the one hand, reduced the amount of memory required to run Windows 95, but on the other hand weakened the walls between the virtual machines.

Under Windows 95, the first physical megabyte of RAM is directly mapped, or in other words copied, into all virtual machines. Now, that's not so bad, as there's nothing wrong with the idea of copying the first megabyte of the basic system software into every virtual machine. The problem is that the relationship between virtual machines and the physical machine is a *two-way* relationship. That means that it is possible to do something stupid on one virtual machine and cause a ripple effect on the other virtual machines.

I guess the easiest way to describe this is simply with an example. Check out the boxed instructions nearby for creatively crashing your machine.

How to Crash Your Machine

Try these steps on a Windows 95 machine—but be darn sure that you're not running anything you care about, because you are going to crash the machine!

1. Open a DOS prompt. (Just click Taskbar, then Programs, then the MS-DOS prompt.)
2. At the prompt, type **debug** and press Enter.
3. Debug's prompt, which is a dash, will show up. At that prompt, type **F 0:0 L ffff 0** and press Enter.
4. The system will stop working.

Is using Debug to crash your Windows 95 machine an unfair test of Windows 95? I don't think so. Try the exact same test on OS/2 or Windows NT and nothing bad will happen. Why couldn't this robustness have been built into Windows 95? The story I have heard is that isolating the bottom 1MB of physical memory would have required that Windows 95's minimum memory requirements go from 4MB, the official amount of memory required for a minimum Windows 95 installation, all the way up to 5MB. The story goes that the Microsoft public relations machine felt that saying that Windows 95 ran on 4MB would help its sales; I've had this story confirmed by a couple of Microsoft employees. It all makes sense, particularly when you consider that IBM was touting their upcoming version of OS/2 that ran well in just 4MB of RAM, but I wish it hadn't worked out this way.

The Hourglass Lives

Before leaving the subject of system vulnerabilities, I should mention the hourglass.

When the hourglass is displayed, that means that the part of Windows that responds to user inputs—mouse clicks and keystrokes—is busy at the moment, and can't handle anything more. This is called having a single input queue, and it's what Windows 3.x had.

The problem with this is that Windows 95 was supposed to have multiple input queues. When the pointer turns into a smaller hourglass with a pointer atop it, you can then start another program while the first program is busy. 32-bit programs can share the input queue. Badly written 16-bit applications don't.

As the Kernel, User, and GDI all have 16-bit as well as 32-bit pieces, there wasn't a way to disconnect the 32-bit subsystem from the occasional piggy 16-bit app. The result is that when a Windows 3.x program puts up the hourglass, you can't talk to *any* application—including the 32-bit ones.

And Speaking of Under the Hood...

Let's leave this chapter with a Stupid Windows 95 Pet Trick. Try this.

1. Right-click the Desktop, and choose New Folder.
2. Name it with the following "title" (don't forget the comma):
   and now, the moment you've all been waiting for
3. Right-click on the folder, choose Rename, and rename it with the following:
   we proudly present for your viewing pleasure
4. Then rename it once more, to **The Microsoft Windows 95 Product Team!**
5. Then open the folder, and you'll see an animated credits screen, complete with music.

Hey, no *wonder* the thing is tens of megabytes in size!

CHAPTER

3

Controlling 95— .INI Files and the Registry

IF you've ever used DOS or Windows, you're familiar with the array of system and hardware configuration files that accompany DOS-based operating systems: AUTOEXEC.BAT, WIN.INI, CONFIG.SYS, and SYSTEM.INI. NT users know that these files were replaced in Windows NT with a centralized configuration database called the *Registry*. Just to make life complicated, however, Windows 95 uses both kinds of configuration files: the DOS ones *and* an NT-like Registry. (Actually, there's more to it than just perversity on Microsoft's part, but we'll talk about the roles of the legacy configuration files in Windows 95 later in this chapter.)

Basically, the Registry holds all configuration information for Windows 95 and Windows 95-ready applications. Older 16-bit apps do not know to use the Registry, unfortunately, so you'll still have .INI files scattered all over your system if you use Windows 3.x programs.

Although both the DOS configuration files and the Registry have a role to play in configuring your Windows 95 environment, they look and work a little differently in Windows 95 than they do in DOS/Windows and NT. In this chapter, we'll talk about what these configuration files look like, how you can use them to tune your system, and how to avoid bollixing up your system while trying to tune it.

The Limited New Roles of
AUTOEXEC.BAT and CONFIG.SYS

You probably know that, unlike previous versions of Windows, Windows 95 is an operating *system*, not an operating environment. It's not a

GUI front end to the DOS operating system (as were previous versions of Windows), but complete unto itself.

Most DOS machines use CONFIG.SYS and AUTOEXEC.BAT to set up the system hardware and operating environment. Although these files can be pretty vanilla if all you want to do is just boot the machine, the more stuff you add to the machine, the more complicated and system-specific they get. Windows 95, in contrast, does not rely on CONFIG.SYS and AUTOEXEC .BAT for system information; a file named IO.SYS and another called the Registry take care of configuring the system as the former pair of files once did.

But if you look at the root directory of your boot drive, you'll notice that you've still got a CONFIG.SYS and AUTOEXEC.BAT. If Windows 95 doesn't need these files to set up your system, then why are these files still there? Two reasons:

- To load any real-mode drivers and TSRs that your computer requires.
- To allow you to tailor DOS sessions for specific DOS programs.

Loading Real-Mode Drivers and TSRs

A few computers, but not all, need to run some real-mode (i.e., DOS) programs that aren't part of Windows 95. The statements corresponding to these programs appear in CONFIG.SYS and AUTOEXEC.BAT, and even if your particular computer requires no such programs, their configuration files will remain on your system, for the unlikely event the need arises in the future.

Creating "Roll-Your-Own" DOS Environments

You can run most DOS programs from Windows 95 and, if necessary, set up an individual AUTOEXEC.BAT and CONFIG.SYS for each one. Thus, if you've got an application that can't run if DOS is loaded high or has some other special requirements, you can set up a custom operating environment for that application.

Although we'll get into the nitty-gritty of running DOS programs under Windows 95 later in this book, for now let's talk a little about how to use `CONFIG.SYS` and `AUTOEXEC.BAT` to give a DOS application a custom-made environment.

Open My Computer and find the icon for a DOS program on your system. Right-click it, and choose Properties from the pop-up menu. A dialog box like the one in Figure 3.1 will appear.

(SNAP, if you're wondering, is a useful screen-capture program for DOS.) Click on the Program tab, and then click the Advanced button at the bottom of the Program screen. You'll see a dialog box that looks like the one in Figure 3.2.

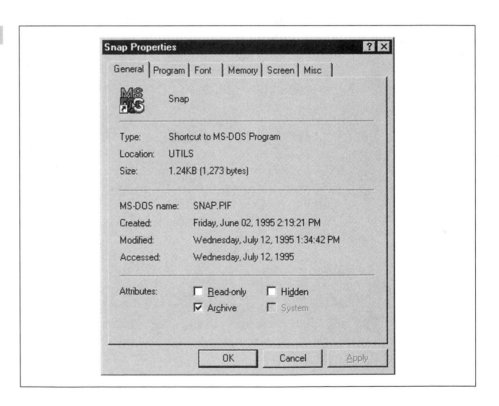

FIGURE 3.2

Advanced screen of
SNAP Properties
dialog box

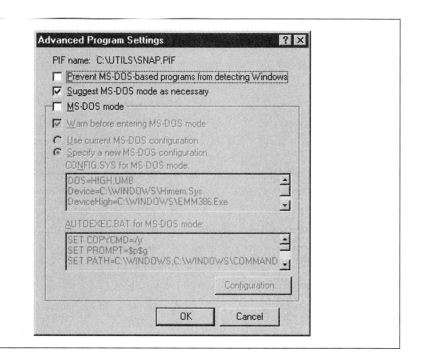

> **TIP**
>
> Don't panic if you turn to the Advanced screen of the Properties tab for a particular DOS app and there's nothing in the CONFIG .SYS or AUTOEXEC.BAT files. You can't see their contents until you've selected MS-DOS mode at least once.

Notice the CONFIG.SYS and AUTOEXEC.BAT files that are listed. Notice also that, by default, *Suggest MS-DOS mode as necessary* is selected, and you must use the vanilla configuration files provided. By default, these files won't do much more than define an operating environment, enable EMM386, define the temporary file directory, and provide mouse support. To change them, you'll need to set the operating environment to MS-DOS mode so that they're no longer grayed out, as you see in Figure 3.3.

FIGURE 3.3

SNAP set to MS-DOS
mode

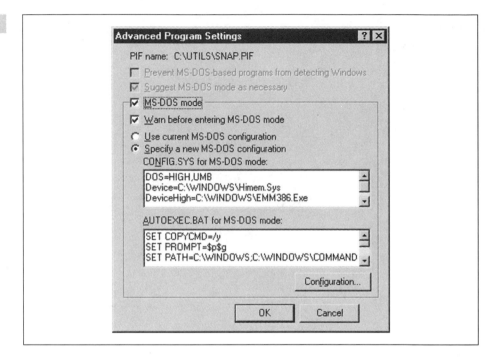

Now, you're ready to customize the configuration files for this program's
DOS session. You can type in the commands you want to load, or you can
select canned configuration information from the screen available after
clicking the Configuration button, as you see in Figure 3.4.

I like the way that this dialog box was set up: Rather than providing you
with a list of statements to add to or delete from CONFIG.SYS or AUTO-
EXEC.BAT, Windows 95 lists the options to activate or deactivate and then
adjusts the configuration files to correspond to your choices. By default,
EMM386 (the memory manager) and mouse support are activated. If
you're not sure of an option's function, right-click on it and its description
will appear in the text box below the list.

FIGURE 3.4

Canned configuration
options

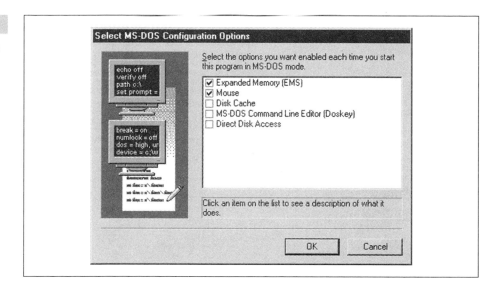

WARNING When editing the CONFIG.SYS and AUTOEXEC.BAT files for a
DOS session, watch what you're doing, and make sure you
make backups before you get started. There's no Restore
Defaults button.

Select the options that you want for the MS-DOS mode of the DOS session and click OK. When you return to the Advanced dialog box, you'll notice that the changes you made are reflected in the configuration files. Notice also that there is no Restore Defaults button, so be careful what you do here. The only way that you can undo changes to a DOS session's configuration files is by canceling out of the application's Properties dialog box altogether. Once you click OK to close Properties you're stuck with the changes that you've made.

Once you've set up the CONFIG.SYS and AUTOEXEC.BAT for that DOS session, return the program's running mode to *Suggest MS-DOS mode as necessary*, the default. If DOS mode is necessary for the program to run well, the configuration files that you set up will run.

Where ARE Configuration Settings Kept?

As you can set up an individual CONFIG.SYS and AUTOEXEC.BAT file for each DOS program on your system, clearly this information isn't centrally located, but is somewhere specific to each DOS program. That "somewhere specific" is the program's PIF (Program Information File), normally stored in the same directory as the program file itself. For example, SNAP's configuration information is stored in SNAP.PIF.

NOTE A DOS program does not need a PIF file to run—it only needs one if you customize its setup in some way, like changing the icon or adding a line to its CONFIG.SYS.

If Windows 95 can't find a PIF for a DOS program, it will look in APPS.INF for configuration for that file and create a new PIF from that information. APPS.INF holds default information for many DOS programs, although it doesn't update itself for new applications that you add to the system. The information in APPS.INF may not be exactly to your liking (for example, if I erase 1-2-3 version 3.1's PIF, the version stored in APPS.INF defines MS-DOS mode for the program), but once Windows 95 has recreated the PIF you can edit it via the Properties dialog, as discussed briefly in this chapter and in detail in Chapter 13.

Using DEBUG to Look at a DOS Program's PIF

PIF files are not readable in a text editor like Notepad, but you can use a DOS program called DEBUG to check out the contents of a DOS program's PIF, if you care to go through the trouble. Before starting up, however, let me issue this warning:

WARNING: *It's very easy to render your machine unbootable with DEBUG. Do* not *experiment with commands other than those listed here unless you know exactly what you're doing.*

I hate to sound grouchy, but I don't want my e-mail flooded with messages from people who've blown away their MBR and can't boot. Please keep your Startup Disk on hand at all times when working with DEBUG.

Enough lecturing—let's check out the contents of SNAP.PIF. First, I'll need to add something distinctive to its configuration so that I can find it easily. Therefore, I'll go into SNAP's Properties dialog, as we just discussed, and manually add the statement

rem elephant=pink

at the end of its CONFIG.SYS. The rem is so I don't mess up the configuration with junk lines.

Now, I'm ready to use DEBUG. I open the DOS prompt and type

DEBUG_C:\UTILS\SNAP.PIF

(All underscores indicate spaces—DEBUG is very picky about syntax.) The cursor changes to a dash, indicating that DEBUG is running.

Next, I need to find out how long SNAP is. I know that the length of a file is stored in register CX, so I'll type **r** to display the contents of all of the PIF's registers. The result looks like this:

AX=0000 BX=0000 CX=04F9 DX=0000 SP=FFEE BP=0000 SI=0000 DI=0000

DS=1B6C ES=1B6C SS=1B6C CS=1BPC IP=0100 NV UP EI PL NZ NA PO NC

1B6C:0100 007853   ADD [BX+SI+53],BH   DS:0053=00

As you can see, SNAP's PIF is 04F9 bytes long (that's hex, translating to 1273 bytes in decimal). That means that I need to search memory, starting from DS 100, for a file 04F9 bytes long that contains the string "elephant." I'll do that with this command:

s_100_l_04f9_"elephant"

That nets me the following:

```
1B6C:05E8
```

This is the segment and offset for part of SNAP.PIF. Armed with this information, I can dump the contents of this part of the PIF onto the screen with **d_1b6c:05e8**. The results are as follows:

```
1B6C:05E0                   64 6C 65 70 68 61 6E 74      elephant
1B6C:05F0 10 2D 20 70 69 6E 6B 0D-0A 91 C3 19 36 30 32 34  = pink....6024
1B6C:0600 36 30 36 20 1a 06 39 35-35 31 19 2E 19 03 03 00  606 ..9551....
1B6C:0610 13 0F 08 0E F5 0F 0F 1B-26 09 D4 D7 AA AD 00 00  .......&......
1B6C:0620 01 1F 01 03 01 07 0B 47-10 17 28 03 0C 53 54 27  .....G..(..ST'
1B6C:0630 00 00 58 3F 12 16 16 12-12 1E 1E 12 12 16 16 35  ..X?.........5
1B6C:0640 35 65 00 00 75 67 69 07-05 03 0D 0F 0D CB CB D7  5e..ugi.......
1B6C:0650 D7 D7 D7 D7 00 AA C7 D7-D7 D7 D7 93 93 93 93 1C  ..............
1B6C:0660 39 00 25 42 02 00 0B 0B                          9.%B.........
```

When you're done looking at SNAP.PIF, type **q** to quit DEBUG and exit the DOS prompt.

To view other information in the PIF, I'd use a smaller number to describe the segment, perhaps substituting **16c0:05e8** in the dump statement. The result would be earlier lines in the configuration files, as they're stored in the PIF in the order in which they appear in the Properties dialog box.

What Is the Registry?

You may still have an AUTOEXEC.BAT and CONFIG.SYS, for odd drivers and configuring DOS programs, but the meat and potatoes of your Windows 95 configuration resides in the Registry. You control the Registry with C:\windows\regedit.exe. Let's take a look; you can see the opening screen of the Registry in Figure 3.5.

This, by the way, is not the way your Registry will look when you first open it. I've expanded some parts of it to illustrate what you may see when working with it. Normally, when you start up REGEDIT, all that you'll see are the icons labeled HKEY-something. HKEY is Microsoft-ese for "*handle* (that is, pointer) to a *key*." Keys are the folders you see.

FIGURE 3.5

Registry branches,
keys, and subkeys

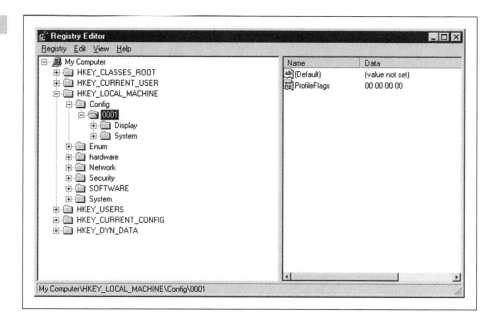

This scary-looking database contains all of the configuration information for your computer and its network connections, your session on the computer, and the sessions of any user that logs into that computer. It's a lot of information, cryptically organized, but understanding how it works and how to get around in it is essential for working with Windows 95.

The Registry is the front end for all Windows 95 configuration data: the system configuration, the hardware configuration, the setup information for Win32-based applications, and user preferences. The actual files where this information is stored are called USER.DAT, SYSTEM.DAT, and (if you're using the Policy Editor, discussed in Chapter 8) CONFIG.POL, but they are not in human-readable form. To see your current user and system configurations all in one place, you'll need to run REGEDIT.

Some of the information in the Registry is always stored on disk, while other information is stored initially in RAM, and thus dynamically reflects changes. For example, if you adjust the configuration of a Plug and Play optical drive, that change appears immediately in the Registry.

Why Have a Registry?

Before you tune out in preparation for a discussion of esoteric techie stuff, know that there is at least one characteristic of the Registry that makes understanding it worthwhile: its compactness. You know how, before installing new software, you had to back up a whole slew of files to make sure that you could restart the computer and/or fix Windows after the changes the new software made to the system rendered it unbootable?

As the Registry contains all Windows 95 system and user information, you only need to back up USER.DAT and SYSTEM.DAT. With the Windows 95 Registry, all you have to do is export these files to another directory or to disk, name them something in English if you like, and then restore them when things go wrong. The only caveat I might make is this: Name the exported versions something that is easily identifiable when they are condensed to the eight-dot-three format that real-mode sessions demand.

What's in the Registry?

The Registry is an ASCII database pulling information from SYSTEM.DAT, USER.DAT, and (if set up) CONFIG.POL. These files are not in a form that is humanly readable, so you can only see their contents or manipulate them via the Registry (or, more usually, the Control Panel or, for CONFIG.POL, the System Policies Editor).

- SYSTEM.DAT contains hardware-related and computer-specific settings.

- USER.DAT contains user-specific information found in user profiles, such as user rights, desktop settings, and so forth.

- CONFIG.POL contains policy information relating to the system and user settings. For example, you can create a system policy controlling how users may configure their displays or the devices that they can share. Any information in the system policies file overrides the information in USER.DAT and SYSTEM.DAT. (CONFIG.POL is not mandatory to a Windows installation.)

The Registry itself contains nothing—as you can see in Figure 3.6, it's just the front end to the database of your system's configuration, a way of seeing the information in a way that makes sense to humans.

If you export the Registry, you'll create a text file with a .REG extension, but this file is only a *link* to the configuration information, not the configuration itself. You can blow away all files with the .REG extension on your machine and nothing bad will happen; your system will just recreate another Registry from the information in the .DAT files. (If you do this, then it won't create another .REG file until you export the Registry.)

NOTE   **The Registry itself contains no system information—it's just the human-readable representation of the information in the .DAT files, which contain information that your system requires to boot, start Windows, and keep it running.**

Conversely, if you erase or rename SYSTEM.DAT and USER.DAT, then your system will not be able to load the Registry on bootup and it'll have to

FIGURE 3.6

How the Registry allows users to access Windows 95 configuration files

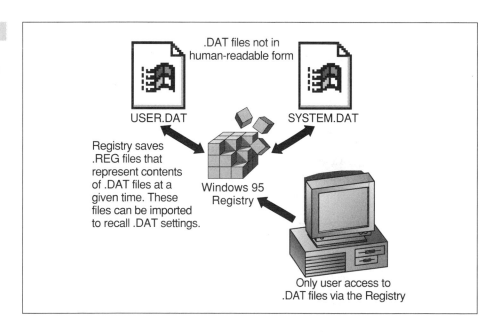

rebuild the files from the backups it makes each time the machine boots successfully. (We'll discuss how that works in the Recovery chapter.)

The contents of the Registry are described in Table 3.1.

What's Not in the Registry?

The Registry does *not* contain setup information for Windows 3.x applications. This is because apps designed for previous versions of Windows don't know how to access the Registry; Win16 applications were designed to work with WIN.INI and SYSTEM.INI and to maintain their own .INI files. So long as you've still got 16-bit applications on your machine, you'll use the .INI files.

Nor does the Registry contain program-specific setup information for DOS programs. If you edit a DOS application's PIF, that information is not reflected in the Registry.

TABLE 3.1 Overview of Registry Contents

FILE NAME	DIRECTORY LOCATION (LOCAL INSTALL)	DIRECTORY LOCATION (NETWORK INSTALL)	CONTENTS	REQUIRED FOR INSTALLATION?
SYSTEM.DAT	C:\windows	C:\windows	Machine-specific information	Yes
USER.DAT	C:\windows	User's home directory	User-specific information	Yes
CONFIG.POL	Logon directory of network server	Logon directory of network server	Hardware and user information determined by policy	No

The Windows 95 Registry is NOT the Same as the Windows NT Registry

Before we go any further with this discussion, NT users should know that Windows 95's Registry is *not* the same as the NT Registry that they've come to know and love. When Microsoft was tailoring the Win32 API for Windows 95, it had to cripple its implementation slightly to permit the operating system to run on 4MB of RAM, as promised. Some Registry functions were among the casualties of this crippling.

The Windows 95 Registry isn't bad, it's just different. It works a little differently, it contains different information, the data is arranged differently, and the syntax is different. That said, your experience working with NT's Registry isn't wasted—you just can't use quite the same skills to work with Windows 95's Registry that you developed for NT's. For example:

- You cannot set Windows 95's Registry to read-only from within the Windows 95 Registry Editor. To make it read-only, you must change the access settings from the Properties dialog box.

- You cannot set group permissions to the Windows 95 Registry from within the application. By default, *anyone* can edit the Registry on the local machine. (This is not a particularly smart way to leave things, as you'll see in this chapter.)

- Windows 95's Registry does not keep *.LOG versions of important files to record changes.

Cautions about Working with the Registry

For those who haven't worked with Windows NT and so skipped the previous section, here are a few things to think about before leaping into editing the Registry:

- **In general, the Registry is *not* where you should be making changes.** Most of the configurations that you can adjust in the Registry have a GUI front end somewhere else, with a Cancel button attached. If you can make the adjustments you want from another dialog box, it's a good idea to do so, for two reasons: (1) you can cancel changes before they take effect, and (2) it's harder to screw up.

- **Know what you're editing.** Before you change any values, make sure that you know what making the change will do to your system. *If you don't know, then don't change it.* The Registry *cannot* distinguish between valid and invalid entries, so, for example, you *could* change the value of the primary network provider from "Microsoft" to "goldfish" and receive no complaints from Windows 95—at least not immediately.

- **Back up before editing.** Using the Export Registry File option in the File menu, you can save your system configuration to disk or to another drive or directory before editing it. This is a very good idea, in case you make a mistake while editing.

'Nuff said. You know that reckless meddling with your system's configuration is dangerous. Keeping that in mind, let's discuss the anatomy of your Registry and how you can safely make changes to it.

The Registry: Pieces of the Puzzle

Like the File Manager, the Registry is organized in a treelike structure. It consists of trees, subtrees, keys, and values, as you can see in Figure 3.7.

- The *tree* is the entire Registry, called My Computer. It consists of six subtrees:
  - Hkey_Classes_Root
  - Hkey_Current_User
  - Hkey_Local_Machine
  - Hkey_Users
  - Hkey_Current_Config
  - Hkey_Dyn_Data

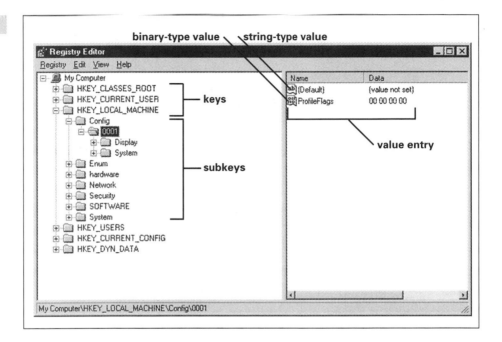

- Each of the *subtrees* controls a different part of your system. For example, Hkey_Local_Machine controls the hardware setup for your machine. (A complete list of the subtrees and their functions appears below.)

- Each of the folders within a subtree is called a *key*. (As you'll notice, keys can contain subkeys and sub-subkeys.) The keys (and subkeys) control the configuration to a specific part of the subtree's function. For example, the key called *Mouse* within the subtree Hkey_Local _Machine contains all the mouse settings.

- The actual settings within the Registry are called *values*, or *value entries*. Each value has two parts: the value name, which identifies it, and the value data, which contains the configuration information. The values may be in either of two formats:

  - Binary (or hex representations of binary numbers), used for most hardware information.

  - String (human-readable text, like "AmiProDocument") used for most software-related information.

It's very easy to make a mistake when editing binary or hex code, so, once we begin the discussion of editing the Registry, stick to editing string values.

Subtree Functions

As mentioned above, the six branches of the Registry divide up the configuration for your computer and where it fits into the network. Table 3.2 illustrates those divisions.

Opening the Registry

If you're like me, you like to play with something when learning how to use it. At the very least, it's nice to have it in front of you. Therefore, at this point you may be saying to yourself, "This talk of the Registry is all very well, but how do I *start* the silly thing?"

First of all, unless you installed Windows 95 from the CD, you *can't*—the Registry Editor is not available with the floppy disk version. Second, by default the Registry Editor is not included on any menus, perhaps so idle curiosity doesn't blow away the system configuration.

If you installed Windows 95 from the CD, you can open the Registry in a few different ways:

- Choose Run from the Start menu and type **Regedit** in the space provided.

- *Or,* open the Windows folder and double-click the icon labeled REGEDIT.

- *Or,* add the Registry Editor to the Start menu. The process is just like adding any other icon—click the Start menu, then choose Settings, then Taskbar. Click the Add button, and type **C:\windows\regedit .exe** in the text box provided. When prompted, indicate the folder in which you want to place the icon, and choose a name for the icon. The Registry Editor will now be available from whichever folder you put it in.

TABLE 3.2	**SUBTREE**	**DESCRIPTION**
Location of Your Computer's Configuration Information	HKEY_Classes_Root	Contains the file associations and OLE links, the information that tells your system, "When the user double-clicks on a file with the extension .BMP, start up PBRUSH.EXE to display the file." Much of this information is duplicated in the Local_Machine subtree, as Root is a duplicate of Hkey_Local_Machine\Software\Classes.
	HKEY_Current_User	Contains the user profile (colors, sounds, applications, etc.) for the person currently logged in to the machine. This subtree is a subset of Hkey_Users (described below).
	HKEY_Local_Machine	Contains information about the hardware installed on the machine and the file associations and port assignments. You'll do most of your work in this subtree.
	HKEY_Users	Contains both the default user profile for someone who hasn't logged in before and the profile for the current user.
	HKEY_Current_Config	Points to Hkey_Local_Machine\Config, the subtree that records the current configuration of the hardware attached to the computer.
	HKEY_Dyn_Data	Contains dynamic information about Plug and Play hardware attached to the computer. The information contained in this subtree is stored in RAM, so you don't have to reboot to update it.

Navigating in the Registry

Navigating in the Registry is pretty simple. When you open the Registry Editor, the six branches are visible. Click on the one you want, and it opens into its keys. Click on the key you want, and you'll see *its* keys (if the key icon has the plus sign in a box that indicates that it has subkeys) and values. Double-click on the entry in the data column of a value to edit it.

The big trick in the Registry lies not in moving around, but in finding where you want to be. When you're looking for something, how do you know where to find it?

Finding things in the Registry is partially a function of logic and experience, and partially a function of the available tools. So far as the logic part goes, where would you look for configuration information about your mouse? Hkey_Current_User doesn't sound very likely, as the mouse drivers for a machine won't change from user to user. Hkey_Local _Machine is a much more likely starter, as the mouse is part of the machine *any* user will use.

Using the Find Tool

When logic won't help you, there's always the Find tool. Think of a word that relates to the configuration information you're looking for (keep it short, as the Registry Editor's style is telegraphic, to say the least) and choose Find from the Edit menu. If the first Find that you come up with doesn't work, press F3 or choose Find Next from the Edit menu, and the Registry Editor will look for the next incidence of that word for you.

Notice that the Find tool is more useful in Windows 95 than in Windows NT, as the Registry is organized differently. Rather than devoting a separate window to each subtree, as Windows NT does, Windows 95 includes every subtree in the same window so you can extend searches from subtree to subtree.

TIP	When searching for a word, start as close to the top of the Registry as possible if you're not certain which subtree you should be looking in. If the word doesn't appear in the subtree in which you started, the Registry Editor will begin searching in the subtree next on the list. If you begin the search in one of the lower subtrees and the word does not appear in that subtree or any of the ones listed after it, the Registry Editor does not go to the top of the list and begin again.

Editing the Local Registry

Editing the Registry is mostly a matter of finding what you want—once you get that far, the rest is easy. The simplest way to explain how to make changes to the Registry is to do it. In this section, we'll go through the process of changing the color of the buttons from the gray of the default Windows color scheme to blue. The process includes three main steps:

- Backing up the Registry
- Editing the configuration
- Restoring the Registry (if necessary)

One problem with the Find tool: It won't search for text in Registry entries. (It *will* search for text in Registry *keys*, however.) You can get around the problem by exporting the Registry to ASCII and then searching the ASCII file.

Backing Up the Registry

Before making any changes directly to the Registry, export it to a safe place (either your local drive or, for extra security, to your computer's Startup disk). If you have this backup copy, you can restore your Registry very easily if you mess up your system. (If you don't, and the corruption is bad enough, you might have to reinstall the operating system. So don't skip this step.)

The easiest way to back up your system's configuration is to export the Registry to disk or to another directory. When Regedit exports a Registry, it is dumping out the entire Registry in a simple ASCII format. Essentially, exporting the Registry converts USER.DAT and SYSTEM.DAT to something you can view, search, and save. Once exported, those versions of the system configuration are not available to the system until you import them. In the meantime, you're able to make all the changes that you like to the Registry information. Take a look at Figure 3.8 to see how this works.

FIGURE 3.8

Exporting a Registry

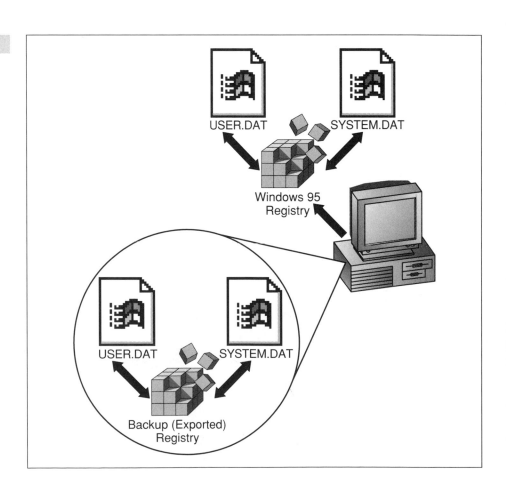

When you export a Registry it maintains a copy of the system configuration files with it. This copy, however, is isolated from the operating system (as represented by the ring around the exported files). Changes made to the current Registry do not affect the exported copies. Therefore, when you replace the current Registry with an exported one, you'll restore the operating system to the way it was when you exported the Registry.

To export the configuration information's front end, open the Registry Editor (choose Run from the Start button on the Toolbar, and type **Regedit .exe**). You should see a screen that looks like the one in Figure 3.9.

Choose Export Registry File from the Registry menu. A dialog box like the one in Figure 3.10 will appear.

FIGURE 3.9

Opening screen of the Registry Editor

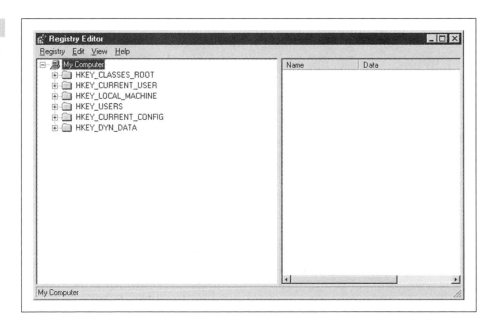

FIGURE 3.10

Export Registry File
dialog box

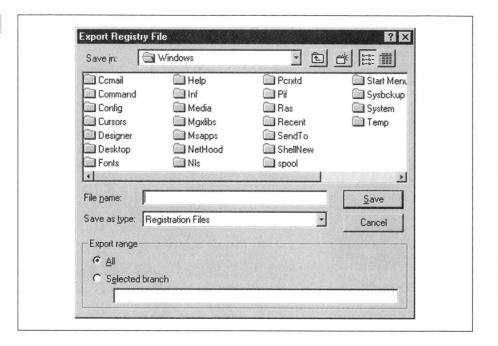

Select the disk or directory to which you want to copy your Registry and type a name for the file in the text box provided. Windows 95 supports long file names when running in protected mode, so this name can be longer than the eight-dot-three pattern you may be used to as a Windows user. As you can see in Figure 3.11, I named my backup copy **Working Registry for TSC on 6-5-95** and copied it to my \backup directory.

Click Save, and the backup copy is saved to that folder. If you open the folder, you'll see the Registry icon labeled with the name you specified.

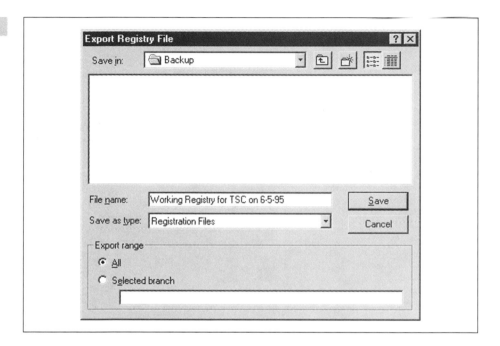

FIGURE 3.11

Export Registry File
dialog box with
export information

Editing the Registry's Contents

Now that we've saved the current configuration, we can mess around with it. Run Regedit to start up the Registry Editor.

As I said earlier, in this experiment we're going to edit the display to change the color of the buttons in the dialog boxes. Off the top of my head, I don't know which key the values that relate to this information are in, so I've got two options: I can guess (the subtree that relates to the current user and the display key within it seem likely contenders) or I can do a search for instances of the word "color" throughout the Registry. The second method seems like less work, so I'll use it.

Position the cursor in My Computer so that the search will extend through every subtree. From the Edit menu, choose Find. You'll see a dialog box that looks the one in Figure 3.12.

Type **color** in the Find What text box and click Find Next. While it's searching, a dialog box like the one in Figure 3.13 will appear.

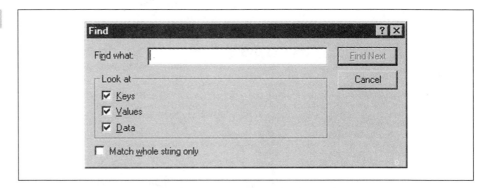

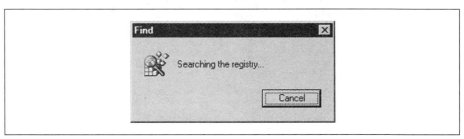

To keep the search as broad as possible, I've instructed the Editor to look at keys, values, *and* data for the keyword, as it does by default. If I checked *Match whole string only*, Regedit would only find "color", but this way matches like "ButtonColor" or "Colors" will count as hits as well. I'll keep it unchecked, as I'm not sure exactly how the word will appear.

The first hit, as you see in Figure 3.14, doesn't look like what I need (I can't manipulate the hex accurately), so I'll click F3 to find the next "Color."

And so it goes, until I find the one I want as in Figure 3.15.

Aha! "ButtonFace" looks like the value name I need. If you've messed around with changing color values numerically, you'll know that the value 192 192 192 indicates a nice medium gray made of middling amounts of red, green, and blue.

FIGURE 3.14

First result of Find action

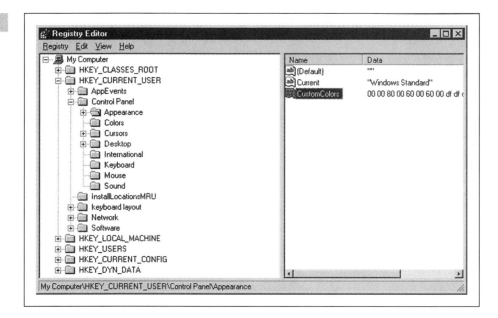

FIGURE 3.15

Section of Registry that controls display colors

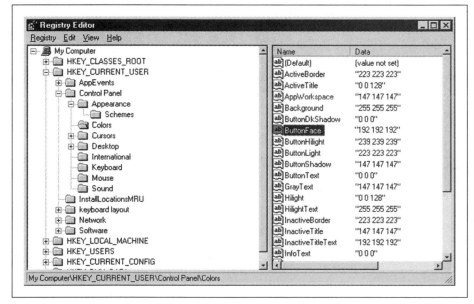

NOTE

Brief digression—0 is least, 255 is most; three 0s would be black and three 255s would be white. You can get a feel for this in Paint. Open the program from the Start menu, and double-click one of the colored squares at the bottom of the screen. That will put you in a dialog in which you can edit the numeric values of the colors and see the results immediately.

To make the tops of the buttons blue, double-click on the word "Button-Face." You'll see a dialog box like the one in Figure 3.16.

Type **0 0 255** in the Value data text box to show no red and no green but full-intensity blue, and click OK. Notice that the button faces are still gray—the change has not taken effect yet.

Exit the Registry Editor and log off (you don't have to restart the computer). When the login dialog box shows up, it will be an obnoxious shade of blue.

Restoring the Registry

As the change you made is pretty easy to remember, you could restore the Registry (and get rid of that obnoxious blue) by searching for "Button-Face" and changing its value data back to 192 192 192. Once you logged off and back on again, the change would take effect.

FIGURE 3.16

Editing a Registry value

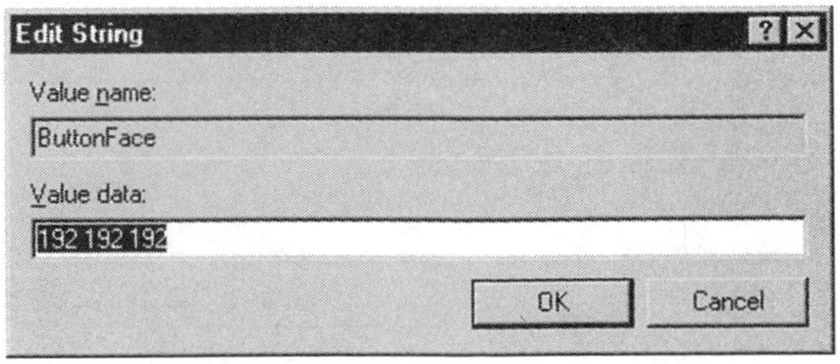

WARNING   You can't reverse an importing action: once you've imported a Registry or a subtree thereof, it replaces whatever was there before. If you want to save a copy of the configuration, export it before you import the old one.

Since we're practicing for real-world changes that may not be quite so easy to reverse, however, let's do a real trial. There are two ways in which you can restore your Registry to the way it was before:

- Import the Registry from the Registry Editor.
- *Or*, activate the icon of the backup in its folder.

In either case, what you're doing is replacing the current configuration with the one you exported. As you recall from earlier in this chapter, when you export the Registry it maintains a copy of what the .DAT files looked like at the time you exported. When you import that saved file, you replace the current configuration with that saved one.

To import a saved Registry, select Import Registry File from the Registry menu and move to the directory where you stored the backup (in my case, C:\backup). You'll see the name of the backup copy as you do in Figure 3.17.

FIGURE 3.17

Importing a Registry

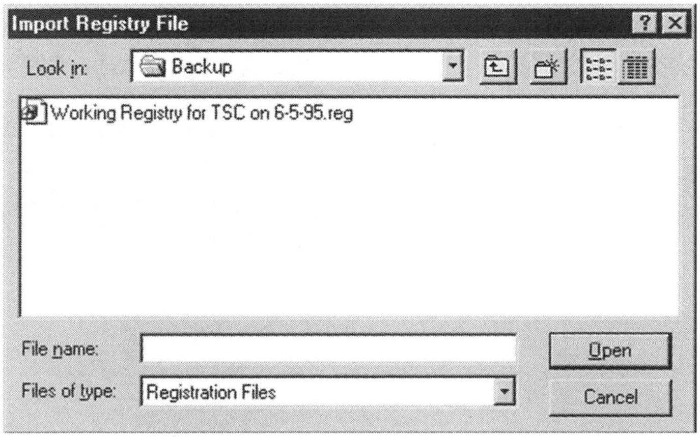

Click Open, and the Registry Editor will replace the current copy of the Registry with the one you just imported. A status box like the one in Figure 3.18 will show the progress of the importing process.

When the file is fully imported, a dialog box like the one in Figure 3.19 will announce the fact.

Importing a saved Registry from its folder is even easier. Open the folder to which you exported the file (as in Figure 3.20) and double-click it.

When you activate the saved file, it imports itself into the Registry, showing the same dialog boxes that you saw with the previous approach.

Whichever method you choose, the system configuration will revert to the one in the restored Registry as soon as you log off and log back on.

What about Duplicate Entries?

The Registry sometimes repeats itself. For example, as we noted earlier, some of the information found in Hkey_Classes_Root also appears in Hkey_Local_Machine. If the same values appear in two different subtrees, which subtree controls?

FIGURE 3.18

Importing Registry status dialog box

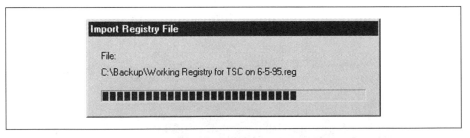

FIGURE 3.19

Import confirmed

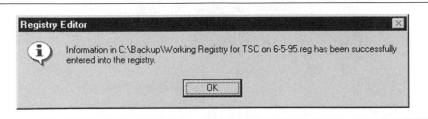

FIGURE 3.20

Folder containing
exported Registry

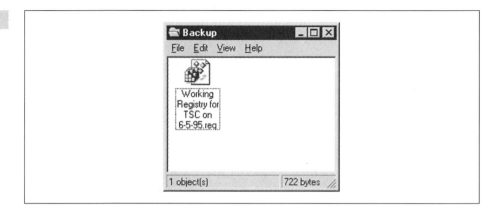

The subtrees of the Registry are arranged in a hierarchy. If the same information appears in more than one subtree of the Registry and you manually change it in only one subtree, then the effect of the change upon the system depends on where that subtree falls in the hierarchy. Generally speaking, system-specific information outranks user-specific information. For example, a setting that appears in both the Local_Machine and Users subtrees will be controlled by what's in Local_Machine. Please note that this only applies to those times when you've edited the Registry directly; if you edit the system configuration from the Control Panel the settings will be updated in every subtree in which they appear.

For example, you can set file associations through the Registry to link files with a particular extension to an application. Four subtrees of the Registry contain value data for file associations: Hkey_Classes_Root, Hkey _Current_User, Hkey_Local_Machine, and Hkey_Users. By default, all files with the extension .1ST (as in README.1ST) are linked with Notepad, so if you activate a file with that extension you'll also open Notepad. If you change the file association from Notepad to Ami Pro (a Lotus word processor), you'll open up Ami Pro when you activate any file with the .1ST extension. But if you edit the file association in one subtree of the Registry at a time, here's what will happen:

- If only Hkey_Classes_Root is set to AmiPro, then .1ST files will open Ami Pro when activated.

- If only Hkey_Current_User is set to Ami Pro, then .1ST files will open Notepad when activated.

- If only `Hkey_Local_Machine` is set to AmiPro, then `.1ST` files will open Ami Pro when activated.

- If only `Hkey_Users` is set to Ami Pro, then `.1ST` files will open Notepad when activated.

> **NOTE**
>
> By the way, this is an excellent example of how you can make an invalid entry into the Registry without it telling you that the change won't work—you just find out when you attempt to use the system with the changes that you've wrought. Ami Pro cannot open any file that is not a valid Ami Pro document with a `.SAM` extension unless you import the file into Ami Pro using a listed filter. If you edit the Registry to open Ami Pro when you activate any file with a `.1ST` suffix, Ami Pro will start up all right when you double-click a `README.1ST` object, but it will not open the file—because it is not an Ami Pro document.

Although there appears to be a contradiction in that the Root subtree and the Local Machine subtree appear to control file associations independently of each other, remember that the Root subtree is really `Hkey_Local_Machine\Software\Classes`, so changes made to Root are changes made to that key and subkey within Local Machine.

Editing a Remote Registry

Why would you need to edit the Registry of a remote machine? It's handy for any of the following situations, where it's easier to fix the problem from your desk than it is to go to the ailing workstation or you *can't* fix the problem from the local machine.

- The person using that machine played with the display settings and turned their screen entirely black.

- You want to copy the same user configuration to several machines.

- A user has connected to the wrong network drives and can't find their files.

Editing the Registry of a remote computer works pretty much the same way as editing a local one: the main difference lies in the process of connecting to the remote Registry in the first place. In this section, we'll talk about how to connect to the remote machine (and some of the potential connection glitches you may encounter) and what you can expect to see when you've connected.

Preparing to Administer a Remote Computer

Before you can edit another computer's Registry, both you and the other computer must have at least one network protocol (like NetBEUI or IPX/SPX) in common and the Remote Registry service set up.

To install the Remote Registry (or any other) service on a computer, insert the Windows 95 CD-ROM in the drive and follow these steps:

1. Open the Control Panel and choose Networks.

2. Click on the Add button, and, in the Select Network Component Type dialog box that appears, double-click Services.

3. From the Select Network Service dialog box, click the Have Disk button. When prompted, specify the path to `\Admin\Nettools \Remotreg` on the CD. You'll see a file called `REGSERV.INF` in the menu. Select it, and click OK.

4. Select Microsoft Remote Registry from the Models list and click OK, then click OK to get out of the dialog box altogether. Windows 95 will search the CD for all the files that it needs to set up the service.

After you exit from the Network dialog, Windows 95 will tell you that you must restart for the change to take effect, but you don't have to reboot then unless you want to be able to use the Remote Registry service right away.

You'll need to install the Remote Registry Service on both the administering machine and any Windows 95 machine to be administered.

Connecting to the Remote Computer

You must initiate a specific connection to a remote machine's Registry in order to edit it. To do so, open the Registry Editor and choose Connect to Remote Registry from the Registry menu. A dialog box like the one in Figure 3.21 will appear.

Type in the name of the computer you want to administer, or, to make sure that you type it correctly and choose from the right domain, click Browse and choose it from the dialog box like the one in Figure 3.22. All machines connected to the network will be displayed, whether or not they're Windows 95 machines or have the Remote Registry service running.

Choose the machine to connect to (in this case, I'll choose AMS) and click OK. Click OK again at the next dialog box to connect to the Registry.

Troubleshooting a Remote Registry Connection

At this point, you should be successfully connected. If you are not, you may see a dialog box like the one in Figure 3.23. If you see this dialog box, make sure of the following things:

- You've connected to a machine running Windows 95.

- The Remote Registry service is running on both machines.

FIGURE 3.21

Connect Network Registry dialog box

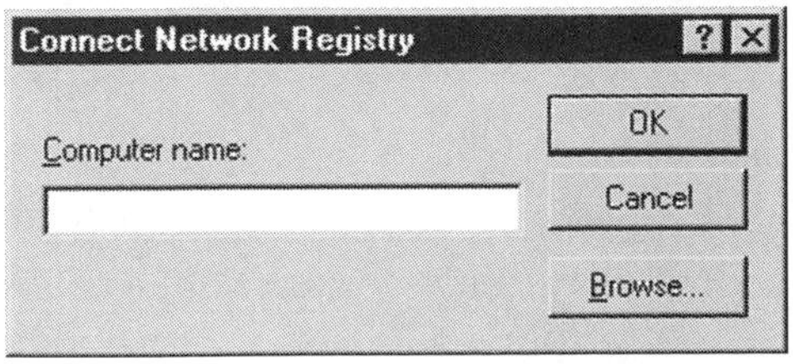

FIGURE 3.22

Browse list for Remote
Registry administration

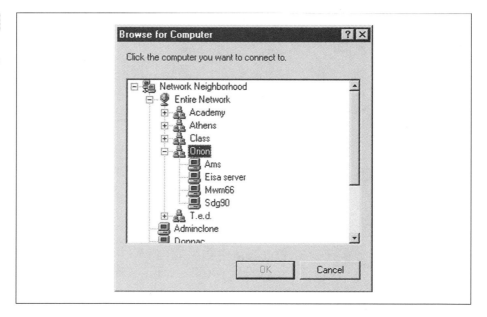

You might see a message telling you that you don't have permission to edit the remote Registry, as in Figure 3.24. You'll see this message if:

- You've logged onto a domain that doesn't have permission to administer the machine's Registry.

- Your account is a member of a group not permitted to administer the remote computer (by default, only Domain Administrators have this permission).

If you're running NT on your network and have more than one domain, you may wonder if establishing a *trust relationship* between two domains

FIGURE 3.23

Unsuccessful attempt
to connect to remote
Registry

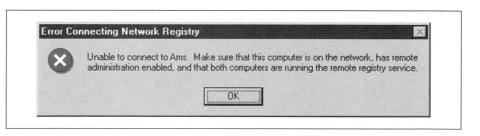

FIGURE 3.24

No permission to edit
remote Registry

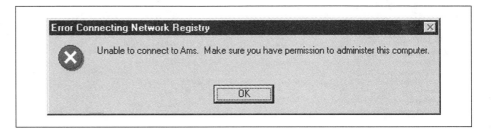

means that the trusted domain can administer machines who have permitted members of the other domain to administer them.

Nope.

No matter what the trust relationships between the two domains are, if you don't log on to the domain with explicit permission to administer the remote machine, you'll see a message like the previous one.

Permitting Other Groups to Administer Remote Registries

The previous section described how to set up a computer for remote administration of its Registry by members of the Domain Administrators group. If, for some reason, members of other groups require this ability, the setup process is a little more involved.

Open Control Panel and click on the Passwords icon. You'll see three tabs: Change Passwords, Remote Administration, and User Profiles. Click on the Remote Administration tab. You should see a dialog box that looks like the one in Figure 3.25.

In this screen, you can see the users and/or groups (by default, only the group Domain Administrators) that currently have permission to remotely administer this machine. Click the Add button to select other remote administrators. You'll see a screen that looks like Figure 3.26, with a list that includes a globe icon and various head icons.

Single heads are individuals; double heads are groups. The globe signifies everyone on the network. Notice that a list box in the upper right corner lets you specify the domain to draw administrators from. It's perfectly

FIGURE 3.25

Setting Remote
Administration options

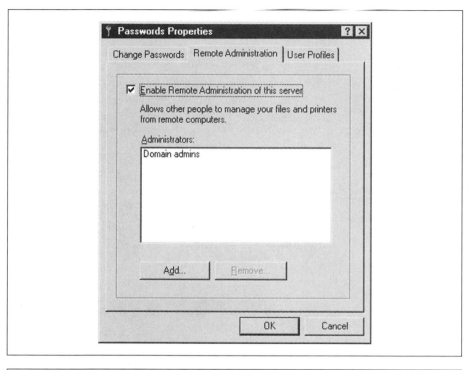

FIGURE 3.26

Adding Remote
Administrators

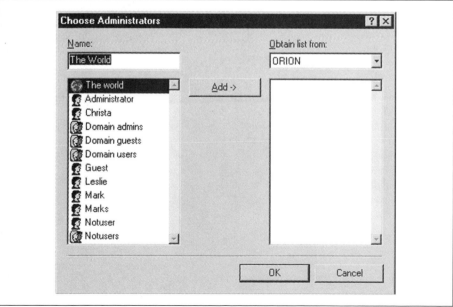

okay to have some administrators from one domain and some from another, thus eliminating the need to set up double accounts for remote administrators. Click on the individuals or groups who you want to be able to administer your computer, and then click Add. If you chose your administrators from more than one domain, the administrator's domain name will appear in parentheses next to his or her name. In Figure 3.27, I've added the group Domain Administrators from T.E.D. and the user Leslie from ORION to the list of those permitted to remotely administer my computer.

Click OK and, as you can see in Figure 3.28, you'll be back at the initial screen, where you can see the two new members added to the list. If Leslie or any member of T.E.D.'s Domain Administrator group log on to a machine with the Remote Registry service running, they will be able to edit my computer's Registry.

FIGURE 3.27

Administrators from two workgroups added to list

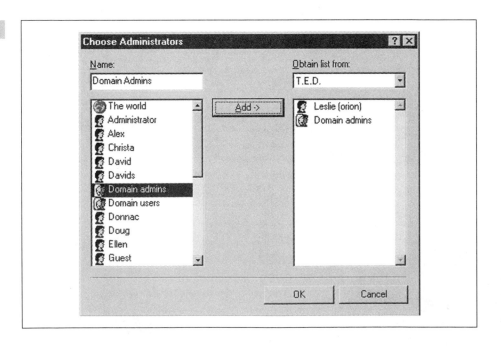

FIGURE 3.28

New list of remote
administrators

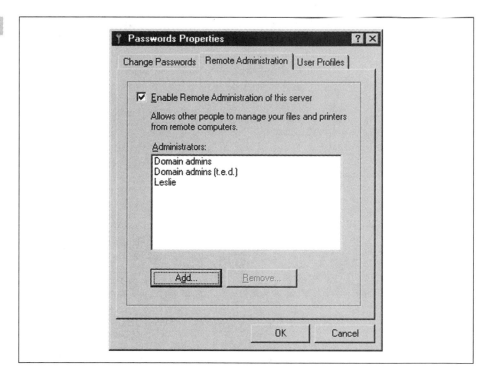

WARNING When choosing the accounts that have access to your Registry,
don't forget that you're giving people the power to destroy your
system's configuration and require you to reinstall. Don't give
this capability to just anyone.

To remove users or groups from the list of a machine's remote administrators, click on the name and click the Remove button. A message box
will appear, asking if you're sure that you want to remove that administrator; click OK to confirm the removal. Even if you have only one administrator in the list, you can still remove it—there's no minimum.

Editing the Remote Registry

If everything went well and you saw no error messages, you're now ready to edit the remote Registry. Your screen should look like the one in Figure 3.29.

From here on out, the editing process is the same as it is for the local Registry. When you've finished making changes, exit the Registry Editor or choose Disconnect Remote Registry from the Registry menu.

WIN.INI and SYSTEM.INI under Windows 95

There are lots of files in the Windows world with the extension .INI, for *initialization*. Excel, for example, automatically creates and maintains a

FIGURE 3.29

View of remote
Registry

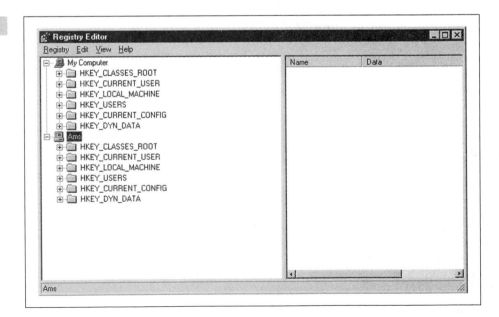

file called EXCEL.INI which tells Excel things like whether to start up in a maximized condition, what the previous few files accessed were, and what user options should be set. Most other applications create their own .INI files—Ami Pro uses AMIPRO.INI, Word For Windows creates WINWORD.INI, and so on.

If a program creates an initialization file for itself, however, that file is for its personal use *only*—other programs don't access it. For general configuration information, Win16 applications access two more general initialization files: WIN.INI and SYSTEM.INI.

Contents of .INI files

It's hard to draw a clear and distinct line between what SYSTEM.INI and WIN.INI do, as WIN.INI has existed since the Windows 1.0 days, and SYSTEM.INI has only been around since version 3.0. Although it's tempting to say that SYSTEM.INI controls the hardware configuration of Windows, and WIN.INI contains user preferences and software configuration, that's not 100 percent accurate. It *is* a decent approximation, however, so use it if you like, just to get a grasp on what these two files do.

The .INI files are all divided up into *sections*. Sections are demarcated by section names, which are surrounded by square brackets. One section, for example, is called [boot]; the [boot] section not only contains references to drivers, it also contains information about some Windows fonts, screen savers, language to use for messages, and which program shell to use.

The New Look of .INI Files

If you installed Windows 95 on top of your previous Windows directory, the installation procedure saved your Windows 3.x SYSTEM.INI and WIN.INI under the names SYSINI.W31 and WININI.W31. The contents of the old and the new files do not match—although they're similar, the entries in the new .INI files reflect the differences between a Windows overlay on DOS and the Windows 95 operating system. The old configuration information was set aside in the .W31 files, and new .INI files created from the information in the Registry.

What's different? The exact entries will vary from PC to PC, depending on your hardware and how you set up Windows, but here's some of the more important differences in each initialization file.

SYSTEM.INI versus SYSINI.W31

SYSTEM.INI, recall, is more or less responsible for recording hardware information. It contains configuration information for drivers, network setup, the display, the process of starting Windows, and so forth.

Thus, when you change the operating system, the display modes it supports, and the way that it does networking, it's not surprising that entries corresponding to those qualities should change also. Many of the important differences occur in the [boot] and [386Enh] sections of SYSTEM.INI. For example:

- The default shell in SHELL= (the program that, among other things, provides the background to Windows) differs from Windows 3.x; in Windows 95 it provides access to user programs with EXPLORER.EXE rather than to PROGMAN.EXE.

- The protected-mode screen grabber (the program that saves the information in your DOS screens when you flip from DOS programs to Windows) is now called VGAFULL.3GR instead of VGADIB.3GR. There *is* no real-mode screen grabber (indicated in SYSINI.W31 as 286Grabber) in the Windows 95 SYSTEM.INI.

- Windows 3.x defined the display font for non-Windows applications displaying either 40 or 80 columns and 25 or fewer lines (EGA80WOA.FON, for example). Windows 95 skips these entries entirely—the display settings for DOS programs are set in their Properties dialog boxes, as discussed in Chapter 13.

- The line allowing Windows to bypass DOS and BIOS to access a Western-Digital hard disk (device=*wdctrl) is now gone, as Windows 95 is its own operating system and doesn't need special statements to permit 32-bit disk access.

- Many Windows 3.x virtual device drivers are rolled into VMM.VXD, so individual statements referring to those drivers are missing from Windows 95.

- The [mci] section, which describes how Windows handles multimedia applications that use the media control interface, has some new entries for video handling.

- SYSTEM.INI under Windows 95 contains an entirely new section devoted to networking, including entries to define how TCP/IP works.

Please note that this list doesn't include *every* difference between a Windows 3.x SYSTEM.INI and a Windows 95 SYSTEM.INI, but these are some of the more important variances. There are some other differences, in that the names of some programs have changed so the entries look different (such as the mouse.drv=Logitech Mouse entry changing to mouse.drv=Logitech), but variations like that aren't really substantial. Of course, if you change your system configuration after installing Windows 95, the contents of the .INI file will change as well.

WIN.INI versus WININI.W31

WIN.INI more or less keeps track of the user setup and application software for Windows. It also keeps configuration information for Windows programs that don't have a .INI file (like Micrografx Designer). It's a much larger file than SYSTEM.INI, containing information about all of your software's fonts and OLE links.

The WIN.INI files for Windows 3.x and Windows 95 are more similar than their respective SYSTEM.INI files. The major changes are as follows:

- Some new entries relating to Windows 95's video capabilities are added to the [mci extensions] section.

- Several entirely new sections have been added, relating to:
  - the Registry
  - the ATM (Adobe Type Manager, not Asynchronous Transfer Mode) workaround for printing
  - new Microsoft applications

In general, however, you don't need to worry about these settings. They're not anything that you should need to change from inside the .INI file—path settings and other like information are more easily edited from the Control Panel or the Taskbar item on the Startup Menu.

Why Do I Have .INI Files?

.INI files have some built-in failings. They can only be nested in two layers (the [section] name and the entries included in the section). They can only be up to 64K in size. If you're using .INI files, backing up your system's configuration requires copying four files (both .INI files, CONFIG.SYS, and AUTOEXEC.BAT). If you've got this wonderful Registry that keeps all of your configuration files in one manageable database (and, even if the entries are cryptic, they're certainly no more cryptic than the entries in a CONFIG.SYS or SYSTEM.INI file), then why do you still *have* WIN.INI and SYSTEM.INI files?

The answer is: for backward compatibility.

Previous versions of Windows relied on SYSTEM.INI and WIN.INI. These two ASCII text files control roughly the same things as SYSTEM.DAT and USER.DAT respectively, so retaining the .INI files might seem to be a waste of time. But applications written for previous versions of Windows don't know how to look in the Registry for the information that they need.

Windows 95 is a 32-bit operating system, but Microsoft realized that it couldn't possibly make Windows 95 incompatible with the 16-bit applications that Windows users have been buying for years. In the interests of avoiding a riot on the front steps of the Redmond compound, Windows 95 was designed to accommodate both 32-bit applications written for 95, which can access the Registry, and 16-bit applications, which *cannot*. Hence, you've still got WIN.INI and SYSTEM.INI files floating around in your system.

If you install Windows 95 on top of Windows 3.x, then the information in WIN.INI and SYSTEM.INI is copied into the Registry during Setup. When you make changes to the Registry, either directly or via one of the graphical tools like the Control Panel, they're updated in WIN.INI and SYSTEM.INI for the use of applications not designed to work with the Registry. Note that your Windows 3.x .INI files (now with .W31 extensions) are not affected by changes to the system Registry.

Generally speaking, you shouldn't need to edit either WIN.INI or SYSTEM.INI directly—most of the settings that they control are accessible via the Control Panel. If you need to fine-tune an application (for example, to change the default source directory to import pictures from), then you'll need to make those changes to that specific application's .INI file. You can edit or view any .INI file in Notepad.

For more information on configuring old DOS and Win16 applications to work with Windows 95, turn to Chapter 13.

CHAPTER

4

Setting up 95— Strategies and Tactics

EVER been through a major software upgrade? If you're like most PC support people, then you probably have—and I'm sure the memories aren't too positive. Now I can't say that a mass migration to Windows 95 will be easy, or even *can* be easy, but there are some right ways and some wrong ways to go about it. In this chapter, I intend to push you in the direction of some of the right ways.

I think the most important part of a successful Windows installation—or, for that matter, *any* new software installation—lies in understanding your options, the pitfalls, and ways to make the transition as automated and smooth as possible.

One thing I should mention about this chapter: As this concerns setting up Windows 95, you'll see references to things that we haven't covered yet; for example, you'll see a number of references to networking concepts, even though we haven't discussed networking yet. I must apologize for that, but there's a kind of "chicken and egg" nature to discussing setup, so I'll ask your forbearance in advance.

Getting Ready for a Windows 95 Installation

Once upon a time, in order to install a piece of software on my system, all I needed to do was create a new directory, copy the files to that directory, add the new directory to the path, and I was done. Well, those days are long gone, and modern installations require more preparation and better documentation. As I see it, the main steps in preparing for a Windows 95 installation are:

- Inventory your hardware.
- Test the hardware.
- Document the hardware.
- Inventory your current software.
- Test Windows 95 compatibility with that software.
- Prepare any PIFs for DOS software.

We'll examine some of those steps in this chapter, and some in later chapters. First, let's look at the hardware.

Inventory Your Hardware

Modern organizations using PC's often do not use a standard suite of hardware, mainly due to the commodity nature of PC hardware. (No one would have guessed this a few years ago, but in most companies it is more common to find standardized software than it is to find any kind of hardware standards.) This means that it is quite likely you will have to install Windows 95 on a wide variety of hardware, and that can pose a problem. You see, Windows 95 is very good about detecting the hardware that you have in a system, but, like any software, it cannot detect *all* hardware. So, to be prepared for the inevitable, you still have the important job of figuring out what hardware you have on your system before you embark on a Windows 95 installation.

Now, when I say that you should inventory your hardware, I don't really mean that you have to know "Compaq model Deskpro M/50, 486 processor"; actually, that kind of information is easy for the installation software to figure out. Here's what you need for your inventory:

- The type of monitor on your system.
- What expansion boards are in your system; in particular, any LAN adapters, proprietary CD-ROM interfaces, SCSI host adapters, video adapters, other unusual hard disk controllers, nonstandard parallel or serial ports, and any internal or external modems.

- What system resources the boards require—I/O addresses, IRQ levels, DMA channels, RAM addresses, and ROM addresses.

- Any network-specific information, like network names, IP addresses, DNS servers, gateways, subnet masks, and the like.

I know that gathering this information isn't fun; believe me, I know, as I've done it many times. But if you don't have the information at your fingertips when you are installing Windows 95, then there is a decent chance that you may be stopped with a difficult question right in the middle of the installation. The result would be a half-installed copy of Windows 95—not a very pretty prospect. Of course, if there is absolutely no way for you to get this information, then go ahead and install Windows 95; as I've said before, its detection software is really quite good. But gathering this information—in particular, gathering the system resource information—is absolutely essential to supporting PCs in the '90s. Even if you aren't going to install Windows 95, the utility of this information should pay for at least some of your time.

What Kind of Hardware Should You Have for 95?

While I'm on the topic of hardware, let's take a minute and talk about what sort of hardware will work with Windows 95, and especially what hardware will work best.

CPU Types

Windows 95 will run on any 386 or later processor. This is not a bogus claim, despite what some people have said about 95 requiring a 486 processor. In my experience, Windows 95 runs as well and as fast on a given piece of hardware as Windows 3.x did. If you liked the way that Windows ran on your old Windows 3.x system, then you'll like Windows 95 on that same system. Does that mean that there *isn't* any reason to upgrade your processor with Windows 95? Well, there *is* one reason: Windows 95 multitasks better than Windows 3.x, which means that you'll be more likely to attempt to multitask in the first place—and once you start multitasking, you'll develop a real need for speed. You can certainly multitask with a 16-MHz 386 processor; but, then, even though the rear bumper on my

Honda Civic is wide enough to accommodate two trailer hitches, I don't imagine that I would enjoy pulling two boats with my Civic. On the other hand, one reason why a *Pentium* may not be warranted is that Windows 95 code has not been optimized for the Pentium processor, so you will not get the maximum power from a Pentium.

Memory

Windows 95 really only needs as much memory as Windows 3.x to get its work done. While the outside of the Windows 95 box claims that you can run Windows 95 in a tiny amount of memory, anyone who has tried to run Windows in either flavor knows that 4MB falls somewhat short of Windows' requirements.

My recommendation is that anyone buying a new system should purchase 16MB of RAM, but if you can only afford 8MB right now, you'll be fine with your current applications.

The question of how much memory you really need is connected to the question, "What programs are you trying to run?" If you do not have a network and you only run one program at a time, then you'll probably be happy with 6MB of memory. Network redirector software, however, can take up to 1MB of memory for its buffers and such, and the increasingly-popular TCP/IP network software requires a bit more than that to run well. What I'm really saying here is, Don't even *think* of attaching to a network if you have less than 8MB of RAM. All of the Windows modules take up memory, whether it's dial-up networking, a mail client, scheduling software, or whatever. You will see that the System Monitor can let you keep track of your system's memory and, to a certain extent, follow which component is using that memory.

Disk Interfaces

When you purchase a hard disk drive, that drive must have an accompanying disk interface; this interface is typically one of two types: SCSI or IDE. IDE is the more popular of the two, mainly due to its price. You can buy a 1GB+ IDE drive for about three hundred dollars as of this writing, but a SCSI drive of the same size would probably cost around five hundred dollars.

In general, however, I often recommend SCSI hardware, largely because of its flexibility. Whereas IDE can only support hard drives and the occasional tape drive or CD-ROM, SCSI supports more devices; it is common to see scanners, tape drives, optical storage devices, CD-ROMs, and, of course, hard drives with a SCSI interface. The benefit, then, of SCSI is that you simply place one board in your system and that one board drives a variety of peripherals.

The fact of the matter, however, is that you probably have IDE hardware on your system, and that's okay—okay, that is, as long as we're talking about Windows 95. If we were discussing a less popular operating system, like NT or OS/2, then it would be a far smarter move to buy SCSI rather than IDE. There is one reason for this: software support. It is much easier to find software support for a CD-ROM attached to a SCSI host adapter than for one attached to an IDE adapter.

NOTE   The way I wrote that looks as though I am saying that you can take a CD-ROM and either attach it to an IDE or SCSI host adapter at your option—but that's not true. When you purchase a CD-ROM, one of the features that you must choose is the CD-ROM's interface type—SCSI, IDE, or proprietary.

Plug and Play

I've mentioned Plug and Play (PnP) before, but as long as I'm talking about hardware that works particularly well on Windows 95, it's worth mentioning that Windows 95 and Plug and Play are a terrific match. On the one hand I don't want to leave you with the impression that you must have Plug and Play-compatible hardware in order to run Windows 95, because you don't, but on the other hand it is certainly true that Windows 95 is enhanced by Plug and Play hardware. While Plug and Play-compatible systems are somewhat unusual at this writing, there is actually a huge number of computers out there that do Plug and Play sort of through the back door, and these are laptop computers. Many modern laptops have PC Card slots, and every PC Card laptop that I have ever seen can function as a Plug and Play computer for Windows 95.

> **NOTE**
>
> There is an exception to that, however; if you have a laptop with a PC Card bus system, but a docking station with normal ISA bus slots, then the Plug and Play part of Windows 95 is stymied a bit by the old ISA slots, as they do not yield to Plug and Play-type system control.

Testing Hardware

Windows 95 is like all advanced operating systems in that it requires a lot of *reliable* RAM. Also, as Windows 95 is a virtual-memory operating system, it requires that the hard disk be as dependable as the RAM; so the secret of getting a machine ready for Windows 95 is to *test your hardware*.

Testing RAM

It's very common for people to tell me that they have tested their hardware thoroughly because they have done one of the following things:

- Ran the memory test that is part of the BIOS.
- Allowed the HIMEM.SYS device driver to test memory.
- Ran the IBM PS/2 advanced diagnostics.
- Ran any basic suite of diagnostics.

And it always surprises people when I tell them this, but most memory diagnostics are of no value. You see, at one time, it was common to buy a bunch of RAM that wasn't reliable, as building RAM on a large scale was new for hardware vendors. There was a general perception in the industry that it was our job as buyers to watch out for ourselves. In the past ten years, however, memory production has become more reliable and so has memory testing by memory sales companies. You can be pretty sure when you buy a memory module today that it has been tested before it was sent to you (probably with better tools than the ones above), which is why the memory tests in the previous list are really pretty pointless.

Modern memory problems are a bit more subtle—but no less frequent. Memory chips tend not to fail by themselves; modern memory areas tend to be interactive in nature (like a memory location that tests fine all by it-self, but when you put a particular bit pattern into another memory loca-tion, an unwanted bit pattern appears in the first memory location). Now, these areas are understood by memory vendors (just ask one what a walk-ing bit error is and they'll know what you're talking about) but they are difficult to detect. Because these errors are interactive errors, vendors often cannot test for them or may lack the time to test for them; that's why *you* have to do it.

I have found only two diagnostic programs over the years that can help find these kinds of memory errors: QAPlus from DiagSoft and CheckIt from Touchstone Software. Both packages are fairly inexpensive and I rec-ommend that you have at least one of them in your software library.

When you run these packages, you must run them from a clean-booted command prompt; that could either be just straight DOS from a boot floppy or a safe-mode command prompt from Windows 95. In any case, you must boot with no device drivers and no memory-resident programs. Additionally, these memory tests have a fast test mode and a slow test mode; run the slow test mode. And don't be surprised if you occasionally come across a system that fails the slow test mode no matter what mem-ory you put in it; the failure can be caused by one of two things. First, and most likely, the memory address support circuitry on the motherboard could be faulty, or, more simply, you might just have a dirty memory socket—try cleaning that socket and re-inserting the memory. Alterna-tively, you will occasionally see a system with faulty static cache RAM. That can be very difficult to test, as I know of only one diagnostic that checks that: AMIDiag from American Megatrends Incorporated; it's another piece of software worth having around.

The reason why it's so important to test memory with Windows 95 is that, unlike DOS, Windows 95 uses all of your memory. You can think of it this way: Imagine you are walking on the second floor of an old house and you are not so certain that the floor is steady, because some of the floorboards may have rotted away. You wouldn't run the hundred-yard dash across such a floor. Instead, you'd gingerly test each board before putting your full weight on it.

It would be nice if Windows tested a floorboard before putting its weight on it—but it doesn't. If your RAM is faulty, then Windows will just crash right through the floor, taking your applications with it. That's why you must provide Windows with a completely sturdy floor in the form of thoroughly tested RAM.

Testing Disks

Now, as Windows doesn't really know the difference between RAM memory and disk memory, your disk must be every bit as reliable as your RAM—which means you need a good disk tester. The only ones that I have come across that I really trust are Steve Gibson's SpinRite program or Prime Solutions' Disk Technician Gold product. Again, you must run these on a clean PC that is only running a command prompt and nothing else.

One more thing to be aware of—these tests take *time*. Testing 16MB of RAM can take three or four hours, and testing 1GB of disk can take *days*. I know it doesn't sound like fun, but unfortunately it's necessary.

Check for Interrupt Conflicts

I may simply be beating a dead horse, but let me reiterate that it's absolutely essential that your system not have interrupt conflicts when installing any modern operating system. Now is the time to go back and make sure that there are no interrupt conflicts. The particular trouble spots to look at include:

- Sound cards set to IRQ 7, which conflicts with the parallel port.
- Ethernet cards set to IRQ 3, conflicting with a serial port.
- A third or fourth serial port added to the system, which shares an interrupt with an existing serial port.
- LAN boards set to IRQ 2 may cause problems; the answer may be to call the interrupt IRQ 9 instead of IRQ 2.

If you do not resolve interrupt conflicts with your PC before installing Windows 95, then you may get some post-installation help from the Device Manager in the Control Panel; you'll learn more about that coming up later in this chapter.

Document Your Hardware

Now that all the hardware works and you have all its resource information in one place, write it all down. After all, you'll need that information again. Since you've done all that work, don't let the effort go to waste.

If you're a small to medium-size shop, you can do what I do in my company. We tape large envelopes on the sides of our computers, and put cards inside the envelopes with information about boards. For example, suppose I installed an Ethernet card on my system. I would then get an index card and write "SMC 8216C Ethernet card installed by Minasi on 10 September 1995; uses IRQ 5, I/O address 300–30F, RAM C0000– C3FFF, no DMA or ROMs." When I need that information in a hurry, it's at my fingertips.

But wait, those of you who have already played with the Device Manager may be thinking, "Can't I get that information from Device Manager?" The answer is maybe yes and maybe no. If everything is working fine, then the answer is probably yes. But if you're mucking around with the system because something doesn't work, then the probable answer is that the Device Manager is confused, and that's why you're doing maintenance on the system in the first place.

Inventory Your Software and Test for Compatibility

Once the hardware is in place, then you'll have to worry about the part of a computer that supplies the most problems—the software. You will need a test computer loaded with both the Windows 95 software and all of the software that you use in your company.

Find Out What Software You Have

This task is simple to explain, but it will take some time to accomplish. The first thing that you need to do is make sure that you will have no 95-related software problems; do this by taking a census of all the software that everyone uses in your company. Now don't just count the big ones, like the word processor, the spreadsheet, the e-mail package, and so on; make sure you also include in your count the little programs like Calendar

Creator or those older clipper programs that have been around for the last eight years. After all, *someone* in your company uses these tools and they'll need to continue to use them once Windows 95 has been implemented in your firm. Another reason why it's important to find the little apps is that they are the programs that probably have not been tested thoroughly under 95; which means they have the greatest probability of not working under this version of Windows.

It is particularly important not to make this into a software licensing witch hunt—you don't want people hiding their applications when they see you coming. Once you have a complete list of all the software that people use in your company, then assemble all of that software on the test machine that I mentioned earlier.

Try Your Software and 95 on a Test Machine

That test machine should be connected to the network, and should be set up so that it mirrors as closely as possible a normal workstation in your company. Then sit down and put each application through its paces under Windows 95, taking notes about things that don't work properly.

Once you have the list of things that don't work properly, go back and try to find fixes. In many cases, all you'll have to do is to tweak the application a bit to solve the problem. When you find that answer, then you should put that into a file with Windows 95 upgrade notes and distribute it via the network; this way, other people don't waste time trying to make something work.

In some cases, you will find that the answer to making the application work under Windows 95 may be a simple patch that you can get from the application manufacturer, perhaps by downloading it from their bulletin board. Again, if that fixes the problem, then you should distribute the patch over your network or whatever other software distribution system you have.

You *may* find that there are some things that simply will not work under Windows 95. Now you have a hard choice: should you implement 95 or not? That will depend on how many applications do not work under 95, how many people depend on them (always remember that people are the most expensive part of a computer system and anything that keeps people from working is probably not worth the upgrade), and whether you can simply make a clean break and stop using the application.

Create PIFs for Your DOS Applications

DOS programs are different from Windows 3.x programs under Windows 95 because DOS programs require PIFs (program information files) to work properly. Building these PIFs isn't hard, but they take a little getting used to. You will learn more about that in Chapter 13.

Doing a Windows 95 Installation

Most of what's involved with a Windows 95 setup is just sticking the CD-ROM disc into its drive, logging on to it, and typing **Setup**. (I *do* hope you're installing from CD-ROM; having to install Windows 95 from floppies is the penalty for adultery in seventeen states, and fidelity rates have greatly improved since the floppy penalty was enacted.)

Once you've done one or two setups, you have probably noticed that running the Setup program is pretty labor-intensive; it insists that you click OK for little things and you have to answer a lot of specific questions about a Windows installation. You can get around that by building an *installation script* or *batch script file*. Having a batch script means that you can just say to the Setup program, "Do it," walk away, then come back a half hour later and find that the installation is mostly done, your system has rebooted, and you're back on-line. (Alternatively, you'll find that you didn't write the script correctly...)

An installation script can be a real timeserver, once you get it written. Unfortunately, many people think that they can learn to write such a file by looking in the Windows Resource Kit. There's nice information in the Resource Kit, and much of it is even accurate; but you'll find there's some information that is also *in*accurate.

There are several ways (according to Microsoft) to build a batch script:

- By hand with Microsoft documentation. This works *if* you know what you're doing.

- Automatically with SETUPLOG.TXT. Every time you install Windows 95, it actually takes the choices that you made and puts them together into a setup batch file. Kind of a neat idea, but it doesn't work without some doctoring.

- With a program called BATCH.EXE located in the admin directory of the CD-ROM. Again, a good idea, and probably the recommended path.

- By modifying the sample batch scripts in the admin\reskit\ samples directory of the CD-ROM. I've had good luck with these, as they are well-documented.

All of these options can be made to work. To my mind, it's essential to put together a batch script or two. The sad fact of the matter is that as your office's troubleshooter you *will* at some point end up reinstalling Windows a few times, just as you would have to do with any other operating system.

NOTE   Not every Windows setup option has a corresponding command in batch setup scripts, but many do.

Structure of an Installation Batch Script

Batch scripts are ASCII files, so you can create and modify them with a text editor. They look a lot like the old Windows 3.x .INI files, with sections separated by section names enclosed in square brackets. A typical batch script includes the following sections:

- **[BatchSetup]**   This is created by the BATCH.EXE program, and it's just version information. Actually, it can be deleted with no resulting problems.

- **[Setup]**   This contains overall instructions on how Setup should proceed, such as an express or a custom setup, prompt before overwriting files, and the like. Most are yes/no kinds of questions, and they're answered 1, which means yes, or 0, which means no.

- **[NameAndOrg]**   Here you fill in the user name and organization information. A related piece of information—product ID number—that you might expect would go into this section goes in [Setup] instead.

- **[Network]**   This handles the network-specific part of the installation, questions such as, "What kind of LAN adapter do you have?" or "Should we use user-level or share-level security on shared directories?"

- **[OptionalComponents]**   This is the list of parts to install, just like the Optional Components dialog box that you see when you run Setup.

There may be others, but these are the basic sections. Now let's take a look inside the sections.

The [Setup] Section

A typical [Setup] section will look like this one:

```
[Setup]
Express=1
EBD=0
ChangeDir=0
OptionalComponents=1
Network=1
System=0
CCP=0
CleanBoot=0
Display=0
PenWinWarning=0
InstallType=1
DevicePath=0
TimeZone="Pacific"
VRC=0
Uninstall=0
ProductID="9999999999"
```

The Express setting is just the Install, Express, or Custom question and, in this case, a 1 means Express (and a 0 means Custom). It's an odd kind of Express setup, however, as the batch script allows you to modify a number of things—which is what *Custom* is supposed to be, right? Display is a related setting; it answers the question "Should I display dialog boxes, or just take defaults?" You'll see Display in all the other sections as well. It seems irrelevant that it's in the [Setup] section, as it doesn't seem to do anything except quickly flash the dialog boxes if you set Display=1. Even though it shows you the dialog boxes, however, you don't get a chance to respond to them, as the Express=1 setting keeps that from happening.

EBD determines whether or not to create an Emergency Boot Disk. ChangeDir says where Setup installs Windows; 0 means to install it into the default directory. Answering 1 requires an extra line, InstallDir=, which points to wherever you want to install Windows. As you probably guessed, OptionalComponents asks whether to install optional components, PenWinWarning asks whether to display a warning about version numbers on a computer with a pen-based interface, and ProductID is the serial number of your particular copy of Windows. For large installations, you probably won't bother putting the specific serial number on each computer.

TimeZone takes a string value like "Pacific"; either look in the Resource Kit for sample values or look in the file named AUTOMATE.INF (it's on the floppies distributed with the Resource Kit). VRC=0 says that when Setup comes across a driver that has a newer date than the one it plans to install, then Setup will just install the newer driver without displaying the prompt. Uninstall says whether or not to save information needed to uninstall Windows 95; a value of 0 is most common, as it means "Don't set up an uninstall option." Alternatively, a value of 5 would set up uninstall, *as long as you install to a directory other than the previous version of the Windows directory*. If you choose 5, then you have to add a BackupDir= command to this section, and you must then specify what directory to save the uninstall information to.

As is too often the case with Microsoft products, the Resource Kit doesn't document all the lines in the .INF setup files. CleanBoot, CCP, and Network aren't explained anywhere, and it's not clear what they do. For example, no matter what you set Network to, it still installs your network drivers if they are available.

The [Network] Section

A typical [Network] section looks like the following:

```
[Network]
ComputerName="aero"
Workgroup="orion"
Description="Compaq Aero laptop"
Display=0
Clients=VREDIR
Protocols=NETBEUI
Services=VSERVER
IgnoreDetectedNetCards=0
Security=domain
PassThroughAgent="orion"
```

Most of this is pretty obvious. Clients, Protocols, and Services are the names of modules to load into Windows 95. Security tells whether to use user-level security or share-level security, and PassThroughAgent tells where to find the user lists for user-level security.

For some reason, following the [Network] section, you get an [NWLINK] and a [NWREDIR] section even if you don't specify that you want a Novell client.

The [VREDIR] Section

If you've chosen the Microsoft network client, then you'll get a section called [VREDIR] that looks like this:

```
[VREDIR]
LogonDomain="orion"
ValidatedLogon=0
```

This just tells the system which NT domain to log on to and whether to log on to the domain as soon as the network logon starts.

Creating Batch Scripts with BATCH.EXE

In most cases, you will be able to get a good batch script assembled by the Batch Script INF Editor, BATCH.EXE, shipped with the Windows Resource Kit.

Start it up, and you'll see a screen as in Figure 4.1.

FIGURE 4.1

Windows 95 batch
setup dialog box

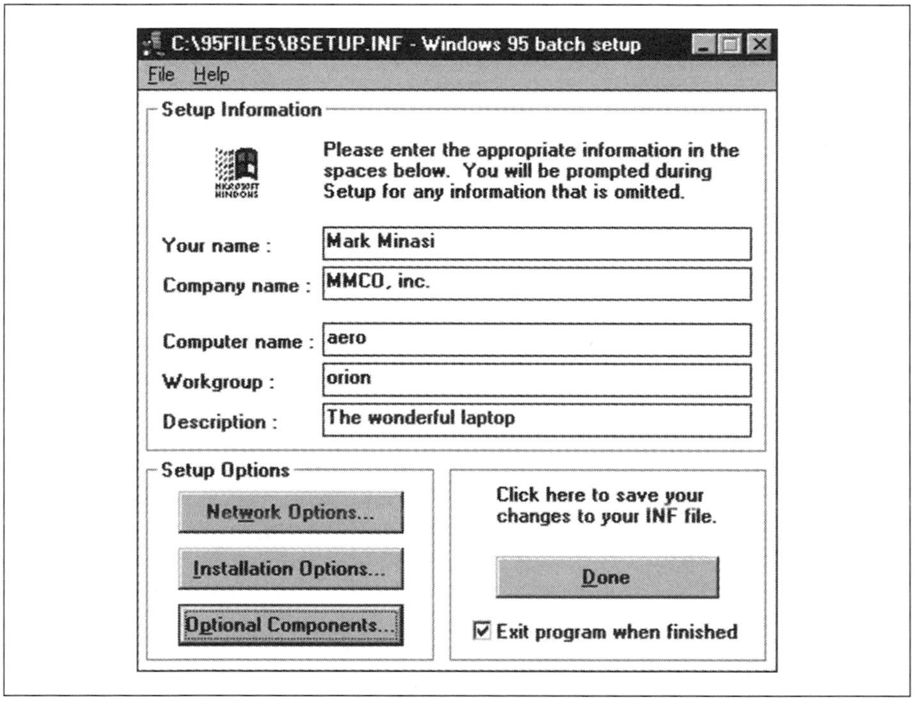

Here I've filled in a few basic pieces of information. From there, click the Installation Options, Optional Components, and Network Options buttons to specify how to install Windows 95.

When you click Installation Options, you'll see a dialog box like the one in Figure 4.2.

I'll talk about *Search source folder* in Chapter 8. *Prompt for startup disk* controls whether to create an Emergency Boot Disk, and the *PenWindows*

FIGURE 4.2

Windows 95 batch
setup—Installation
options

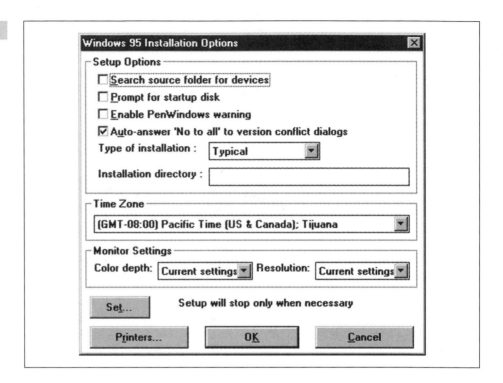

warning is the same as you read earlier in this chapter. Ditto for the *Auto-answer* option, *Type of installation*, *Installation directory*, and *Time Zone* options. *Monitor settings* lets you control how the display will look, and the *Set dialog box* controls at what points, if any, the Setup process should stop and prompt for action.

Clicking the Printers button results in a dialog box like the one in Figure 4.3.

This little stink bomb is located a few dialog boxes down into BATCH.EXE, and it's a lulu. It answers the question, "What kind of printer do you have?" Of course, you can tell Setup to stop and to prompt you while you set up Windows 95, but that's what you're trying to avoid in the first place. What you want to be able to do is to say in this dialog box, "I've got an HP series 4 on LPT1," but it's not that easy.

Printer Name is easy; it is that printer's name, which can be whatever you set it to (like "Printer next to Lunchroom"). If you share that printer, then

FIGURE 4.3

Windows 95 batch
setup—Printers

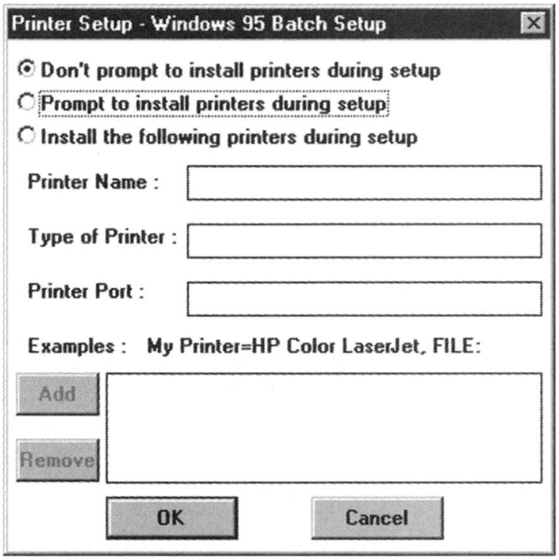

Printer Setup - Windows 95 Batch Setup

○ Don't prompt to install printers during setup
○ Prompt to install printers during setup
○ Install the following printers during setup

Printer Name :

Type of Printer :

Printer Port :

Examples :   My Printer=HP Color LaserJet, FILE:

Add

Remove

OK   Cancel

it's the name that the printer will use to advertise itself on the network. Printer Port is a port name like LPT1: that tells where the printer is attached. If the printer is a network printer, then you must construct a Universal Naming Convention (UNC) name. I'll explain UNC names in the next chapter, but briefly, they look like this:

*servername**printername*

So, for example, if you wanted to use a printer named LASERJET on a server named BIGSERVER, then you'd specify a printer port of \\BIG-SERVER\LASERJET.

The annoying part of all this is the Type of Printer field. You must fill that with the *exact* name of the printer, using the same name that you'd see in Setup's Add Printer Wizard.

For example, suppose I'm setting up an HP series 4 on a server named MWM66, and say its network name is laser16. (I'd find that stuff out from a network administrator. If yours aren't helpful, find out what kind of beer they drink and get them a six-pack.) Basically I'm just attaching to a shared printer, and I'll call it netprint4. In the Printer Name field, I type **netprint4**. In the Printer Port field, I assemble the server and printer name into its UNC name, **\\mwm66\laser16**. Then I have to find the proper type of printer. The easiest way goes like so:

1. On a Windows 95 workstation, click the Start button, then Settings, and Printers. The Printers window will appear.

2. Click on Add Printer to start up the Add Printer Wizard.

3. Click on Next to see the dialog box like the one in Figure 4.4.

FIGURE 4.4

Add Printer Wizard

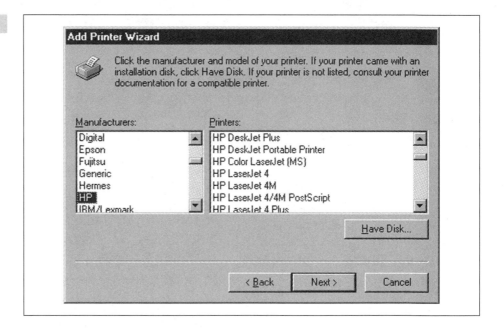

4. Browse around and find the exact printer name, like HP LaserJet 4 or HP Color LaserJet (MS).

5. Click Cancel and then close up the Printers window.

6. Now I know that the printer's true name is HP LaserJet 4, so I type that into the Type of Printer field.

7. Finally, click Add, or your work won't be saved. You'll see the line "netprint4=HP LaserJet 4,\\mwm66\laser16" in the multiline field in the Printer Setup dialog box. Yeah, it's sort of cumbersome for an easier operating system.

Back in the Batch Setup dialog box (Figure 4.1), the Optional Components button is pretty self-explanatory. For now, click the Network Options button and you'll see a dialog box like the one in Figure 4.5.

FIGURE 4.5

Windows 95 batch setup—network options

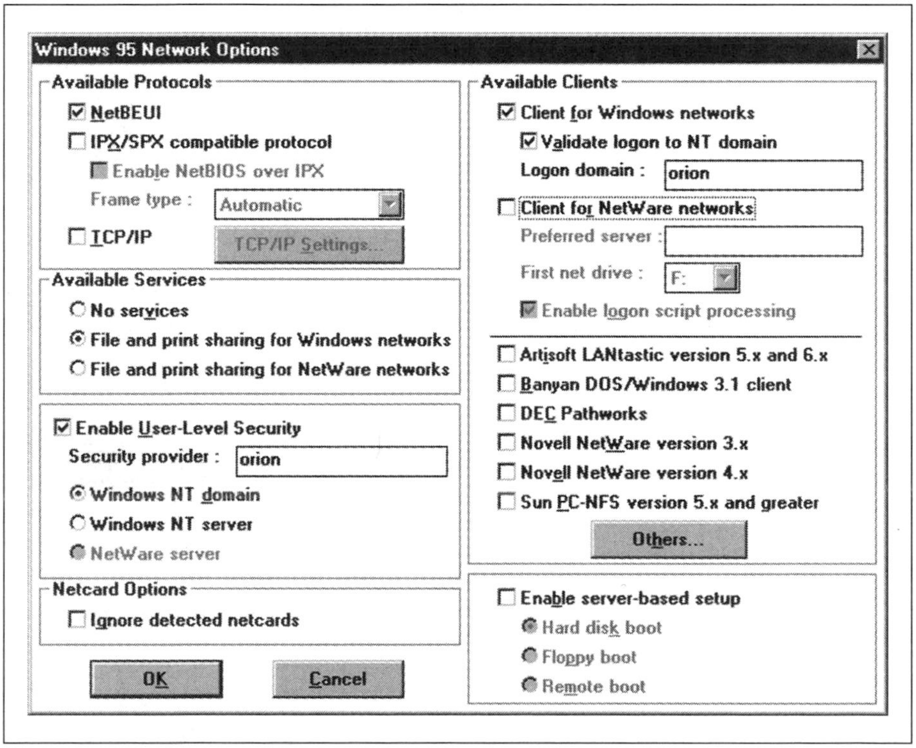

I realize that some of these options may be a bit techie for some readers, but they'll make sense after you've read the upcoming chapters on networking.

First, select a network protocol. The three mainstream protocols around which Windows 95 users will build their networks are NetBEUI,

IPX/SPX, and TCP/IP. In my example, I've built a small network, so I can use NetBEUI, the simplest of the three protocols.

Next, a Windows 95 workstation can also act as a low-powered server visible in either a Microsoft enterprise network or a Novell network. You can choose to act as a workgroup server in a Microsoft network, a Net-Ware 3.x file server, or not to share resources on the network at all. In many cases, the latter option is the right one, as it simplifies the network (there's less traffic from workstation-based servers advertising their wares) and saves memory on your workstation.

The panel below the Available Services panel allows you to choose whether to share with either share-level or user-level security (discussed in Chapter 5); oddly enough, this option remains enabled even if you choose not to share at all. If you select user-level security, this allows you to choose which particular users can use your shared disks, printers, or whatever.

If you choose to limit sharing to particular people, then you have to know who those people are in the first place. Windows 95 knows how to read user lists from a NetWare 3.x server or a Microsoft network server.

N O T E Actually, Setup can read a user list from a NetWare 4.x server if that server has bindery emulation enabled.

Netcard Options are self-explanatory; Available Clients allows you to install the software necessary to use the network services offered by Net-Ware and/or Microsoft network servers. This is also where you specify which server to log on to (in the case of a NetWare network) or which domain to log on to (in the case of a Microsoft NT network). The next panel loads support for less-popular network systems. In Chapter 8, I'll discuss in some detail the last check box, *Enable server-based setup*, when I show you how to set up Windows 95 off a server.

Then, once you've filled in all the dialog boxes, save your work. From the main window, click File, then Save As, and save the file with a .INF extension.

Building Batch Files for Many Machines

BATCH.EXE is a nice system, but it sounds like it's almost as much work as running Setup. How can it be leveraged? With Batch-Mode Save.

BATCH.EXE has an option that will mass-produce .INF files, creating .INF files that are identical to one another in all ways save that they specify different machine names and, optionally, IP addresses. (IP addresses are used on TCP/IP networks.)

It's unfortunate that you can only modify machine names and IP addresses, as it would be nice to customize user names and other things, but it's better than nothing. Here's how you get it to work.

First, build an ASCII file with all the machine names, one name to a line. If you want to add an IP address, then put it after the machine name, separated by a comma. The file might look like this:

```
mach001
mach002,199.3.2.4
markspc
```

Notice that you needn't put IP addresses on every line. Now save the file, calling it anything with the .TXT extension. From BATCH.EXE, click File, then Batch-Mode Save, and you'll be prompted to enter a file name for the machines; tell it the name of the ASCII file. BATCH.EXE then automatically writes a sequence of .INF files that are numbered numerically—names like A0001.inf, A0002.inf, A0003.inf, and so on.

Here's the problem part: When you need to find the .INF file for a particular machine, you must remember that the 14th script is file A0014.INF and that the 14th machine is Joe Smith's.

Things You Can't Control with an Installation Batch Script

Installation batch scripts have existed since Windows 3.0, but to tell you the truth, I never used them because writing them was just about impossible due to lack of documentation. In contrast, I find that I like Windows 95 batch scripts quite a bit. In fact, I like them so much that I find the things that you *can't* do with them frustrating. One of the most important things that you can't set with an installation batch script is *ghosted connections*.

Under Windows for Workgroups, you could create persistent network connections, which are network drive mappings that would come up automatically every time you logged on to the network. It simplified logon scripts, as you didn't have to worry about setting up everyone's logical drives every time they logged on to the network. They had the down side, however, of making logons a bit slow, as the workstation had to go out and find every server and re-establish connections as soon as you logged on.

With ghosted connections, Workgroups would put off re-establishing connections until you actually tried to do something with the mapped drive. It not only sped up logons, but it was convenient for workstations that only attached to networks now and then, via Remote Access Services (now known as *Dial-Up Networking*).

Under Windows 95, it's still possible to use ghosted connections: just go to Control Panel, Networks, then select Client for Microsoft Networks, and Properties. Under Network logon options, you'll see an option labeled Quick Logon, which essentially gives you ghosted connections. Click OK, back out of the windows you've opened, and, the next time you log on, the system won't complain about all the connections it can't find, as you have not yet activated Dial-Up Networking. This option cannot be enabled with a batch logon script, nor is it the default, requiring some adjustment by hand if you want it on your workstations.

Preserving DOS with Windows 95

Windows 95 offers you a dual boot option whereby you can continue to run your older DOS. All you need to do to preserve the dual boot option is to install Windows 95 into a directory other than the original Windows directory.

Once you've done that, just press F8 when you see the "Starting Windows 95" message, and you'll see the option *Start previous operating system*. Choose that and DOS returns.

If you didn't choose dual boot to begin with, then here's all that Windows 95 needs in order to be able to boot back to DOS:

- The original IO.SYS must be in the root, and must be named IO.DOS.

- The original MSDOS.SYS must be in the root, and must be named MSDOS.DOS.

- CONFIG.SYS and AUTOEXEC.BAT from DOS should be renamed to CONFIG.DOS and AUTOEXEC.DOS.

- The file MSDOS.SYS (which is ASCII) should include, in the [options] section, the line BootMulti=1.

If all that's in place, then you'll see the option to boot another operating system when you press F8.

By the way, if you install NT, then it has an operating system picker that works with 95. OS/2's Boot Manager also works fine, but a word to the wise: Do not install Windows 95 and OS/2 on the same logical drive—they can damage each other.

Ensuring That Your System Uses 32-Bit Drivers

Recall from Chapter 2 the discussion of virtual device drivers, or VxD's. I mentioned there that Windows 95 will also use older 16-bit drivers if necessary. One of the neat things about 32-bit drivers is that they can usually emulate 16-bit driver functionality. This means that your DOS sessions get access to your network cards, CD-ROMs, or whatever, *without* losing free memory space to drivers, save for a 3K-sized driver called IFSHLP.SYS which extends IFS functionality to DOS sessions. (Recall that the IFS controls both disk-based and network-based file systems.)

Ordinarily, those 32-bit drivers get loaded automatically when you install Windows 95. But Windows 95's Setup program is a mite conservative, and so sometimes it may elect to continue to use the old 16-bit drivers. This costs you performance, sometimes stability, and less memory for DOS sessions.

You can combat that with this tip: Once you have Windows 95 installed, rename your old AUTOEXEC.BAT and CONFIG.SYS. Then reboot. Once it no longer gets instructions to load 16-bit drivers, then it'll fill in with whatever 32-bit drivers it has.

So with all this in mind, setting up batch installations should be a snap. Wait—you're still unsure about some of those network options? Turn to the next chapter, on networking 95, to fill in your network information gaps.

CHAPTER

5

Essentials of Networking 95

UNLIKE many earlier versions of Windows, 95 includes an entire network operating system built right into it. You can build a network with nothing more complicated than a bunch of Windows 95 machines.

However, that's probably not a good idea for many organizations, and instead many of us use servers running software made by Novell (NetWare), Microsoft (NT Server), IBM (OS/2 LAN Server), Banyan (VINES), or DEC (PathWorks). The presence of those servers means, first of all, that you'd like Windows 95 to be a *client* of those networks, and, secondly, that you'd like 95 to perhaps act only as a *supplementary* server.

All networks have their own paradigm, and the argot that goes with that. For example, Novell's networks have always been strongly oriented toward workstation/server architecture. Microsoft's networks grew out of a peer-to-peer network approach, and show the earmarks of that today, even though they have evolved to a workstation/server model as good as Novell's.

In this chapter, you'll learn the basic concepts that you'll need in order to introduce your 95 workstations to a Microsoft network or even to *create* a network with 95 workstations.

Microsoft Networking Overview

In a network, machines all have different kinds of roles. One of the most important distinctions is whether a machine is a workstation, a server, or both.

- A *server* is a computer on a network that runs software that makes it possible for that computer to offer *resources* on the network. Resource refers to space on a disk or use of a printer, but can also refer to the use of a modem or a program on the computer.

- A *workstation* is a computer that can use the resources made available by a server.

We usually tend to think of servers as powerful computers stuck off in a room someplace, tended to by systems administrators, but that's not necessarily the case, for better or for worse. Windows 95 computers can actually respond to many of the same commands that a larger server like a LAN Manager, NT, OS/2 LAN Server, or even a NetWare machine would respond to.

Common Server Software Types

In modern networks, you see servers of the following kinds:

- Peer-to-peer servers
- NetWare servers
- UNIX-derivative servers
- SMB-type (Server Message Block) servers

Peer-to-Peer Servers

Peer-to-peer networks are systems that allow you to share data from your workstation to other machines on the network. The main value of peer-to-peer networking is that it seems cheap; you don't have to buy a separate machine to act as a server and you don't have to buy the $1000+ software to make that PC a server.

In my opinion, it's always penny-wise and pound-foolish to do peer-to-peer. Servers are important machines, as many people depend on them to get their work done. Using a workstation as a server means that you have someone pounding away at that important shared machine. If that someone happens to discover some new and interesting bug in Word for Windows, then they may end up crashing their PC—and everybody else's network sessions, too. Additionally, if the person working at the server does something computer-intensive on their workstation, like rendering some complex graphic or recalculating a big spreadsheet, then, again, everybody is slowed down—and some people may end up thinking that the network has frozen altogether.

N O T E

My objections to peer-to-peer networks don't mean that it isn't a good idea now and then to transport data from one workstation to another on the network, and the peer-to-peer capabilities of Windows 95 will be useful there.

NetWare Servers

Among file servers, Novell NetWare 3.11 and 3.12 are the most popular server types; Novell software is said to run on about two-thirds of the corporate servers. Novell also sells NetWare 2.2, built for 286-based servers, and NetWare 4.10, for larger networks.

Novell's NetWare is a proprietary operating system that was mainly intended to respond quickly to network requests. Its head-down, eyes-forward approach to networking has made for servers offering the high performance to which they owe their large market share. Windows 95 machines can act as clients to a NetWare network and can also mimic a NetWare 3.x server. NetWare servers communicate with their clients and with other servers using messages formulated in a language known as NetWare Core Protocols (NCP).

UNIX-Based Servers

The multitasking nature of UNIX makes it an ideal platform upon which to build a server. UNIX-based servers fall into two categories: Banyan VINES and NFS servers.

Banyan is a company based in Massachusetts that builds a product called the Virtual Networking System, or VINES. For years, VINES was the only real alternative if you wanted to build a large enterprise network. Built atop UNIX, VINES uses networking software that is a variation on a popular set of programs collectively called the TCP/IP suite; Banyan calls theirs the VINES Internet Protocol (VIP). VINES has about five percent of the server market.

People who just want to take a garden-variety UNIX machine and make it appear as a file server to other PCs can run a program called the Network File System, or NFS, first developed by Sun Microsystems. You just put NFS server software on a UNIX machine, install compatible NFS client software on the PC, and the PC can use files on the UNIX machine as if it were a local drive.

SMB-Based Servers

Since 1985, Microsoft has sold and licensed server software built around a different language than NCP. Microsoft's server language is called Server Message Block, or SMB. SMB networks will be of main interest to us in this chapter.

Let's look at a simple Microsoft peer-to-peer network and, at the same time, introduce some concepts upon which we'll build.

As you've already read, the whole idea of a network is to share things: share space on a large disk drive, share a particular file on that disk drive, share a printer. Suppose we have a small office that needs to do some sharing, as you see in Figure 5.1.

FIGURE 5.1

Simple sharing setup

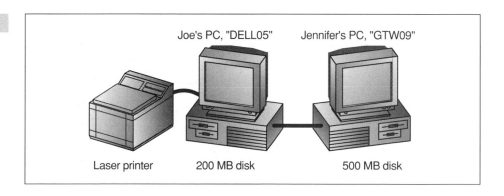

Joe's PC, "DELL05"   Jennifer's PC, "GTW09"

Laser printer   200 MB disk   500 MB disk

Now, in our simple office, Jennifer has more storage capacity on her machine than Joe does on his, but Joe has the office laser printer attached to *his* PC. Each PC has an inventory control number, like DELL05 or GTW09.

Both Jennifer and Joe work on the office accounting system, so they need to share the accounting files—either that or they'll have to pass floppies around. Since Jennifer has more disk space, they put the accounting files on her machine. So, the network problems that we need to solve are:

- Sharing Joe's printer with Jennifer.
- Sharing Jennifer's disk with Joe.

Let's solve their problem with a basic Microsoft (SMB) network. With this type of network, Jennifer just puts her hard disk on the network and Joe puts his printer on the network. Assume both of them are running Windows 95 on their systems.

Here's an important concept in Microsoft networking: You must name each machine in the network, whether it is a server or a workstation. You also must name each user (let's use Joe and Jennifer). Since the PCs need names, we may as well name the PCs with their inventory numbers.

TIP

It's a bad idea to name machines after their users, as PCs may get re-assigned.

Basically, we get Joe onto Jennifer's disk and Jennifer onto Joe's printer like so:

1. Jennifer tells the Windows 95 networking software, "Take the \acctng subdirectory on my C: drive and offer it to anyone who wants it. Call it ACCTNG." ACCTNG is then called, in Microsoft enterprise networking terminology, the *share name* of that drive on Jennifer's machine (GTW09), and it's the name that others will use to access the drive over the network. I'll show you exactly how to do that in a few pages, but for now remember the important things: a machine named GTW09 is sharing a resource called ACCTNG.

2. Joe then tells the networking software on his PC, "Attach me to the ACCTNG resource on Jennifer's machine." For years, PC workstation operating systems haven't understood networking, so we've had to introduce network resources in the back door by showing these resources as *logical drives* or, in the terminology of some networks, *mapped drives*; we might say that the ACCTNG resource is *mapped* to local drive D: for Joe. Joe doesn't know whether ACCTNG is all of Jennifer's drive or just part of it. Joe's networking software then says something like, "You're now attached to ACCTNG on Jennifer's machine. It will appear to you as local drive D:."

Actually, I should mention that Windows 95 doesn't require drive letter mapping. I mention it because virtually every previous PC operating system required it, and because most applications to this day can still only address network resources by letter names. Again, Joe doesn't *have* a D: on his machine; he only has network software that takes read and write requests for a mythical drive D: and reformulates those requests into network communication to Jennifer's machine.

And, while I'm on the subject, the actual name of this network resource is \\GTW09\ACCTNG. Notice the format of this term; it's called a *Universal Naming Convention* name, or a UNC name. The two backslashes are a warning that the name following is a *machine* name; the backslash after that refers to the *share name* ACCTNG, rather than the directory name.

3. Joe, meanwhile, runs his network software and tells it to share the printer on his LPT1: port, giving it a name—again, a share name of JOLASER. Joe's machine is called DELL05, so the UNC name of that printer will be \\DELL05\JOLASER.

4. Jennifer then tells her networking software to attach JOLASER, on Joe's machine, to her LPT1: port.

From now on, whenever Jennifer tells an application program to print to a LaserJet on LPT1:, the network software will intercept the printed output and will direct it over the network to Joe's machine. The networking software on Joe's machine will then print the information on Joe's printer.

I know I left out some of the "how do we do this?" information; it's coming later, I promise. I just wanted to illustrate with that example that:

- Machines and people in a Microsoft network have names.

- Shared resources in those networks also have names.

- You specify network resource names with UNC names, in the UNC format *servername**sharename*.

- One way (and the most common way) to share network resources is to give them bogus local names, like D: or LPT1:.

I started this section by discussing what kinds of machines can be servers in the Microsoft world. Let's name them now:

- Windows 95 workstations

- Windows for Workgroups workstations

- NT workstations

- NT Servers

- A LAN Manager server

- OS/2 LAN Server

- DOS-based machines running LANtastic

- OS/2 Warp Connect machines

All of these servers use SMB type communications.

Network Workstation Types

A networked machine running any of the following cannot act as a server; it can only function as a workstation:

- Windows 3.x

- DOS

- OS/2 1.x and 2.x

You can see that pretty much all modern PC operating systems allow for workstation functionality. Unfortunately, that can make for headaches for support people. It's possible to restrict people from sharing, but we'll take that up in Chapter 8.

Lengths of Different Network Names

For bizarre historical reasons, machine names, people names, and passwords are each established according to different rules in a Microsoft network.

Machine names can be up to 20 characters long. You can include spaces, but I recommend against it; I've run into some bugs in 95 software (and NT, for that matter) when handling machines with blanks in their names.

Passwords can be 14 characters long. You can use nonletter characters, so you can have a password like "eyes.blue" with a period in the middle of it. Microsoft does not offer a means of forcing a user to use a nonletter value in their password—at least not that I know of. Uppercase and lowercase count: password and PASSWORD are two different passwords, and they couldn't substitute for each other.

Sharing Files and Printers under 95

95's GUI makes it simple either to share directories or to use shared directories.

Offering Resources on the Network

For example, suppose I want to share the Windows directory on my computer. I just open up My Computer, open up the C: drive, and right-click on the Windows folder (directory). If you've enabled sharing, one of the options you'll see on the menu is Sharing; choose it, and you'll see a dialog box like Figure 5.2.

FIGURE 5.2

Sharing dialog box

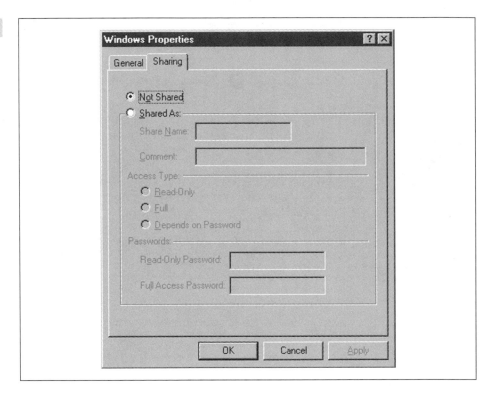

Share it by clicking the radio button labeled *Shared As:* and the dialog box like the one in Figure 5.3 will appear.

Now, this is what you see if you've selected share-level access control. It allows you to do three things: you can give the directory a share name (remember those from a few pages back, like ACCTNG?), you can determine whether people who attach to this directory can only read it or read it and write to it, and, optionally, you can set a password.

This is a nice, simple sharing approach which is virtually identical to the sharing options under Windows for Workgroups. But there's a major lack of control here, as the password option doesn't really have a lot of power to keep the wrong people from using your shared resources. Sure, you can set a password, but it's the same password that *everybody* uses, and it's easy for that kind of password to get out and around to people you might not even know.

FIGURE 5.3

Sharing dialog box:
Shared As

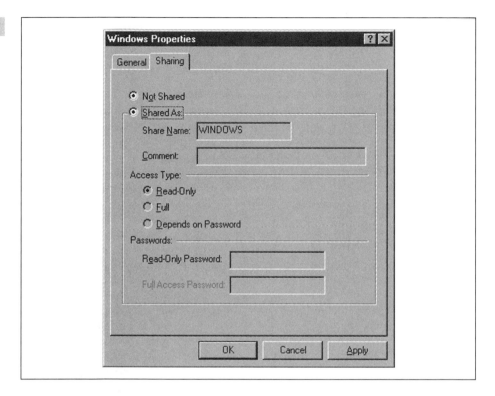

With Windows 95 it's possible to control access in such a way that only a user named Janet or Paul, for example, may access one of your *shares* (i.e., one of your shared resources). You can restrict access to one of your shares in this way:

1. Open the Control Panel.
2. Open the Network applet.
3. You'll see three tab sheets: Configuration, Identification, and Access Control. Choose Access Control.
4. On the Access Control sheet, click *User-level access control*.

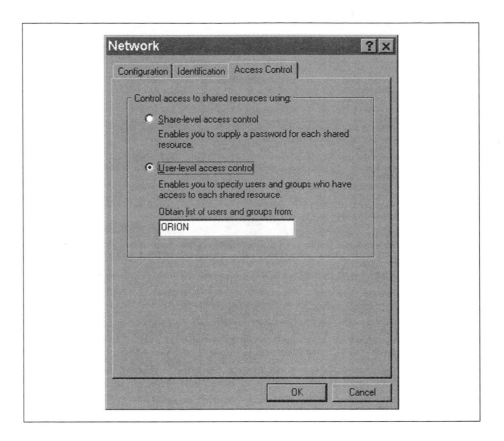

5. In the field *Obtain list of users and groups from:*, fill in the name of your NetWare server (version 3.x or 4.x), your NT Server, or your NT domain controller that contains the network names of the users to whom you are granting access. (In the case of my example, I filled in the name of my NT domain, ORION.)

<table>
<tr><td>**N O T E**</td><td>If 95 can't immediately find the server or domain you've specified, it'll prompt you for more details, so that it knows which of the three types (NetWare server, NT Server, or domain) to expect.</td></tr>
</table>

Now with user-level access control enabled, you'll see a different Sharing page in the Windows Properties dialog, like the one in Figure 5.4.

FIGURE 5.4

The Sharing page in the Windows Properties dialog box has changed

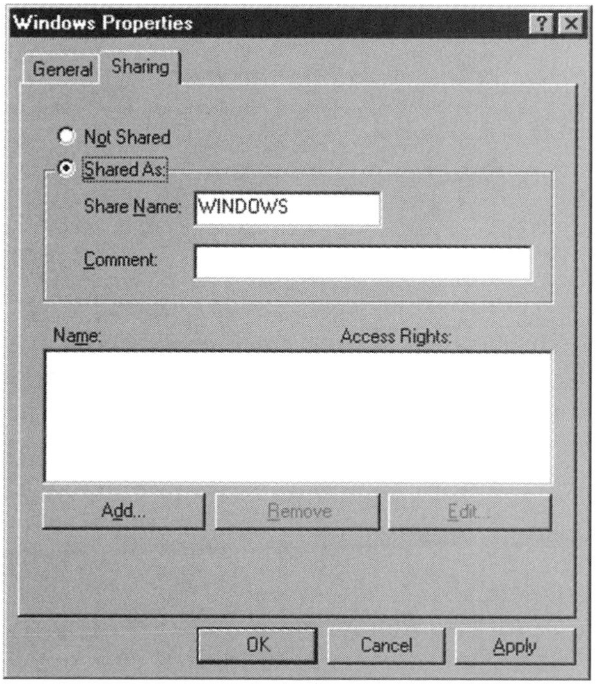

Compare this to the tab page you saw in Figure 5.3, and now you see that there's a place to specify names rather than a general-use password. You can add a name to the list by clicking the Add button, which shows a dialog box like the one in Figure 5.5.

FIGURE 5.5

Giving access to your
shares by adding users

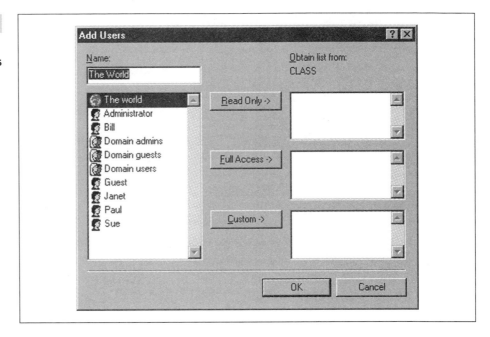

In this example, I've taken a list of users from an NT domain. The NT domain has groups of users, called *local groups*, which do not appear on this list. The list of people you see here are members of a *global group*.

As you see, you can give either read-only, full, or custom access for any particular person; just highlight the person and click the appropriate button. If you click Custom, then you see a dialog box like one in Figure 5.6.

With this dialog, you can fine-tune a user's access to your shares.

Using Network Resources with 95

Now, that was how you share something under 95, but how do you use a share that someone else is offering? Well, 95 makes using network resources simple, as you access all shared resources with the same interface, whether it's a Novell, NT, or 95-shared resource.

First, open up Network Neighborhood. It will show you the computers that it's heard from recently, as you see in Figure 5.7.

FIGURE 5.6

Granting particular
rights to a user

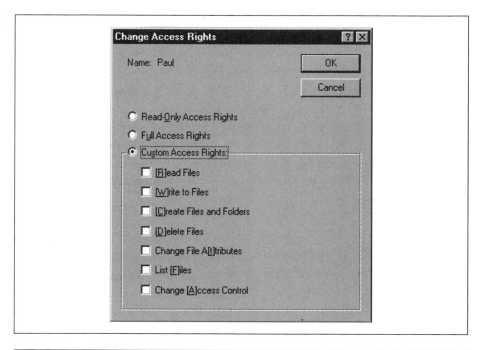

FIGURE 5.7

Network
Neighborhood

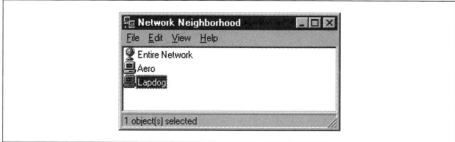

I want a directory on the server named Lapdog, so I open that up and I
see a window like in Figure 5.8.

So I see that there's a resource (a directory) called 95class available on
that server. I could actually see that resource by opening that folder (I'll
get to that later), but for now let's just map it to a drive letter, since many
programs won't know how to look for a resource named with the UNC
convention. I map the resource to a drive letter by right-clicking on the
folder and choosing Map Network Drive, which brings up a dialog box
like the one in Figure 5.9.

FIGURE 5.8

Network
Neighborhood:
Lapdog

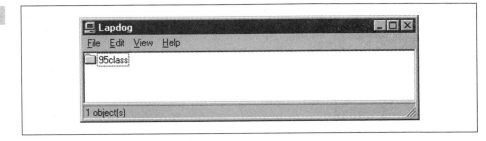

FIGURE 5.9

Map network drive

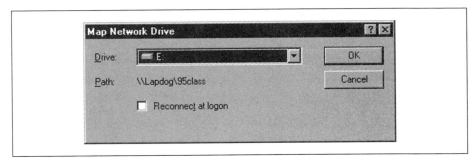

Notice the UNC name in the dialog, \\Lapdog\95class. Here, I can choose a drive letter to map to that share and decide whether I want this to be reconnected every time I log on. Click OK, and from that moment it seems as if I have a local drive named E:.

Avoiding Drive Mappings

As I've said before, you map drives to make older programs happy. But if you're just getting used to Windows 95's network options, then you may be missing some possibilities. Here are a few other approaches.

Use Shortcuts

If you have a network resource that you use frequently, create a shortcut to it. Drag it to your Desktop, and when you click on it you'll do an implicit login.

Replace Drive Letters with UNC Names

Whenever the only programs that will be using the shared resource don't have a problem with UNC names, enter that rather than a drive letter in dialog boxes. For example, my word processor looks for its style sheets on drive H:, which is really \\OURSERVER\BIGDRIVE. Having to remember that H:, not F: or G: or some other letter, is the drive my computer uses for word-processing resources makes remembering to map every new machine to that drive a bit of a pain; plugging in the UNC can be easier, because it's more clear what that drive comprises. You also may find that you're running out of drive letters; with UNCs, that's not a problem.

Use UNC Names in Batch Files

I use a personal information manager called Lotus Organizer and keep all my information in a file called BASE.OR2. But, as I travel, I want to keep my Organizer files with me. I have a machine on my desk called DESKTOP, and my laptop is called LAPTOP. My problem, of course, is that often I must shuttle the BASE.OR2 file between my desktop and my laptop. They're networked, so I share the ORGFILES directory on DESKTOP and copy the files to and fro that way.

Prior to Windows 95, I moved the file from my desktop to my laptop with the following batch file:

```
net use e: \\desktop\orgfiles
copy e:base2.org c:\orgfiles
net use e: /delete
```

The two net use commands are used to establish and to destroy the connection between the laptop and the desktop. I only have to create the bogus E: drive to make the copy command happy.

Under Windows 95, it's one line:

```
copy \\desktop\orgfiles\base.or2 c:\orgfiles
```

TIP

Get in the habit of *not* thinking in terms of mapped drive letters. Use shortcuts and UNC names to get the job done where possible.

Network Software: Drivers, Protocols, and Redirectors

Making networking work in anything but the simplest network environment means understanding the real meaning of an overused word: *compatibility*. Compatibility—or the search for it—is the source of words such as TCP/IP, NetBEUI, ODI, NDIS, redirector, and the like.

Now, you've probably been introduced to something called the OSI seven-layer model. I have something simpler—my three-layer model.

A Network Software Overview

Looking at networks from a high-level point of view, you see that LANs have the basic job of letting the applications programs (WordPerfect, Lotus 1-2-3, Quicken, or whatever) utilize the network hardware to get at data on the network; you see that in Figure 5.10.

In order for the application to use data, messages must go across network boards and through the network software that runs both in the client and the server machines. The network software can be explained in many ways, but I find it easiest to imagine it in a three-part fashion. The first, and easiest, piece of software to understand is the network board driver, as you see in Figure 5.11.

Network Board Drivers

Drivers decouple the network board from the network operating system. For example, suppose you have a Token Ring-based network. When you

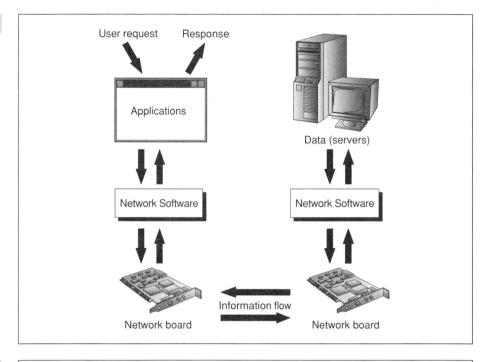

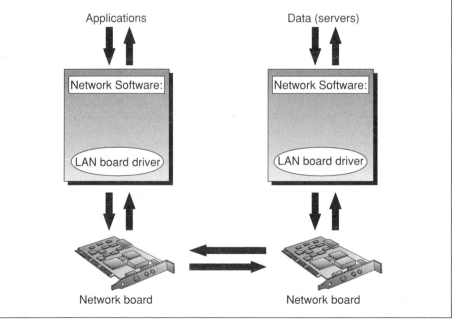

first create your network, you may start off buying boards from IBM, but you don't want to be locked into them—or into any other vendor, for that matter. But you wonder whether a competitor's token ring boards, like the Madge or 3Com token ring boards, will continue to work with your network.

The first place that 95 needs compatibility, then, is in the network boards, or "cards." A person responsible for troubleshooting networked machines needs the ability to incorporate any kind of network card into their network system, whether that card is an Ethernet, Token Ring, ARCnet, FDDI (Fiber Digital Distributed Interface), or any other board; your system must be able to incorporate boards from virtually *any* vendor.

The board driver must know such things as which IRQ a LAN board is set to, which I/O address the LAN card uses, and how to interface with the higher-layer network software.

Network Services: Redirectors and File System Mounters

Above the board driver, up at the top of the network software, is the *redirector*. It's just one of a family of network-aware applications called *network services*. A redirector fools applications into thinking that the application is getting data from a local drive rather than from the network.

For example, consider the case of WordPerfect 5.1 reading a document from a network drive. From WordPerfect's point of view, there is no network. Instead, it knows that there are one or more disk drives available, with names consisting of a letter and a colon, as in A:, B:, C:, and so on. WordPerfect was not designed to accommodate storage devices that don't have names like A: or D:. So there must be a layer of software placed between WordPerfect and the network; this software's job is to present a letter-and-colon face to WordPerfect when supplying data stored on the network. WordPerfect thinks that it is addressing local drives, but its requests for information from drives with names like D: are *redirected* to network requests, as in, "Get the data from the share named WPFILES on the server named SEYMOUR" (or \\seymour\wpfiles in UNC terminology); the redirector software does that, as you see in Figure 5.12.

FIGURE 5.12

Network overview
with redirector

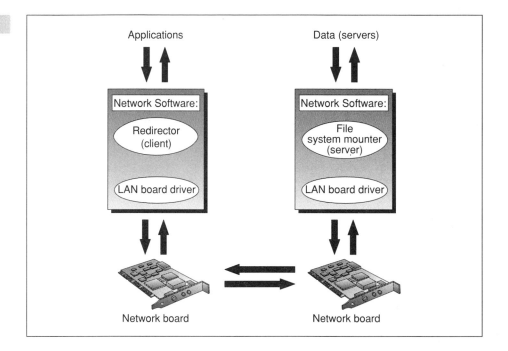

The redirector is only half of a client-server team of software. The redirector is the piece that goes on the client or workstation, and the *file system mounter* is the piece that goes on the server. There are several file system mounters in the network world. The best-known are Novell's NetWare File System, UNIX's Network File System (NFS), and Microsoft's file system mounter, which they usually just call the server. The redirector on the client and the file system mounter on the server must match, or the client can't use the server's resources. Those are the components that speak SMB, NCP, or other server command languages.

In the Internet world, you may have servers running an NFS server, in which case any workstation that wants to access it must run NFS client software. In the Novell world, the servers run a program called NFS.NLM to support the Novell File System mounter, and the workstations run a client program called NET3, NET4, NETX, or the like in order to communicate with the Novell server.

Windows 95 ships with these redirectors:

- Microsoft client
- NetWare client (from Microsoft)
- NetWare 3.x client (from Novell)
- Banyan Windows 3.1/DOS redirector
- SunSoft NFS client version 5.0

Windows 95 ships with other network services, like the SNMP agent. You can find out what services are active by opening up a command line and typing

net service /list

Network Protocols

Third in the trio of network software components is the network *protocol*. In general, a protocol is just a standardized set of rules, which are standardized for the sake of compatibility. For example, when I call you on the phone, there is a protocol that says, "When you hear the phone ring and you pick it up, then *you* should talk first, not me." It's just the common agreement in our culture as to how to communicate by phone.

In fact, this is the middle piece of the network software setup. I left this middle piece for last, as it's the most abstract of the three. You might think of the setup this way: The board driver keeps the LAN board happy, the redirector keeps the applications happy, and the *transport protocol* glues the two of them together by establishing the rules of the road for network communications. The transport protocol's position in our network software system is illustrated in Figure 5.13.

Just as we couldn't use the phone without some agreements about how to use it, NT needs a common communications language, so that all of the machines on an NT network can talk to one another without confusion. Also, because it aims to work with different types of networks, NT needs to be able to speak the networking languages used by those other kinds of networks, so it needs to be something of a polyglot. Those networking *protocols*—protocol is a somewhat more accurate term than

FIGURE 5.13

Network overview
with transport protocol

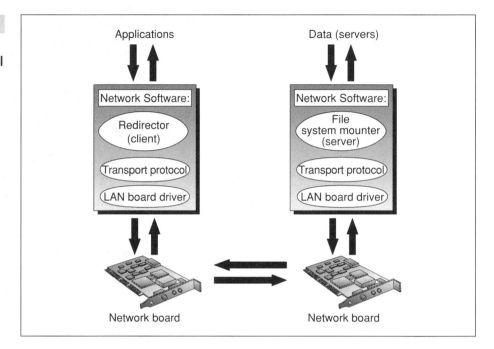

language here—differ widely because they were each originally designed to do different things; also, most of these network protocols were never designed with compatibility with other kinds of networks in mind.

There are a number of transport protocols, and unfortunately every vendor has its own favorite protocol. Here's a quick overview of the ones you'll run across.

NetBIOS and NetBEUI

Back when IBM first started marketing their PC Network, they needed a basic network protocol *stack*, which is an implementation of a board driver, transport protocol, and redirector. They had no intention of building large networks, just small workgroups of a few dozen computers or fewer.

Out of that need grew the Network Basic Input/Output System, or Net-BIOS. NetBIOS is just 18 commands that can create, maintain, and use connections between PCs on a network. IBM soon extended NetBIOS with the NetBIOS Extended User Interface (NetBEUI), which basically is a refined set of NetBIOS commands. However, over time the names NetBEUI and NetBIOS have taken on new meanings.

- NetBEUI now refers to the actual transport protocol. It has been implemented in many different ways by different vendors, to the point where, in some ways, it is the fastest transport protocol for small networks.

- NetBIOS now refers to the actual set of programming commands that the system can use to manipulate the network—the technical term for such a set of commands is an Application Program Interface, or API.

NetBEUI is the closest thing to a native protocol for NT. Unless you tell your system to use another protocol, NetBEUI is one of the protocols that the NT Setup program installs by default; IPX/SPX, discussed next, is the other. But as I said above, NetBEUI should be your protocol of choice for small networks: it's the fastest one around.

IPX/SPX

The most popular local-area network type in the world is Novell NetWare. When the Novell folks were building NetWare, they decided to build their own protocol rather than use an existing protocol. The Novell protocol is named IPX/SPX, for Internetwork Packet Exchange/Sequenced Packet Exchange. Since it is the protocol used most often on NetWare networks, and since Microsoft wanted their software to be somewhat compatible with NetWare networks, Microsoft designed Windows 95 to include an IPX/SPX implementation.

NOTE NetWare is actually based on a Xerox protocol called Xerox Networking Services, or XNS.

IPX/SPX wasn't originally a Microsoft-supported network, but it's now one of the default protocols under 95; NetBEUI is the other.

TCP/IP (Transmission Control Protocol/Internet Protocol)

The famous "infobahn," the information superhighway, is built atop a protocol created over many years by the U.S. government. The protocol is actually a protocol stack, called the *TCP suite*. The TCP suite is a very efficient, easy-to-extend protocol whose main strength has been in *wide-area* networking; it glues together dissimilar networks and brings together similar networks that are separated by distance and low-speed connections. It's one of the best-supported, well-designed internetworking protocols around.

Traditionally, however, microcomputer networks haven't used TCP/IP as a *local-area* network protocol. But that's changing, particularly with the release of the TCP/IP suite in NT Server version 3.5, what I call "turbo TCP/IP."

Multiple Transport Stacks

Two things should be obvious by now. First of all, there is no single best network protocol. Second, you may want to run all four of the protocols described above.

You can.

One of the values of the Microsoft networking model is that it supports *multiple* transport protocols, as you see in Figure 5.14.

In Figure 5.14, you see that the client machine has four transport protocols loaded and the server has one protocol loaded. This could happen if the client machine connected to more than one server—the IPX stack might talk to a Novell server, the NetBEUI stack might allow the workstation to talk to an NT Server, and the TCP/IP stack might talk to an Internet mail router.

Network Binding Interfaces

To make all of this work, we need a way to attach the network boards to the transport stacks—to *bind* the network transport layer to the LAN

FIGURE 5.14

Multiple transport
protocols

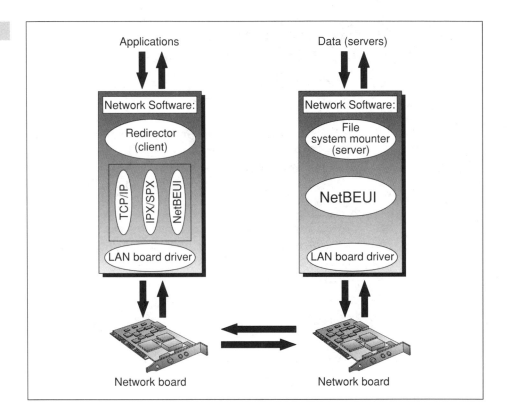

board's driver. (That's the definition of binding: to create a software connection between, essentially to marry, a network card driver and a network transport protocol. I'll talk more about binding a few paragraphs down.) That leads to the need for a very important, standard, interface—the interface between a LAN board driver and a transport stack. There are two competitors for the title of world-standard binding interface: Microsoft's NDIS and Novell's ODI.

Network Driver Interface Specification (NDIS) Version 3.1

Microsoft's standard defines the interface between a network card driver and a protocol stack with an interface called the Network Driver Interface Specification, or NDIS. NDIS-compliant drivers are easy to find for most network boards, so availability is a strong plus for NDIS. Furthermore, there are NDIS-compatible versions of the NetBEUI, TCP/IP, and SPX/IPX protocol stacks.

NDIS 3.0 drivers are particularly attractive in the DOS/Windows world because they load in extended memory, away from your precious lower 640K.

NDIS 3.1 drivers added two important features. First, they are hot-swappable, which means that they work with PC Card network boards: you can install a PC Card board after bootup and Windows 95 will load its driver, protocol, and redirector on the fly. Second, they are used for both NT 3.51 and Windows 95.

Open Data-link Interface (ODI)

Novell's answer to the binding problem is a different standard, one named the Open Data-link Interface, or ODI. At the moment, I haven't seen Windows 95-compliant ODI drivers, save for the old 16-bit ones.

Binding in General

What, exactly, does the word *binding* mean in a network context? Consider this: it's possible to have multiple boards, protocols, and clients. It wouldn't be impossible to have a computer arranged like so:

- An Ethernet board and a modem (a so-called dial-up adapter)
- NetBEUI, IPX/SPX, and TCP/IP protocols
- Microsoft network software and Novell network client software

Look at the possible flows of information: data can arrive to a PC from either the Ethernet card or the serial port/modem, it can then flow through one or all of three protocols, and then it can funnel through one of two clients. Do the math and you'll see that there are 12 different ways for data to flow through a PC.

Not all of those ways make sense, however: it would be silly to place the NetWare client atop NetBEUI, as NetWare uses IPX/SPX the majority of the time, and TCP/IP in a much smaller percentage of cases, but never, to my knowledge, NetBEUI. Similarly, if I only use the modem to connect to the Internet, then there's no point in sending data that arrives via the modem through the NetBEUI and IPX/SPX protocols.

Network binding is the term for defining which connections between board drivers, protocols, and clients make sense. You control binding via the Network applet of the Control Panel. Open the Control Panel, double-click on Network, and examine the Configuration dialog box, as you see in Figure 5.15.

FIGURE 5.15

Network Configuration
dialog box

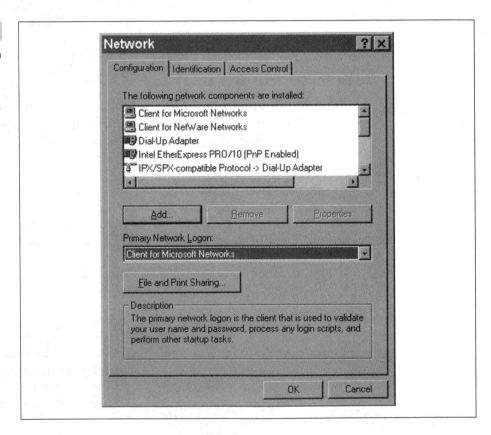

You control which board drivers are bound to which protocols by clicking on the adapter, then clicking Properties. You'll see a dialog box that includes a tab labeled Bindings, as you see in Figure 5.16.

FIGURE 5.16

Dial-up Adapter
properties

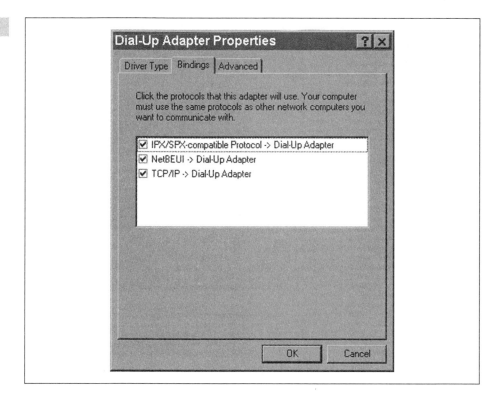

Notice that this is the dialog box for the dial-up adapter, and that it's bound to each of the three protocols. To unbind, just uncheck the boxes.

What if you find that a protocol wasn't bound to an adapter to begin with? Then just click the adapter, then Add, and then Protocol. Add a protocol (even if you're already using it), and it'll be bound to the adapter.

You control which protocols bind to particular clients by clicking on a protocol and Properties. Most of the common-sense bindings are already in place—for example, the Microsoft client for NetWare networks only binds to IPX/SPX—but you can disconnect unnecessary ones and speed up your networking; after all, there's no reason to be bound by the defaults.

Network Applications Interfaces (API's)

As you've already read, most applications are unaware of the network or networks that they use. But some, like e-mail or groupware programs, *must* be cognizant of the network, and exist only *because* of the network. They need to be able to plug in and communicate with other programs running on other machines in the network.

Programmers build network-aware programs so they can be tailored to sets of commands that a network offers to applications programs; those sets of commands are called API's.

Let's use driving a car as a metaphor for using an API. When you're driving a car, you may actually have no idea what occurs under your car's hood—you just push down the accelerator and the car goes faster. Driving consists of just a few basic commands: brake the car, accelerate the car, shift the car's transmission, and so on. There is no basic command built in to a car that lets you "back the car out of the driveway," and yet you can still back a car out of a driveway; you just assemble a number of the basic commands into the actual action of backing a car out of a driveway. You have, in a sense, built a program with your car's API.

There are three API's that you'll probably come across in the 95 networking world:

- NetBIOS: A simple set of 18 commands implemented on an NT network. It is Microsoft's native network API.

- TCP/IP Sockets: The preferred API for working over an internet.

- Novell Sockets: Novell's API.

API's are important to network-aware programs. Microsoft's redirector ("Client for Microsoft networks") is a program that won't function in a PC unless there is a copy of NetBIOS running in that PC. Originally, only NetBEUI included NetBIOS, but now Microsoft has implemented an IPX/SPX that includes NetBIOS, and a TCP/IP that includes NetBIOS, so now you can run the Microsoft redirector whether your network runs the IPX/SPX, NetBEUI, or TCP/IP protocols.

Now that I've explained networking as a three-part suite of software, you might be able to make more sense of what Windows 95 provides in the way of info about your network configuration. Open up the Control Panel and click the Network icon, and choose the Configuration tab if it isn't already displayed. You'll see a dialog box like the one in Figure 5.17.

FIGURE 5.17

Network configuration dialog box

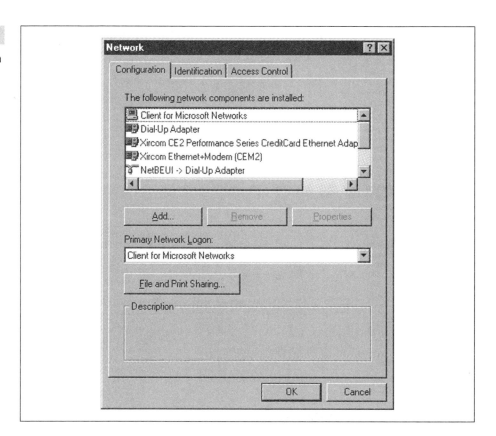

You may have to scroll to see all your components. On my computer, the following components are listed:

- Client for Microsoft Networks (redirector)
- File and printer sharing for Microsoft Networks (file system mounter, server end)
- NetBEUI Dial-up adapter (protocol binding)
- NetBEUI Xircom Ethernet+Modem (protocol binding)

- NetBEUI Xircom CE2 Performance Series CreditCard Ethernet (protocol binding)
- Xircom Ethernet+Modem (board driver)
- Dial-up adapter (board driver)
- Xircom CE2 Performance Series CreditCard Ethernet (board driver)

This is how a Windows 95 system can interact with so many networks: modular protocols, board support, and redirectors.

Browsing

Years ago, I used the IBM PC LAN program, which is the first version of what eventually became the NT Server and Windows 95 networking code. It was a nice, primitive network operating system. If you wanted to access a drive shared by a server, you said to the PC LAN program, for example, "Attach me to drive E: on the machine named AVOCADO." Nice and simple, but it had a major flaw: how did you find out in the first place that the server was named AVOCADO and that the drive that it was offering was called E:? The answer is, *you just had to know the name of the resource before you could use that resource;* there was no "scan the network to find out what's available" feature to the network. (An IBM guy once explained to me that this was "a security feature." Now, why didn't *I* think of that?)

I wanted a kind of net scan command, something that would shout to the other systems, "Hey! Whaddya got?" As it turns out, that's not very simple. The whole process of offering services on a network is part of what's known as *name services,* and they're not easy to offer.

Solving the Browse Problem

How would you make a workstation know about every service on the network? There are several approaches.

Static Service Lists

The simplest approach to letting workstations know what's available to it over the network would be to put a file with some kind of services database on every workstation, a kind of yellow pages of system capabilities. For example, you might have an ASCII file on every PC that says, in effect, "There is a file server on machine BIGPC with a shared disk called BIGDISK, and the computer named PSRV has a shared printer called HP4SI."

This has the advantage of being very simple to understand. To add a new resource, just modify the service list file.

It has the *disadvantage*, however, of being static. When any changes are made to the system, some poor fool (that would be *you*, the network administrator) has to go around to all the workstations and update the file. If there were two hundred workstations on your network, then you'd have to actually travel to each workstation and copy the static service list file to that workstation's hard disk.

This method sounds too primitive to use, but it's not completely useless. In NetWare 3.x, you identify yourself to your desired server via information in NET.CFG. That's a hard-wired server name, and would require a fair amount of editing on every workstation if you wanted to rename an important server; this is why, I suppose, you don't rename servers often in a NetWare world.

Periodic Advertising

Another approach is an occasional broadcast. Every 60 seconds, each resource on NetWare 3.11 tells the rest of the network about itself by shouting, "I'm here!" Novell calls this the Service Advertising Protocol (SAP). This is a very good idea and it works great in many cases.

It's not a perfect answer, however. Its problem is that its broadcasts take a long time to get around in an enterprise network, and can clog up the network if that network has a large number of services that are advertising. (Imagine if every store in the U.S. were to remind you that they exist *every minute* or so—you'd spend so much time responding to advertising that you'd get nothing else done, and your mailbox would be full.) That means that periodic advertising might work okay on small to medium-size

LANs, but on larger networks it would be unworkable. Adding to the problem is the fact that many router systems don't pass broadcast messages, so advertisements may not get from segment to segment.

> **N O T E**   Windows 95 supports SAP; it can advertise its shared services if you tell it to act as a NetWare server.

Name Servers

Yet another approach, and the one used by most enterprise network products, is to assign the task of keeping track of network services to one or more computers, called *browse servers* or *browse masters*. With this system, different parts (usually different geographical parts) of the network each have these browse servers, and the browse servers update each other's service information periodically. It requires a bit of setting up, but it's one of the most logical ways to keep track of network services.

Microsoft's Answer: Browse Services

Microsoft decided (perhaps rightly) that name servers were hard to set up, particularly in a peer-to-peer network environment where services would be up and down as the day went on (like on a Windows 95-based network when users periodically reboot their workstations), so they developed a different approach, called *browse services*.

In Microsoft browse services, there are computers called *browse masters* that perform functions like those of name servers. What's different about the Microsoft browse master concept (by the way, there are also browse backups, machines that back up the browse master) is that there's no one computer fixed as the browse master; it changes according to certain conditions, in a manner that I'll soon describe.

NOTE In some Microsoft literature, browse masters are called *master browsers*, so you may see either term.

You can see the information provided by a browse master—a *browse list*—when you're in the Network Neighborhood. Open up the Network Neighborhood folder, and it will look something like Figure 5.18.

FIGURE 5.18

Network
Neighborhood

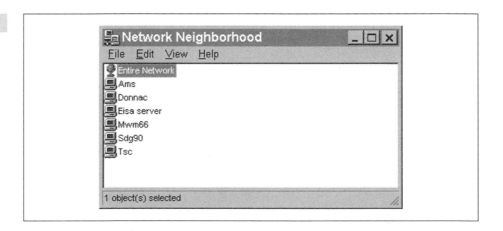

This browse list shows you what machines are nearby (I'll tell you in a minute what I mean by "nearby") as well as offering you access to the entire network. The machines Ams, Donnac, Eisa server, Mwm66, Sdg90, and Tsc are all servers in the sense that they offer resources—shared printers or directories.

How Browsing Works

Chances are that you've used Network Neighborhood dozens of times and never wondered how it worked; most likely, it just *worked*.

But if you ever saw the flashlight shine back and forth for a few minutes, followed by a blank folder or a "Network is not available" message, then you probably wondered just how the thing works—or *doesn't* work.

First of all, browsing is an example of a *client/server* software system. Your Windows 95 workstation runs the client software, which interrogates the browse master.

The browse master runs the other half of the operation, the browse server software. As I've already told you, you needn't anoint one PC as the browse master. Actually, the PCs all get together and jointly determine which of their number should be the browse master. It could be yours!

Electing a Master Browser

If there is no master browser, then there is an *election* to determine which computer would best be master browser. Elections are held when the master browser is powered down gracefully. Consequently, if the master browser is simply turned off, then it may take a good while (almost an hour in some cases) before another one becomes active.

If you're not a master browser, then you're a backup browser (browser backups in some documents), a potential browser, or you've opted out of the whole election process. (I'll show you how to do that in a minute.) Backup browse servers also help remove some of the load from the master browser, as they can respond to browse requests.

When an election occurs, the master browser is chosen with a scoring system that works like this:

- NT Servers beat NT workstations, which beat everything else (i.e., Windows for Workgroups clients or LAN Manager servers).

- If there is a tie, then it goes to the *primary domain controller*, which is an NT server that acts as the overall security monitor for an NT network. The primary domain controller holds all the user accounts.

- If there still is a tie, then the election goes to a Preferred Master (a setting that you can make on a computer running NT). And, while Microsoft isn't too clear about it, machine type plays a role—Pentiums are preferred over 486s.

- If there are no NT machines responding, then the election takes place among the Windows 95 workstations that have their Maintain-ServerList setting set to either auto or yes.

It's that last part you should be worried about.

"If Nominated, I Will Not Run": Avoiding Browse Mastering

Windows 95 workstations should *not* be browse masters. The reason why is simple: If they become a backup browser and announce that they are available as a backup browser, then workstations can become dependent on them for browsing capabilities. Once a workstation has chosen a browser, it doesn't know enough to get a second opinion from another browser if the browse list that it receives looks screwy. Furthermore, if the master browser is an NT server and a 95 machine is acting as a backup browser but isn't logged on to the NT machine, the 95 backup browser can't obtain browse lists from the NT master browser. The result: empty browse lists.

Another potential problem: On my network, I have a 95 workstation running on a Pentium and a master browser running on an NT Server, which is running on a 486. While I'm not certain that the processor type is the root of the problem, I found my 95 workstation claiming that it was the master browser when my NT Server machine had already won the election. The existence of two machines claiming to be master browsers confused the network considerably. The answer was to tell my 95 workstation to just stay out of browse master elections.

Elections can take a lot of time on your network. You can simplify the election process and cut down on the number of elections by forcing a Windows 95 computer to never be the master browser.

Forcing a Machine to NOT Be the Master Browser

On a Windows 95 machine, go to the Control Panel, click on Network, then on File and Printer Sharing, then Properties. On the Advanced tab, you'll see Browse Master, which offers Auto, Enable, or Disable; go for Disable.

On a Windows for Workgroups machine, add this line to the [network] section of `SYSTEM.INI`:

```
MaintainServerList=No
```

The default value of MaintainServerList is auto, which means "make me a master browser if you need me to be one." A value of yes means "if there's a tie when electing browse masters, make me the master browser."

For NT workstations, there is a corresponding Registry entry,

```
MaintainServerList
```

which goes in

```
HKEY_LOCAL_MACHINE\System\CurrentControlSet\Services\
Browser\Parameters
```

It is of type REG_SZ, and its value can be true or false.

Understanding the Neighborhood: Workgroups

What is a network neighborhood? It's just a way of keeping the size of the browse list manageable.

You've learned that every Windows 95 workstation can be a server in the sense that it can share resources. That means that every 95 workstation in your company would show up—perhaps thousands of machines—whenever you requested a browse list! As servers re-announce themselves to the browse master every 12 minutes, you could have a very busy browse master.

Worse yet, there's no *point* in making everyone aware of everyone else. After all, we tend to work in *workgroups*, smaller groups of people who share data. Any organization is composed of many of these workgroups, whether formally or not. From a management point of view, I think of workgroups as being characterized by this notion: 95 percent of the data generated in a workgroup is distributed to (and is, in the main, only interesting to) the rest of the workgroup. Only about five percent of the data generated by a workgroup is shared with other workgroups.

The result: a monstrous, slow browse list that is mainly useless dross to people who want only to see the other computers in their workgroup, not every computer in the company. So what's the answer?

Simple: Create a computer analog to the workgroup. What the heck—let's even *call* it a workgroup. It's just a group of people who want to see each other's resources, but don't care much about resources outside of the workgroup.

When I was getting started in Microsoft enterprise networking, I had a good bit of trouble understanding the difference between a *workgroup* and a *domain*. Part of my confusion about workgroups, as it turns out, came from the fact that there isn't much to a workgroup. Here's my definition of a workgroup:

> **A workgroup is a collection of computers that share resources (printers, disk space, and files) and that share the same *browse list*.**

A workgroup is a *logical* notion, not a physical notion. You could, for example, have any number of workgroups on a single network segment. Conversely, you can sometimes spread a workgroup across several network segments.

When you open up Network Neighborhood, you see the browse list for your workgroup. If you open up Entire Network, then you get a list of workgroups in your network, as you see in Figure 5.19.

FIGURE 5.19

Network Neighborhood's browse list for your workgroup

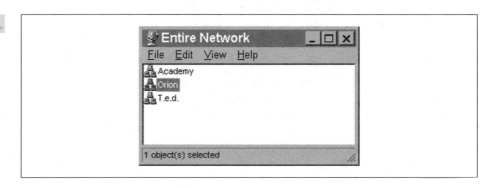

In my network, I have three workgroups: Academy, Orion, and T.e.d. If I double-click on one of those, then the browse list for that workgroup will come to my workstation.

Keeping the Browse List Short

Dividing the company's resources into workgroups helps to keep the browse lists small, but they're still cluttered with machines that aren't really servers (for example, Windows 95 machines or Windows for Workgroups workstations). Of the machines on the browse list you saw a few figures ago, only Eisa server and Mwm66 were servers. The rest were workstations, and in the main they were just cluttering up the browse list.

> **TIP**
>
> To save about 300K of RAM, think about disabling file and print sharing on your Windows 95 workstations. (You can also keep your users from sharing files and printers via the System Policy Editor, which we'll meet in a later chapter.) You disable the function by opening up the Control Panel and choosing Network. Pick *File and printer sharing for Microsoft networks* and click the button labeled Remove. Then reboot the system. You're no longer on the browse list, and you've saved yourself all that RAM.

Understanding and Troubleshooting Browser Issues

Browsing is significant in that it can slow down your workstation's response time and clog your network with unnecessary traffic. It can also frustrate your users if it doesn't respond quickly enough. The following paragraphs offer some browser troubleshooting information.

Browsing in General

The browsing service in Microsoft enterprise networks makes it possible for a workstation to see what the network has to offer. A few specifics about browsing:

- The master browser designates one backup browser for about every 15 computers.
- If you run multiple transport protocols, then each transport protocol needs its own set of browsers.
- Backup browsers verify their database with the master browser every 15 minutes.
- Servers first announce their existence to the master browser, then they re-announce their existence at short intervals. Eventually they settle down to announcing themselves only once every 12 minutes.

Refreshing a Browse List

In general, browse requests are resolved by either the master browser or a backup browser, so you never know who's provided your browse list. But you can force the system to browse you via the browse master with the command-line command net view.

Why Isn't My Resource on the Browse List?

You can experience browsing trouble (i.e., no browse list available or incorrect list) if computers do not exit Windows gracefully—that is, if they just get shut off without first exiting Windows. That computer may appear on the master browser's list for up to 45 minutes, even though it's not literally available as a resource. Even worse, if a *browser* terminates unexpectedly, then it may become impossible to browse for over an hour.

TIP

Remember that if you can't see something on the browser, it's not a big deal. If you know the UNC name for the resource—the name like \\markspc\c—then you can always just punch in that value and if it's available you'll get connected with no trouble, even if the browsers are all confused.

Let's look at how the browse service works in a bit more detail. It may take up to 51 minutes for the browser to notice that a resource has disappeared. This means that the browser may erroneously report that something is available when it is not. Why does that happen?

When a server (the computer offering the shared resource) is running, it announces itself to the master browser every 12 minutes. When the server stops, the master browser won't assume it has gone away for 3 announce periods, or 36 minutes. This would make it sound like the longest that you could ever wait for the browse list to work properly and eradicate a no-longer-available resource would be 36 minutes. But what if your browser is a *backup browser*? The backup browser polls the master every 15 minutes. The longest possible time for a backup browser to query the master is 15 minutes later, thus the worst case time for a server to disappear from the browse list is 51 minutes.

New services, in contrast, are announced to the master browser immediately, but, again, the backup browsers may hear of them as much as 15 minutes later, so the longest that it should take for a new service to appear on the browse list is 15 minutes.

By the way, when I said above that servers re-announced themselves to the master browser every 12 minutes, I simplified the truth a bit. The whole truth is that when a service first starts up, it announces itself more frequently. The service announces itself at intervals of 1, 4, 8, and 12 minutes after it is started, and after it reaches 12 minutes, it announces every 12 minutes afterwards.

Another reason why you might not see a resource is that its server may be using a different protocol from your workstation. You see, the services offered by the NetBEUI-using machines are maintained on a different browse list than the services offered by the TCP/IP-using machines. There is a different master browser for each transport protocol.

If you are running TCP/IP and resources do not appear on the TCP/IP browse list, it may be because the IPX and/or NetBEUI protocols are hogging the network's attention. If you can, remove the other protocols and the TCP/IP browser will work more smoothly.

NOTE   By the way, how does the network know to hold an election if someone just pulls the plug on the master browser, and the master browser doesn't get a chance to force an election? The answer is, the next time another computer asks for browse information and doesn't get a response, that computer forces an election.

TIP   If you take the other protocols off the PC, then be sure to re-enable MaintainServerList on some other machine, or NetBEUI and IPX will be without browsers.

Integrating 95 Workstations into an NT Domain

If you have an NT-based network, then you'll find accessing NT resources to be fairly easy. There are a few things to know, however, to simplify accessing resources or to save you time trying to do something that you can't do.

If you're going to log on to an NT domain, then you should tell your workstation to log right on to the domain. You know that password that you created to log on to your workstation? That's not necessarily your domain logon password. Now, if you chose a user name and a password for your 95 workstation that are the same as your domain name and password, then you're okay.

When you first log on to your 95 workstation, 95 doesn't log on to the domain. You don't log on to the domain until you try to "access a resource controlled by the domain," according to the manuals. Resources controlled by the domain are shares offered by *NT machines*—NT Server or NT workstations—where the machines have been explicitly added to the domain when installed. If Windows for Workgroups or Windows 95 machines offer resources, then those are *not* controlled by the domain.

If this still isn't clear, let's ask the question, "Why would you want a resource controlled by the domain?" The answer to that is simple: it makes it easier to administer the network. If you have 20 NT Servers scattered around your building, then you can control shares on any one of them by just sitting down at one of those servers and running a program called the Server Manager. From Server Manager, you can remotely force another NT machine to stop sharing something, to start sharing something, or to change the rules on who gets access to the share. *That's* convenience.

So the practical reason for a machine to join a domain is that the machine becomes capable of remote administration. This sounds like a good thing, and it is—so good, in fact, that you may want to be able to do this with your 95 workstations.

Unfortunately, you can't.

One of the major differences between 95 and NT is security. 95 machines cannot join a domain. 95 *users* can *log on* to a domain—but their *machines* cannot *join* a domain.

I've already said that you don't actually log on to a domain until you try to access a share controlled by the domain. This probably happens when you start up and reconnect to your permanent shares. You can, however, alternatively choose to use Quick logon, where you don't connect to a share until you actually try to use it. If there was a problem with the domain login, then you wouldn't find out about it until then.

For that reason, it may make sense for you to log directly on to the domain when you start up your system. You can do that like this:

1. Open the Control Panel. Double-click on the Network applet.
2. Choose *Client for Microsoft Networks* and click the Properties button.

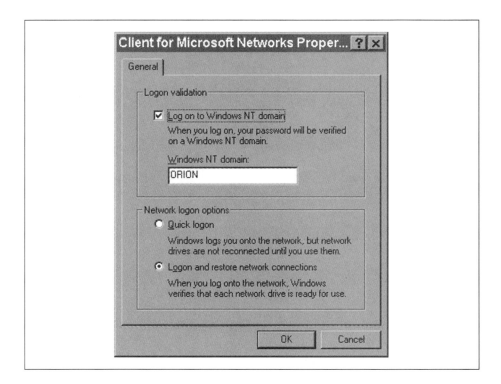

3. Click the *Log on to Windows NT domain* box and fill in the name of the domain, then click OK.

This may not make a great difference, but it may sometimes simplify figuring out why you can't get to your shares, as you'll get a message that the domain refused you a login. One bonus of doing the domain logon is that your login screen not only offers you the chance to fill in the name and password; it also lets you choose which domain to log in to.

CHAPTER

6

Windows 95 and Novell NetWare

WITH Windows 95, Microsoft has included various ways to connect to the Novell NetWare environment. Microsoft has provided a true 32-bit client that is big on performance and light on memory, but if you need closer compatibility with NetWare, or if your mainframe-connectivity VLMs or application-specific VLMs need full support, you can load your current network client software, and it will interact directly with Windows 95.

Microsoft Connections versus Novell Connections

To make Windows 95 coexist with NetWare, you have three options: You can use *Microsoft Client for NetWare Networks* (which I'll call MS Client for short), *Microsoft Service for NDS*, or *Novell NetWare Client*. Your primary decision is, do you want to use a Microsoft solution or a Novell solution? The following sections will help you to decide.

MS Client

Microsoft Client for NetWare Networks provides a complete 32-bit driver for connectivity to the NetWare world. This 32-bit driver can run completely in Windows protected mode. In addition, the driver requires only minimal overhead for conventional memory, which is important because conventional memory is still sacred under Windows 95. Finally, the complete set of software needed to make MS Client for NetWare Networks do what it does is provided with Windows 95.

Those are the hot reasons why the MS Client for NetWare Networks method makes sense; here are some others:

- **Novell script processing** Client for NetWare Networks will process the system login scripts and individual login scripts created by the network administrator of the Novell network. (Please note that MS Client for NetWare Networks does not support NetWare Directory Services (NDS) in the current iteration of Windows 95. Therefore, on 4.x servers the script processing will only take place if bindery emulation has been enabled on the server. Microsoft is promising to add this feature at a later date. I would look for it on the quarterly Tune-up packs that will be released by Microsoft.)

- **Long filename support** If you enable OS/2 naming support on your Novell server, you can save files with names up to 254 characters in length. With the OS/2 naming support enabled, your NetWare server will appear as a High Performance File System (HPFS) volume to the Windows 95 clients.

- **Storage of user profiles** You can save your user profile information on the Novell server.

- **Single peripheral systems** Because you are using the 32-bit drivers for connectivity, you can use the dial-up services that are part of the Microsoft enterprise network. On most of Microsoft's products this is referred to as remote-access service, but in Windows 95 it is known as dial-up networking. If you use MS Client for NetWare Networks, dial-up networking will allow you to attach directly to the Novell servers and process NetWare login scripts remotely. More on this in Chapter 7.

In order for MS Client for NetWare Networks to interact with Windows 95, you will need a set of DLLs and virtual device drivers (VxD's), all of which are provided with Windows 95 or can be downloaded from Microsoft.

MS Service for NDS

Another Microsoft solution is the *MS Service for NDS* (NetWare Directory Services), which you can download from Microsoft. If you are looking at the list above and are thinking that the Microsoft solution will give you the memory benefits that you need, but you also need the NDS support that is essential for a NetWare 4.x environment, then you should consider MS Service for NDS. It provides all of the functions listed above for MS Client, as well as support for your VLMs, and network administration capability with NetWare 4.x.

Novell NetWare Client

Although it's true that MS Client for NetWare Networks may talk directly to Novell servers with few problems, if you need to talk to many different *types* of servers that are using IPX as their primary protocol, you really should use *Novell NetWare Client*. MS Client is a viable option for client connectivity in terms of attaching to NetWare for file and print services, but it does not support the specialized VLMs needed to run the network administration utilities.

If you choose to connect to NetWare via Novell NetWare Client, you ensure driver compatibility with NetWare. To install Novell NetWare client, you can use the ODI driver provided on the disk that came with your network interface card. Novell NetWare Client is also preferable if you attach to different *types* of servers.

As you evaluate ways to integrate with NetWare, you will find that there are two approaches to using the Novell NetWare Client option. Keeping in mind that Novell no longer provides direct support for IPX-NETX, but that IPX-NETX is still a large percentage of the current Novell installed user base, one approach is to support the IPX-NETX drivers that are prevalent with NetWare 3.x. Or you can load IPXODI-VLM combinations, an approach that provides direct support for NDS. You can't take both approaches, however.

N O T E   Not all the software needed to install IPXODI-VLM combinations is provided with Windows 95; some of the drivers must be installed from the NetWare disks.

N O T E   As this book is being written, Novell has its own 32-bit driver solution in beta testing. By the time you read this, there may be yet another integration solution from Novell incorporating the full range of 32-bit driver support.

Setting Up MS Client for NetWare Networks

All of the MS Client for NetWare Networks drivers are included with Windows 95. The installation process assumes that you are using MS Client for NetWare Networks as the only method of communicating to a Novell server. If you choose to run MS Client for NetWare Networks in conjunction with the Novell NetWare Client software, look for the discussion later in this chapter. Now let's take a look at how to install MS Client for NetWare Networks.

Installing MS Client for NetWare Networks

Actually, this installation is really straightforward.

1. Remove the NetWare drivers from the AUTOEXEC.BAT file.
2. Choose the Network option in the Control Panel.
3. Select Add...

4. Select Client from the list in the *Select Network Client Component* area.

5. Select Microsoft as the Manufacturer.

6. Select Client for NetWare Networks, the second option on the list shown in the Figure 6.1.

FIGURE 6.1

Network options for
your client software

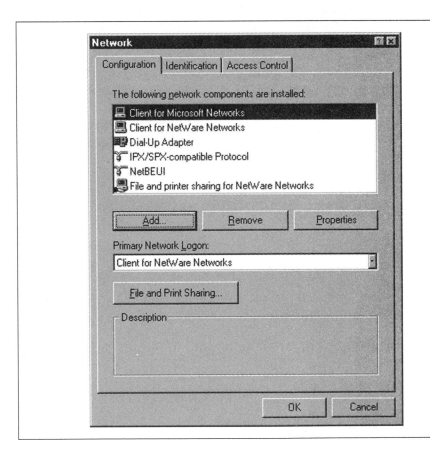

To enable printer and file sharing, click the *File and Print Sharing...* button and select your preferences, as seen in Figure 6.2.

This will install the appropriate drivers on your system and also will make the appropriate changes in the Registry. As you learned earlier, changes

FIGURE 6.2

File and Print Sharing

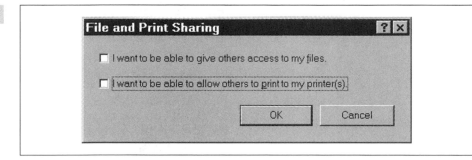

to the Registry require you to restart the computer; once you shut down and restart, the changes will take effect.

You have now completed the easier part of setting up MS Client for Net-Ware Networks. The harder part is configuring the client software to work properly with your system. Your next big hurdle will be choosing the *network binding interface* (NBI) that you want to use with Windows 95 and NetWare.

Choosing a Network Binding Interface

As discussed in Chapter 5, the network binding interface is the glue that enables your network interface card's device drivers to handle multiple protocol stacks. The NBI that Microsoft prefers is the *Network Driver Interface Specification*, or NDIS. The binding favored by Novell is called the *Open Datalink Interface* (ODI). Unfortunately, you can only load one. So which one should you choose? The choice can be difficult, but it is not fatal, as you can switch back and forth between the two relatively easily (please note the weasel word "relatively").

NDIS drivers *should* be your choice if you need to ensure that your computer system stays in protected mode for all of its communication needs. However, if you are using a program or TSR that requires the actual IPX/SPX protocol stack, and not the Microsoft emulated version, then you may need to use ODI. (An example of programs that fall into this category would be most DOS terminal emulation programs.) Keep in mind that choosing the ODI option will take up more conventional memory than NDIS, as NDIS drivers can load in extended memory. (ODI drivers cannot.) In addition, there are no Plug and Play drivers for ODI. Let's take a look at how to set up these drivers.

1. Select the Network icon in the Control Panel.

2. Choose Network Adapter from the list.

3. Select the Driver Type tab.

4. You will see the dialog box shown in Figure 6.3, with three options: Enhanced mode (32-bit and 16-bit) NDIS driver, Real mode (16-bit) NDIS driver, and Real mode (16-bit) ODI driver. Select the appropriate binding interface and click OK to continue.

FIGURE 6.3

Dial-Up Adapter Properties—choosing NDIS or ODI drivers

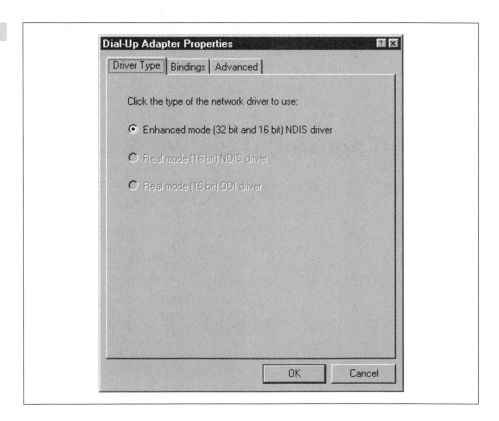

This updates your system software and requires you to shut down and then restart your system for the changes to take effect.

Using MS Client for NetWare Networks

Here are a few additional things to know about MS Client.

- Loading MS Client for NetWare Networks will only allow you to communicate via IPX/SPX. If you are looking for support for other protocols besides IPX/SPX, you will need to load a different client. For example, if you want to communicate via TCP/IP, you might load MS Client for *Microsoft* Networks instead, which includes support for the TCP/IP protocol.

- When using *File and Printer sharing for NetWare Networks*, please remove the Lastdrive= statement from CONFIG.SYS. If you put the Lastdrive= statement in CONFIG.SYS, the highest value that you can use is Z. This means you can only have 26 connections.

N O T E

MS Client for NetWare Networks has support for 32 connections, and functionality for 32 drive mappings is already enabled when you load it.

- Unfortunately, if you are a fan of the NWPOPUP, you will need to get rid of it. However, the Microsoft utility WINPOPUP will now serve this function and will display both NetWare and Microsoft broadcast messages.

- Due to the architectural design of Windows 95, whenever you create a NetWare network map (using the Map command), these mappings will apply to all virtual machines, even if you created the map in a virtual machine.

As we leave this discussion of troubleshooting MS Client for NetWare Networks, let's discuss which Novell functions you can and cannot perform.

If you are a NetWare 3.x administrator, there is good news for you. All of the NetWare utilities to which you are accustomed are still supported in the MS Client software. Even SYSCON (the network administration utility) works just fine; simply go to the DOS prompt, map a drive to the \public directory, and use the NetWare command as always.

If you are a NetWare 4.x administrator, we have some good news and some bad news. Most of the reporting commands, like Slist and Userlist, will work just fine under MS Client; however, the administrative functions of a 4.x server require NDS compliance, which MS Client does not support. If you need to remotely administrate a NetWare 4.x server under Windows 95, your only viable connectivity option is to run Novell NetWare Client.

Setting Up Novell NetWare Client

When installing Novell NetWare Client you first need to decide whether to support IPX-NETX (also referred to as *monolithic IPX*) or IPXODI-NETX or IPXODI-VLM. In either case, you need the latest drivers from Novell. The following are lists of all the files needed.

Novell files needed for a monolithic IPX install:

- IPX.COM
- NETWARE.HLP
- VNETWARE.386
- NETWARE.DRV
- NETX.EXE
- VIPX.386

Novell files needed for an IPXODI-NETX (NetWare 3.12) install:

- ODI driver from NIC manufacturer
- NETWARE.DRV

- VNETWARE.386
- LSL.COM
- NETX.EXE
- IPXODI.COM
- NETWARE.HLP
- VIPX.386
- NWPOPUP.EXE

Novell files needed for an IPXODI-VLM (NetWare 4.x) install:

- ODI driver from NIC manufacturer
- VLM files for the various services that the client will be running
- NETX.VLM

Now here are the steps to installing the Novell NetWare Client software.

1. Install the Novell drivers as usual.

   For ODI, the following lines should be in your AUTOEXEC.BAT or STARTNET.BAT file:

   ```
   |s|
   [NIC ODI Driver]
   ipxodi
   NETX
   ```

   (In the last line above, substitute VLM as needed instead of NETX.)

2. Choose the Network option in the Control Panel.
3. Select Add.
4. Select Client from the list in the Select Network Client Component area.
5. Select Novell as the Manufacturer, as shown in the Figure 6.4.
6. Select NETX or VLM as the workstation shell.

As usual, you will need to shut down the system and restart for the changes to take effect.

FIGURE 6.4

Select Novell under
Manufacturers.

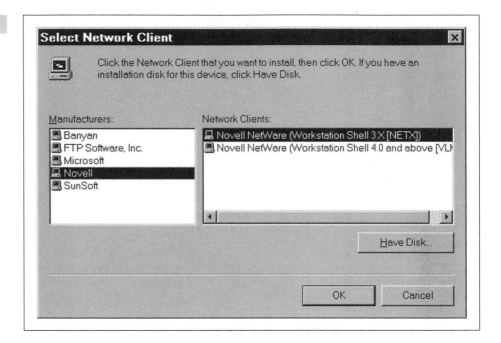

If you are working with a legacy system, and, therefore, ODI is not an option, here are the steps to enable monolithic IPX-NETX support in Windows 95:

1. Inherent in the nature of monolithic IPX is that it must be the only network option installed. Go to the Control Panel, click the Network icon, and remove all installed networking components.

2. Click Add.

3. Click Select Network Component.

4. Select Novell as the Manufacturer.

5. Select Novell IPX Monolithic Driver.

You will need to shut down and restart to have the changes take effect.

Enabling Long Filename Support on the Novell Server

As discussed earlier in this chapter, in order to enable long filename support on the NetWare server, you need to load the OS/2 name space support. Here's how you do it:

1. At the NetWare server prompt, type

   Load os2

   add name space os2 to volume sys

2. Add the following to the STARTUP.NCF file:

   load os2

3. Down the server, and at the C: prompt, copy the OS2.NAM file from the NetWare disks or CD-ROM. Place this file in the same directory as SERVER.EXE.

4. Type **SERVER** to restart the NetWare server.

Making Windows 95 Appear as a Novell Server

You may find yourself in a position where not everyone in your office uses Windows 95, but everyone does use NetWare. If you use a Windows 95 machine, you may want to share information from your machine with the rest of the network. The conventional way of doing this is to simply share the information through the Windows Explorer; this way people can access the data if they use WfW, Windows NT, or a machine running MS DOS Client. But what if the person accessing your machine only has Novell drivers loaded? You can make your Windows 95 machine and share appear as a Novell server and volume on the network.

Let's take a look at this process.

1. Ensure that you have loaded the IPX/SPX-compatible protocol.

2. In the Control Panel click on Network.

3. Select Add, then choose Service.

4. Select Microsoft as the manufacturer (as in Figure 6.5), choose the service *File and Printer Sharing for NetWare Networks*, then click OK.

FIGURE 6.5

Choosing File and printer sharing for NetWare Networks

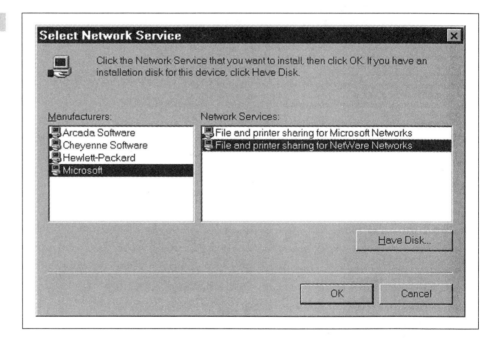

Please note: You cannot load the *File and Printer sharing* for both Microsoft Networks *and* for NetWare Networks.

5. Now, click on *File and Printer Sharing for NetWare Networks* in the components lists, select Properties, and enable SAP Advertising. Click OK. This will broadcast the Windows 95 machine as a Net-Ware server to the Novell network.

6. Your Windows 95 machine does not have its own security database for validating user access to itself as a NetWare server, so it must share a user list with a known NetWare server. Click on the Access Control tab and select User-level access. Provide the name of the Novell server that will be used to validate users' access to this Windows 95 "NetWare" server.

7. The final step is to restart Windows 95. (As usual, the system will prompt you to reboot.)

Now, to share resources with the NetWare world, you simply go to the Windows Explorer and share resources as you normally would. Since you have selected User-level access, you will now see the option *Add users to a share*. When you click on the Add button, a list of NetWare users and groups will appear in the pick list. At this point, you can give the users read-only, full, or custom access to this share.

If you are a NetWare client, accessing this share is as easy as mapping a drive. Keep in mind that the Windows 95 machine is the server name and the share is the volume name. So, if you have a Windows 95 machine called GTW09 and shared directory called WIN95SHR, at the NetWare client you would type the following:

map x:=GTW09\WIN95SHR:

At that point, if your system prompts you for a login name and password, provide them as they appear on the NetWare server list.

CHAPTER

7

Wired 95— Remote Access with Windows 95

ONE of the biggest features Microsoft introduced as an integral part of Windows 95 is *dial-up networking*, which is the ability to remotely attach to a major network via a telephone or leased connection. This ability has many advantages.

One advantage is that it is convenient. If you leave the office and decide to continue working on a project at home, often you discover that files that you need were not saved to the floppy disk that you brought home with you. One option is to get back in your car, drive back to work, and retrieve the files from the network. But wouldn't it be so much easier and convenient to dial up your network from home and download the files? That's what's known as telecommuting.

Another advantage is remote administration. If you are a network administrator with a pager (and there are very few of you without pagers), you often get that dreaded page at 2:00 a.m. If a user locked himself out of the network (for example, he was having a bad typing day and mistyped his password three times), it becomes your job to either unlock his account or give him a new password. (Please note: If someone is actively working at 2:00 a.m., this must be a *very* important project.) Without dial-up networking, you must drive to the office and fix his user account. With dial-up networking, all you have to do is drag yourself to your computer at home, dial up the network, and perform the administrative task from home. Then, and most importantly, you get to go back to bed.

Now all of this probably sounds terrific, but you must be wondering, "How difficult is this to set up?" If you have ever worked with modems and telecommunications, you're probably fearing the adventure ahead of you. Good news! Once you get the terminology down, installing dial-up networking is not that difficult.

Let's begin with one of the largest issues—using remote-access software versus using remote-control software to communicate with your remote network.

What Is the Difference between Remote Control and Remote Access?

Once you've made the decision to let your users telecommute, you need to decide between the telecommuting methods of *remote control* and *remote access*. Both methods have similar hardware requirements: a modem, a telephone line, and a PC at the home office. The difference lies in the way in which the telecommuters access the office network. The method you choose depends on the kind of work that the telecommuters will be doing and the software that they use to do it.

Remote Control

Remote-control computing is a method of telecommuting in which the remote users actually *use* a network computer, controlling it via modem from their homes or outside offices. Thus, this kind of telecommuting requires a modem, a phone line, remote-control software, a remote PC, and a *host PC*, which is an office workstation specifically designated for dial-in use.

The Puppet Master

Remote control allows the remote user to take control of the host PC in the office via modem. The remote PC works as a front end for the remote user, letting him or her key in data and see the results on their monitor, while the only things traveling between the central office and the remote office are the input and the output. All the work is being done by the host PC in the central office—it has the applications, its processor is performing the calculations, and so forth. The remote PC does not need to have any of the necessary applications on it, it just uses the host machine's.

Remote control is best for non-GUI applications that mainly involve keyboard data entry. It becomes much slower when using mouse-intensive or graphics-intensive programs, such as Windows itself or any Windows application. To alleviate this problem, some remote-control software (such as ReachOut from Ocean Isle Software) only transmit GUI screen *changes* to the remote PC. This cuts down on traffic, at least in theory.

Disadvantages

In addition to its slowness with Windows, remote control has a few other disadvantages:

- The need for more than one PC for telecommuters—the remote PC and the host PC.

- The need for extra cabling (each machine needs its own connecting cable), power, cooling, and space.

- If the host machine locks up, then the remote user can't reset it.

- People using the host machine as a workstation tie up its use as a host.

- Security concerns. (Remember, remote control means that an office machine is logged on to the network.)

Remote Access

Remote access (also known as remote-node access) makes the remote PC a node on the network, rather than the controller of a network PC. The remote PC does all the processing necessary. The remote PC should have on its hard drive all the applications that it will need, so as to keep the data transfer to a minimum.

So Near, and Yet So Far

Remote access to a network requires a modem, a phone line, a remote PC, and remote-access software on both ends of the connection. In effect, remote access makes the remote PC a node on the office LAN. The phone line acts as a cable which connects the remote PC to the network interface card at the office. To log on to the network, the remote user dials up the remote access server (which, depending on the type of network your company is running and how the server(s) are configured, may or may not be the same computer as the file server). Once connected, the remote users must log on to the network just as they would if using one of the office PCs. (The security measures involved vary from product to product.)

Once logged on to the network, remote users can use the network just like any other user can, according to their user rights. When the remote users access files, they work on them at the remote computer, only accessing the file server to save the file or get a new one. Therefore, if the user is running Windows or other graphical user interface (GUI) applications, remote access is a faster option than remote control. Of course, it will still take remote users longer to access files on the server than it will take local users, as remote users must use telephone lines for transmission instead of fast network cable. This is obviously more of a problem with bigger files. When accessing an 11K memo, it's no big deal. Accessing a 1MB *book*, however, will take significantly longer. Since the user is running the application on the remote PC, however, at least the GUI application screen needn't travel through the phone lines; only the data needs to make the trip.

Which Is Better?

When the time comes for you to decide between remote control and remote access, consider the following points:

- What are the user's requirements? Which applications is the user running and what work does the user do?

- What hardware is compatible, and what is your computer's memory capacity?

- How will each option work with your LAN?

Essentially, when choosing between remote control and remote access, you're stuck with a choice between downloading screens (no big deal for DOS applications, but worth noting for Windows) and downloading files. No matter how you slice it, telecommuting is not, at this point, as fast as working in the office.

One option is not to limit yourself to one choice—many companies use remote control in some situations and remote access in other situations.

What Are the Setup Options for Dial-Up Networking?

The most common method of implementing dial-up networking will be via a modem. I strongly recommend that you use a modem that is following a useful standard, for example Hayes compatibility. You definitely want to avoid modems that only talk to their evil twins, like the High Speed Transmission (HST) modems which only talk to other HST modems.

Dial-up networking (DUN) does not limit you to connecting via modem. You can use DUN to attach a cable between two machines, which turns them into a small network. DUN supports a direct connection via parallel cable or null modem cable.

Dial-up networking also supports *Integrated Services Digital Network* (*ISDN*) connections. In order to use ISDN for dial-up connection, you must make sure that ISDN is supported in all the locations that you will be calling to and from.

NOTE   Dial-up networking is the same as *Remote Access Service* (RAS), with which you are familiar if you have used Windows for Workgroups 3.1x or Windows NT. Dial-up networking in Windows 95 is more powerful and flexible than WfW's RAS but not as complete as Windows NT's RAS.

What Connection Protocols Are Supported by Dial-Up Networking?

PPP   The protocol of choice for connecting with dial-up networking is the Point-to-Point Protocol (PPP). Microsoft has designed most of its remote access and dial-up connectivity around this protocol. At the speeds most of us will conduct our dial-up networking

(128Kbps or less), the primary advantage of PPP is that the connection does error checking of data and data compression during the transmission process. This makes for faster and more secure data transfer. Another reason to consider using PPP is that it is quickly becoming an industry-wide standard.

If you are using PPP you can connect to a network using IPX/SPX, TCP/IP, NetBEUI, or any combination of the three. Because of its power and flexibility, PPP is the default protocol when installing dial-up networking.

NetWare Connect Novell uses software known as NetWare Connect to allow remote clients to dial up to the network. Windows 95 comes with a NetWare Connect client which allows your Windows 95 machine to attach to a NetWare Connect server directly, without going through a Microsoft gateway of any type. Even though Windows 95 machines can connect to a NetWare Connect server, it is not a reciprocal relationship; NetWare Connect clients cannot dial in to a Windows 95 server.

RAS Dial-up networking supports RAS as implemented by Windows for Workgroups 3.11 and Windows NT 3.1. (Windows NT 3.5x now defaults to using PPP.) You may see this RAS option referred to as *asynchronous NetBEUI* in some systems' help files or in network documentation.

SLIP An older protocol standard is the Serial Line Interface Protocol (SLIP). Unlike its PPP counterpart, SLIP does not perform error checking or data compression while transmitting data; the responsibility is placed on your hardware to perform these functions. This is not a bad thing, since most 14.4Kbps and 28.8Kbps modems *do* perform these functions.

NOTE   Microsoft recommends against using SLIP except when dialing up a UNIX network that is using a dial-up server with TCP/IP.

What Are the Different Combinations for Connection Protocols and Network Protocols?

There are two parts to dial-up networking: the dial-up *server* and the dial-up *client* (the remote user's machine). Let's take a look at the various combinations from that perspective. The information is summarized in Table 7.1.

TABLE 7.1

Various Combinations of Connection and Network Protocols

CLIENTS	SERVER
TCP/IP over SLIP	UNIX remote server, Internet (SLIP Router)
IPX over NetWare Connect	NetWare Connect Server
IPX, NetBEUI, and/or TCP/IP over PPP	Internet (PPP Router), Windows 95, Windows NT RAS Server, and NetWare
NetBEUI over RAS (Asynchronous NetBEUI)	Windows 95, Windows NT, Windows for Workgroups 3.11, and LAN Manager Servers

How Do I Install Dial-Up Networking?

Installing dial-up networking is a two-step process:

1. First, you must install the dial-up networking software onto your client machine and onto your host PC or server.

2. Then you must configure the dial-up networking software as either client or server.

Installing Dial-Up Networking on the Network

Let's look at how to install the dial-up networking software on your company's host PC or server:

1. Click on Control Panel.

2. Select Add/Remove Programs.

3. Select the Setup tab.

4. Click the Communications option and then select Details.

5. Select *Dial-up networking* from the list.

You will be returned to the main window to continue with the setup—select the Next button, then.

Configuring the DUN Network Connection

Good news! You do not have to restart your system in order to configure dial-up networking.

Installing Dial-Up Networking on the Client Machine

The first step to installing dial-up networking software on a remote machine is to install all the *protocols* the remote user might need and bind them to the *dial-up adapter*. On the remote machine, go to Control Panel, choose Network, and select the dial-up adapter your remote machine will be using.

The next step is to create a new Dial-Up Networking (DUN) *connection*. Instruct your remote user to go to the DUN folder in My Computer and, within the folder, choose the Make New Connection option. The user should supply any information needed and click OK. This creates a Connection icon in the Dial-Up Networking folder.

Once the user has created the DUN connection, he or she can double-click the Connection icon at any time to dial up to the network. It may ask for the name of the server or domain they want to log on to, as well as a password. DUN will then dial the location, verify the user name and the password, and if everything checks out, allow access to the server. At this point, the user can now do anything they normally could if they were local to the network (only more slowly).

At the risk of repeating myself, I strongly recommend that remote users do not attempt to run applications across the DUN connection; they should only go DUN to get data files and information. For example, if you choose to start a network copy of Word for Windows from your remote DUN location, it could easily take over 45 minutes for the application to begin, because the entire program would have to be transported via modem to the memory of your remote DUN machine.

TIP

Dial-Up Networking is designed with data in mind. The best implementation of DUN would be a remote DUN machine that has the applications loaded locally.

The recommendation also applies to remote administration. Load a copy of your network administration utilities locally on each remote DUN machine you expect to administer the network from. Of course, if you choose to follow this advice, be aware that the network vendor may require you to buy additional licenses of the network administration utilities. Many network vendors sell the utilities in sets.

Configuring a DUN Client Connection

To configure a DUN client connection, simply right-click the Connection icon that was created in the preceding section and select Properties.

Your first major decision here concerns the type of server you will be dialing up via this connection. If you typically dial to the same site, but you know that sometimes you'll want to connect via RAS (asynchronous NetBEUI) and other times you'll want to connect via NetWare Connect, use Make New Connection and create two separate connections. Then whenever you go to make your connection, you can choose from a pair of Connection icons.

You can see your choices for Type of Dial-Up Server in Figure 7.1.

Let's take a look at the different options available on this screen:

- **PPP** Used for dialing to RAS servers that are using TCP/IP, IPX, NetBEUI, or any combination of the three. DUN will automatically detect which of the three to use based on the protocols you select at the bottom of the screen.

- **NRN** Used for connecting to a NetWare Connect Server.

- **WFW/WIN NT** Used when dialing into a Windows 95 dial-up server, NT RAS Server, or WfW RAS server.

- **SLIP** Used for any implementation of SLIP of the TCP/IP protocol.

FIGURE 7.1

Type of Dial-Up Server
dialog box

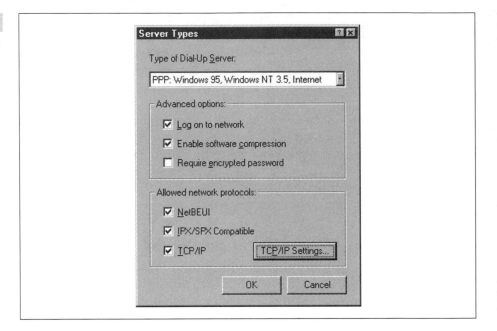

- **CSLIP** Used for any implementation of compressed SLIP connections. (Your network administrator should specify whether or not you need to use SLIP or CSLIP. The protocol must match what the dial-up server is using.)

- **Log on to network** This option, which is enabled by default, will dial up and log you into the network using the username and password you typed in when you logged into Windows 95. If this option is deselected, it will ask you for a logon name and password every time you attempt a new connection.

- **Enable software compression** This option will compress the data before it is sent to the modem (or the like) for transmission.

- **Require Encrypted Passwords** This option enables a feature known as the Challenge Handshake Authentication protocol (CHAP). CHAP will be discussed in greater detail later in this chapter.

This screen is also where you specify the protocols that you want the DUN connection to support. If you want to configure a connection to the Internet, click on the TCP/IP settings. This option will ask for information that you may need to get from your network administrator or your Internet service provider.

How Do I Test the DUN Connection?

Once you have configured your DUN connection, just double-click and the connection will be made immediately. You should see the lights of your modem flashing, and, if you have enabled the modem speaker, you should hear that distinctive squelching noise which indicates that Windows 95 is negotiating a connection.

Using Microsoft's Universal Naming Conventions (UNCs), you should now be able to access any network resource for which you have permission.

> **TIP**
>
> When you are connected to a network, you can go to the *Connected To* window and see the number packets sent, number of packets received, and the overall status of your connection.

Once you have established a connection for the first time, dial-up networking will be activated in any of the following circumstances:

- When you select a network resource that is not part of your network
- When a UNC directs you toward a network resource (for example, \\server\public_)
- When an application calls for a network resource

Shortcuts to Popular Network Information

If you need to dial up to many different networks, shortcuts are a great way to organize all of your frequently visited sites. It also gets you quickly to the information on those networks that you use most frequently.

Without shortcuts, I have to take the following steps every time I want to connect to my home directory at work:

1. Open the My Computer folder.

2. Open the Dial-Up Networking folder.

3. Select my connection. (In my case, it's MMCO Office.)

4. Provide a password.

At this point the system starts to negotiate the connection and to authenticate me to the network. After validation, I map a network drive to my home directory on the network (as discussed in Chapter 5) and then I can access my files.

All this gets a little tiresome quickly, and this is where shortcuts come to the rescue. To create a shortcut to my home directory, I still follow the above steps the very first time I connect, but I let Windows 95 automatically create a shortcut to the directory by clicking and dragging my network home directory folder to the desktop.

From that point on, if I want to get to my home directory then I just double-click on its shortcut. Windows 95 will now automatically call the network, validate me to the network (assuming my Windows 95 logon and network logon are identical), and take me to my home directory. If I am already connected to the network, the shortcut is still a useful way to fly directly to my home directory.

Installing the Windows 95 Server

Many users familiar with Windows NT Remote Access Server may be wondering, "What's the difference between NT's RAS and Windows 95's Server?" There are two differences:

- Whereas the Windows NT RAS is included when you purchase Windows NT, the Windows 95 Server is not included with Windows 95. If you want to install the Windows 95 Server, you need to purchase an add-on package known as Microsoft Plus!, which retails for $50.

- Connections: Windows NT can support up to 256 simultaneous connections; a Windows 95 Server can only support one connection at a time.

The first step to enabling Windows 95 Server is to install the Microsoft Plus! software. With Microsoft Plus! installed, do the following:

1. In the Connections menu, a new option, Dial-Up Server, will appear.

2. In the Dial-Up Server configuration window, click *Allow caller access*.

3. Set the Security option. You can define a password that anyone calling to this Windows 95 machine must provide in order to access the shared resources of the DUN server system. Alternatively, if you are implementing user-level security, you can specify the users that can access this machine.

4. Select *Server Type*. This option defaults to PPP, which supports TCP/IP, IPX, and NetBEUI. By selecting this option, a determination is made during the negotiation of callers to this DUN server machine. If PPP cannot negotiate a viable connection, the DUN server will automatically switch to RAS for NT and Windows for Workgroup clients.

Once you click OK, your system is now waiting to receive calls.

What about Security?

We have discussed some of the things to be considered in order for a DUN to work and to interact properly. But once you have DUN up and running, there are a few security concerns you might want to deal with.

For example, Jennifer, dialing up from home, can locate another user, say Joe, who is currently logged into the DUN server, and kick him off. All she has to do is take these four simple steps:

1. Go to My Computer.
2. Select Dial-Up Networking.
3. Select Dial-Up Server.
4. Click the Disconnect User button.

In the same vein, if Joe hasn't been kicked off yet, he can take a preemptive strike against everybody, by remotely turning off the server! All he has to do is follow the first three of the steps above and then click No Caller Access.

Fortunately, once you have DUN up and running, there are a few security features you can enable.

Password Authentication Protocol (PAP)

The first level of security is established during the connection. If you have selected PPP as your server type on both the client and the server, then you can utilize a technology known as the Password Authentication Protocol (PAP). Before the invention of PAP, the server, client, and user held the following conversation:

Server (to client): *Do you use PAP?*

Client (to Server): *No.*

Server (to Client): *What is the user's name?*

Client (to User): *What is your logon name?*

User (to Client): *Frank.*

Client (to Server): *The user says his name is Frank.*

Server (to Client): *Great, what is the user's password?*

Client (to User): *What is your logon password?*

User (to Client): *Doghouse.*

Client (to Server): *The client says his password is Doghouse.*

Server (to Client): *Thank you.*

This conversation would take place every single time the user wanted to log in to the network remotely. There is no encryption of information being sent back and forth. With some network servers, you may actually have to create a script file so this conversation can be automated. In either case, it still requires that the network administrator understand how to create the script file. Scripts in theory are very straightforward, but in practice the syntax can vary from hardware device to hardware device and from network operating system to network operating system.

If both your server and the client are using PAP, then the conversation goes something like this:

Server: *Do you use PAP?*

Client: *Yes.*

Server: *Great, then please send over the username.*

Client: *Frank.*

Server: *Great, please send over the password.*

Client: *Doghouse.*

Server: *Thank you.*

This entire conversation took place without any interaction on the part of the user. If it took any time at all, all the user saw was the hourglass while this conversation took place in the background. Unfortunately, just as you saw the password *Doghouse* in the conversation presented above, the password was sent as a simple text string across the communication line. When I last looked in Webster's dictionary under the word *security*, this wasn't part of the definition. If you are looking for a secure validation, you want to use CHAP.

NOTE Now before we discuss CHAP, I would like to mention SPAP in passing. The makers of the Shiva Modem have their own Authentication protocol known as Shiva Password Authentication Protocol (SPAP). Windows 95 supports SPAP for dialing into a Shiva Server.

Challenge-Handshake Authentication Protocol (CHAP)

As said previously, CHAP allows for secure validation. If the server and client have CHAP enabled, the following conversation takes place:

Server: *Do you do CHAP?*

Client: *Yes.*

Server: *47*

Client (to itself): *Let me factor the password by 47 and send the encrypted version across the line.*

Client (to Server): *Kjsyao7r* (representing the password doghouse).

Server: *Thank You.*

Now, since the server sent a *challenge code* (47 in the example above), it knows that it will use the same number as the challenge factor to decrypt the password and then validate it. The power of CHAP is that when the first client logs in the challenge code may be 47, but when the next client logs in the challenge code dynamically changes. Since the challenge code is constantly changing, the passwords are encrypted using a different key every time.

To enable CHAP, just select Require Encrypted Password when configuring the client *and* when configuring the server. If Server Type is PPP, DUN will attempt a PAP conversation by default, unless Require Encrypted Passwords is selected.

Access to Resources with DUN

DUN allows you to specify how people may gain access to the DUN server.

- The first option is share-level security. This permits you to assign passwords to each resource that you share. You can set a password for read-only access and a different password for full-control access. The downside of this configuration is that a user may have to memorize many passwords. If you are looking for centralized control, you will want to set user-level permissions instead.

- When you set user-level permissions, Windows 95 will look for a Windows NT or NetWare server to validate a user. The user has to be a valid user of Novell network or a NT domain in order to gain access to your machine. Windows 95 still controls read-only or full-control access to the resource, but enforces these security parameters by users, not by resource.

How Do I Create a Direct Serial Connection?

Users aren't limited to actually dialing in via a phone line to set up a network connection; they can connect their remote computer directly via a serial cable. To create a direct serial connection, the first thing that you need is an acceptable cable. Any of the following will do:

- Serial null modem cable
- LapLink cable
- InterLink cable
- 25-pin parallel cable (all wires must be present)

Of the four types of cables, the parallel cable will provide the fastest throughput between machines.

Once you have made a physical connection between the machines, take the following steps:

1. Choose *Add/Remove programs* in Control Panel.

2. Select Communications in the Components list.

3. Select Direct Cable Connection.

A new icon, titled Direct Cable Connection, will appear in the My Computer window. Please make sure this icon appears on both machines before attempting to establish a connection.

The first time you click on Direct Cable Connection, the Direct Connect Wizard will appear and allow you to designate one machine as the host machine and the other machine as the guest machine.

CHAPTER

8

Supporting Windows 95 Clients on a Network

YEARS ago, people looked to PCs as an alternative to mainframe computing. When justifying the purchase of a PC, they often cited cost. "PCs are cheaper than mainframes," they said, and they were right—as long as they were only talking about the cost of the hardware.

The last twenty years of desktop computing have taught us that the real cost of owning PCs lies in supporting them. So anything that makes supporting PCs easier is a real plus.

Windows 95 doesn't solve all of a support person's remote support headaches, but it's an improvement over Windows for Workgroups or (ugh!) regular old Windows 3.1 with network drivers added. In this chapter, you'll see how you can leverage your network investment to simplify support in the following ways:

- You can simplify Windows 95 installation over a network.

- You can set up your 95 workstations to boot from shared directories on the network.

- You can use system policies to restrict user access to Windows 95 features.

- You can use user profiles so that your desktop follows you wherever you go on the network.

- You can use Net Watcher, Network Monitor, and System Monitor to watch network activity and remotely administer resource sharing over a 95 network.

Setting Up 95 for Network Installs

The prospect of walking around your company with a CD-ROM disc, or, more likely, a knapsack full of floppies to install 95 probably doesn't sound like much fun (and, coincidentally, it's *not*). You can use your *network* to make installing 95 easier in three ways:

- You can install the entire 95 system on your user's local hard disks from a network.

- You can set up 95 so that *most* of it sits on a shared directory on the server and only about three to four megabytes sits on the user's local hard disk.

- You can even set up a workstation so that it needs only a floppy to start from, and the Windows 95 installation doesn't touch the workstation's hard disk. The process *is* buggy, but you can get it to work with persistence.

In this section, you'll see how to do those things.

There are basically three groups of files that you need in order to get Windows working over a network:

- The very large shared directory (about 75MB) of Windows files. You'll usually run them from the server, but if you want you can install them entirely onto a local hard disk when doing a network installation.

- A directory containing the user's personal Windows-specific files, including the SYSTEM.DAT part of the Registry, your temporary files, and the like. This is called the *machine directory*. It ranges from 1.5MB to about 4MB in size, and each machine that can boot Windows 95 has a machine directory. The machine directory can sit on either the PC's local hard disk or the server.

- Files required to boot the user's computer up to the point where it can access the server. I call these the *boot files*; there's no official

Windows name for them. Every computer must have these boot files on either the local hard disk or a floppy disk, or, in the case of machines with remote-boot LAN adapters, on the server. These files are about 1.5 MB.

Installing 95 onto a Local Hard Disk from a Server

Installing 95 from a server is simple. Just copy all the contents of the CD-ROM's win95 folder to a directory, set the directory to read-only (just in case...), and then go to each user's workstation and connect to the shared directory. Run Setup as usual and you're done.

Installing 95 to Share a Directory on the Server

Suppose I want to install my workstations so that they boot 95 mainly from the server? Setting up 95 on a workstation entails three (or, optionally, four) steps:

1. Set up a shared directory that contains the Windows files, which will be used both for workstation setup and for people to start up Windows 95 every day.

2. Optionally, create a separate share which will hold a machine directory (a kind of home directory for each machine) on your network.

3. Create standard setup scripts.

4. Optionally, on each workstation, take the following steps:

   - Set up simple DOS-based or Windows 3.x-based network client software.
   - Log on to the shared directory.
   - Run Setup.

Those few steps have a variety of options within them; let's take a look at what those options are and how to use them.

Getting Ready: Build a Share and Then Run NETSETUP

In order to *run* Windows 95 from a network, you must first create a shared directory with the decompressed 95 files. First, go to your server and create a share in which you can store the shared files. In my examples, I'll use a share called W95SHR on my primary domain controller, named EISA Server. (Yes, there's a blank in the name. I wish I'd never done *that*, believe me, but you'll see more about that later...)

Then tell Windows to copy and decompress itself from the shipped file cabinets. You do that with NETSETUP.EXE, which you'll find on the CD in the \admin\nettools\netsetup directory. Don't try to install it with the Control Panel—it won't work. Instead, just open up the admin \nettools\netsetup folder on the CD-ROM and double-click on the NETSETUP.EXE file. Start it up and you'll see a screen, as in Figure 8.1.

FIGURE 8.1

Setting up 95 installation paths

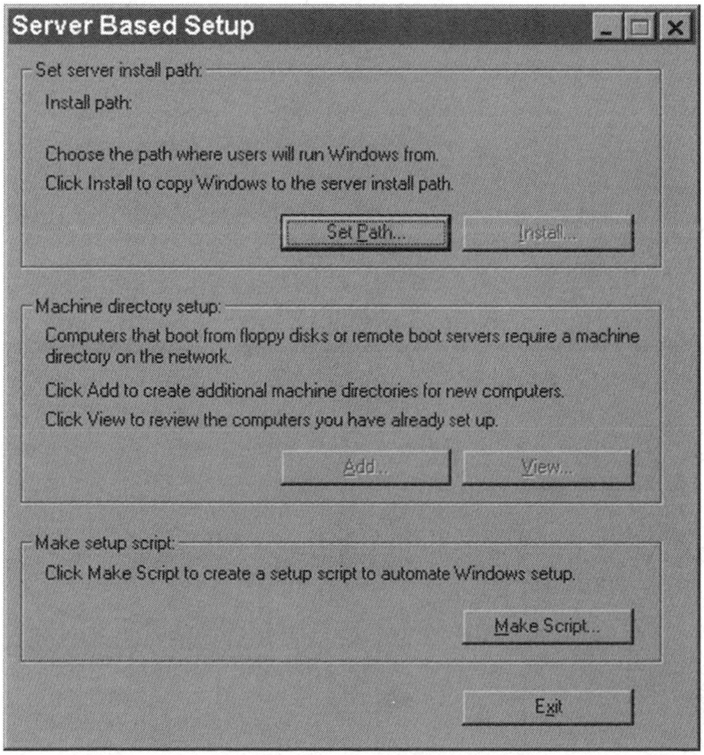

Click Set Path, and you'll be prompted for the name of the shared Windows directory to create. This name must be a UNC name, like \\myserver\w95shr. It would be nice to call it a name like \\myserver \Windows 95 shared directory, but that would make your life tougher when it comes time to access the directory when upgrading from DOS or Windows 3.x. If the share doesn't yet exist, then you'll get an error message; Netsetup cannot create an entirely new share. If, on the other hand, the share exists but the directory doesn't, then you'll be prompted as to whether or not to create it. When you have that taken care of, click Install and you'll see a dialog box like Figure 8.2.

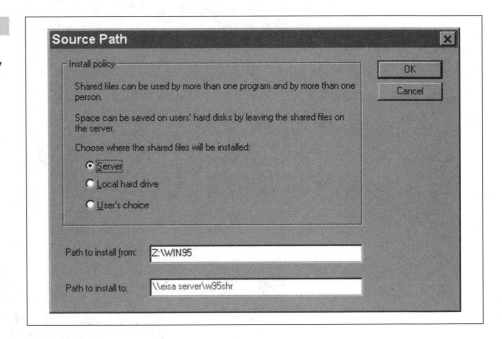

You're running Netsetup now, and you (or others) will run regular old Setup for each workstation to put Windows 95 on a workstation, or on a workstation and server working together. In the Group Install policy, you control whether Setup will allow someone to copy the files onto their local hard disk. I'd pick *User's choice*, as it doesn't affect your site license whether people run 95 from the server or if they copy it to their workstations. (You see *Server* chosen in the Figure 8.2 because it is the default, before I changed it.)

The options *Path to install from:* and *Path to install to:* should be self-explanatory. (In case you're wondering, Z: is the CD-ROM on my system.)

As you can see in Figure 8.3, once you click OK, you'll see the next important dialog box, which concerns default batch files.

This creates a setup batch script with more details than you saw in the Batch Script Editor you met in Chapter 4. You do *not* have to do this now. If you do *not* create the default script the first time, you can do it later by reinvoking Netsetup, specifying the path name of the shared Windows installation you previously created, and then clicking that Make Script button at the bottom of the dialog box. Read ahead a few paragraphs before you decide to click Create Default; my recommendation is that you click Don't Create Default.

The dialog box that you see is more akin to the System Policy Editor, about which you will learn more later in this chapter, than it is to BATCH.EXE. It looks like the one in Figure 8.4.

While this is supposed to be doing a job like BATCH.EXE's, it doesn't do the same kind of job that BATCH.EXE does (and not nearly as well). I'll explain how to use this Server Based Setup Default Properties dialog, but my recommendation is that you just skip this step and choose Don't Create Default in the previous dialog box.

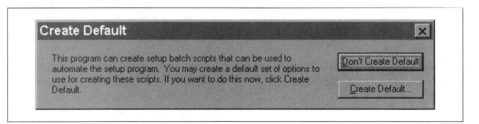

FIGURE 8.3

Choosing batch file scripts

FIGURE 8.4

Choices for batch
script setup

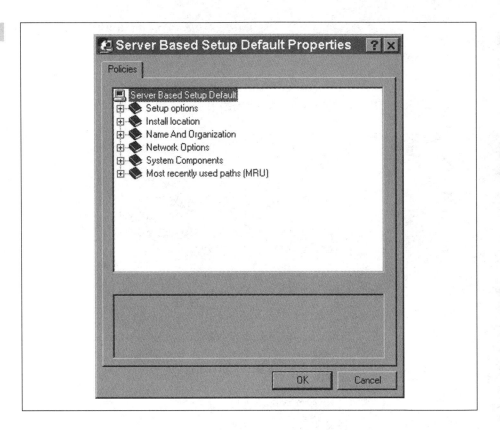

Setup Options

In the Choices for Batch Script dialog box (Figure 8.4), click the Setup
Options volume and you'll see controls relevant to the overall setup. Most
of them are either self-explanatory or similar to the BATCH.EXE dialogs,
but there are a few pitfalls. With Automated Install, you can set up the
installation to be free of user input; that's an option that you can set inside
Setup Options. With Setup Mode, you choose whether the setup is Custom, Typical, or whatever.

Install Location

Here is where you specify that Windows should be set up so that it runs
from the server, rather than the workstation's local hard disk, and whether
or not it boots from a floppy.

Name and Organization

This lets you pre-enter information, such as the name of your organization. You can fix it so that the user never sees the information upon Setup or you can just provide defaults.

You then enter the product identification number and Netsetup starts copying information to the shared directory. (Again, in my example, I've put that directory on a server called EISA Server, on a share called W95SHR.)

Network

In this section, you can ensure that people log on to the domain, specify the workgroup to join, and other similar things. There's useful stuff here, but the interface is terrible, so you'll end up fixing it by hand, as I'll next explain.

Adjust the Script

Click OK, and Netsetup will copy and expand over 75MB of files to your shared directory. You can exit Netsetup at this point and examine the script that it wrote if you allowed it to; if not, then now's a good time to run BATCH.EXE.

You'll find a file called MSBATCH.INF in the shared Windows directory. It's set to read-only, so you'll need to reset that bit before editing it. And you'll want to edit it. As I've said, Netsetup just falls down a bit on getting the .INF file correct, requiring you to look back to Chapter 4 and tweak the commands to get them right. For example, it lets you specify protocols and client software, but you're supposed to fill in the names, rather than choose them from a list. Protocol names are NETBEUI, NWLINK (the 95 name for IPX), and MSTCP. Redirector names are VREDIR (the client for Microsoft networks) and NWREDIR (the Microsoft client for NetWare networks). If you were to load all three protocols and both clients, then the line in the .INF file should end up looking like the following two lines.

```
Clients=VREDIR, NWREDIR
Protocols=NETBEUI, NWLINK, MSTCP
```

Other important settings include HDBOOT, which should be set to 1 if you're going to start your Windows machine from the hard disk or 0 if you're going to boot either from a floppy or directly off the server with a remote-booting LAN board. ReplSetup should equal 1 if you're starting from a remote-booting LAN board, and 0 if you're booting from a floppy; the whole setting is only relevant if HDBOOT=0.

Just by way of example, here's an MSBATCH.INF that I use for my network, with comments:

```
[Setup]
Express=1
InstallDir=" g:\mwm66"
EBD=0
ChangeDir=0
OptionalComponents=1
Network=1
System=0
CCP=0
CleanBoot=0
Display=0
PenWinWarning=0
InstallType=1
DevicePath=1
TimeZone=" Eastern"
Uninstall=0
VRC=0
NoPrompt2Boot=1

[NameAndOrg]
Name=" Mark Minasi"
Org=" MMCO, inc."
Display=0

[Network]
ComputerName=" MWM66"
Workgroup=" orion"
Description=" 95 workstation"
Display=0
Clients=VREDIR
Protocols=NETBEUI
IgnoreDetectedNetCards=0
HDBoot=1
RPLSetup=0
WorkstationSetup=1
```

```
DisplayWorkstationSetup=0
Security=domain
PassThroughAgent=" orion"

[VREDIR]
LogonDomain=" orion"
ValidatedLogon=1

[OptionalComponents]
" Accessibility Options" =0
" Briefcase" =0
" Calculator" =1
" Character Map" =0
" Clipboard Viewer" =0
" Desktop Wallpaper" =0
" Document Templates" =1
" Games" =0
" Mouse Pointers" =0
" Net Watcher" =0
" Object Packager" =1
" Online User's Guide" =0
" Paint" =1
" Quick View" =1
" System Monitor" =1
" System Resource Meter" =1
" Windows 95 Tour" =0
" WordPad" =1
" Dial-Up Networking" =1
" Direct Cable Connection" =1
" HyperTerminal" =1
" Phone Dialer" =1
" Backup" =0
" Defrag" =1
" Disk compression tools" =1
" Microsoft Exchange" =0
" Microsoft Mail Services" =0
" Microsoft Fax Services" =0
" Microsoft Fax Viewer" =0
" Central European language support" =0
" Cyrillic language support" =0
" Greek Language support" =0
" Audio Compression" =1
" CD Player" =1
" Jungle Sound Scheme" =0
" Media Player" =1
```

```
" Musica Sound Scheme" =0
" Robotz Sound Scheme" =0
" Sample Sounds" =0
" Sound Recorder" =1
" Utopia Sound Scheme" =0
" Video Compression" =1
" Volume Control" =1
" Additional Screen Savers" =0
" Flying Windows" =1
" The Microsoft Network" =0
```

Express=1, display=0, and NoPrompt2Boot=0 all minimize the number of mouse clicks you must do to get through the installation. Verify=0 keeps Setup from complaining if you are *re*installing Windows 95 on a machine. I still haven't figured out CCP, and ProductID is obvious. InstallType=1 is Typical, ebd=0 says to skip making an emergency boot disk, and Uninstall=0 says it's not necessary to keep the uninstall information—it usually isn't meaningful for network setups, and certainly not for floppy-based boots. Installdir tells where to install the Windows files to; this will turn out to be important for network installations.

In [network], the two references to WorkstationSetup tell Setup to do a network install using the shared binaries on w95shr, rather than to copy all of the Windows files to the local hard disk. HDBOOT=1 and RPL-Setup=0 say that you should set up to boot from the hard disk. That's not necessary; it's just how I have it set up. I'm loading the Microsoft network client (VREDIR) and the NetBEUI protocol.

I built this file with BATCH.EXE. The built-in batch file creator in Netsetup produced a file that required a pile of work to make it look like this (which is, again, why I recommend using BATCH.EXE).

Restart NETSETUP and Create Machine Directories

It's nice that you can take all of those Windows 95 files and put them in a single shared directory, rather than having to burn up tens of megabytes on the C: drive of every hard disk in your organization. But not everything can be shared. Registries, program groups, desktops, .INI files from legacy apps, and temporary and swap files are some examples of things that are specific to a particular person or workstation.

You're probably familiar with the idea that users on a network have home directories, which are directories on the server that no one can access except for its owner. As users move around, user-specific information can live in the user's home directory. But where does the machine-specific stuff, like swap files, temp files, and SYSTEM.DAT, live? It is in a kind of home directory for a particular workstation, called a *machine directory*. Each machine needs a place to put this information. On a stand-alone installation, it's mixed in with the other Windows files. On a networked installation, it can sit on a small directory called windows on the workstation's C: drive or it can be on a directory on the server. Obviously, floppy-based systems must put their machine directories on a server.

Another way of understanding machine directories is to keep in mind that they are also the *installation directory* of Windows 95. When Setup asks where to install Windows 95 to, you should point Setup to the machine directory—but I hope to have you avoid that manual labor; we'll make installing 95 over the network as automatic as is possible.

Go to your network and create a directory which will hold all of the machine directories; I called mine, uncreatively, Machine. Share that directory so that it's visible on the network.

Now return to Netsetup and click the Path button. Fill in the UNC name of the shared Windows directory that you created before. (It's w95shr in this example, not machine, remember—you now want the shared Windows directory, not the machine directory.)

In the machine directory setup part of Netsetup, click Add, and you'll see a dialog box like Figure 8.5.

I'll set up just one machine for now, but notice that there's a procedure here for setting up multiple PCs in one pass—I'll get to that later. I've created a share on EISA Server called Machine which will contain these machine directories.

I want to set up a machine called MWM66, so I fill in the name of the machine and the name of the directory where it'll keep its information, as you see in Figure 8.6.

I've said this before, but it's important to create the machine directory before running this, as I've had Netsetup give me a GPF a few times when I asked it to create the machine directory. Unfortunately, if you GPF out

FIGURE 8.5

Adding a machine
directory

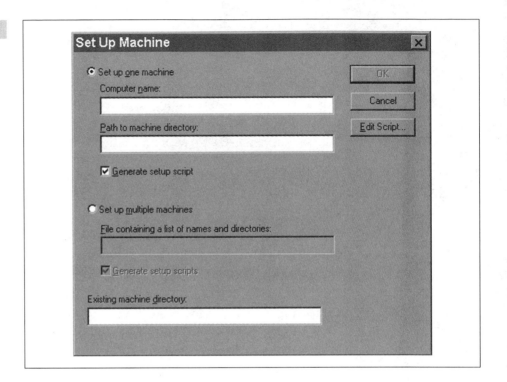

of Netsetup the first time you run it—when it creates the shared directory—then you have to zap the directory and start all over again or it won't let you create new machine directories.

And here's a bug alert: the *Path to machine directory:* field must contain a UNC name, as that's all this dialog box will accept. Unfortunately, that puts a UNC name into a script file that Netsetup creates, and running that causes an error. More on this in the next section called "Fix the Script File."

If you click the Edit Script button (*don't!*) then Netsetup brings you back to the script-builder dialog that you saw several figures back, allowing you to fine-tune a script for a particular machine. *Do not* click this button, as it will make you build a script from nothing; it won't carry over any of the settings that you specified earlier in the *default* script. If you just click OK, then it'll take your default MSBATCH.INF (the one you spent all that time fixing) and shove in the machine directory and machine name.

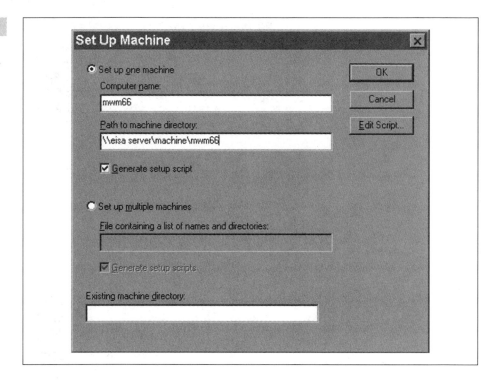

Once you've clicked OK to end Netsetup, you'll find that the machine
directory has been created and the directory contains only an MSBATCH
.INF file.

Fix the Script File

Once again, don't trust the network setup program. It tells your system
to install Windows 95 to a machine directory named \\eisa server
\machine\mwm66. The actual line in the .INF file is InstallDir= "\\eisa
server\machine\mwm66"

This seems like it should be correct, but it isn't, invariably leading to
a Setup error about being unable to create \\eisa server\machine
\mwm66. Instead, go back and change the script file to say:

InstallDir="g:\mwm66"

or something like that, and just remember to map the \\eisa server \machine share to G: before commencing the Setup process. Yes, it's dumb, but I've tried doing setups from inside Windows 3.11, DOS with the MS Workgroup Connection, and DOS with the MS Network Client for DOS version 3.0, all with the same error message. And, by the way, don't try to save yourself a step by specifying "g:\mwm66" while still in Netsetup—it won't take direct drive-letter entries.

Setting Up the Workstation

Once you have the shared directory and any machine directories set up, you'll need to go to the workstation to do a *pull* installation. It's called a pull installation because you run a program on the workstation to pull the files from the server onto your workstation.

> **N O T E**   There is, in contrast, a *push* installation which you can accomplish without leaving your desk—but that requires that your firm use Server Management System (SMS) or a similar tool.

Running Windows 95 off the server seems a bit of a chicken-and-egg problem: how do I load an operating system off the server when I have to load software to see the server in the first place? The answer is that your workstation must run a kind of mini operating system, basically DOS, with a small real-mode redirector, to get started. There's an AUTO-EXEC.BAT and a CONFIG.SYS just like in basic MS-DOS, and it includes the Net Start and Net Use commands you need to attach to the shared Windows 95 directories.

So, that means that step one in getting your workstation to run the Windows 95 Setup program is to load some network client software under your old operating system (unless you're just upgrading or reinstalling Windows 95).

TIP

I have encountered a fair number of network-related Setup crashes, most often when I get to the Copying files stage of an installation for floppy disks. (You know, the bang the drum *slooooowly* part of Setup.) They're often trap "D"s on the DOS extender. The DOS extender that's blowing up is in EMM386.EXE, so it might seem like a good idea to just not load EMM386—but then you often don't have enough RAM to run Setup. I don't seem to get this problem when my redirector is the MS Network Client for DOS version 3.0, so I strongly recommend that you run that. These problems seem most prevalent when I'm making a system that can boot entirely from a floppy, so if you're doing workstation installs that will boot from the local hard disk, then you probably don't have as much to worry about.

Once you're connected to the network, map to the shared Windows directory and to the machines directory. In my example (this is easiest to understand with an example), I mapped F: to the shared Windows share and G: to the machine share. Move to the shared Windows directory and run Setup, specifying the machine directory and the MSBATCH.INF file that was created there. For example, I've mapped the network volume that contains my shared Windows files to F: and my machine directory share to G:, so I go to my shared directory and type **f:setup g:\mwm66 \msbatch.inf**

Now, even though we're going to use a setup batch script, let me describe what you'd see if you *didn't* prepare a batch script. The setup looks like a normal Windows setup, except for a few important dialog boxes.

The first new dialog box is labeled Server-based Setup. Choose *Set up Windows to run from a network server* in order to use the shared files. If you don't check that, then Setup will just create a stand-alone installation on your hard disk by copying files from the shared Windows directory. If you choose *Set up Windows to run from a network server*, then you'll get another dialog box, labeled Startup Method. It offers three options:

- Start Windows from my hard disk
- Start Windows from a floppy disk.
- Start Windows from the network (remote boot server).

In most cases, you'll choose the *from my hard disk* option.

Then Setup asks for Machine directory, prompting "Type the name of the directory where you want to put files and settings for this computer. Then click Next to continue." Again, this dialog box will not accept a UNC name; it must be a drive letter and directory name. I specify G:\mwm66, as that's the machine directory that I've created for this computer.

Setup finishes the first part of the Setup Wizard, copies some files, and reboots. Unfortunately, in the case of *my* network, the reboot failed; you may come across this as well. If you're like me and put a space in the name of your server, then Windows 95 Setup isn't too bright. It puts Net Use statements into your AUTOEXEC.BAT, without quotes:

```
net use f: \\eisa server\w95shr
net use g: \\eisa server\machine
```

This doesn't work. I just edited the AUTOEXEC.BAT file (yes, there's still one of those, and it's essential to booting Windows 95 from the network) to put quotes around the UNCs, so the commands look like this:

```
net use f: "\\eisa server\w95shr"
net use g: "\\eisa server\machine"
```

I rebooted, and Setup could finish up its work. The result: a windows directory on my C: drive with 1.4MB of files on it, and mwm66, in the Machine share, has 1.3MB in it.

Now let's get back to the setup script. Despite the notion that this has to be a hands-free installation, there are a few places where you'll have to press a key or respond to Setup:

- You get an initial "Press Enter to run Setup" message, which requires you to hit Enter.

- After Setup runs ScanDisk, you have to press X to exit ScanDisk.

- The license agreement requires an Alt+Y acknowledgment.

- Setup may complain about the presence of OS/2 or NT on the system; you must respond to those dialogs.

- When the pre-GUI part of Windows 95 loads and initially logs you on to the network, you have to enter your name and password.

- You must again log in from the GUI once 95 is up. As a matter of fact, that's a down side of running Windows off a shared directory: You have to log in twice every time you start up Windows.

Review: .INF Settings for Network Setups

Before moving on to floppy setup options, let's take a minute and focus on the particular special settings you'll need in order to direct your system to do a network setup. The commands you have to know are:

- **Installdir** This goes in the [setup] section; all of the other commands go into the [network] section. This points to the machine directory, and it should be a drive-letter name, not a UNC name.

- **WorkstationSetup** When set to 1, this tells Setup that you'll run Windows from the shared Windows directory every time that you start Windows.

- **DisplayWorkstationSetup** When set to 0, this suppresses dialog boxes, assisting in building a hands-free setup.

- **Clients and Protocols** This names the network redirectors and transport protocols.

- **HDBoot** When set to 1, this instructs Setup to put the boot files on the PC's local hard disk. If set to 0, it tells Setup either to prepare a boot floppy or to set up an area for a network boot via a LAN card with a boot ROM.

- **RPLSetup** If you've set HDBoot to 0, this tells whether to boot from floppy (set the value to 0) or LAN card (set the value to 1).

By starting from a working script and changing these values as appropriate, you can modify scripts to do any kind of installation that you like.

Setting Up 95 for Floppy-Based Boots

You can take these installations a step further and tell Windows 95 to put *all* of your files in the machine directory, and just build a floppy disk that you can use to start 95. Just go to the MSBATCH.INF file that you're using to drive Setup and change HDBOOT=1 to HDBOOT=0, and be sure that there's also a RPLSetup=0 line in the same section. You'll be prompted to create a floppy disk even if you put EBD=0 in the file, as this is a bootable floppy with a small network redirector on it.

That process generally works well, but I've found a few problems with it. As my problems may simply be due to my not having done something right, you might not experience these troubles; if so, all the better. But if you *do* run into trouble creating a floppy-based boot, take a look at this section.

Check AUTOEXEC.BAT

As I've said a number of times before, when the Setup program writes out AUTOEXEC.BAT files, it doesn't construct proper Net Use statements for servers that have spaces in their names.

Ignore the DBLSPACE Error Message

When I boot from the floppy that Windows Setup built, I get the following message:

> You are loading the incorrect version of DBLSPACE.BIN for this version of MS-DOS. Since this configuration is untested, you should correct this problem as soon as possible. Press ENTER to continue starting MS-DOS.

For the life of me, I have no idea what this is all about. But I don't use DBLSPACE (and in fact I'd imagine that nobody with a hard-diskless workstation would either), so it seems not to be a problem.

Be Careful Editing MACHINES.INI

Before your PC can start floppy-booting 95 from your network, the PC must be able to find its Registry.

Unfortunately, however, the Registry is too big to fit on a floppy, so 95 does a little kludge called Setmdir upon bootup. Setmdir assists in the process of loading 95 from the network by pointing your PC at the network location where it can find the Registry. The AUTOEXEC.BAT that my system automatically generated looked like this:

```
snapshot /s
net start
net logon /savepw:no /y
net use f: \\eisa server\c
path=f:\w95shr\;f:\w95shr\command
setmdir
```

Snapshot helps Windows 95 change your system over to protected mode, but don't worry about it; it has nothing to do with fixing your MACHINES .INI file. The Net commands start up the network and map the F: drive to my server so that the Path commands can help my bootup disk find the bulk of the Windows 95 files.

The problem comes with Setmdir.

Its name is short for *set machine directory*. Suppose you put all your machine directories on a server called Wally, on a share named Macshare, in directories named machine\pc1, machine\dellpc, machine\billspc, and so on—Setmdir is the program that lets the 95 startup routine find it.

The trick to how it does that is that all Ethernet and Token Ring boards have unique 48-bit ID numbers (which become 12-digit hexadecimal numbers), and a program called Setmdir looks up a computer's machine directory via that ID number. For example, the hexadecimal representation of the Ethernet ID on the machine I'm currently working on is 00608CDE8F48, and its machine directory is \\eisa server\c \machine\mwm66—*that's* the connection that Setmdir must make.

You could have hundreds of machines booting from floppies, so you'd have to somehow keep track of which machine used what machine directory. Windows 95 organizes all of this data by keeping it in a file called MACHINES.INI on the shared Windows 95 directory.

Let's see how I told 95 where to find the machine directory. I create an entry in MACHINES.INI with the name **[00608CDE8F48]**. It contains one parameter called **sysdatpath**. (Don't type sysdat*a*path—leave that last *a* off of *data*.) I added a Net Use command to my AUTOEXEC.BAT just so I have G: mapped to the machine share. The entire MACHINES.INI entry looks like this:

```
[00608CDE8F48]
sysdatpath=f:\machine\mwm66
```

But what if I didn't want to do the extra Net Use? You can add a mapping line after the sysdatpath line. If the machine directories were on the share named Macdata on server Wally, in a directory named machine\mwm66, then I'd add a line to map \\wally\macdata and use that map to refer to machine\mwm66, like so:

```
[00608CDE8F48]
sysdatpath=x:\machine\mwm66
x=\\wally\macdata
```

So, remember: You only need to do the extra mapping lines if your machine directories aren't already on the same share as your shared Windows files.

Just to be sure that this is clear, suppose I were going to install a second PC. First, I have to find out what its Ethernet ID is. If the machine is already running a Microsoft network client, then I probably can just go to the command line and type **net diag /s**. I'll be prompted for a network name, but I just press Enter. I see a screen like the one in Figure 8.7.

All you care about here is the *Permanent node name*, 0000C0573E82; that's the Ethernet ID. Suppose this machine's name is SDG90 and it has a machine directory in machine called sdg90. As that, too, is on my \\wally\macdata share, my MACHINES.INI now looks like this:

```
[00608CDE8F48]
sysdatpath=x:\machine\mwm66
x=\\wally\macdata
[0000C0573E82]
sysdatpath=x:\machine\sdg90
x=\\wally\macdata
```

FIGURE 8.7

Finding a machine's
Ethernet ID

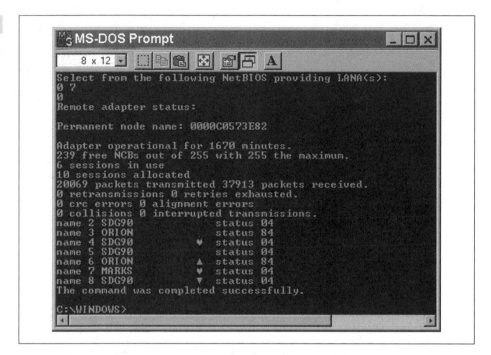

```
MS-DOS Prompt                                    _ □ X

8 x 12 ▼   □ ▦ ▦   ▦ ▦   ▦ ▦   A
Select from the following NetBIOS providing LANA(s):
0 7
0
Remote adapter status:

Permanent node name: 0000C0573E82

Adapter operational for 1670 minutes.
239 free NCBs out of 255 with 255 the maximum.
6 sessions in use
10 sessions allocated
20069 packets transmitted 37913 packets received.
0 retransmissions 0 retries exhausted.
0 crc errors 0 alignment errors
0 collisions 0 interrupted transmissions.
name 2 SDG90              status 04
name 3 ORION              status 84
name 4 SDG90          ♥   status 04
name 5 SDG90              status 04
name 6 ORION          ▲   status 84
name 7 MARKS          ♥   status 04
name 8 SDG90          ▼   status 04
The command was completed successfully.

C:\WINDOWS>
```

NOTE Remember, the only reason that I did the x=\\wally\macdata lines was because the machine directories were on different shares from the shared Windows ones.

Don't Log On as the Machine

For some reason, the simple network redirector wants to log you on with a user name that's the same as the machine ID. That's not going to work, because (at least on my NT-based network—you know, my *Microsoft* NT Server-based network?) there's no automatic process for creating a user named 00608CDE8F48. So, if you log in as that person, your bootup will bomb, as the attempts to network shares will fail.

Now, I could imagine situations where this would be a *good* thing—perhaps you want to create machine accounts with different rights than the users who will log on to them—but the Microsoft documentation is silent on these matters.

NOTE   If you've been skipping past this discussion because you boot from your hard disk with help from the network, then think again: it's really convenient to be able to create a floppy that will boot a machine entirely off the network without needing any help from the hard disk.

Using User Profiles

One major way to make your Windows 95 installation more network-enabled is with *user profiles*. They're a trifle complex, so I want to introduce them in three steps:

- First, you have to understand what a user profile is and what it includes.

- Next, I'll show you how to enable your system to use user profiles—Windows 95 installations don't use them by default.

- Finally, you'll see how to keep user profiles on the network, so that they can follow users wherever they go.

Introduction to User Profiles

You may have noticed that Windows 95 asks you to log on to your machine, sometimes even if you don't have a network. The reason for that is so Windows can keep track of who's on the computer at the moment. Ordinarily, that's not information of any value. But with user profiles, it can be quite useful.

Suppose, for example, that you are a person who shares a PC with other people; perhaps you only use the PC a few hours a day, as do the two or three other people who use that PC. It can be frustrating to spend time getting your desktop set up just the way you like it, only to find that the next time you attempt to use the PC the last person who used it rearranged everything.

You may recall that the Registry is stored in two files, named USER.DAT and SYSTEM.DAT. The USER.DAT information is where the user profile information is stored, and, normally, there's only one USER.DAT on a machine, sitting in the windows directory. But, if you tell your system to allow multiple profiles (I'll show you how in a minute), then Windows will create a new directory, called \windows\profiles, which will then contain folders for each person. In Figure 8.8, you can see that on my system, I have a profiles directory with folders for a user called Mark and another called MarkS (my supervisor account). Inside each directory is a USER.DAT file; there's a USER.DA0 file in MarkS because I've used that account more than once, and so the normal backup file got created.

What's kept in a profile?

- Desktop settings, including colors, background, and any shortcuts *on the desktop*; shortcuts that aren't on the desktop won't be saved as user-specific shortcuts.

- Program groups, both names and contents.

- Virtually anything set with the Control Panel.

- Persistent network connections.

- Applications settings for apps that are 95-aware and write information to the Registry.

FIGURE 8.8

Contents of \Profiles directories

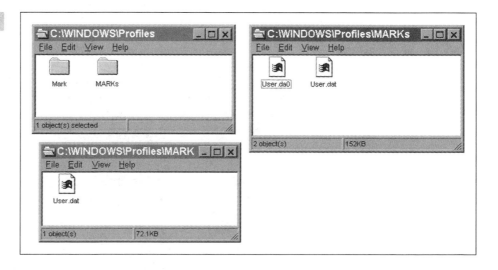

Pre-Windows 95 apps don't use the Registry, so any settings made to them are global across all users on a machine. For example, say that I log on to my computer as Mark, change the default document directory for Ami Pro, and then log off. If I log back on as MarkS, then Ami Pro will still be using the default directory that I set it to when logged on as Mark; this is because Ami uses one of the old-style .INI files to keep its settings and there's no user-specific setting capability. In contrast, if I were running the Windows 95 version of WordPro, and Mark changed WordPro's default directory, then that wouldn't affect MarkS's use of WordPro. This is because WordPro would store its configuration information in the Registry and Mark would have a different Registry from MarkS. (I suppose you could call this multiple profile disorder.)

Using Profiles

To enable Windows 95 to use profiles, start the Control Panel and open up the Passwords applet. Choose the User Profiles tab, and you'll see a dialog box like Figure 8.9.

Click the *Users can customize...* radio button. You may also want to select *Include desktop icons...* and *Include Start menu...* to complete the separation between users. I usually check *Include desktop icons* and not *Include Start Menu* because that selection means that when I install a new program as one user, then I don't see it as the second user. Keep the second one unchecked, and any new programs installed by any user will be available to all users of that machine.

Networking Profiles

This works very nicely, as I can create two personas for myself—the Mark account is my mild-mannered author/lecturer self, equipped with a crowded desktop of all the tools I use in my normal work, but none of the powers and abilities of a network administrator. The MarkS account has a simpler desktop, as it's only used when there's a network problem, and I must step into the computer's telephone booth, emerging in my uniform with the big red S (for Supervisor) on the chest.

FIGURE 8.9

Enabling user profiles

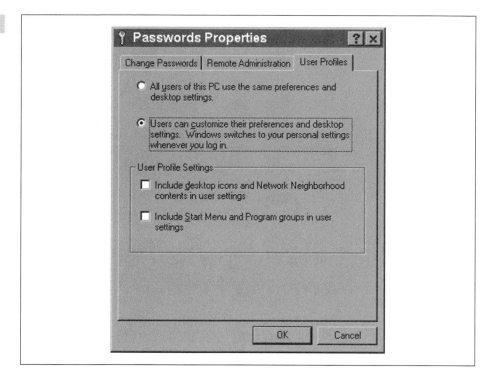

But when I go to a computer other than my own, I'm back to Square One. That computer has no knowledge of my profiles. Obviously, what I need is to network those little suckers. But how?

Quite easily, actually. It's one of those things that they engineered into Windows 95 for minimum pain and suffering. Basically, if you have a network and a home directory, then 95 automatically keeps the profiles in your home directory and looks for them when you log on. There are a few considerations you should be aware of, however:

- If the program groups rove with you on the network, then you may find yourself with a lot of pointers to programs that don't exist.

- You must have a network that you explicitly log on to; in particular, an NT or Novell network will work best.

- This will slow down your logins somewhat; I find that I usually have to wait about an extra 15 seconds to suck up the profile from the network.

All you have to do to make this work is to establish a home directory on your primary logon network. In the Novell world, it's in the MAIL directory; on an NT network, it's the USERS directory. You as administrator needn't do anything to start the system using networked profiles—95 detects the presence of a home directory and uses it, even if there are profiles on the local hard disk. The profiles on the network take precedence.

If you have an NT network, then this won't work unless you log explicitly on to the domain; if you've forgotten how to do that, here's how: You open the Control Panel, then Network, and click Client for Microsoft Networks, then Properties. You'll see a check box labeled Logon validation, which instructs Windows to log you on to an NT domain. Fill in the name of the domain, restart the computer, and you're in business.

Forcing People to Use a Particular Profile

Look in a user's home directory (if they're using profiles) and you'll find the file USER.DAT, the user-specific part of the Registry. You can forever freeze a user's profile settings by renaming USER.DAT to USER.MAN. The extension denotes a *mandatory* profile. The existence of a mandatory profile overrides other profiles, and when users log in, they'll get the settings in their USER.MAN file. If they make any changes to their 95 desktop, then the changes will remain in effect until they log out—but the changes won't be saved and aren't used the next time they log in.

To build a profile from scratch, you'll have to log on as a user, set up the desktop as you like it, and then save it so you get the USER.DAT to work from. It's a bit cumbersome, and it's probably why you'll opt for the System Policy Editor rather than mandatory profiles as a control mechanism.

By the way, user profiles exist under Windows NT as well, but they are different things altogether; there's no relationship between a 95 profile and an NT profile, unfortunately.

Controlling Desktops from the Network

Mandatory profiles are one way to exercise control over user's desktops, but they're not a really easy-to-work-with method. Windows 95 provides some other ways to control desktops. Before going on, however, I should warn you: we're about to embark on a controversial subject. But it's one that deserves a bit of discussion, if only because it seems that no one else talks about it when discussing a tool in Windows called the *System Policy Editor*.

The System Policy Editor allows a network administrator to exert a tremendous amount of control over what users can and can't do with their workstations. The big questions are: Is that right? and Should people be able to control the things on their desktops?

I'm not one hundred percent certain how I feel about this. If I were a parent of a small child, then I might like to be able to control what my child could or couldn't do with the computer, simply to protect the child from themself. But as a "power user," I would bridle at the idea of some network administrator telling me what I could and couldn't do with my computer.

On the other hand, I have *also* been a network administrator, and there are a lotta people out there who just plain don't *want* to become computer experts—they find the monstrous array of options that they're given from simply clicking the Start button to be annoying. They'll *welcome* you simplifying their user interface.

And, finally, let's face it: there are definitely some people in the workforce who waste their own time and their employer's time by playing games or tweaking their systems. We all know the guy who has a different silly bitmap every day or the woman who delights in showing you her latest set of bizarre system sounds. The computers with which we work on our jobs *aren't* our computers. They're bought and paid for by our employers, and those employers have a right to tell us that we can't play Solitaire when we're supposed to be on duty. The System Policy Editor isn't one of those tools that watch you on a minute-by-minute basis to see how many keystrokes or mouse clicks you produce—that would be, in my opinion, an invasion beyond the standard employer/employee relationship—but, in the end analysis, the decision is one that must be made by each company on its own.

How Desktop Control Works

There are several avenues for remote control.

- You can remotely view and modify Registries, provided that you have loaded support for remote Registry control on each workstation that you want to remotely control. (It's a service in the \admin \nettools\remotreg folder on the CD-ROM.)

- You can use mandatory user profiles to define how a workstation operates when a particular user logs on to the workstation. As you've seen, these profiles do not keep users from changing the Windows desktop while using the computer; they just keep the users from *saving* any changes. So, there's some control here, but not a lot. You must set up each desired user workstation to use these profiles.

- You can make certain profiles mandatory and unchangeable with the System Policy Editor, which creates a file called CONFIG.POL.

In the following sections, you'll learn more about these options (other than mandatory profiles, which we've already covered).

The System Policy Editor

As you know, Windows 95 builds a new Registry every time you start up your system, constructing it out of USER.DAT and SYSTEM.DAT for most users. Now, if you *also* have a CONFIG.POL file in the right place (I'll define the right place in a minute, I promise), then Windows will use restrictions in CONFIG.POL to modify how it builds the resulting Registry.

Using system policies requires that you have a network, and that people log on to the network; a loose association of Windows machines doing peer-to-peer networking can't use system policies. The overview on creating and using system policies is the following:

1. Install the System Policy Editor off your Windows 95 CD-ROM; it's in the `\admin\apptools\poledit` directory.

2. Create a policy file with the Policy Editor.

3. Save it as `CONFIG.POL` into your `netlogon` directory on an NT system or into the `\sys\public` directory on the user's preferred NetWare server.

4. Ensure that all your workstations log on to an NT domain or a NetWare preferred server.

And that's it. Now let's take a closer look.

Installing the System Policy Editor

First, you have to install the editor and some support files. Just open up the Control Panel, choose Add/Remove Programs, and click the Windows Setup tab. Click the Have Disk button, and then direct it to the directory that contains the Policy Editor, most likely `\admin\apptools\poledit`. You'll get the option to install both the Policy Editor and something called Group Policies; take them both. The Policy Editor will now be in `programs\accessories\system tools`.

Building a Policy

Let's see how to use this tool to start to control how people work with Windows 95. My example assumes that you have an NT-based network, but it'll work on Novell in just about the same way.

Start up the Policy Editor. Click File, and New File. You'll see a screen like Figure 8.10.

The Policy Editor lets you make either policies that are specific to particular people or blanket policies with the Default User or the Default Computer.

FIGURE 8.10

Blank user profile file

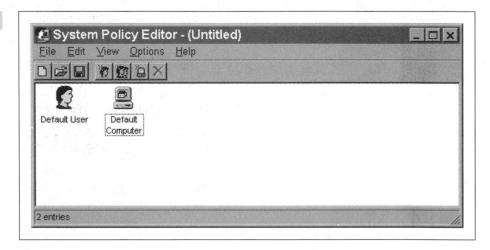

FIGURE 8.11

Preliminary user
properties dialog box

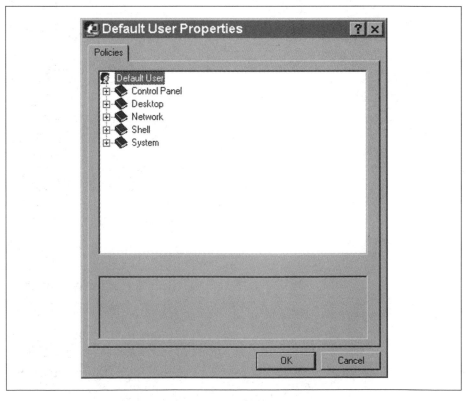

Let's set everyone's wallpaper to Rivets and take away their ability to change it (heh, heh). Wallpaper is a user-specific item, so we'll find it by double-clicking on Default user. You'll see a screen like the one in Figure 8.11.

The wallpaper is a Control Panel item, so open it up and you'll see Display as an option. Choose that, and you'll see a dialog box like Figure 8.12.

FIGURE 8.12

No display policy

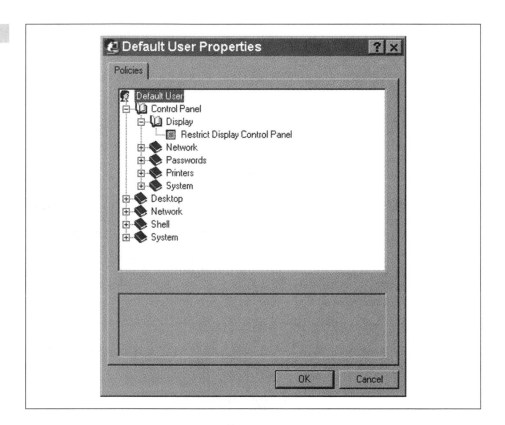

We're going to remove the user's ability to change their backgrounds, so we're restricting the Display part of the Control Panel. Notice that the check box is gray; that means that this option is neither enabled nor disabled—gray means there is no policy about this. Check the box, and you'll see a dialog box like the one in Figure 8.13.

FIGURE 8.13

Display policy in effect

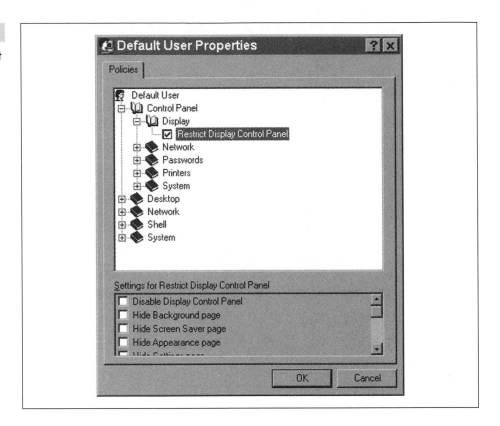

Once the box is checked, you get a panel on the lower part of the dialog box that enumerates the things that you can control. One of them is Hide Background page; check it.

Now you've removed all users' abilities to modify their wallpaper. Next, let's set the actual wallpaper. The wallpaper itself is part of the Desktop, so open up the Desktop branch and check the Wallpaper box. You'll see a dialog box like Figure 8.14.

The lower pane now lets you select a wallpaper—the drop-down list box will show you which files are available. Now you're done, so click OK.

Now all you need to do is to save this to the proper place. Its name should be CONFIG.POL. As I'm running an NT network, I save the file in the NETLOGON share on my primary domain controller, in a directory called c:\winnt35\system32\repl\import\scripts. On a NetWare

FIGURE 8.14

Setting a mandatory
wallpaper

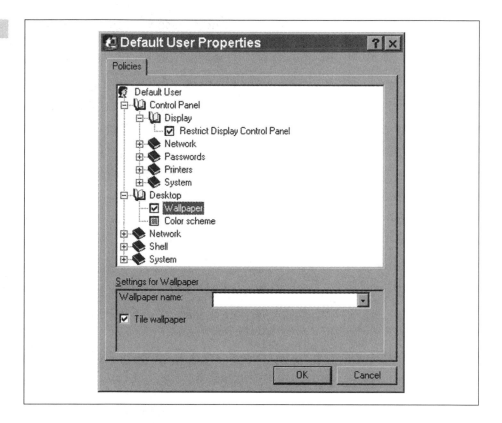

server, I'd just put it on my users' preferred server's sys\public
directory.

Exit the System Policy Editor and exit Windows. When you return to Windows and log on to the network, you'll see that you have the Rivets wallpaper and no way to change it.

Note that I did *not* have to have user profiles enabled in order to do this;
all I had to do was to ensure that I logged on to the domain.

Defeating a Policy

Hmmm... now suppose I'm a smart, but evil, user. I want to *change* my
wallpaper, dammit! Let my pixels go!

There is a way around it, also with the help of the System Policy Editor. I (the evil user) start up the System Policy Editor. This time, however, I click File/Open Registry. I see a user and a machine, just as before—except *this* time what I'm seeing refers to my machine. I double-click on the User, and I see the same categories as before: Control Panel, Desktop, Network, Shell, and System. I click on Desktop and there's the wallpaper. I change it, and the change takes place immediately; no more rivets!

Keeping Users from Defeating Policies

Okay, you're now thinking, "Gee, thanks, Mark; I was getting all excited about these system policies, but now you tell me that any user can defeat them with their own copy of the System Policy Editor. *Now* what do I do?" If you're in the System Policy Editor at the moment, take a look at `default user\system\restrictions`. One of the things that you can restrict is called *Disable Registry editing tools*. Click that one, and neither Regedit nor the System Policy Editor works.

Your next question will no doubt be, "ummm ...what happens when I—I mean, a *friend* of mine—disables the Registry editing tools just for fun, but now can't do anything about it, because it's no longer possible to run Regedit or System Policy Editor?"

First, if you put the restriction in `CONFIG.POL`, rather than in the Registry of a particular machine, and if you applied it to a particular user, rather than all users, then you can just log on as someone else, run the System Policy Editor, and then change the setting.

Alternatively, you could set the policy named *Only Run Allowed Windows Applications*, and leave out Regedit and Poledit.

If you did it for *everyone*, then just log on to the network as a supervisor and take it out of the `Netlogon` or `\sys\public` directory. Use the backups from the day before as a starting point for rebuilding where you were. (`CONFIG.POL` is not an ASCII file, so it wouldn't be very easy to splice out *just* the no-edit rule.)

If you did it in the local Registry, then you might try booting up from the Windows 95 startup disk and running the simple Registry editor that comes on that disk. Delete the RestrictRun entry from the following key:

```
hkey_current_user\software\microsoft\windows
\currentversion\policies\explore
```

What If You Want CONFIG.POL Somewhere Else?

You've already seen where the policies file CONFIG.POL should go. But what if you want to put it somewhere else? You can do that, by telling your Registry to find CONFIG.POL in another location.

The System Policy Editor is also a Registry editor. From the File menu, choose Open Registry, and you see a subset of Registry entries. Change where your computer gets its CONFIG.POL from with the following changes:

1. Open up Default Computer.
2. Open up Network, then Update.
3. You'll see an option called Remote Update; choose it (as shown in Figure 8.15).
4. Where you see Update Mode, select Manual. Then, in the field labeled Path for manual update, put the path—the manual says a UNC name is required, but a drive designation seems to work sometimes—and there you should enter the location and name of the policy file. Include the name of the file; it shouldn't be \\server \share; it should be \\server\share\config.pol.

This can be useful for network systems that aren't NetWare or NT-based.

Things That Go Wrong: Troubleshooting Policies

In the process of learning about how system policies work, I managed to do a few dumb things that kept my experiments from working. Here are

FIGURE 8.15

Choose Remote Update

a few suggestions on things to look for if you're having trouble getting a policy to work.

You Get No Policy Effect at All

It's like you didn't do anything. You can cause this in a number of ways.

- Most likely is that you have a Novell network, and you've put the .POL file in the correct \sys\public directory, but you're using the *Novell* client/redirector software, not the Microsoft NetWare Client software. You must be using the Microsoft NetWare client to automatically download policies. If you're *not* using the Microsoft client, then you'll have to use manual downloading and point to the server in question *using UNC names*. For example, if your Net-Ware server's name is Master, and you've put the CONFIG.POL file in a directory named `policy` on the `sys` volume, then the path to the file is `\\master\sys\policy`.

- If you're running NT servers, then it is likely that your network client isn't logging on to the NT domain.

- With any other kind of network (that is, with anything other than a Novell network or NT servers), you have to enable manual downloading.

- One possible problem is a failure to read the policies correctly, whether through a network error or via a file corruption. In the very same screen where you select manual or automatic downloading, there is a check box which will instruct 95 to display error messages if there's a problem reading `CONFIG.POL`.

- While messing around in the Policy Editor, you may have edited your own Registry and disabled policies altogether. In the Settings for Remote Update screen, the one that, again, selects manual or automatic download of policies, the *default* is to *automatically* download policies. If, when playing around with the Editor, you disabled the Remote Settings box altogether, then your system will not get or obey system policies.

You Change a Policy, but the Old One Remains in Effect

Remember that the System Policy Editor can directly edit a Registry as well as the policy file. You can go directly to a workstation and make a policy that is local to that machine only. For example, suppose you impose some ugly wallpaper, but then go back in the System Policy Editor and remove the wallpaper, as well as restore the user's ability to change the wallpaper.

So the user reboots, finds that he or she is still stuck with the dumb wallpaper, and can't change it. To make things more confusing, *other* users are now freed from the wallpaper, and are using their newfound powers to set their wallpaper to all kinds of bitmaps.

Go to the user's machine and pull up their Registry with the System Policy Editor, or just access it over the network if you have remote administration enabled. Look at the Registry entries to see if you've disabled something. For example, in the Wallpaper case, look in the Local User definition under Desktop and Control Panel. Locally set Registry restrictions seem to take precedence over any found on the network `CONFIG.POL`.

There's Something in the Registry That You Want to Control, but There Are No Settings for It in the System Policy Editor

All the `CONFIG.POL` file does is to provide a kind of a mask that your Windows 95 workstation uses when building its Registry (an operation that it does every time you log on). There are dozens of entries in the Registry, but not all of them are in the System Policy Editor.

Or, at least, none of them are in the System Policy Editor *by default.* You see, the System Policy Editor works off a *template*, a file that tells it which Registry entries to play with. You can modify that by building your own templates; see the section "Using Templates" later in this chapter for more information.

You've Locked Yourself Out of the Computer with Policies

If the computer won't let you do much of anything, try this.

First, boot in Safe Mode Command Prompt. Export the Registry to a file using Regedit (yes, it works in text mode). Just type

Regedit /e tempreg.txt

Then, edit `TEMPREG.TXT`. Look in `hkey_local_machine\system\currentcontrolset\control\update`; you'll see a value entry that looks like the following:

```
"UpdateMode"=dword:00000001
"NetworkPath"=""
```

Just change `00000001` to `00000000`.

Rebuild the Registry with this file, erasing any current Registry entries like so:

regedit /c tempreg.txt

Then just reboot. You're fixed.

Group Policies

It would obviously be too cumbersome to create specific policies for every user. As both NT and Novell support the notion of groups of users, Windows can leverage those groups by allowing you to set policies for entire groups.

Someone can even be a member of more than one group, with different policies. You just rank the groups in terms of their importance, and whenever there's a conflict then the policy of the more important group prevails.

There's only one trick to this: In order for this to work, you must install the file GROUPPOL.DLL on each of the network's workstations. The Policy Editor then lets you rank the relative importance of the various groups.

Custom Folders

Your control of a desktop doesn't stop there. You can customize five special folders:

- The Programs folder
- The Network Neighborhood
- Desktop icons/shortcuts
- The Start menu
- The Startup folder

You can control all of these through settings in the System Policy Editor. Look at the power of this: You can control exactly what items appear on your users' menus, and, via the Startup folder, control what programs run on your users' machines. Additionally, you can remove the MS-DOS prompt, the Run option from the Start button, and drives from My Computer, leaving no backdoor way to start other programs. Again, this may be good or bad, depending on your corporate culture.

Using Templates

Think of the System Policy Editor in this way: Insofar as it modifies Registries, it's kind of an alternative Registry Editor. But it's more than that, as you know if you've ever *used* Regedit—Regedit is about as user-unfriendly as programs get. In contrast, the System Policy Editor presents a subset of the Registry in an easier-to-read fashion.

In a sense, that's also what the Control Panel does. So how are the Control Panel and the System Policy Editor different? Well, first of all, the Control Panel only works with Registry settings; it doesn't create constraints (policies). Second, the Control Panel isn't really configurable, save for the fact that you can remove things from it—you can't add things.

Add things? Yes. Open up the System Policy Editor and you see a number of settings—all controls for parts of the Registry. But *which* parts of the Registry? Ones specified by a file called ADMIN.ADM.

ADMIN.ADM is a *template*, an ASCII file written in a programming language defined in the Resource Kit. Summarized, there are several parts to a template:

- A *class* is the subtree, like Local User or Machine.

- A *category* is just a name used to group a number of Registry items. For example, if you wanted to organize your policies so that there was a small book icon for "color," which controlled the colors of a number of disparate keys, then you'd end up taking keys from different parts of the tree. Each category entry creates one of the book icons. You can nest categories.

- *Policy* is the description for the particular value entry that you're going to modify.

- *Keyname* is, as you'd imagine, a Registry key name like `software \microsoft\windows\currentversion\policies\explorer \restrictrun`. It specifies the target of the editor item.

- Valuename is the actual name of the value within the specified key.
- *Part* tells the System Policy Editor what kind of interface item to use—a check box, list box, or whatever.

This is perhaps understood best with an example. Here, I've opened the System Policy Editor, double-clicked on User, opened Control Panel, and within that found Restrict Display Control Panel. The dialog box appears as in Figure 8.16.

FIGURE 8.16

Options for restricting display

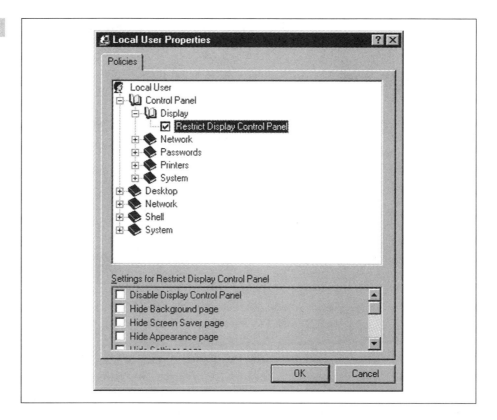

Here's the fragment of code that handles this.

```
CLASS USER

CATEGORY !!ControlPanel
  CATEGORY !!CPL_Display
    POLICY !!CPL_Display_Restrict
    KEYNAME Software\Microsoft\Windows\CurrentVersion \Policies\System
      PART !!CPL_Display_Disable CHECKBOX
      VALUENAME NoDispCPL
      END PART

      PART !!CPL_Display_HideBkgnd CHECKBOX
      VALUENAME NoDispBackgroundPage
      END PART

      PART !!CPL_Display_HideScrsav CHECKBOX
      VALUENAME NoDispScrSavPage
      END PART

      PART !!CPL_Display_HideAppearance CHECKBOX
      VALUENAME NoDispAppearancePage
      END PART

      PART !!CPL_Display_HideSettings CHECKBOX
      VALUENAME NoDispSettingsPage
      END PART
    END POLICY
  END CATEGORY     ; Display
```

CLASS USER defines the part of this file that describes the User icon. Category !!ControlPanel says, first, create a book icon, and second, name it something defined by !!ControlPanel. !!ControlPanel is a string variable defined later in the file as:

```
ControlPanel="Control Panel"
```

The characters "Control Panel" are then displayed next to the book icon.

POLICY !!CPL_DISPLAY_RESTRICT says to display CPL_DIS-
PLAY_RESTRICT, which I found later in the program to equal Restrict
Display Control Panel. You see that is displayed in the top pane, but there
are several potential ways to restrict the Display Control Panel. As it turns
out, they are all values within the software\microsoft\windows\cur-
rentversion\policies\system key.

The triples that appear next look like

```
PART !!CPL_Display_Disable CHECKBOX
VALUENAME NoDispCPL
END PART
```

Each one of these triples describes a value that can live within the key. The
string variable is just the label to put in the dialog box, and CHECKBOX
says to just put a check box in place, rather than an edit field or list box
or whatever. VALUENAME says, "Once you have the value checked or
not checked by the user, then this is the name of the actual value to stuff
in the Registry."

Templates make the System Policies Editor an incredibly flexible tool;
you can even use it to control Registry entries created by third-party vendors. The main problem with it is that Microsoft hasn't documented all
of *their* Registry entries. (Grumble, grumble; they did it for NT, though,
and that's been tremendously helpful.)

Let's build a sample template for an imaginary Registry entry. Suppose I
have a software company named MarkSoft, and all of my programs open
up with a welcome banner. You can modify that welcome banner by adding a value called WText to system\marksoft\currentversion\set-
tings; you put text in there to control the welcome banner. A template
file might look like this in its entirety:

```
CLASS USER
CATEGORY !!GenlSettings
    POLICY !!WelcomeBanner
    KEYNAME Software\Marksoft\CurrentVersion\Settings
        PART !!WelcomeText EDITTEXT
        VALUENAME WText
        END PART
    END POLICY
END CATEGORY
[strings]
```

```
GenlSettings="General settings"
WelcomeBanner="Welcome banner"
WelcomeText="Text to display in welcome banner"
```

Now open the System Policy Editor and click Options ➤ Template, and tell it to read your file—save it with the extension .ADM so it's easier for the Editor to find it. Click File ➤ Open Registry, then open the User class, and you'll see a screen like Figure 8.17.

Fill in the text and save it. Restart, and start up the Registry Editor, and you see an entry for MarkSoft, as you see in Figure 8.18.

I won't deny that building your own templates won't be something that you'll do every day. But what's truly exciting (to me, anyway) is that this is a powerful support tool that I can shape to my own needs. Other utility vendors could learn from this.

FIGURE 8.17

Adding an entry to a template

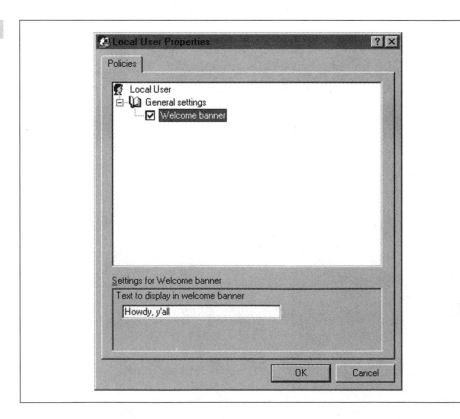

FIGURE 8.18

New entry displayed
in Registry

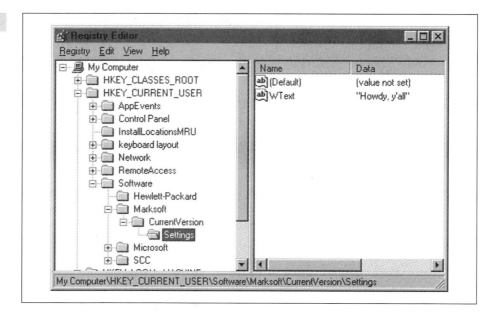

Remote Registry Modification

Both Regedit and the System Policy Editor offer the ability to modify remote Registries from the one they're running on. That's a great support tool, but there's a catch: The remote computer has to *allow* you to modify its Registry across the network before you can do it.

You allow that by installing a kind of tiny server program on each workstation, a program that allows a workstation to share its Registry over the network—even if the workstation hasn't enabled file and print sharing. In addition, you must install the same service on the machine you'll use to administer the Registries, if it's not one of the workstations.

The tiny server program is one of many network service programs that you can load in Windows. You have to do a little hunting for this one, however; it's on the CD-ROM in the \admin\nettools\remotereg directory. Just start up the Control Panel, then Network, then Add, then Service, then point the dialog box at the above directory.

By the way, it should be obvious that you must be running at least one of the same protocols on the workstations as on the support person's machine, as all of the network layers must match for the communication to work.

To access a remote Registry in the System Policy Editor, click File and Connect, then point to the machine whose Registry you want to modify. In the Registry editor, click Registry, then Connect Network Registry. The Registry editor even lets you view and modify multiple Registries from different machines simultaneously.

You can use the System Monitor across the network to monitor PCs other than the one you're working on, so long as the machines have the Remote Registry service activated.

Peeking over the Net: Net Watcher, System Monitor, and Network Monitor

Microsoft includes some network-based monitoring tools that, although they are not a complete suite of tools, are nonetheless a nice set of "free" network applications.

The System Monitor

The System Monitor allows you to log activity on your system. You can keep track of kernel activity (percent utilization of the CPU, number of virtual machines active, number of threads running), the file system, network client, network server software (number of bytes read, written, data rates per second), and the system's memory manager (amount of free memory, disk cache statistics, virtual memory statistics). While none of these are amazingly important, the fact that you can monitor them at a distance may be of value. For example, if a user complains that their machine is running too slowly, then a quick look at memory might reveal that their computer is extremely low on memory and is paging like crazy.

You can monitor a remote computer in a few ways, but the easiest is just to open up the Network Neighborhood folder, find the computer that you want to monitor, and right-click it. Choose Properties from the menu that results, and you'll be offered the option to run either Net Watcher or System Monitor, or to remotely control sharing on the remote computer's hard disk. Not just anyone can do this, however—you must have administrative rights to that machine and be running the Remote Registry service to access this information on another machine.

Using Network Monitor

Network Monitor lets you keep an eye on the flow of data on the network. It's a neat tool for keeping track of how busy the network is.

Well, that's the *good* part about it. The mildly evil part of Network Monitor is that, to really work as fully intended, it requires the System Management Server (SMS) on your system. As SMS requires NT Server, SQL Server, and a machine with a minimum of 64MB to run, it's a *whole* 'nother story...

The Network Monitor is on the CD-ROM in `admin\nettools\netmon`. In the Network applet of the Control Panel, click Add, then Service, then click the Add button, and choose Microsoft. Click Have Disk and fill in the directory for the Network Monitor (someone *did* claim that Windows 95 made things easier, right?). You'll see Microsoft Network Monitor Agent, so click OK until the Control Panel shuts up; your system will then reboot.

What you will see when you reboot (well, actually, you won't see it unless you look for it) is a new set of objects to monitor in the System Monitor. You'll have a new set of items under the heading Network Monitor Performance, and you'll be able to monitor the following:

- Ethernet broadcasts per second
- Ethernet multicasts per second
- Ethernet frames transmitted per second
- Ethernet bytes transmitted per second

In much the same way that you might listen to a traffic report to find out how busy a highway is, these new objects in System Monitor can allow you to see how congested your network is—an essential tool for answering the question, "Why is the network slow?"

Net Watcher

Every Windows 95 workstation is potentially a server. Not a very *powerful* server, but a server nonetheless. And if people are using your shared resources, then it might be nice to know who those people *are*.

You can do that with Net Watcher. It allows you to:

- Display who is using your shares
- Create new shares or delete existing shares
- Control sharing on remote computers

If you're used to NT Server networks, then think of this as an extremely lame version of the Server Manager program.

Windows 95 not only provides built-in networking—a somewhat *de rigueur* feature of operating systems these days—but also includes a number of network support and management tools gratis. They probably won't end up being the tools of choice for big networks, but they're a start for those who can't afford expensive third-party tools.

CHAPTER

9

Fixing Windows 95 Crashes— Failure Recovery

THE new generation of Windows is not rock-solid, although it handles crashed applications and resources better than its predecessors did. As you can't just boot the computer to DOS when Windows is misbehaving anymore (well, normally—turn to the end of the chapter for more information), this chapter will discuss how you *should* proceed when Windows falls down and can't get up. We'll talk about what's happening during the nearly invisible boot process, what components are loaded during the process, how you can track the loading, and methods to boot your PC that allow you to circumvent Windows when it's having a bad day.

Windows 95 Boot Sequence

When Windows 95 doesn't boot, it's easier to figure out why if you know what's *supposed* to happen during the boot process. This is somewhat new territory to former DOS and Windows users, so hang on.

Once you've got power to the system, the boot process takes place in four stages:

1. Loading the BIOS
2. Loading DOS drivers and TSRs (for backward compatibility only)
3. Initializing static VxD's in real mode
4. Starting up the protected-mode operating system and loading any remaining VxD's

BIOS? VxD's? Let's look at each of these in turn and figure out exactly what's going on at each stage.

Boot Step 1: BIOS Initialization

Once your system is getting power, there has to be some functioning computing hardware to use that power. As you know, at the heart of most PCs is a single circuit board called the *motherboard*. The motherboard contains the CPU, some memory, and the circuitry required to transfer data from one point on the board to another—you can recognize this circuitry by its pieces, which include the bus, the direct memory access hardware, and the interrupt controller. Most of these pieces must be functioning properly for anything at all to work on the motherboard.

Part of the memory included on the motherboard is in the form of *ROM* chips—*Read Only Memory*. ROM contains an important set of software called the *BIOS* (*Basic Input Output System*).

ROM and Bootstrapping

Why do we need the BIOS? It has to do with how CPUs work. When a CPU powers up, it doesn't know how to communicate with anything—the keyboard, display, disk drives, you name it. Before it can communicate with, say, a hard disk, a CPU needs a program in memory that tells it *how* to communicate with a hard disk. Virtually all PC programs must be read from disk before the PC can run them. This leads to a chicken-and-egg problem: The CPU needs disk-reading instructions before it can read anything from the disk, but the disk is where it loads its programs from. Where, then, does the CPU find that first disk-reading program when you first turn on the computer? That's where ROM comes in. The first disk-reading program is contained in the ROM's BIOS, the instructions that tell the CPU how to communicate with its parts.

What's a Plug and Play BIOS?

If you read the Windows 95 Resource Kit, you'll see that Windows 95 is designed for Plug and Play BIOSes, which can automatically detect Plug and Play boards in the system and configure them to use the appropriate DMA channels, interrupts, and I/O channels. Even if your PC's BIOS does not support Plug and Play, it will work with Windows 95: you'll just have to configure any add-in boards by hand using the methods discussed in Chapter 10.

N O T E In product literature, Microsoft rather endearingly calls BIOSes that do not support Plug and Play "legacy BIOSes." The fact is, *most* current BIOSes do not support Plug and Play.

How the BIOS Works

Regardless of whether your PC's BIOS supports Plug and Play, BIOS in-structions are hard-wired into the ROM chips. Although RAM chips lose their contents when you shut down power on a PC, *ROMs* do *not* forget. That means that the BIOS is always available, even if some of the hard-ware it controls is inaccessible.

A part of the BIOS that is used only when you first power up the com-puter is responsible for inventorying and initializing the parts of your PC: figuring out what's there, testing the parts to make sure that they work, and preparing them to do their jobs. Now, this gets a little involved, so let's take the process one step at a time.

There are five steps to the BIOS initialization process:

1. Test some low memory.
2. Scan for other BIOSes.
3. Yield to other BIOSes.
4. Inventory the system.
5. Test the system.

Test Low Memory

In order for the BIOS to function, it needs to work with some RAM. Therefore, the first thing that most BIOSes do is test the bottom part of the system's RAM. If that test crashes, then most BIOSes can't recover. Therefore, if your PC won't boot, one troubleshooting step is to replace the lowest bank of RAM to see whether the problem is that the BIOS has no RAM to use. Unfortunately, this is not an option if the lowest bank of RAM is *soldered* on the motherboard (as is the case with some PCs).

Scan for Other BIOSes

The BIOS in your PC can't support every possible piece of hardware—LAN boards, unusual video boards, you name it—so the important functions of inventory and initialization have to go somewhere else. That is why many add-on boards have some ROM on them; you may have noticed this when installing them.

The main system BIOS allows the add-on boards to do *their* inventory and initialization first. But before that can happen, the main system BIOS must *find* those BIOSes. It does that by examining memory for BIOS *signatures* in the ROM area of memory, i.e., the addresses between 768K and 960K. Once it finds a BIOS, it can go to the next step.

Yield to Other BIOSes

Once it's found a BIOS on the add-on board, the main system BIOS passes control to the BIOS on the add-on board so that it can do whatever inventory and initialization it requires. Add-on BIOSes get to do their job before the main system BIOS.

Notice what that means: The ROM instructions on an add-in board get to run before either the system BIOS *or* the operating system. *This means that a malfunctioning board can keep your PC from booting.*

For example, consider a VGA board. It has a BIOS chip on it that contains a setup routine. That setup routine announces that the board is up and ready by putting a copyright notice on the screen. When your PC is booting, the VGA message appears *before* the memory test occurs and before the PC checks for the drives. Again, the point here is that this VGA ROM assumed total control of the system fairly early in the boot process, as will each ROM on add-in boards.

Inventory and Test the System

Once all of the add-in ROMs have gotten their time, *and assuming that their programs ran properly and returned control to the main system BIOS,* then the main system BIOS will inventory the items that it controls; these items will vary from system to system. At a minimum, the system BIOS must inventory and initialize the system memory. What does "inventory and initialize" mean here? You've seen at least one example of it a million times: the memory test. For another, ever notice the quick flash of the drive lights on the floppy and hard-disk drives? That's the BIOS doing an inventory of the storage devices.

CMOS Setup Information Read

Before we go on to the next step, where the system actually loads CONFIG .SYS and AUTOEXEC.BAT, I shouldn't neglect to at least mention the final part of the BIOS initialization, the reading of the setup information. If you've set up new computers, or added equipment to existing computers, you're aware that most computers built with 80286-or-later CPUs store a partial inventory of the computer's hardware in a chip called the *setup chip* or *CMOS chip*. Part of the BIOS's inventory process, then, involves reading that setup chip. Not *all* of the PC hardware inventory is in that chip, only the total amount of memory, the types of disk drives on the system, the type of video adapter, and whether or not the computer is equipped with a coprocessor. The chip also contains the battery-backed clock/calendar that initializes the system clock.

The CMOS is worth mentioning because this setup chip causes a *lot* of PC trouble calls. If the battery is dead, the setup information gets lost. The computer can't access the hard disk if doesn't know the hard disk's type, and consequently cannot boot if the setup chip is bad or has a dead battery. Now, while the lack of setup information *sounds* like something that's pretty obvious, it's often not obvious to the person who's reporting the trouble; so keep an eye out for it when you're on the site trying to fix the computer.

People are sometimes confused when their hard disk drive type has disappeared from the CMOS but the clock still keeps good time. How can it be that *some* of the CMOS is damaged while some is still good? It's actually quite simple. The clock is kept by a clock circuit, and the other information is kept by a memory. Memories need more power than clock circuits do. As a result, there may be a long period where your system's battery has enough power for the clock but not for the memory.

Boot Step 2: Loading Real-Mode Drivers

Once the BIOS is loaded, your PC can "see" its hardware. Now it's time to load the drivers that allow the PC to *use* the hardware. Under DOS, CONFIG.SYS contained the hardware profile. Windows 95 handles the process a little differently. When your system boots, Windows 95 polls the devices in the system to detect their hardware configuration, including the following things:

- interrupt usage
- port usage (as in COM1 or LPT2)
- computer identification
- docking-station data (if applicable and available)

Windows 95 compiles the current configuration information it accumulates into a 2-byte *hardware profile* for each device. A hardware profile is a pointer to the configuration information for that device.

NOTE In the interests of backward compatibility with 16-bit applications, Windows 95 loads the CONFIG.SYS and AUTOEXEC.BAT files at this stage of the boot process, even though it does not need these files to operate (the information in them is contained in the Registry).

Boot Step 3: Initializing Static VxD's

The third stage of the boot process loads Windows-specific device drivers (static VxD's) and WIN.COM, which supervises the loading process.

What are VxD's?

What *is* a static VxD, and why would I want to initialize one? Well, a VxD is a Windows device driver. Since the early days of operating systems, it's been clear to the designers of those systems that the part of the operating system that directly controls and manipulates the peripherals—printers, video, disk drive, etc.—should not be embedded in the operating system itself, but rather should reside in separate programs. These programs are called *drivers*. By separating the driver functions into separate programs, operating systems designers make it easier to add support for a new peripheral at a later date. Otherwise, every time that HP (for example) offered an improved driver for one of its printers, you'd have to buy—and install—an entirely new operating system.

Windows 95 is no different from older operating systems in this respect. You cannot assemble a bare-minimum Windows configuration without including drivers for the video display, the mouse, the keyboard, and, if present, a network. Windows 95 distinguishes between *real-mode drivers*, which set up some system-critical functions like the ability to boot from a SCSI drive or see upper memory, and those that Windows uses to control devices when it's in *protected mode*.

In order for Windows to control devices while in 386-Enhanced mode, it must have programs that allow Windows to treat those devices as virtual devices. Let's take the display screen as an example. Virtualizing the screen means that fifteen DOS programs can all simultaneously modify what *they* think is on the display screen, while in reality none of them is getting to the actual display screen. To work this display magic, Windows has a *Virtual Display Driver* (or VdD) that permits applications to modify the *virtual* display. There's a Virtual Mouse Driver (VmD), a Virtual Keyboard Driver (VkD), and so on. As all of these drivers have names that start with a V and end with a D, but contain something that varies in the middle, they have the generic name VxD's.

Windows 95 subdivides VxD's into two classes: *static* and *dynamic*.

- *Static VxD's* are those that Windows loads on bootup—the ones that control things like the memory manager, the configuration manager, other device loaders, and so forth. In older versions of Windows, VxD's were loaded in the [386enh] section of the SYSTEM.INI file on a device= line. In Windows 95, most of the common VxD's are rolled together into one file called VMM32.VXD. You can add additional VxD's to the system by adding them to the system\vmm32 directory. Windows 95 will load any virtual device drivers found in that directory in place of those in VMM32.

- *Dynamic VxD's* (protected mode device drivers) are for devices like disks and network cards that must be loaded at a certain time and in a certain order. Unlike static VxD's, which are loaded by VMM32, each type of dynamic VxD is loaded by a device loader designed for that type of device. For example, the device loader for disk drivers is called IOS. You can identify dynamic VxD's in the Registry by their value names: They all begin with DevLoader. Dynamic VxD's are not loaded until the final stage of the boot process.

Loading Static VxD's

VMM32.VXD loads static VxD's in three steps. The process looks like this:

1. VMM32 loads all the drivers specified in the Registry, including all drivers not directly linked to any specific piece of hardware.

2. If VMM32 finds a Registry entry with the value name StaticVxD, then it loads that device driver and initializes it. By default, all of these entries are included in hkey_local_machine\system\current-controlset\services, but VMM32 would also load any others that it found elsewhere.

3. Finally, VMM32 scans the [386enh] section of SYSTEM.INI for device= lines and loads any drivers that it finds there. Entries in SYSTEM.INI take precedence over those in the Registry.

NOTE Since entries in SYSTEM.INI take precedence over equivalent entries in the Registry, be cautious about editing SYSTEM.INI— if you specify a device= statement for which no device exists, you'll cause an error.

Boot Step 4: Loading the Operating System

After all the static VxD's are loaded, VMM32 switches the processor to run in protected mode, rather than real mode. At this stage of the game, the Configuration Manager figures out what devices are loaded. If your PC has a Plug and Play (PnP) BIOS, the Configuration Manager loads the information from it; otherwise, it looks to see what's already loaded and then loads the dynamic VxD's described in the previous section. If your PC has a Plug and Play BIOS and you're using PnP cards, the Configuration Manager then makes sure that none of the devices are conflicting with each other. If your PC does not have Plug and Play BIOS, then Configuration Manager can't prevent device conflicts: if you assign the same interrupt to two add-in cards, you'll run into device conflicts like those you'd expect.

After the Configuration Manager has established what devices are on the system, you'll see the login dialog box. Enter your name and password, and the final components of Windows will then load in the following order:

1. KRNL386.EXE loads the underlying operating system.
2. GDI.EXE and GDI32 load the graphic interface for the operating system.
3. USER.EXE and USER32 load the user interface, including such items as Network Neighborhood and Explorer.
4. Resources used by Windows 95, such as fonts, are loaded.
5. The entries in WIN.INI are checked.
6. The Desktop configuration, including colors and dialog fonts, is loaded.

Once you've logged on, the items in the Startup folder are processed, and your system is now up and running. And if it's not? Well, that's what the rest of this chapter is for.

Dissecting BOOTLOG.TXT

When you installed Windows 95, a file called BOOTLOG.TXT was created in the root directory of your boot drive. In part, it looked a bit like this:

```
[0008199D] INITCOMPLETESUCCESS = VCOMM
[0008199E] Dynamic load device C:\WINDOWS\system
\serial.vxd
[000819A0] Dynamic init device SERIAL
[000819A2] Dynamic init success SERIAL
[000819A3] Dynamic load success C:\WINDOWS\system
\serial.vxd
[000819A9] INITCOMPLETE = VCOND
[000819AA] INITCOMPLETESUCCESS = VCOND
[000819AB] INITCOMPLETE = VTDAPI
[000819AC] INITCOMPLETESUCCESS = VTDAPI
[000819AD] INITCOMPLETE = VFLATD
[000819AE] INITCOMPLETESUCCESS = VFLATD
[000819AF] INITCOMPLETE = VPMTD
[000819B0] INITCOMPLETESUCCESS = VPMTD
[000819B1] INITCOMPLETE = DiskTSD
[000819B2] INITCOMPLETESUCCESS = DiskTSD
[000819B3] INITCOMPLETE = voltrack
[000819B4] INITCOMPLETESUCCESS = voltrack
[000819B5] INITCOMPLETE = HSFLOP
[000819B6] INITCOMPLETESUCCESS = HSFLOP
[000819B7] INITCOMPLETE = ESDI_506
[000819B8] INITCOMPLETESUCCESS = ESDI_506
[000819B9] INITCOMPLETE = SERENUM
[000819BA] INITCOMPLETESUCCESS = SERENUM
[000819BB] INITCOMPLETE = LPTENUM
[000819BC] INITCOMPLETESUCCESS = LPTENUM
```

Although this doesn't look very useful, if you can decipher the information herein it can give you a clue as to what's going on with your system.

When Is Bootlog Created?

You don't get a new BOOTLOG.TXT every time you restart your system. Instead, one is created when you *first* install Windows 95; unless you install something new or are trying to isolate a boot problem as described in the following section, you don't need to create another one. When you do need one, you can create one by choosing the interactive system startup (by pressing F8) and selecting the *Create boot log* option from the menu, or by typing **win /b** from the command line to start up Windows. Essentially, you should probably keep a printout of your BOOTLOG file around for reference (you can't diagnose sick if you don't know what healthy looks like), but you don't need a new one every day.

What Can You Learn from Bootlog?

Since BOOTLOG is created only if your system boots successfully, you can use your handy printed copy of a successful boot's BOOTLOG to narrow the field of possible suspects when your system doesn't boot. For example, if you read a BOOTLOG created when your system booted successfully and notice that some of your VxD's did not load during that bootup, you can probably assume that those VxD's are not suddenly responsible for your system not being able to boot properly at a later date. The system worked before without 'em; it's not likely that it's suddenly going to freeze up now unless something *else* has changed.

You can also use BOOTLOG for troubleshooting if your system boots successfully but not all of its components start up. Reboot, create a new version of the file, and scan it for errors, as described below.

Reading BOOTLOG

BOOTLOG is divided into five parts that correspond roughly to the stages of the boot process:

- Records of loading real-mode drivers
- Records of loading VxD's (Windows device drivers, remember)
- Records of initializing system-critical VxD's

- Records of initializing devices dependent on VxD's
- Records of successful initializations

Let's look at each of these sections in turn.

Section 1: Loading Real-Mode Drivers

As you'll remember from the description of the boot process earlier in this chapter, before Windows 95 starts up it loads the DOS drivers that you used in earlier versions of Windows, so as to ensure that all of your old applications can use them. Below is a short list of some possible failures and the entries that you should look for in this short section of BOOTLOG if you encounter these failures. If the entry is missing, make sure that you have the corresponding statement in your CONFIG.SYS—for example, if you don't have access to memory beyond 640K, check for a HIMEM.SYS entry in CONFIG.SYS.

Problem: No extended (XMS) memory in which to run Windows.

BOOTLOG Entry: loadfailed=c:\windows\himem.SYS

Implication: Only the lower 640K of memory is available to your programs—you can't run Windows without extended memory.

Problem: Incorrect DOS version. (Message appears when you try to run programs or drivers that worked before.)

BOOTLOG Entry: loadfailed=c:\windows\setver.EXE

Implication: You can't run some DOS programs because they're not included in the version of DOS that the system thinks you have.

Problem: Windows 95 won't boot from a bus-mastered hard drive.

BOOTLOG Entry: loadfailed=c:\windows\dblbuff.SYS

Implication: If your boot hard-disk controller uses bus mastering, you can't boot from C:.

Problem: `IFSHLP.SYS` message appears briefly at command prompt; Windows won't run; and system locks up.

BOOTLOG Entry: loadfailed=c:\windows\ifshlp.SYS

Implication: The Installable File System Helper (which loads device drivers for Windows 95) did not load. Only the minimal file system in `IO.SYS` is available. You can't run Windows in this case either, as VFAT won't run.

Section 2: Loading VxD's

This section of BOOTLOG logs the results of every attempt to load VxD's. Note that these drivers are not *initialized* until the next section; these entries only record whether or not the drivers were even loaded into memory.

If you run into problems, make sure first of all that each Loading statement has a corresponding LoadSuccess= statement, like the sample lines below.

```
[000815B3] Loading Vxd   = VMM
[000815B9] LoadSuccess   = VMM
[000815C3] Loading Vxd   = vnetsup.vxd
[000815C6] LoadSuccess   = vnetsup.vxd
[000815C7] Loading Vxd   = CONFIGMG
[000815CA] LoadSuccess   = CONFIGMG
```

As we discussed earlier, remember that your system can successfully boot and work fine even if you see some Fail entries in BOOTLOG, so record the boot process while it's still working so you have some basis of comparison.

Table 9.1 lists a couple of specific VxD Load statements that you'll want to watch for if you run into problems.

Please note that, if VSHARE does not load successfully, do *not* add it to your CONFIG.SYS. Instead, since VSHARE is one of the VxD's rolled into VMM32, simply ensure that it's included in the section of the Registry labeled Hkey_Local_Machine\CurrentControlSet\Control\VMM32Files.

TABLE 9.1

Loading VxD's

IF YOU HAVE THIS PROBLEM...	...LOOK FOR THIS MESSAGE IN BOOTLOG
Cannot access DoubleSpaced or DriveSpaced (compressed) drives.	loadsuccess=c:\dblspace.bin
Sharing violations occur.	loadsuccess=vshare

NOTE Even if VSHARE loads successfully, sharing violations can still occur. A successful load, however, at least narrows the field.

Section 3: Initializing System-Critical VxD's

The next section of BOOTLOG records the system's attempts to initialize vital VxD's, those that it requires to run at all. This longish section begins where the entries begin to look like this:

```
[0008168D] SYSCRITINIT = VMM
[0008168E] SYSCRITINITSUCCESS = VMM
[0008168F] SYSCRITINIT = VCACHE
[00081690] SYSCRITINITSUCCESS = VCACHE
```

Unlike the previous section, which only recorded the loading process, your system will not start up if there are any Fail entries in this section. Only those VxD's that loaded successfully will be initialized.

Section 4: Initializing Device VxD's

The fourth section of BOOTLOG records the system's attempt to initialize VxD's that relate to devices. The entries herein look something like this:

```
[00081714] DEVICEINIT = VMM
[00081715] DEVICEINITSUCCESS = VMM
[00081717] DEVICEINIT = VCACHE
[00081718] DEVICEINITSUCCESS = VCACHE
```

Some device VxD's are composed of a bunch of smaller drivers. The entries for these devices will look something like this:

```
[0008175B] DEVICEINIT = IOS
[00081776] Dynamic load device C:\WINDOWS\system
\IOSUBSYS\apix.vxd
[0008177E] Dynamic load success C:\WINDOWS\system
\IOSUBSYS\apix.vxd
[0008177F] Dynamic load device C:\WINDOWS\system
\IOSUBSYS\cdfs.vxd
[00081786] Dynamic load success C:\WINDOWS\system
\IOSUBSYS\cdfs.vxd
[00081788] Dynamic load device C:\WINDOWS\system
\IOSUBSYS\cdtsd.vxd
[0008178E] Dynamic load success C:\WINDOWS\system
\IOSUBSYS\cdtsd.vxd
[00081790] Dynamic load device C:\WINDOWS\system
\IOSUBSYS\cdvsd.vxd
[00081796] Dynamic load success C:\WINDOWS\system
\IOSUBSYS\cdvsd.vxd
[00081798] Dynamic load device C:\WINDOWS\system
\IOSUBSYS\disktsd.vxd
[0008179E] Dynamic load success C:\WINDOWS\system
\IOSUBSYS\disktsd.vxd
[000817A0] Dynamic load device C:\WINDOWS\system
\IOSUBSYS\diskvsd.vxd
[000817A6] Dynamic load success C:\WINDOWS\system
\IOSUBSYS\diskvsd.vxd
[000817A8] Dynamic load device C:\WINDOWS\system
\IOSUBSYS\voltrack.vxd
[000817AE] Dynamic load success C:\WINDOWS\system
\IOSUBSYS\voltrack.vxd
[000817AF] Dynamic load device C:\WINDOWS\system
\IOSUBSYS\necatapi.vxd
[000817B6] Dynamic load success C:\WINDOWS\system
\IOSUBSYS\necatapi.vxd
[000817B8] Dynamic load device C:\WINDOWS\system
\IOSUBSYS\scsi1hlp.vxd
[000817BE] Dynamic load success C:\WINDOWS\system
\IOSUBSYS\scsi1hlp.vxd
[000817C0] Dynamic load device C:\WINDOWS\system
\IOSUBSYS\rmm.pdr
[000817C5] Dynamic load success C:\WINDOWS\system
\IOSUBSYS\rmm.pdr
[000817C7] DEVICEINITSUCCESS = IOS
```

This series of entries records the initialization of the device loader, which then loads a slew of internal files. The bottom entry shown here (device-initsuccess = ios) tells you that the IOS device loader successfully loaded all of its files.

The Windows Startup Menu

If Windows doesn't boot properly when you start up the machine, and re-booting once doesn't work, you can manage the boot process with the Startup menu. Using the seven selections available, you can boot your PC in almost any way that your heart desires. (Quiet, you in the back who are claiming that there are really eight selections—we'll get to that later in this chapter.)

Contents of the Startup Menu

You can switch to the Startup menu while your computer is booting, after the system identifies the drives and you see the message "Starting Windows 95...." Press F8 when you see that message, before the logo appears. You'll see a menu like DOS 6's MultiConfig menu. If the last time you successfully booted your machine it was set up to access a network, it will include networking options, as follows:

1. Normal
2. Logged (\BOOTLOG.TXT)
3. Safe mode
4. Safe mode with network support
5. Step-by-step confirmation
6. Command prompt only
7. Safe mode command prompt only

If the system boots up too fast for you to hit F8 before the logo screen comes up, you can increase the interval during which you can access this menu by adding the line **Boot Delay=** to the [options] section of MSDOS.SYS and providing as a value the number of seconds to wait. For example, BootDelay=5 gives you five seconds to press F8 and get the Startup menu before Windows starts up. When you've edited the file, that section should look something like the following:

```
[Options]
BootGUI=1
Network=1
BootDelay=5
```

So far, so good. Now let's find out what each Startup option does, what happens when you choose them, and why you should prefer one over another.

Normal

Choose the default option, Normal, and normal is what you'll get: the system will continue booting as though you hadn't interrupted it with the F8 keystroke. This is useful if you pressed F8 by mistake, so you don't have to reboot again.

Logged (\BOOTLOG.TXT)

As with Normal, the second option directs the system to boot normally. In the background, however, Windows 95 will create a record of the boot process (as discussed earlier in this chapter) so you can watch for failed processes. Select this menu item if something isn't working right in Windows and you can't track down the problem child, but the problem isn't serious enough to warrant a more restricted system startup. You can also use this option to review the boot process when things are going well.

Safe Mode

If you choose option 3 from the Startup menu (or press F5 at the "Starting Windows 95…" message), then your PC will bypass CONFIG.SYS and AUTOEXEC.BAT; it *will* load the Registry and HIMEM.SYS so that Windows can start up in a vanilla configuration: VGA mode, no network drivers, and only the drivers needed to get Windows going. When Windows has started up, your display will appear as you left it (that is, the color scheme and fonts will not revert to Windows Default), except that it will appear in VGA mode and the words *Safe Mode* will be written in the four corners of the screen.

During the startup process, 95 will alert you to the limitations of safe mode with a dialog box like the one in Figure 9.1.

Click OK, and you'll log in to the machine. Note that you won't log into your domain or workgroup, because safe mode does not support networking.

Safe mode is for those times when you suspect that your system's configuration is messed up, but perhaps not enough to entirely prevent you from using Windows. It's good for any of the following situations:

- Windows 95 hangs after the "Starting Windows 95..." message appears.

- Windows 95 stalls for an extended period at startup.

- Something isn't working properly or works differently than you expected.

- The video does not display correctly (resolution, not color scheme).

- Your PC suddenly slows down or begins stalling repeatedly.

For example, if you accidentally changed your display to a configuration that your monitor can't handle (difficult to do, given the way that you change video resolutions in 95, but possible if you really try) or if you've added a new driver to your startup files that's playing havoc with your

FIGURE 9.1

Warning notice for running Windows in safe mode

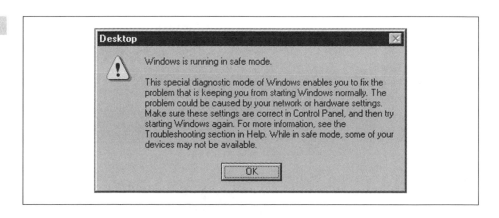

system, then safe mode can get you far enough to correct the problem. Remove the errant driver or restore the resolution to a configuration that works, and then restart your computer.

One really annoying thing about working in safe mode (or safe mode with networking, for that matter) is that 95 doesn't deal well with persistent connections that aren't currently working. It continually polls, looking for the mapped drives, and if it doesn't find them it alerts you to the fact— over and over. It's highly irritating when you're trying to fix the problem, whatever it is, and Windows insists on tugging on your hem and complaining, "Hey, I *still* can't find drive D: mapped to serverted\public." In the interests of your own sanity, make disconnecting from all persistent connections one of your first priorities when you're working in safe mode. Open the My Computer folder and right-click any drives with a red × on them, and choose Disconnect from the pop-up menu that appears. You'll have to remap those connections once you get the system started normally, but that's better than living with Windows nagging you about the connections that it can't find.

When you exit a safe mode session of Windows, your options are a bit more limited than you're used to. When shutting down, you must either shut down entirely or restart the computer in Windows 95. Although restarting the computer in DOS mode is listed as an option, you can't do it, and if you try you'll see an error message like the one in Figure 9.2.

Remember, choosing *Restart the computer in MS-DOS mode* from the Shut Down menu doesn't restart the machine, it exits the graphical user interface and leaves the basic operating system in place—there's no VMM32 running, just DOS.

FIGURE 9.2

You can't run DOS
programs in safe mode

Similarly, you cannot log off a network and then back on again from regular safe mode. For that you need the second safe mode option, *Safe mode with network support*.

Safe Mode with Network Support

Choosing menu item 4 from the Startup menu (or pressing F6 at the "Starting Windows 95…" message) starts Windows 95 in safe mode, but also loads `NETSTART.BAT` to enable networking. This is essentially the same as running Windows in safe mode except that you have (as the logon text puts it) "limited network functionality."

It's pretty limited. Your persistent connections won't load at startup, and you can't connect to the network drives from the Network Neighborhood object either. If you log off and log back on again, you log on only to the machine, not to the network. Don't try to run Net Start from the command line, as you'll be told that you can't start or stop the network from a DOS prompt. And, as we discussed just a minute ago, you can't choose MS-DOS mode from the Shut Down menu, as programs that require DOS mode cannot run in safe mode.

Essentially, *Safe mode with network support* from the Windows Startup menu is for the same kinds of situations as *Safe mode*. If something goes fairly wrong with your system setup, but not so wrong that you can't fix it if you can get into Windows, this is a good option to choose.

Step-by-Step Confirmation

Choosing menu item 5 (or pressing Shift+F8 at the Startup menu) allows you to review each of the startup files and choose whether to implement them when starting up the computer. This enables you to review the following processes:

- Loading the Registry
- Creating `BOOTLOG.TXT`
- Running the files in `CONFIG.SYS` (confirming each separate entry in the file)
- Running `AUTOEXEC.BAT` (confirming each separate entry)

Choose whether or not to activate each process by pressing Enter for Yes or Esc for No. If you activate all the options, Windows will start up normally, except that you won't see the initial logo.

You should use this step-by-step confirmation option to start up Windows if you think that a particular driver or configuration setting might be causing your bootup problems. As this is a line-by-line process, it's best if you use this when you already have a pretty good idea what the problem is.

Command Prompt Only

Choosing this option allows you to start up Windows from the command prompt, and so lets you add switches to WIN.COM. The following can be useful when you need to isolate an incorrectly configured setting. The syntax is as follows (the brackets, of course, merely indicate options):

```
win [/B] [/D:[F] [M] [N] [S] [V] [X]]
```

- **/B** creates a BOOTLOG.TXT file that records operating system messages generated during system startup.

- **/D:** is used for troubleshooting when Windows 95 does not start correctly. The following switches may be used with /D:

  - **F** turns off 32-bit disk access. This is equivalent to 32Bit-DiskAccess=FALSE in SYSTEM.INI.

    Briefly, 32-bit disk access increases throughput on Western Digital-compatible disks by bypassing the BIOS. It may cause bus-mastered disks to be unstable, so try disabling it if you're having trouble with hard disk crashes. 32-bit disk access is less problematic than it was under Windows 3.x, however.

  - **M** starts Windows in safe mode. It's equivalent to choosing item 3 from the main Startup menu.
  - **N** enables safe mode with networking. It's equivalent to choosing item 4 from the main Startup menu.
  - **S** specifies that Windows 95 should not use the ROM address space between F000:0000 and 1MB to break out of a virtual machine mode. This is equivalent to SystemROMBreak-Point=FALSE in SYSTEM.INI. Use this switch if Windows 95 stalls during system startup.

Sometimes, third-party memory managers scramble ROM so that it makes a less predictable jumping point to move between real mode and protected mode, and this can cause Windows problems. If you have this problem and want to keep using the memory manager, add the line to your SYSTEM.INI.

- **V** specifies that the ROM routine will handle interrupts from the hard disk controller. This is equivalent to Virtual-HDIRQ=FALSE in SYSTEM.INI. Use this switch if Windows 95 stalls during system startup.

We'll talk more about the **V** setting elsewhere in this book, but, in brief, it causes Windows to switch to real mode whenever it needs to access the disk. It's not the best solution, but if you want to keep using that ultra-fast disk controller and its manufacturer (like most of them) has not created a VdD for it, you may discover that you don't have a choice.

- **X** excludes all of the adapter area from the range of memory that Windows 95 scans in looking for unused space. This is equivalent to EMMExclude=A000_FFFF (memory addresses 640 through 1024) in SYSTEM.INI.

Using the **X** switch keeps Windows from using *any* upper memory, so, if you're having problems with memory conflicts, think of this less as a cure than as a diagnostic tool. If this switch keeps Windows from crashing, check your documentation or start excluding ranges of memory addresses to identify the reserved memory that Windows is stomping on.

Once you've started Windows from the command line, it will start up as usual, except that you won't see the beginning logo and it seems to take a little longer than a normal startup.

Safe Mode Command Prompt Only

Select item seven from the Windows Startup menu or press Shift+F5 at the "Starting Windows 95…" message, and you'll load safe mode from the command prompt. At first, it may look as though you've booted to DOS. Don't be fooled, however: type **Ver** and the system will assure you that you're running Windows 95. Your capabilities here are pretty much those of a DOS session, however: you can start up the network, map your drives to other machines, and so forth. Getting anything done here requires a certain level of proficiency with the command line, but if you're able to get around the keyboard it's a useful mode if something's gone so badly with your system that even your VGA drivers no longer work.

From here, you can:

- Copy the .DAT files of the Registry or other system files from disk or a network directory, if your local ones are corrupted or missing
- Pull drivers from other machines to replace missing ones
- Copy or move files between drives and directories just as you would from the File Manager or the My Computer object

Generally speaking, anything that you can do from a DOS command prompt you can do from the Windows 95 prompt.

Restoring a Registry

As we've discussed elsewhere, Windows 95 keeps its system information in a file called the Registry (SYSTEM.DAT and USER.DAT). If there's no system information, then there's no Windows. Therefore, it's important to back up a working copy of your system's Registry and to know how to restore it when something happens to the original. In the best case, Windows 95 will automatically restore your Registry on bootup (we'll discuss *how* in just a minute), but you can also restore it by hand if necessary in one of the following ways:

- Run Setup and verify system files.
- Run Regedit from the command prompt in real mode and import a saved copy of the Registry.
- Run the Registry Editor from Windows and import a backed-up Registry from another location.

First, we'll discuss why you shouldn't need to use any of these options, and then how to make them work if you *do*.

Gone, but Not Forgotten: How Automatic Restore Works

Every time that Windows 95 boots successfully, it backs up SYSTEM.DAT and USER.DAT to SYSTEM.DA0 and USER.DA0, respectively. If the Registry is missing on bootup, Windows 95 will restore the Registry files from the backups. Any unsaved changes that you made to the Registry during your last session will be lost, but at least you'll have a recent copy of the configuration files.

NOTE   This is similar to the Last Known Good configuration that NT users are accustomed to.

If you'd like to see how this works before you have to do it under pressure, move SYSTEM.DAT and USER.DAT from the \windows directory to a floppy disk, write-protect the disk, and set it safely aside. (Technically, you don't need to do this, but *I'm* not blowing away my Registry information on purpose without backing it up.) Then restart the machine.

When the machine starts up, it'll first flip to the familiar logo screen, but then it rethinks the situation and sends you to the Windows Startup menu. You'll see the message "Windows has detected a registry/configuration error." Selection 3 from the menu, *Safe mode*, will be highlighted, and you have 30 seconds if you want to choose another mode in which to start up Windows. ***Don't***. Instead, press Enter so that you can restore the Registry. The logo screen and then the Windows Startup menu will appear again, but just wait patiently through it.

Windows will start up in safe mode, using the default color scheme since there's no configuration information to tell it otherwise. The Registry Problem dialog box will appear, as you can see in Figure 9.3, warning that Windows can't access the system directory and telling you that you should restore the Registry and restart.

Helpfully, the dialog box also informs you that you shouldn't just shut down (if you did, then you'd blow away the .DA0 files that contain the way

FIGURE 9.3

Registry Problem
dialog box

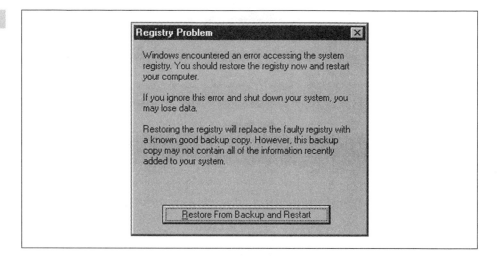

you'd last left your configuration and you'd be stuck with the current vanilla configuration). Finally (this is a big dialog box), it tells you what
you'll get when you restore the Registry files.

Click the button on the bottom that says Restore from Backup and Restart. A dialog box like the one in Figure 9.4 will appear, asking if you
want to restart the computer now (as is required to completely restore the
Registry files).

Unless you have some pressing reason to not reboot at this time, choose
to restart. The computer will shut down and then restart as normal, having replaced the missing .DAT files with the .DA0 backups.

Of course, both of these methods require working .DA0 files. If you have
neither SYSTEM.DAT nor SYSTEM.DA0, you'll see a message informing you

FIGURE 9.4

Confirm system restart

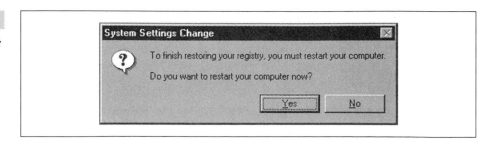

that the Registry services are not available for this session. This innocuous-sounding statement means that most Windows operations will fail, as the Registry contains the brunt of your system's configuration. If you see this message, you'll need to rebuild the Registry, using one of the methods described below.

Restoring the Registry by Hand

If you corrupt or destroy your system's Registry, then you have a few different options depending on what the problem is and how you prepared for the eventuality. Here are some common situations:

- You accidentally imported an incorrect Registry to replace your good one, but you have a backup.

- You accidentally erased your .DAT and .DA0 files, but you backed up the Registry to the local disk or a floppy.

- You erased your .DAT and .DA0 files, and you *don't* have backups.

Replacing the Current Registry

If Windows boots normally and the problem is merely that you don't like the last change you made, you may be able to get away with simply importing the Registry and having done with it—*if* you exported a working configuration before you made the change. The following steps show you how to do this.

1. Once Windows has started up, run REGEDIT.EXE to start up the Registry editor.

2. Choose Import Registry File from the Registry menu.

3. Move to the directory where you exported the working Registry, and select the proper one. (This is where those long file names that Windows 95 supports come in handy. You can give exported copies good, descriptive names like *Configuration before installing new TCP/IP drivers* or whatnot.)

4. Click OK, and you'll import that Registry over the old one. Note that any changes that you'd made to the system configuration since exporting the Registry will be lost.

If you hadn't exported the Registry but include it as part of your backup routine, you can restore SYSTEM.DAT and/or USER.DAT from the backups. Just copy them over the existing files (or insert them into C:\windows) and reboot. Once again, any changes that you made to the system since backing up will be lost.

Please note that, if Windows 95 booted successfully then there's no point in renaming the .DA0 files to .DAT files in an effort to restore the configuration. Remember, Windows 95 re-creates the .DA0 versions every time that it boots successfully. If the new Registry booted, that's what's in the .DA0 files, even if something's wrong with it.

Rebuilding the Registry with SETUP.EXE

All right, Windows 3.x users: what happens if you accidentally delete or corrupt a system file? If you're lucky and you know what you did, you can copy the file from your backups, but sometimes nothing will do but to re-install the entire operating system. Although it's not that tricky a job if you've done it a few times, it's certainly time-consuming, and you can probably think of better ways to spend those precious work hours.

If your system configuration is corrupted and you can't restore it from the .DA0 files, you may be able to restore the corrupted or missing files from the installation CD or diskettes. You can run Setup from safe mode or protected mode; the only catch is that, to run it from safe mode, your CD must be locally available—no network support, remember.

If you run Setup after you've already installed the operating system, it will ask if it should reinstall Windows 95 or just verify installed components. If you want to verify installed components, Setup examines the setup log and reruns the installation process without completely copying all system components. During this process, Windows 95 checks the already installed files against the files on the installation disks. If the file on the computer is missing or has metamorphosed into its evil twin, Setup will reinstall that file. Since only corrupted or missing files are reinstalled, this speeds up the process immeasurably.

Just to run Setup, you'll need at least 10MB of free space on your hard disk—even if you don't restore any files.

Please note that running Setup to restore the Registry will restore the files to their original configuration from when you first installed Windows 95. Most of the time, this will be okay, but it's worth keeping in mind.

Living Dangerously: Using the Command Prompt

If you have to, you can run Regedit from the command prompt and import or export Registries or edit the Registry (.REG files, not .DAT files) with a text editor.

This is potentially really, *really* dangerous, because:

- The command line is neither intuitive nor forgiving—that is, if you do something you didn't intend, you can't undo it easily.

- The Registry looks different in EDIT.COM than in its natural habitat so it's easy to get disoriented.

- Not only can the Registry still not tell a valid entry from your grocery list, it lets you wantonly edit and delete trees, keys and subkeys, not just values.

Reserve using the command prompt for those times when you're (a) really sure of what you're doing, and (b) have no other choice. No other choice in this context means that you can't run Windows at all.

You can do pretty much anything from the command prompt that you can using the GUI Registry Editor. Table 9.2 shows some actions and syntax examples.

Be *very* careful about replacing the Registry with another file (the **/c** switch). If you import a Registry file that is a branch of the entire Registry, it will only replace the branch to which it corresponds. On the other hand, if you *replace* the Registry with a file that contains only a branch of the entire file, then your system's Registry will consist only of that branch. For example, if you export hkey_current_user as newuser.reg and then

ACTION	EXAMPLE
Export the entire Registry to a file (`NEWREG.REG`).	Regedit /e newreg.reg
Export one branch (`hkey_local _machine`) of the Registry to a file (`NEWBRNCH.REG`).	Regedit /e hkey_local _machine newbrnch.reg
Import a Registry file (`NEWREG.REG`).	Regedit newreg.reg
Import the Registry file `NEWREG.REG`, made from a specific `SYSTEM.DAT` and/or `USER.DAT`, located (respectively) at *systempath* and *userpath*.	Regedit /L: *systempath* /R: *userpath* newreg.reg
Replace the current Registry with a previously exported one (`NEWREG.REG`).	Regedit /c newreg.reg

replace the registry with `newuser.reg`, you will blow away all of your hardware configuration information and default user setups. It's probably safer to stick with importing and exporting Registry files, and relegate the Replace function to the "interesting but overkill" closet.

To replace a missing Registry, type the following:

Regedit *backup registry path and filename*

where *backup registry path and filename* is where you previously exported the Registry to. Don't forget that, if you used a long file name for the exported Registry it will be listed in its shortened form when you're in real mode. For example, `Backup Registry made on 8/31/95.reg` will become `Backup~1.reg` when it's abbreviated to the eight-dot-three format.

If you can't avoid it, you can edit the Registry with EDIT.COM. Type

Edit c:\windows\testconf.reg (or whatever the name of your Registry is)

and you'll see output that looks like the following:

```
[HKEY_LOCAL_MACHINE\SOFTWARE\Classes\.ME]
@="txtfile"

[HKEY_LOCAL_MACHINE\SOFTWARE\Classes\123Worksheet]
@="1-2-3 Worksheet"

[HKEY_LOCAL_MACHINE\SOFTWARE\Classes\123Worksheet
\protocol]

[HKEY_LOCAL_MACHINE\SOFTWARE\Classes\123Worksheet
\protocol\
StdFileEditing]

[HKEY_LOCAL_MACHINE\SOFTWARE\Classes\123Worksheet
\protocol\
StdFileEditing\SetData
Formats]
@="NotesDocInfo"

[HKEY_LOCAL_MACHINE\SOFTWARE\Classes\123Worksheet
\protocol\
StdFileEditing\verb]

[HKEY_LOCAL_MACHINE\SOFTWARE\Classes\123Worksheet
\protocol\
StdFileEditing\verb\0]
@="Edit"

[HKEY_LOCAL_MACHINE\SOFTWARE\Classes\123Worksheet
\protocol\
StdFileEditing\server]
@="c:\\123r4w\\programs\\123w.EXE"
```

Reading these entries is similar to reading command-line file and directory information—the name of the branch is on the far left, and the keys and subkeys progress downward from left to right, like this:

branch\key\subkey\subkey\subkey

The part of the entry that reads @="Edit" or the like is the value name.

When using a text editor, do *not* edit any part of the Registry other than the value data. It's even easier to mess up your system's configuration here than it is in the GUI Registry Editor, as that application will not permit you to edit anything other than value data in the first place. Using a text editor, you could destructively edit the names of keys and subkeys, or delete them altogether, and you'd never get any warning that you might've just trashed your system—until it's too late.

Creating and Using a Startup Floppy

Like DOS, Windows 95 permits you to boot from a floppy in case of emergency. The only catch is that your computer's A: drive must be the 3½-inch drive, as the startup files take up more than 1.2MB, and a 5¼-inch floppy can't hold that much data. The emergency floppy contains files for booting up and (hopefully) fixing your computer, as you can see in Table 9.3.

You can create the startup floppy either while installing Windows 95 or, if you delete or lose the floppy, afterwards.

- To create the floppy *during* installation, have a junk floppy (i.e., one not containing anything you want to keep) on hand and insert it as directed.

	FILE NAME	FUNCTION
TABLE 9.3 **Contents of Startup Floppy**	ATTRIB.EXE	Assigns attributes (such as archived, read-only, hidden, or system file) to files.
	COMMAND.COM	Provides an operating environment. Executes AUTOEXEC.BAT and NETSTART.BAT.
	DRVSPACE.BIN	Permits the boot disk to recognize a drive compressed with Drvspace.
	EBD.SYS	Utility for the startup disk.
	EDIT.COM	Text editor for editing startup files (including the Registry, but only as a last resort—see precautions in this chapter).
	FDISK.EXE	Configures the partitions on a hard disk. With the /MBR switch, can also rebuild (but not *fix*) the MBR without destroying the data on the disk.
	FORMAT.COM	Formats the partitions on a disk.
	IO.SYS	The real-mode operating system that replaces DOS. Reads the small portion of SYSTEM.DAT on the startup disk. (Note: This is not the same IO.SYS used with DOS—that file is now called IO.DOS.)
	MSDOS.SYS	Contains information for backward compatibility between Windows 95 and MS-DOS applications. (Note: This is not the same MSDOS.SYS used with DOS—that file is now called MSDOS.DOS.)
	REGEDIT.EXE	Used to import, export, or replace all or part of the Registry.
	SCANDISK.EXE	Disk analysis and repair utility for common disk and file errors such as lost clusters, bad clusters, and cross-linked files.
	SCANDISK.INI	Initialization file for Scandisk.
	SYS.COM	Copies IO.SYS, MSDOS.SYS, and COMMAND.COM to the drive you specify.

- To create a startup floppy *after* installation, open the Control Panel, choose Add/Remove Programs, and select the Startup Disk tab.

    1. Click on the Create Disk button, and the system will begin to set up the startup files. When it's ready to write the startup disk, you'll see a dialog box like the one shown here.

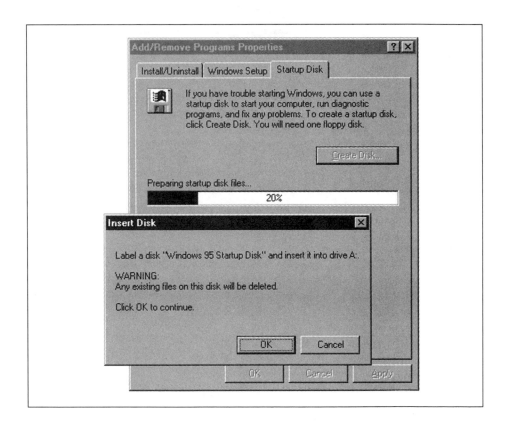

    2. Insert a disk as prompted (I recommend writing the date on the disk label as well as naming it with the Label option), and the system will create the disk. To make troubleshooting easier, it's a good idea to copy CONFIG.SYS, AUTOEXEC.BAT, WIN.INI, SYSTEM.INI, and a copy of your system's Registry onto this disk. Do that, and your startup disk will contain all the files that you need to fix your hard disk and replace your configuration.

Keep the startup floppy write-protected and labeled, so you don't delete it accidentally. If your computer will not boot normally, you'll need this disk around just to get the system going.

Booting to DOS

Okay, I lied earlier: if you really want to, it's possible to make your computer capable of booting to DOS. It just requires either some previous planning (and a lot of empty space on your hard disk to contain 40MB of operating system files) or some post-installation tweaking.

Installing Windows 95 for Dual Boot

When installing Windows 95, you have the choice of either installing the operating system to a new directory or installing it into your old Windows directory over the previous installation (as Microsoft recommends). If you go with the default, then Windows 95 overwrites Windows 3.x and absorbs any previous system settings that apply to it. This is convenient, but (as noted at the beginning of this chapter) it limits your options if something goes wrong with Windows 95.

If you decide to install to a new directory instead of going with the default, specify the new directory during installation. This will preserve your old Windows installation. Other than that, the installation process will proceed normally.

When you've finished installing Windows 95, remove the read-only attribute for MSDOS.SYS and open the file in Notepad. In the [Options] section, add the line **BootMulti=1**. When you've finished, the active portion of MSDOS.SYS should look something like the following:

```
[Paths]
WinDir=C:\WINDOWS
WinBootDir=C:\WINDOWS
HostWinBootDrv=C

[Options]
BootGUI=1
Network=1
BootMulti=1
```

Reboot and press F8 when you see the "Starting Windows 95..." message. You'll now see an eighth option in the Windows Startup menu: *Previous version of MS-DOS*. Choose that item, and DOS will boot.

Booting to DOS

Although the Windows 95 Resource Kit describes an elaborate process for setting up dual DOS/95 booting after installation, the sad fact is that it doesn't work—renaming the command interpreter with a DOS extension seems to make it unreadable, and loading COMMAND.COM doesn't work either.

However, you can still boot to DOS if necessary, using the old-fashioned method of creating a DOS bootable floppy. Go to a *DOS*-based machine and create a system disk (this *must* be a DOS machine, not a Windows 95 machine). Insert the disk in drive A: and reboot, and your system will boot to DOS, and you'll have access to any DOS programs on your system. Kludgy, but it works.

CHAPTER

10

Installing and Supporting New Hardware

ONE of the major pluses of an advanced operating system like Windows is its ability to centralize device control. Under DOS, a high-performance video board required a number of separate video drivers—one for 1-2-3, one for WordStar, one for Harvard Graphics, and so on. With Windows 3.x, in contrast, one Windows driver served all of the Windows applications. DOS was still important under Windows 3.x, however, because most hardware installation programs were DOS-based, and nearly all of the diagnostic programs that you found for new hardware were DOS programs.

Windows 95 changes the story on device support, as it does away with DOS, requiring that you find some other way to install and test the new hardware. Ultimately, even that won't be necessary, as the world will move more and more to Plug and Play, or something like it.

Until the promises of Plug and Play start coming to fruition, most of our existing systems require that we install boards the old-fashioned way, flipping DIP switches, moving jumpers, or running proprietary software programs.

Even on those antediluvian boards, however, Windows 95 offers a plus: the *Device Manager*, a central repository of information about your system's hardware configuration. In this chapter, you'll learn how to make the Device Manager understand what kind of hardware is in your system, how to configure boards in a 95-based system, and how to best keep track of your system's hardware information under 95.

Elements of Hardware Installation

No matter what operating system you're working in, the boards you install in your system must be compatible with other boards. *Compatible* in this sense means that they don't step on each other's toes. And that's where IRQs, DMAs, and the like come into the story.

When I was a kid, there was a kind of standing joke about Christmas Eve. Parents would buy their kids all kinds of stuff, and the stuff would come in boxes, arranged in a way that no one could ever duplicate: once you took the pieces of the toy out of the box, you'd never be able to repack it the way it came. The really fun part, however, was the incredibly bad documentation that came with the toys; I think a couple of comedians in the early 60s made their entire living parodying these "assembly instructions."

The folks that made all that toy documentation needed somewhere to go as the years wore on, and it appears they moved to circuit board documentation. These documentation writers all assume that you already understand five pretty important things. Those five things are:

I/O addresses These tell you which address the circuit board uses to communicate with the CPU.

DMA channels These are used to speed up I/O to and from the system's memory. (Note that your system is severely limited in how many boards can be hooked up to use DMA.)

IRQ levels Hardware devices must use these to interrupt the CPU to force it to service them in some time-critical fashion.

ROM addresses Many boards include some of their low-level control software in ROM. The ROM requires a memory address, which must not conflict with other ROMs or any RAM in the system.

RAM buffers Some add-in cards maintain a little RAM (8K to 64K) on board to hold data temporarily. That RAM should not conflict with any other RAM or ROM in your system.

In the first half of this chapter I'll give you the scoop on these obscure-sounding resources.

I/O Addresses

Stop and think for a minute about how the CPU talks to some other piece of hardware, like a serial port, a disk controller, or a keyboard controller. You already know how the CPU talks to one kind of hardware—the memory. You know that the CPU can know which part of what memory chip it's talking to, because each location in memory has its own unique *memory address*.

Other hardware has addresses as well, but they're not memory addresses; they're a completely different set of addresses called input/output addresses, or *I/O addresses*. Some people call them port addresses or hardware addresses. Think of the CPU as having two windows on the outside world: the memory addresses and the I/O addresses.

Much as the CPU can read and write memory addresses, it can read and write I/O addresses. There are fewer I/O addresses than there are memory addresses, a lot fewer: Any computer built with a 386 or later processor can address 4096MB of RAM, but only 64K of I/O addresses. That's not all that limiting, really; most of us won't be attaching a thousand keyboards to a single PC.

I/O addresses allow a CPU to tell its peripherals apart, as you can see in Figure 10.1.

In this example, the CPU communicates with the RAM on its left via memory addresses. It communicates with other peripherals—a keyboard controller, a serial port with a mouse on it, and an Ethernet LAN card, in this simplified example—via their I/O addresses. The keyboard controller sits at address 64, the serial port at 3F8—there's an F in the number because it's a *hex* number, which I'll get to in a minute—and the Ethernet card is at address 300.

FIGURE 10.1

Distinguishing
peripherals with
I/O addresses

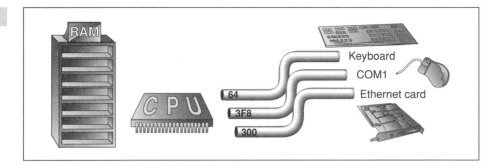

What this means is that when the CPU wants to send some data to the
Ethernet card, then it drops it down the tube labeled 300, rather than the
one labeled 3F8 or 64. (There aren't really tubes in a computer, of course;
I just like the imagery of the CPU communicating with its minions via
old-fashioned pneumatic tubes.)

It's Hex, But There Are No Spells

A quick word on the hex notation: you'll see that both memory addresses
and I/O addresses tend to be reported in *hexadecimal*, or *hex*, an alternative
way of writing numbers, preferred by techies because it lends itself to working with bytes.

Briefly, hex is just another way to represent numbers. We're all comfortable
with counting in the *decimal system*—the normal way of numbering: **0, 1, 2,
3, 4, 5, 6, 7, 8, 9**... that does it for the single digits; what comes next? Well,
we're used to the next number being a ten (**10**), which is the first number—
0—with a **1** stuck on the front of it. The number following that (eleven) is
the number that usually follows **0** (**1**, in case you've forgotten), except again
with a **1** stuck on the front of it to produce the familiar **11**, and so on.

Decimal has 10 single-character number symbols, which is why it's also
called *base 10*. Hexadecimal is based not on 10, but on *16*, and so hex needs
16 single-character number symbols. It starts off with the familiar **0**
through **9**, so it's got the first ten numbers. But after **9** comes **A**—hex uses
the letter A to represent its eleventh digit. As you'd imagine, **B** comes next,
and so on to **F** as the sixteenth digit. Therefore, the way you count in hex

is like so: **0, 1, 2, 3, 4, 5, 6, 7, 8, 9, A, B, C, D, E, F**... and then **10**. See, hex has a 10 just like the decimal system; it just arrives later.

For example, suppose I were to tell you that the COM1 serial port uses an address range from 3F8 through 3FF. (I can hear Ford Prefect of *The Hitchhiker's Guide to the Galaxy* answer, "Why? Do you think you're *likely* to tell me that?") How many addresses does COM1 then take up? Well, you know that 3F8 is the first address. After 3F*8* comes 3F*9*. Just like all the numbers you've ever known, the rightmost digit is the one that changes as the number gets bigger; 9 comes after 8, so 3F9 is the next value. Just a minute ago you learned that 9 is followed by A, so the next address would be 3FA, then 3FB, 3FC, 3FD, 3FE, and finally 3FF. (Why *finally*? Because the range is from 3F8 through 3FF, so when you get to the 3FF, you stop.) Go back and count them up, and you'll see that a serial port uses eight I/O addresses.

What does it do with all of those addresses? Several things. First of all, a serial port can both transmit and receive bytes at the same time. One address holds received data and one holds outgoing data. Of the other addresses, some will be used for status information, such as, "Does the modem have a connection to another modem?" Some will be wasted— wasted because it's easiest for a circuit designer to take either eight or sixteen addresses, due to a peculiarity in the PC hardware. If you designed a board that only required seven I/O addresses, you'd still take eight of them.

Common I/O Address Uses

That's probably a bit more than you actually wanted to know. What you really need to know about addresses is "How do you know which ones are currently taken?" Well, you can start off with Table 10.1.

Many devices have only one I/O address that they can use. Using the example of COM1 again, part of the very definition of COM1 is that it uses I/O addresses 3F8 through 3FF. Other devices may allow you to use any of a range of addresses; for example, most sound cards default to address 220, but will allow you to reconfigure them to use some other address if 220 is not available. Reconfigure a COM1 serial port, in contrast, and it's no longer a COM1 serial port.

TABLE 10.1	HEX ADDRESS RANGE	USER
Common I/O Address Uses in PCs	00–0F	DMA Controller 8237 #1
	20–21	Programmable Interrupt Controller 8259A #1
	40–43	Timer 8253
	60–63	8255 Peripheral Controller
	60–64	Keyboard Controller (AT only) 8742
	70–71	Setup RAM access address (AT only)
	80–8F	DMA page registers
	A0–A1	Programmable Interrupt Controller #2 (8259 AT only)
	A0–AF	NMI Mask Register
	C0–DF	8237 DMA Controller #2 (AT only)
	F0–FF	Math Coprocessor (AT only)
	1F0–1F8	Hard disk controller
	200–20F	Joystick controller
	210–217	Expansion chassis
	220–22F	FM Synthesis Interface (WAV device), Sound Blaster default
	238–23B	Bus mouse
	23C–23F	Alt. bus mouse
	278–27F	LPT2
	2B0–2DF	EGA
	2E0–2E7	GPIB (AT only)
	2E8–2EF	COM4 serial port
	2F8–2FF	COM2 serial port

HEX ADDRESS RANGE	USER
300–30F	Ethernet card
300–31F	Prototype card
320–32F	Hard disk controller (XT only)
330–33F	MIDI port (common location)
378–37F	LPT1 printer port
380–38F	SDLC card
3A0–3AF	BSC card
3B0–3BF	Monochrome adapter
3BC–3BF	LPT3
3D0–3DF	Color/Graphics adapter
3E8–3EF	COM3 serial port
3F0–3F7	Floppy disk controller
3F8–3FF	Com1 serial port

NOTE The key to understanding why this information is important is to know that this address cannot be used by any other device: the rule is, only one device to an I/O address. To understand why this is so, I'll steal an old analogy.

I/O Address Conflicts

Think of I/O addresses as being like post office boxes. Say the keyboard has P.O. box 64. When the keyboard has data for the system, it puts the data in box 64. When the CPU wants to read the keyboard, it looks in box 64. Box 64 is, in a very real sense, a better definition of the keyboard from the CPU's point of view than the keyboard itself is. If you plug a new board into your system, and that board uses I/O address 64, then the new board won't work, and, in addition, the keyboard will cease to work as well—you can't run two devices off the same I/O address.

Now, in reality, no one's going to design a board that uses address 64, because everybody knows that's the keyboard's. Not only that, but everybody knows you have to have a keyboard. But what about a case where you have a conflict in *optional* boards?

For example, I recently installed a Sound Blaster 16 on a PC that was already equipped with an Ethernet card and a SCSI host adapter. The Sound Blaster 16 includes a circuit called a MIDI interface, and it happened to be set at I/O address 330. Unfortunately, 330 is the I/O address used by the SCSI host adapter, so I got a disk boot failure when I turned my system on. There actually was nothing wrong with the *disk*; it was the disk's host adapter *board* that couldn't work due to the conflict with the Sound Blaster 16. Checking the documentation, I found that the sound card's MIDI circuit offered either address 330, which it was currently using, or 300. I set the address to 300 (by using a *jumper*, which is what the Sound Blaster 16 uses to set its MIDI address), reinstalled the board, and had the situation as shown in Figure 10.2.

Now my CPU's I/O address 300—that particular post office box—is shared by the MIDI circuit on the sound card and the Ethernet card. The system didn't complain when I booted up, because my system doesn't need either the sound card or the Ethernet card in order to boot. But when I tried to configure the sound card, it failed. You can see why in Figure 10.3.

FIGURE 10.2

Sharing I/O addresses between an Ethernet card and a sound card

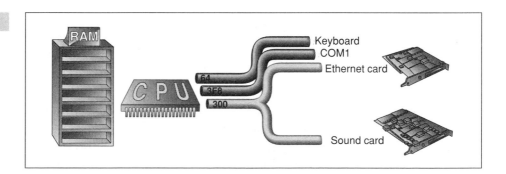

FIGURE 10.3

I/O conflict between an Ethernet card and a sound card

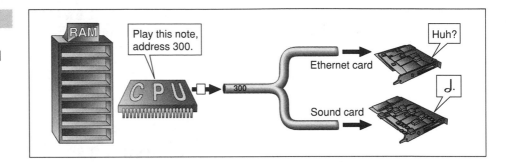

A "play this note" message went into I/O address 300. The Ethernet card has no idea how to respond to this request, and indeed may not be prepared for any requests at all. Worse yet, the electrical signal from the CPU gets split up two ways, so it may not be strong enough to actually get to *either* board.

Why did Creative Labs, the creator of the Sound Blaster 16, build a deliberate conflict into its card? The answer is, they didn't. There is no official standard for SCSI host adapter I/O addresses; Adaptec uses 330 for some of their boards, Trantor uses 350, Iomega offers a range from 320 through 350, and I'm sure other SCSI vendors have other options. Ethernet cards *tend* to sit at address 300, but that's not set in stone. What I'm saying is that the most common conflicts will be between the types of boards that appeared after the mid-80s, because, since then, there has been no central coordinating force in the PC hardware industry.

How did I solve my conflict, by the way? Well, the Adaptec board offered me 330 or 300 as my only choices, as did the sound board. The Ethernet board offered 300, 310, 320, 330, or 340. I didn't want to mess with the Adaptec board, because it was the hard disk interface, and if *it* became conflicted then I'd lose access to the vitally important hard disk—so I left the SCSI board at 330. That meant that the Sound Blaster 16 had to go to 300. The Ethernet board then played the peacemaker, as I set it to address 310.

More and more, I find that board manufacturers are moving from jumper settings to software settings, but in this case, the SCSI board and the sound board set their addresses with jumpers, and the Ethernet card set its I/O address with software. Which do I prefer? Well, software is, of course, nice. But suppose the sound board came preset to 330, as it did, and required that I run some software in order to get it to switch addresses? That would be a real pain. Think about it: I'd install the sound board at 330 initially, as I had no choice. That would disable my hard disk, requiring that I juggle floppies in order to run the program that would set a different address for the sound board. To add insult to injury, the setup program for the sound board only works once it's installed on the *hard* disk. I just might decide that getting past *that* gauntlet wouldn't be worth it, and scrap the board altogether. In contrast, all I *actually* had to do was to move a jumper. So there are pros and cons to both sides.

> **N O T E**
>
> I've already said this, but let me repeat: You probably won't have a clue which DIP switches do what unless you have the documentation, so be sure to latch onto any switch-setting documentation you've got.

What would I have done, by the way, if the Ethernet card was set at 300 and wouldn't accept any other addresses? How would you resolve that problem? *You may not be able to resolve all I/O address conflicts*, as not all boards even give you the chance to change I/O addresses. It's hard to believe, but some boards are hard wired to use only one I/O address range. I had a LIM board that conflicted with a clock/calendar, but unfortunately neither board gave me a chance to change the I/O address. One board had to be removed—the conflict couldn't be resolved.

1K Addresses versus 64K Addresses

I mentioned that there are 64K I/O addresses. The ISA bus, however, only implements 1,024 addresses. The bottom 256 (hex locations 000 through 0FF) are only available to components on the system board. Plug-in expansion boards must use the top 768 locations (hex 100 through 3FF). Therefore, expansion boards will only allow you (if they are designed properly) to set your I/O addresses somewhere between 100 hex and 3FF hex.

MCA, EISA, PCI, and VESA slots support all 64K I/O addresses. But if you're installing a board in a system that contains a hybrid of EISA, PCI, or VESA slots as well as *ISA* slots, then you may run into a conflict. These non-ISA slots don't just support up to address 3FF hex (1K); they support up to address FFFF (64K). Note that extra digit—it's important.

There aren't many that do this currently, but some boards use I/O addresses above 3FF, and some ISA buses get confused about this. Suppose, for example, that you have some garden-variety ISA board in a hybrid ISA/VESA system at address 2D8, and a VESA local-bus video accelerator board at address E2D8. 2D8 and E2D8 look like different addresses, and they *are* different addresses—but *not* to some *ISA*-based machines. Because it's a hybrid PC, the commands to read or write data over address 2D8 might be destined for a VESA slot, or they might be intended for an ISA slot. In contrast, commands dealing with address E2D8 *must* be intended for a VESA slot, as it's impossible for address E2D8 to be relevant to an ISA slot. Unfortunately, there are hybrid motherboards that repeat *all* I/O address communications over *all* bus slots. As ISA only understands three address digits, sending a request referring to E2D8 to an ISA bus slot gets "heard" by the ISA slot as a request for address *2D8*. The result? Now you have an I/O address conflict with the ISA board at 2D8.

The bottom line is that when you're installing a board in a hybrid system, take a minute and make sure that there aren't conflicts between the four-digit I/O addresses and the three-digit I/O addresses.

I hope it's obvious by now that you can make your life a whole lot easier if you write down the I/O addresses used by your devices. Otherwise, installing a new board can be a real nightmare.

DMA Channels

Once a hard disk controller gets some data from the hard disk, that data's got to be stored in RAM. The same thing gets done when new data comes in on a local area network card. Big blocks of sound information must be zapped out to a sound card in a smooth, reliable fashion in order for that card to produce pleasant-sounding voice or music sounds. The data originates in the system's memory, and it has to get to the sound board.

A fundamental problem in computer design is getting data from memory (RAM) to or from a hard disk controller, LAN board, video capture card, sound board, video card—in short, to transfer data between memory and a *peripheral*. ("Peripheral" is easier to write than "LAN card, disk interface, etc.," so I'll stick to that from here on in.)

Programmed Input/Output (PIO)

The simplest way to move data between a peripheral and memory is via *programmed input/output*, or *PIO*. With PIO, the CPU sends commands to the peripheral through an I/O address or addresses. Let's see how that gets done with a simple example.

Suppose the CPU wants some data from a part of one of the disk drives. Data on disks, as you'll learn in the disk section, is organized into *sectors*, blocks of data that are 512 bytes long. When a PC accesses data from a disk, it can't take it in 1- or 2-byte chunks; the smallest amount of data that the CPU can ask for is a 512-byte sector. Suppose the goal for the moment is to get sector 10 from the disk and to put it into RAM. The first step is for the CPU to tell the disk interface to get the data; on many disk interfaces it does that on I/O address 1F0, as you see in Figure 10.4.

The disk interface then responds to the request, pulling the 512 bytes off the disk drive. The interface then tells the CPU that it's ready, and the CPU now has the task of getting the data from the disk interface to the RAM. Assuming that the disk interface works with the CPU via a 16-bit bus instead of a 32-bit bus (which is still, unfortunately, true in 90 percent of the PCs), the CPU requests the first two of those bytes, as you see in Figure 10.5.

The CPU then stuffs that data somewhere in RAM, as you see in Figure 10.6.

Moving those two bytes takes time, as does figuring out where to put the *next* two bytes. The CPU then requests two more bytes, puts them in RAM, figures out where the next bytes will go, and so on. Will this work?

FIGURE 10.4

PIO part 1: Requesting data from the disk interface using I/O addresses

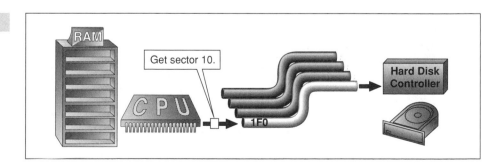

FIGURE 10.5

PIO part 2:
Requesting first part
of data from the disk
controller

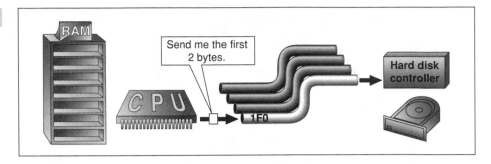

FIGURE 10.6

PIO part 3: Putting
data into RAM

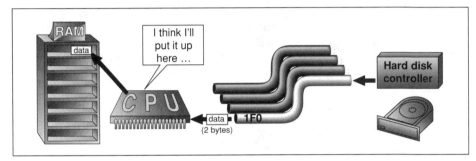

Yes, undoubtedly. Is it fast? Well, not always. Can we make this faster?
Certainly. Read on.

DMA (Direct Memory Access)

Now let's take a look at how PC CPUs access floppy disk drives. Suppose
I want to read sector 20 off of a floppy disk. Things start out very much
the same as before, as you see in Figure 10.7.

FIGURE 10.7

DMA part 1:
Requesting data from
disk controller

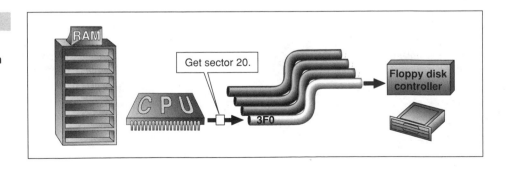

The floppy disk controller is at address 3F0, so the CPU sends the initial command out over that address. Ah, but when the floppy disk controller has the data ready, then it knows that having the CPU pick up two bytes and put them down and then pick up two *more* bytes and put *them* down, and so on, takes time. If the idea is to get the data into the RAM, why not cut out the middleman? The process is depicted in Figure 10.8.

First, there's a diversionary tactic, allowing something other than the CPU to control the bus; then, as you see in Figure 10.9, the data gets delivered to the RAM directly.

Okay, I admit that the floppy disk controller doesn't really distract the CPU; actually, it says to the CPU, "May I have direct access to the memory?" Some of the wires on the bus are DMA Request (DREQ) lines and some are DMA Acknowledge (DACK) lines. A board requests direct access to the memory bus with a DREQ line, and the CPU responds with a DACK. The idea here is to keep more than one peripheral from seizing the bus; there are multiple DMA request/acknowledge lines, more commonly called *DMA channels*.

FIGURE 10.8

DMA part 2: Diversion of the CPU by the disk controller

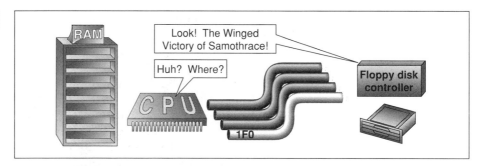

FIGURE 10.9

DMA part 3: Using the DMA channel to put data directly into RAM

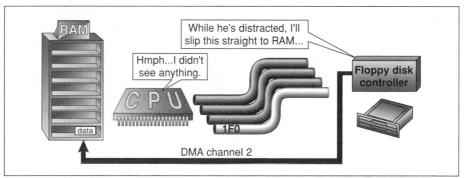

The original PC had a single DMA controller chip, the 8237. It allowed up to four DMA channels, and to this day 8-bit ISA slots only have four DMA channels available, numbered from 0 to 3.

The original PC used channel 0 for *dynamic memory refresh*. Briefly, here's how it works. There are two kinds of memory: dynamic and static. Dynamic sounds better than static, but it isn't. When you tell a static RAM (SRAM) something, it remembers it until you turn off the power or change it. Think of memory as a container of liquid, and static RAMs are ceramic mugs. You put water in them, it stays there. Dynamic RAMs (DRAMs), on the other hand, are like water cups made out of thin sheets of paper; they leak. Put data into a DRAM and it will forget whatever you tell it within 4 milliseconds (ms).

As a result, old PCs had to drop everything and do a RAM refresh every 3.86 ms. This took 5 ticks of the clock out of every 72, or about 7 percent of the PC's time. Of course, if the CPU were doing a lot of INs, OUTs, internal calculations, or the like, then you wouldn't notice the slowdown, as the whole idea of DMA is to work in parallel with the CPU. (Wouldn't static RAMs make a slightly faster computer? Yes, ...but they're more costly, lots more costly.) In more modern PCs, the RAM refresh is handled by a separate circuit. DRAMs still need to be refreshed in modern systems, but the CPU isn't involved, so no DMA is required, and channel 0 is free on most modern PCs.

On the older PCs I was referring to a minute ago, the hard disk controller used DMA channel 1, but most modern disk interfaces don't use DMA, they use PIO for reasons I'll explain in a minute; as a result, channel 1 is available on modern PCs. The floppy disk controller has employed channel 2 since PC days, and it still does; so don't assign anything else to channel 2. In general, channel 3 is unused.

Modern machines with 16-bit ISA, MCA, EISA, PC Card, PCI, or VESA slots have two DMA controllers, and thus eight DMA channels to the XT's four.

NOTE

Notice that the above implies that you only have *one* free DMA channel on an old XT-type machine, but seven available DMA channels on most modern PCs—just leave channel 2 for the floppy controller, and you're in good shape.

To DMA or Not to DMA?

You're probably wondering by now what I left out of the story. I just got finished explaining that DMA allows for faster transfers of data between peripherals and memory, and modern machines basically don't use DMA. (You're supposed to go "*huh?*" at this point.)

DMA is pretty nifty, except for one thing. In order to assure backward compatibility, the AT's designers held DMA operations to 4.77 MHz— the original PC's clock speed. Lest you skim over this because it sounds like a history lesson, *ISA bus machines still do DMA at 4.77 MHz*. Honest. If you have a shiny new 200 MHz Pentium Pro-based system on your desk and you do a DMA operation on it, the whole shootin' match slows down to just under *three percent* of that 200 MHz clock speed. The best the other buses do when DMA-ing is 8 MHz on DMA. What's the answer? Bus mastering; but I'll get to that in a minute.

Anyway, that's why you'll see that some boards give you a choice as to whether to DMA or not.

So, in summary, if you have an expansion board that needs a DMA channel,

- The only one available is generally DMA channel 3 on the old PCs.
- If you're installing a 16-bit board, try whenever possible to use the extra 16-bit-only DMAs—channels 4 through 7—to leave room for the 8-bit boards in your system.
- If you're out of DMAs, see if the board offers the option to disable DMA. Disabling them might be slower, but it might be faster. On most modern computers (above 25 MHz), PIO will probably be faster than DMA. Try it both ways to see.

You can see common DMA uses in Table 10.2.

CHANNEL	USE
0	Dynamic RAM Refresh (XT—free on AT)
1	Hard Disk Controller (XT only—free on AT), or commonly used by sound boards in AT architecture
2	Floppy Controller
3	Unused, but also used on many 16-bit sound boards (they use two DMA channels)
4–7	Available on modern PCs

Bus Mastering

This is a slight digression, but it's important, it fits in here, and I'll keep it short.

You just learned that DMA is a neat idea that is hampered by an historical error—4.77 MHz. DMA actually has another problem, although it's not one that would be immediately apparent.

DMA can transfer data from a peripheral to RAM, or RAM to a peripheral, with neither transfer requiring the CPU's intervention. But DMA can't transfer data from a *peripheral* to a *peripheral* because such an operation would be two DMA operations: peripheral to RAM, followed by RAM to peripheral.

Many boards built for the EISA, MCA, or PCI buses can do *bus master transfers*, allowing them to bypass not only the CPU, but RAM as well, transferring data between peripherals at the maximum speed that the bus supports. Bus mastering, then, can speed up a system in two ways. You see this diagrammed in Figure 10.10.

ISA supports bus mastering, but only allows one bus master board in an ISA system. EISA, MCA, and PCI systems allow multiple bus masters. It's a feature worth exploiting.

FIGURE 10.10

Bus mastering

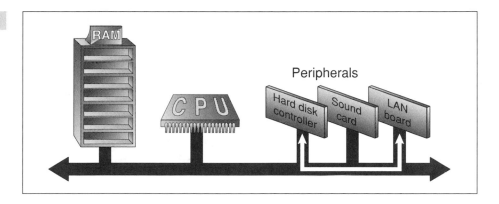

IRQ (Interrupt Request) Levels

In the DMA section, I was describing PIO. After the CPU made the request of the disk controller for the data, I then said "the disk interface then tells the CPU that it's ready…"—which was a trifle sneaky on my part. As far as the CPU is concerned, it initiates all conversations with peripherals; they "speak when they're spoken to." A peripheral gets the CPU's attention in one of two ways: *polling* or *interrupts*.

Polling

To illustrate polling, let's look at how DOS controls a parallel port in order to print data. The printer is massively slower than the CPU, so there has got to be some way to handshake the two. Things start off as you see in Figure 10.11.

FIGURE 10.11

Printing data through
the parallel port

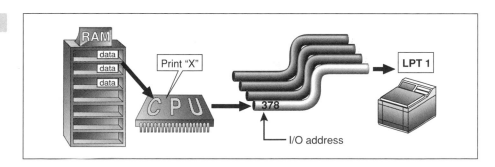

Data travels through I/O address 378, the address of LPT1, and is deposited from there into the printer. The CPU then keeps an eye on the printer, as you see in Figure 10.12.

The CPU just sits there at the pneumatic tube (forgive me) numbered 378, repeatedly checking for an indication from the printer, much as someone expecting a letter might run out to the mailbox every ten minutes. (I'd include the lyrics for that song that goes, "Wait a minute, Mr. Postman...," but then we'd have to get the copyright permission, and it's too much trouble. You might just want to hum along to get into the polling frame of mind.)

The CPU essentially sits on address 378, asking, "Are you ready now? How about *now*? How about NOW?..." It's a big waste of the CPU's time, but this polling method of waiting for an I/O device to finish its work is simple to design. Besides, in a single-tasking world like you see in DOS, the CPU doesn't have anything else to do anyway; it is singly focused on servicing the parallel port. Eventually, as you see in Figure 10.13, the port responds.

FIGURE 10.12

Polling of the printer by the CPU

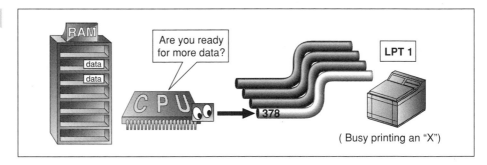

FIGURE 10.13

Response of parallel port to polling

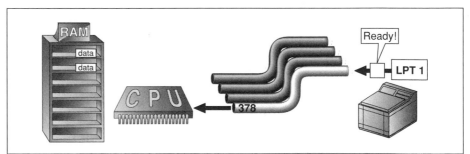

The CPU now sends another byte to the printer, and it begins all over again. As I've said, the process is wasteful but simple, and it works fine in the single-tasking DOS world.

Hardware Interrupts

But what about a multi-tasking world, such as most of us live in today? And even if you work single-tasking, there are many peripherals on your PC, and the PC can't poll them all. That's why hardware interrupts are built into the PC.

You can see how interrupts work if we look back to the discussion of how the CPU gets data from the disk interface. Recall that the CPU stuffed a "get some data" request down I/O address 1F0. Now, it takes time for the disk to return the desired data. Why not let the CPU use that time to do other things, as in Figure 10.14?

The disk interface is in its "own private Idaho," as the CPU is likewise off in its own world. But most modern disk controllers have a circuit running between themselves and the CPU, a circuit called an interrupt request level, or IRQ level. (Actually, some really high-performance SCSI host adapters don't do this.) The disk interface wakes up the CPU, as you see in Figure 10.15.

Once the CPU has been interrupted, it knows to start getting the information from the disk controller, as I described in the discussion of PIO a few pages back.

FIGURE 10.14

CPU works on other things while waiting for disk controller

FIGURE 10.15

Using IRQ levels
to get the attention
of the CPU

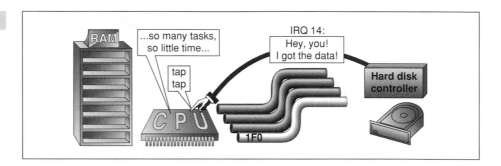

How Interrupts Work

PC interrupts were originally handled by an Intel 8259 *prioritized interrupt controller* (*PIC*); nowadays, there's no discrete 8259 on your system, it's just built into the motherboard's chipset. The 8259 is prioritized in that it has eight interrupt levels numbered from 0 to 7, and lower numbers get higher priority. That means that if interrupt 3 and interrupt 7 both ring at the same time, it's interrupt 3 that gets handled (serviced in PC hardware lingo).

When an interrupt occurs, the 8259 forces the CPU to put its current work on hold and immediately execute a program that allows it to handle the interrupt. Such a program is called, appropriately, an interrupt handler or an interrupt service routine. For example, in the disk drive example, when IRQ14 occurs, then the CPU jumps to a small program that tells it how to grab the data from the disk controller (via PIO, in the case of most PC disk interfaces), stuff it into some RAM, and return to whatever it was doing before it was interrupted.

The original PC had only one 8259, with eight interrupt lines, and that PC's bus implemented lines 2 through 7; interrupts 0 and 1 weren't on the bus because they were pre-assigned. IRQ0 is attached to a timer circuit that creates an interrupt about 18 times per second. IRQ1 is attached to the 8042 keyboard controller. Driving the keyboard interface via interrupts is a good idea, because the keyboard controller is pretty dumb. It has no memory to speak of, and so every time a keystroke arrives at the controller, it must hand off this keystroke to the CPU (who then puts it in the keyboard buffer) before another keystroke comes in. Essentially, once the keyboard controller gets a keystroke, it wants to say to the CPU, "HEY! STOP EVERYTHING! COME SERVICE ME **NOW** BEFORE

THE USER PRESSES ANOTHER KEY!!!!" And so it "rings the bell"—it activates its interrupt line, and the CPU stops doing whatever it's doing and executes the program that moves the keystroke to the keyboard buffer.

PCs since the AT have all been equipped with a second 8259, bringing the total of interrupts on most PCs up to 16. You can see the common uses for that in Table 10.3.

If you're installing a board, and it needs an IRQ, look first to IRQ2 on a PC or IRQ5 on an AT. If those aren't available, try 3—if you don't have a COM2, there's no conflict.

Conflicts on COM Ports: "Sharing Interrupts" Examined

I've already said a couple of times in this book that you can have COM1 or COM3, but not both, and that you can have COM2 or COM4, but not both. *Now* I can explain it.

As you saw in the preceding interrupt table, IRQ3 is assigned both to COM2 and to COM4. So if you had both COM2 and COM4, they'd have to share IRQ3.

The problem with that scenario is that sharing interrupts isn't possible on many PC add-in cards. Blame it on the ISA bus; it does not support sharing IRQs. In fact, it's unlikely but possible that inserting two boards using the same IRQ level into the same ISA-based system could permanently damage both boards.

Newer buses allow for IRQ sharing: MCA, EISA, PC Card, and PCI bus slots all allow interrupt sharing, if the boards going into those slots are designed to accommodate shared interrupts—but not all are, unfortunately. VESA doesn't support it. The preponderance of ISA and VESA systems out there means that for most of us, IRQ sharing is out. So where did COM3 and COM4 come from? The original PS/2 machines were designed with, of course, an MCA bus, and so IBM saw that a third party could design an add-in card that offered a third and perhaps fourth serial port. They wanted software support for it, so DOS 3.3—the version of DOS released with the PS/2 in April 1987—included support for COM3 and COM4. People started asking for it, and so vendors built COM3/

TABLE 10.3

Common IRQ Uses in the PC Family

INTERRUPT LINE	DEVICE	COMMENTS
0	Timer	
1	Keyboard	
2	Cascade to IRQ9	On some systems, IRQ2 is the gateway to IRQs 9–15; avoid it if possible.
3	COM2	Can also be COM4, but only one of the two.
4	COM1	Can also be COM3, but only one of the two.
5	XT hard disk controller, LPT2	Hard disk interface used only on XTs, or alternatively for LPT2 on the unusual machine with LPT2. This is free on most modern PCs, and is the "catch-all" IRQ for bus mice, sound cards, LAN boards, etc.
6	Floppy disk controller	
7	LPT1	
8	Clock	
9	Possible cascade to IRQ2	May not be available; see text.
10		Generally available.
11		Generally available.
12	Motherboard InPort	If your PC/laptop has a built-in mouse port, it probably sits here.
13	Coprocessor	This interrupt is required even if your CPU has a numeric coprocessor built in.
14	Hard Disk	
15	Unused	Generally available.

COM4 support into their machines, even though it was a silly idea on an ISA board.

> **NOTE**
>
> If you have a mixed-bus system, like PCI and ISA, or EISA and ISA, then if ISA uses an interrupt, you can't share it through the advanced bus. For example, if an ISA board uses IRQ3, then none of the EISA boards can use IRQ3. On the other hand, if in that case no ISA board used IRQ4, then any number of EISA boards could use IRQ4—they could, that is, if the boards were designed to share IRQs, *and* if the *drivers* for the boards supported interrupt sharing. (How can you find out? It'll be in the documentation. Unfortunately, there are very few add-in cards that support IRQ sharing.)

IRQ 2 and IRQs 9 through 15

A lot of people buy themselves grief by putting their network cards on IRQ2. Don't do it. IRQ2 was available back on the 8-bit PC/XT type designs, but it serves a valuable role in modern PCs.

The PC/XT systems had a single interrupt controller, an Intel 8259 chip. The 8259 could support up to eight interrupt channels, and the original PC/XT systems hard-wired channels 0 and 1 to the system timer (a clock circuit that goes tick every 15 ms) and the 8042 keyboard controller.

The system was wired with those interrupts because IBM wanted to make sure that the keyboard and the timer had high priorities; you recall that on an 8259, when two interrupts occur at the same time, the one with the lower number gets priority.

In 1984, the first 16-bit PC compatible system was released—the IBM AT. The proliferation of add-in devices on the market made it clear that eight interrupt levels just wasn't enough. So, as I've mentioned before, IBM decided to add another 8259. The problem was that just slapping the extra 8259 onto the motherboard might present some backward-compatibility problems, so IBM decided to kind of slip in the extra 8259 via the back door, as you can see in Figure 10.16.

FIGURE 10.16

Adding an extra 8259
for more IRQ levels

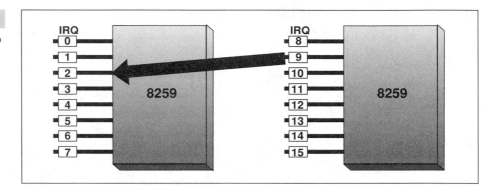

The way they did it was to take the new IRQs 8 through 15 and route them through IRQ9, then connect IRQ9 to IRQ2. Result: Whenever IRQ8 through 15 is triggered, IRQ9 goes off, which makes IRQ2 look like *it* went off. The PC's BIOS then knows that whenever IRQ2 appears, that *really* means to check the second 8259 to find out which IRQ *really* rang the bell. By the way, they also freed up IRQ5; it's no longer needed by your AT-or-later hard disk controller.

Some Advice on Choosing IRQs

This implies a few things. First, don't use IRQ2, as it already has a job: it's the gateway to IRQs 8-15. Many people set their network cards to IRQ2 and then wonder why their system randomly hangs. If you *do* use IRQ2 for some circuit board, then you may have some driver software set to IRQ9. IRQ9 and IRQ2 are electrically equal under this system, as they're tied together.

It also means that it's a good idea to avoid IRQ9, if you can.

Other things to consider when choosing interrupts:

- Because interrupts 8 through 15 slide into the architecture via IRQ2, they essentially inherit IRQ2's priority level. That means that IRQs 8 through 15 are of higher priority than IRQs 3 through 7.

- Safe IRQs are 5, 10, 11, and 15; avoid the others. You'll probably need to use these for your:

  - Sound card. If it's an 8-bit card, then your only option is IRQ5.
  - A LAN board.
  - SCSI host adapter, although some bus mastering SCSI host adapters (like the Adaptec 2742) can actually forgo interrupts, needing only a DMA channel.

NOTE Whatever you set your boards to, *write it down!* You'll need the information later.

Earlier, I suggested taping an envelope to the side of a PC and keeping important floppies there. Here are some other things to put in there. Each time I install a board (or modify an existing board), I get a new piece of paper and write down all the configuration information on the board; for example, I might note "Intel EtherExpress 16 card installed 10 July 1994 by Mark Minasi; no EPROM on board, shared memory disabled, IRQ10 used, I/O address 310 set." The Device Manager can help here, as it will print out a report of the hardware in your system; I'll discuss that later in this chapter.

I've mentioned this earlier, in the I/0 address discussion, but let me repeat: some boards don't have jumpers and DIP switches. This means that *there is no way to get them to work with conflicting boards*. For example, a client that I regularly visited had installed an IBM 5251 (System 36 terminal emulator) board and an old Quadram Quadboard in a PC. The printer port on the Quadboard and the terminal emulator wanted the same resource—which one, I'm not sure. In any case, neither had jumpers. One had to be thrown away. Moral: Find out if the expansion boards that you buy have adjustable DMA, IRQ, and I/O addresses.

I hesitate to mention this, but sometimes device conflicts can be solved by doing surgery on the boards. Just lobotomize the chips that are performing the function you wish to defeat. An example I have seen a couple of times is in serial ports. A client wanted me to set up a multifunction board in a PC with clock, memory, printer, and serial ports. He already had a board installed which provided both serial ports COM1 and COM2. The jumpers on the multifunction board allowed me to set the multifunction board's serial port to either COM1 or COM2, but not disable it altogether. What to do? A chip called the 8250 UART (Universal Asynchronous Receiver/Transmitter) is the heart of most serial ports. I found the 8250 on the multifunction board and removed it. The problem was eliminated. *Please don't try this unless you understand what you are doing.*

ROM Addresses and RAM Buffers

In addition to I/O addresses, DMA channels, and IRQ lines, there is a fourth source of conflict: ROM addresses. Some controller cards (like EGAs and hard disk controllers) require some ROM onboard to hold some low-level code. The XT controller board's ROM started at C800:0000. As before, a possibility exists that two different boards may require some software on board, and if the two boards *both* try to locate their ROM at the same location in the PC's memory address space, neither one will work.

Fortunately, some boards include jumpers to allow you to move the start address of the ROM. Most of the major boards that include ROM, like the EGA, VGA, XT-type hard disk controller, and the like, should *not* have (if it's even possible) their ROM addresses changed. Too many pieces of software rely on their standard addresses. The boards you'll see that typically include ROM are:

- Video boards, which have ROMs addressed at either address C0000 or E0000. It's usually not a good idea to move these addresses around.

- High-performance disk interfaces, which, like 32-bit IDE host adapters or SCSI host adapters, have ROMs on them; these ROMs can be moved if the board permits.

- Token Ring network adapters, which have some ROM on them; it is moveable.

- Any kind of LAN board can have ROM on it, if the PC boots from the network and not from its local hard disk. It's unusual, but some companies use this "diskless workstation" approach.

- Some high-end sound boards may have ROM on them; the ROMs contain prerecorded sounds, like samples of pianos, violins, or flutes.

- All PCs have some ROM at the top 64K of the first megabyte, the memory range from F0000 through FFFFF.

There are two things to be concerned about when configuring memory on add-in cards. First is the obvious one: Make sure that two different boards don't have memory configured to the same address.

The second thing you have to be concerned about is the effect of adapter memory on your *DOS memory manager*. Memory managers must know exactly which areas of memory are already filled up with adapter RAM or ROM, or the memory manager will overwrite the RAM or ROM, causing lots of potential system failures.

Most adapter RAM and ROM ranges vary, so I can't document them for you here, but you can see the unchanging ranges in Table 10.4.

Note the PCMCIA reference: PC Cards can take up to 64K of memory, and if you have two PC Card slots, that can mean that the entire C0000 through DFFFF range is taken.

	FUNCTION	ADDRESS RANGE (HEX)	ADDRESS LENGTH
TABLE 10.4 Common ROM and RAM Buffer Addresses	XT Hard Disk Controller	C8000–CBFFF	16K
	EGA	C0000–C3FFF	16K
	VGA	C0000–C7FFF or E0000–E7FFF	32K
	LIM Boards (may vary)	D0000–DFFFF	64K

Resolving Installation Conflicts: An Example

I'll provide you with as many installation examples as I can. Later, we'll look at the installation documentation for a few boards. But before we go on, I'd like to relate a few brief examples of installation problems and solutions that I encountered while putting a half-dozen Ethernet LAN boards into some computers. These things happened to me under DOS and older Windows, but the moral of the stories remain the same: Be careful when installing hardware.

The first LAN card I installed was an Ethernet board that used everything we've discussed—an I/O address range, a DMA channel, an IRQ channel, and some shared RAM. I left the I/O address at 300 hex, as that wouldn't conflict with the computer into which I was installing the board. The IRQ I chose was IRQ5, avoiding the more commonly used IRQ2. I avoid IRQ2 because it *can* be used in some systems, but the fact that it cascades to IRQs 8 through 15 makes me a bit nervous; in the past, using IRQ2 has caused conflicts with Windows. I set the DMA to channel 1, and put the shared RAM between CC000 through CFFFF, as I knew that it would not then conflict with the hard disk controller ROM between C8000 and CBFFF.

When I plugged the board in, however, it refused to function. A little fiddling around made me realize that the DOS memory manager that I was using was placing its memory at the same addresses as the shared memory on my LAN board, which in turn was clobbering the LAN board. I told the memory manager to exclude the range of addresses from CC000-CFFFF; the board worked fine after that. In Windows, you'd do that with the Device Manager, which I'll show you shortly.

I set the second board identically, and it refused to work. A quick check of my notebook reminded me that a sound board was using IRQ5, causing a conflict. The LAN board offered only IRQs 2 through 7, and I didn't want to use any of them, as I'd like to avoid 2 if I can, and 3 through 7 were busy, so I needed an alternative approach. A quick look at the sound board showed that it could support any IRQ up to IRQ10, so I reset the sound board to IRQ10, leaving IRQ5 free for the LAN board. Problem solved.

Trouble appeared on the next machine as well. After inserting the LAN board, not only did the LAN board not work, the video screen showed some odd colors upon bootup. It was a special Windows accelerator board, so I checked its documentation. The accelerator, as it turned out, employed the I/O address range 300 through 30F, causing a conflict with the Ethernet card. I reset the I/O address on the Ethernet card, and all was well with *that* machine.

The next computer booted up okay, but I got strange flickers on the video screen whenever I tried to test the Ethernet card with the test program supplied with the Ethernet board. The Ethernet card was failing its tests, also, so I looked more closely, and realized that I'd never opened this particular computer before.

This computer was equipped with a super VGA board. Almost all super VGA boards have an autoswitching feature that they'll optionally support, a feature whereby they automatically detect what video mode the currently running software needs, and then switch to that mode. This feature should be disabled, for two reasons. First, it causes OS/2 and Windows NT to fail, as well as a number of other programs. Second, the autoswitch mode requires that the video board use a combination of interrupts 2 and 9, which is less than desirable because it steals a much needed interrupt; in some cases, it causes a system to falsely report memory error. This super VGA card, as you can imagine by now, had the interrupt enabled, allowing for super VGA. I removed the interrupt jumper from the board—its location varies, and you must consult the documentation for your board before trying to remove the interrupt jumper. The Ethernet board ran without a hitch afterward. By the way, if you *are* planning to check your super VGA documentation to find out whether the interrupt is enabled, be aware that some manuals refer only to the interrupt and some refer only to autoswitching. If you can't find one, look for the other.

By now, as I approached the final machine, I was trying to *anticipate* problems. The LAN board placed in this last machine, like its comrades, refused to work at first. I struggled with this for a while, idly running diagnostic programs on the entire system. As I've explained before, I reasoned that if I could figure out what *didn't* work on this system that had worked *yesterday*, that would give me a clue about what the board was conflicting with. (Of course, there was the possibility that the board just plain didn't work, but the earlier experiences of the day seemed to render that doubtful.) Then I noticed that the diagnostic programs failed to notice that the PC had a mouse. Eureka! I recalled at that moment that this particular machine didn't have a serial mouse, unlike most machines in my office—it had a *bus* mouse. A bus mouse requires an interrupt-using circuit board of its own, and I was fairly sure that I'd set the interrupt on the bus mouse interface board to IRQ5. Not wanting to remove the cover from the PC unless necessary, I tried loading the mouse driver, and got the error message "interrupt jumper missing." I opened up the PC, checked the mouse board, and sure enough, it was using IRQ5. With its interrupt changed, I replaced the mouse board, and the last of the LAN boards was fired up and ready to go.

I don't want to discourage you with this story. I just want to underscore how important it is to keep documentation of what's installed in your current machines, and to share a war story with you that may give you an idea or two the next time you're having trouble making a new board behave.

Soft Setup versus Hard Setup Boards

How do you select one interrupt over another? On older boards, you flip DIP switches or move jumpers. On more and more boards, however, you run a program to control these settings.

If you get a board that has no switches, that is only set up with a diskette, then is that a Plug and Play (PnP) board? No, not necessarily. Plug and Play refers to a particular method of building a board, a way that does, indeed, use software configuration—but not every board that uses software configuration is a Plug and Play board.

Installing and Configuring New Boards with 95

Let's get down to the brass tacks of putting a board into 95 and making it work. The three parts of doing that are:

- Installing the board and physically placing it inside the machine.
- Configuring the board's resources.
- Finding, loading, and configuring a driver for the board.

In the ideal world, you just install a board, Windows detects it, and all is well. Sometimes that even *happens*, but usually there are complications. Answer these questions before installing a board:

- Does Windows have a driver for the board right there on its CD? Check the WinNews area of CompuServe or the Microsoft Network for a listing of the supported hardware. Whether your copy of Windows will support a particular board is determined partially by which Tune-up Packs you have installed in Windows, if any.

- Is the board Plug and Play? If not, make sure you know how to set its resources. If the board is Plug and Play, but your system isn't, *then enable Plug and Play anyway*. Windows 95 can often take control of the configuration of a Plug and Play board even if the BIOS doesn't support Plug and Play. (One example of this is the Intel Ethernet Pro cards. Even though they're ISA Plug and Play cards, you can stick them into any machine and Windows 95 will set the board's IRQ and I/O addresses. That's because the Ether Pro card isn't a *boot* device, at least not for most people. You get much of the power of Plug and Play on a non-PnP system for cards that aren't boot devices.)

- If there isn't a driver right on the CD, is there a Windows 95-compatible driver? If not, you can try a real-mode driver, but I don't recommend it.

The 95 Hardware Installation Roadmap

The most important question about hardware installation under Windows is, "Does the board support Plug and Play?"

Handling Plug and Play Hardware

If the board is Plug and Play, then there's usually not much to do—just plug it in and Windows will detect it. The worst thing that may happen is that Windows won't have the driver for it, so you'll have to supply a disk. In some cases, the system is complex enough that Windows can't make the board work on the first boot. If that's the case, try booting Windows two or three more times, giving the Windows Configuration Manager a chance to shuffle resources around. If things *still* don't work, then treat the Plug and Play board like a legacy board, as covered below.

Slight digression here: Not everything that claims to be Plug and Play *is*. For example, all PCI boards are *supposed* to be Plug and Play, but I've run into some troubles with PCI boards, particularly since they often do not ship with a configuration disk. These boards seem to *assume* that you'll be running them in a PnP system with a PnP operating system like Windows 95. Boards that have been tested to work in a Windows 95 environment and are Plug and Play are often indicated by a *Windows 95 Ready* sticker on their boxes.

NOTE And one other thing about Plug and Play boards: Don't forget that a certain percentage of new circuit boards are just plain no good. I've never seen a figure on it, but twenty years of experience with microcomputers has led me to expect that about ten percent of the add-in cards are dead right out of the box.

What that means is that you're going to need some kind of test program, and, at least at the moment, the majority of board-level diagnostic programs are DOS-based. While most DOS-based diagnostics will work fine under Windows 95 in command-line safe mode, a few will not—for example, 3Com advises that the diagnostic program they have available as of this writing is not designed for use in this mode in Windows 95 and will not work. So keep a bootable DOS floppy around, just in case.

Handling Non-Plug and Play Boards

Installing a non-PnP board may pose some more trouble.

First of all, typically you have to set its resources so that it doesn't interfere with an existing board—no IRQ, DMA, I/O, or memory address conflicts. *Do that before you run Windows*.

For example, suppose you're installing a sound card. Sound cards often require a few I/O ranges, an IRQ level, and a DMA channel or two. Once you install the card, you have to make sure that the card doesn't step on the resources of any existing boards. If you just shove the board into the system, turn it on, and boot Windows, then you may get some nasty error messages (for example, if the built-in factory settings on the board conflict with your network board), and the conflict that you've just created will keep you from getting onto the network. Instead, try booting Windows to Safe Mode Command Prompt and set the resources from there.

Again, just a reminder: How you set resources for a board depends on the board. Some use jumpers and DIP switches, and others use software setup—you'd only use Safe Mode Command Prompt if you needed to run a software setup routine. And when you're finished setting resources on a board, *write them down*.

Next, you must first get Windows to recognize that the hardware is installed, and second, tell the Windows drivers what resources the board is using. Windows will often be able to figure out the resources, but you can hand-enter them with the Device Manager, as I'll describe in a few pages; for now, let's see how to get Windows to recognize the new board.

Windows has a set of excellent hardware detection routines, and it can detect about 80 percent (my figure, not Microsoft's) of the non-Plug and Play boards around. That's a staggering piece of work, and my hat's off to whoever wrote the code. In some cases, the hardware detection code is assisted by Windows 3.x, which means that if you were running Windows 3.x when you installed Windows 95, the 95 setup program just queried any existing 3.x drivers about the existence of add-in cards.

You may find, however, that you have to *tell* Windows that you have a new piece of hardware, and exactly what kind of hardware it is. You do that with the Hardware Installation Wizard, in the Control Panel. Open the Control Panel, and then double-click on Add New Hardware. You'll see a dialog box like in Figure 10.17.

Click Next, and you'll see the next screen, as in Figure 10.18.

Again, Windows has some nifty detection hardware, and it wants to show it off here—but *don't*. The detection software must, by its very nature, do some mildly risky things, things that *could* lock up your system or, in the worst case, damage data on your hard disk. Detection's fine for the whole-sale hardware driver installation that occurs upon the initial Windows setup—and you, of course, backed up your data prior to installing Windows, so data loss isn't an issue. But if all you're doing is installing a mouse or a sound board, then you *know* what kind of hardware it is; after all, you just installed it. Click No, then Next, and you'll see a dialog box like in Figure 10.19.

FIGURE 10.17

Add New Hardware Wizard

FIGURE 10.18

Add New Hardware
Wizard, detecting
the hardware

FIGURE 10.19

Manually selecting
the hardware

NOTE

I guess I haven't underscored this point before, but you'd go through this process for virtually *any* new hardware, not just a board; for example, you'd use this to add a new mouse, printer, or modem. If you know the name of the hardware manufacturer but aren't sure how to classify the board, then choose *Other devices*; it's a listing of all of the drivers, but is organized by manufacturer.

Once you click Next, you'll enter an installation module that's specific to the particular piece of hardware that you're installing. You may have to fill in device names, as is the case with network cards or printers, and you may have to fill in resource information, perhaps IRQs, I/O addresses, or memory addresses. Then the system will reboot, and the board will usually work. The only other possibility is that Windows may not have the driver for the board, in which case you'll have to supply the diskette with the board driver. Once you've done that, don't forget to use the Device Manager to tell the driver what resources the new board uses; see the upcoming section "Modifying Hardware Resources" to see how.

Speaking of drivers, however, it wouldn't hurt to check to see if there are more up-to-date drivers available for your new add-in board. Most vendors have a bulletin board, or, for those who are connected to the Internet, an ftp site. In the majority of the cases where I've installed a new board, I've found that the vendor has newer drivers available than the ones that came in the box.

To update a driver for an already installed device, use the Device Manager.

Running the Device Manager

Once you have your hardware configuration set up, you'll sometimes need to examine it or modify it. You can do that, with the Device Manager (DM). You get to the Device Manager by opening up the Control Panel, double-clicking on the System icon, and then choosing the Device Manager tab. You'll see a dialog box that looks like Figure 10.20.

FIGURE 10.20

Control Panel's
Device Manager

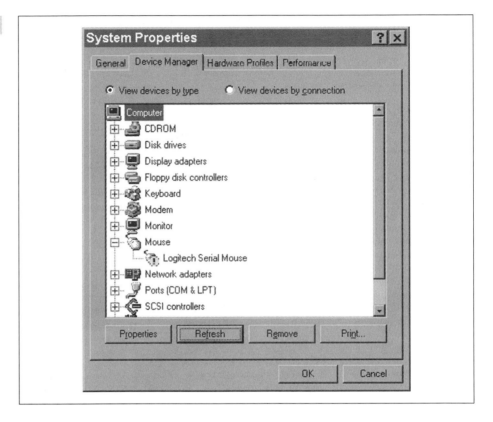

FIGURE 10.20

Control Panel's
Device Manager

The Computer icon branches off into the different kinds of devices on
your system. Any malfunctioning devices are expanded and highlighted
with a yellow or red exclamation point icon to indicate some kind of failure. In the example above, you see that in the Mouse devices category, my
Logitech Serial Mouse is failing in some way. (In this case, it's nothing to
worry about. The problem is that I'm using the Logitech Sensa mouse; it
works fine, but there's no driver for it, so I'm using the old Windows 3.x
drivers, and Windows 95 is complaining about it.)

You'll use the Device Manager to do a number of things:

- The DM will let you remove a device from your Windows
  configuration.

- The DM spotlights troublesome hardware, as you saw in the previous example.

- You use the DM to tell Windows what resources (I/O addresses, DMA channels, IRQ levels, RAM addresses, and ROM addresses) a board uses, if the board isn't Plug and Play.

- You use the DM to install an updated device driver.

- The DM will print out a summary of your system's hardware.

Removing a device is easy; just click the device then click Remove. Ask the Device Manager to print out a system summary with Print, and you'll see a report like the one in Figure 10.21.

FIGURE 10.21

A system summary provided by Device Manager

```
Resource Summary Report
******************** SYSTEM SUMMARY ********************
Windows version: 4.00.950
Computer Name: Poorly designed clone
Processor Type: Pentium
System BUS Type: ISA
BIOS Name: American Megatrends
BIOS Date: 12/15/93
BIOS Version: Unknown
Machine Type: IBM PC/AT
Math Co-processor: Present
Registered Owner: Mark Minasi
Registered Company: Mark Minasi and Company
******************** IRQ SUMMARY ********************
IRQ Usage Summary:
   00 - System timer
   01 - Standard 101/102-Key or Microsoft Natural Keyboard
   02 - Programmable interrupt controller
   03 - Communications Port (COM2)
   04 - Communications Port (COM1)
   05 - Creative Labs Sound Blaster 16 or AWE-32
   06 - Standard Floppy Disk Controller
   08 - System CMOS/real time clock
   09 - Adaptec AHA-294X/AIC-78XX PCI SCSI Controller
   11 - Intel EtherExpress PRO/10 (PnP Enabled)
   13 - Numeric data processor
******************** IO PORT SUMMARY ********************
I/O Port Usage Summary:
   0000h-n-000Fh - Direct memory access controller
   0020h-n-0021h - Programmable interrupt controller
   0040h-n-0043h - System timer
   0060h-n-0060h - Standard 101/102-Key or Microsoft Natural Keyboard
   0061h-n-0061h - System speaker
   0064h-n-0064h - Standard 101/102-Key or Microsoft Natural Keyboard
   0070h-n-0071h - System CMOS/real time clock
   0081h-n-0083h - Direct memory access controller
   0087h-n-0087h - Direct memory access controller
   0089h-n-008Bh - Direct memory access controller
   008Fh-n-008Fh - Direct memory access controller
   00A0h-n-00A1h - Programmable interrupt controller
   00C0h-n-00DFh - Direct memory access controller
   00F0h-n-00FFh - Numeric data processor
   0201h-n-0201h - Gameport Joystick
   0210h-n-021Fh - Intel EtherExpress PRO/10 (PnP Enabled)
```

FIGURE 10.21

A system summary
provided by Device
Manager (continued)

```
    0220h-n-022Fh - Creative Labs Sound Blaster 16 or AWE-32
    0270h-n-0273h - IO read data port for ISA Plug and Play enumerator
    02F8h-n-02FFh - Communications Port (COM2)
    0300h-n-0301h - Creative Labs Sound Blaster 16 or AWE-32
    0378h n 037Ah - Printer Port (LPT1)
    0388h-n-038Bh - Creative Labs Sound Blaster 16 or AWE-32
    03B0h-n-03BBh - ATI Graphics Pro Turbo PCI (mach64)
    03C0h-n-03DFh - ATI Graphics Pro Turbo PCI (mach64)
    03F2h-n-03F5h - Standard Floppy Disk Controller
    03F8h-n-03FFh - Communications Port (COM1)
    FF00h-n-FFFFh - Adaptec AHA-294X/AIC-78XX PCI SCSI Controller
******************** UPPER MEMORY USAGE SUMMARY********************
Memory Usage Summary:
    000A0000h-n-000AFFFFh - ATI Graphics Pro Turbo PCI (mach64)
    000B0000h-n-000BFFFFh - ATI Graphics Pro Turbo PCI (mach64)
    000C0000h-n-000C7FFFh - ATI Graphics Pro Turbo PCI (mach64)
    000C8000h-n-000CA7FFh - Adaptec AHA-294X/AIC-78XX PCI SCSI Controller
    A0000000h-n-A07FFFFFh - ATI Graphics Pro Turbo PCI (mach64)
    FFBFF000h-n-FFBFFFFFh - Adaptec AHA-294X/AIC-78XX PCI SCSI Controller
******************** DMA USAGE SUMMARY ********************
DMA Channel Usage Summary:
    01 - Creative Labs Sound Blaster 16 or AWE-32
    02 - Standard Floppy Disk Controller
    04 - Direct memory access controller
    05 - Creative Labs Sound Blaster 16 or AWE-32
```

NOTE

By the way, I often get asked, "How did you get that printout
into your document?" Simple: I installed a printer called Generic
TTY and printed to a file. The result was an ASCII file that I could
easily incorporate into a word processing document.

Now, for years, I've been teaching classes in DOS memory management,
and I've been telling people *not* to believe printouts like the one above.
The reason for that is that software can't be trusted to completely detect
hardware, as I suggested when I advised you to not let Windows detect your new hardware. However, I'm going to modify my "don't let software tell you about hardware" advice here: You *can* trust the Device
Manager's reports for hardware you're *using*. As I've said before, the nice
thing about hardware support for Windows 95 is that all the drivers are
in one place, and that place—the Registry—is where the Device Manager
goes to extract its information. If the hardware is working, then you can
trust the Device Manager. In my case, since my sound board is making
noise and recording things correctly, then I trust the reported information
about the sound card. As the video board is working, I trust the video
board information, and so on.

But I still don't trust the DM completely. If I had installed a LAN card and the card wasn't working, then I wouldn't trust anything the DM was telling me about the LAN card. Also, my computer has an Intel Smart Video Recorder Pro in it, complete with functioning drivers. The Pro is set at I/O address 350, IRQ15, and even *works*—albeit with old Windows 3.x drivers—but nary a word of it in the Device Manager report.

Modifying Hardware Resources

Once you've installed a non-Plug and Play card, you have to set its resources, both on the board and in the drivers.

Updating Device Drivers

Device drivers are an ever-changing thing. LAN board drivers, printer drivers, video drivers, and mouse drivers are four pieces of software that seem to change a few times a year. One of the things that you can do to make your system more reliable is to check with your hardware's vendors periodically to see if they've updated their drivers. Then you should get the new drivers, either by ordering them directly from the manufacturer or by downloading them from a manufacturer bulletin board, a communications service like CompuServe, or off an Internet ftp site.

Once you have an updated driver, you can tell Windows 95 to use it in this way:

1. Open up the Device Manager.
2. Click on the particular device whose driver you want to update.
3. Click on Properties. You'll see a dialog box like the following one.

For this example, I've chosen my display adapter. Be aware that, for some reason, you won't see a Driver tab for every piece of hardware. On my computer, I found a Driver tab for my sound card, SCSI adapter, display card, joystick, mouse, parallel and serial ports, and keyboard. In contrast, there wasn't a driver tab for the floppy drives, network card, CD-ROM, modem, or monitor. In most cases, that isn't a problem—I'm not aware of alternative floppy or monitor drivers—but for the modem and network cards, that implies that you refresh the drivers by deleting the modem or

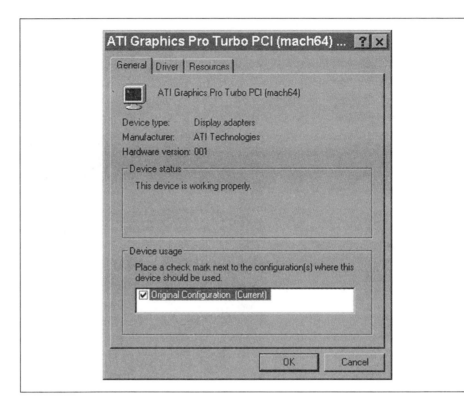

the card and then reinstalling it with the new driver; this is a somewhat cumbersome process.

By the way, since I've mentioned updating network drivers, here's an important tip: For some reason, when you delete a board and then reinstall it, the protocols get reinstalled but the client software doesn't. As a result, all of your persistent connections don't work, which leads to panic, unhappiness, and the like. Just take steps to make sure the client software is reinstalled, and all will be well.

Now, to continue:

4. Click on the Driver tab, and you'll see a dialog box like the following:

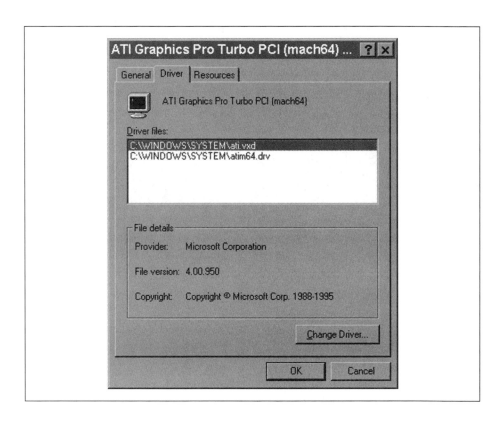

5. Now all you have to do is to click Change Driver, and yet another dialog will appear. Click *Have disk...*, insert the diskette with the new driver (or direct the dialog box to the directory with the new driver), and you will update the driver.

Working with Plug and Play Systems

One of the two or three most important things about Windows 95 is its support of the Plug and Play architecture. The idea with Plug and Play is that when you install a board into a Plug and Play-compliant system, the system would:

1. Recognize the board. ("This is an Adaptec 2942W SCSI host adapter.")

2. Ask the board what IRQs, DMAs, I/O addresses, RAM addresses, and ROM addresses it needs. ("It requires an interrupt, a 256-byte block of I/O addresses, and a 16K ROM range.")

3. Ask the board what range of IRQs, DMAs, I/O addresses, RAM addresses, and ROM addresses it can *use*. ("It can use IRQ 5, 7, 9, 10, 11, or 14, any 256-byte block from address 60K to 64K, and any ROM address from C0000 to E0000.")

4. Set those things (IRQ, etc.) so that they don't conflict with anything already in the system.

5. Ask the board for identification information, which the system can then use to tell the operating system to search for and configure the necessary drivers.

This is a step better than the basic software setup boards, because with them you have to run the setup program. With Plug and Play, in contrast, you don't do anything (in theory, anyway); you just insert the board.

In 1993, Microsoft, Intel, and Compaq proposed the standard called Plug and Play. The idea behind PnP is that board manufacturers would add circuitry to their add-in boards so that the automatic setup and the resource query (resource here means IRQ, DMA, I/O address, ROM address, or RAM buffer address) capabilities of EISA and Micro Channel would become available to machines with ISA buses. The PC's operating system could then configure and query boards directly, eliminating the need to pop the top of the PC except when actually removing or inserting a board.

The *catch* about Plug and Play is that you can't retrofit it on an existing system; it has to be built into a computer when you buy it. Furthermore, you must have an operating system, as I mentioned a page or two back, that *understands* Plug and Play, or you won't get most of Plug and Play's benefits. Of course, if you're this far along in the book, though, you know you're okay, as Windows 95 is a Plug and Play operating system.

To "do" Plug and Play, you must have:

- A system with a Plug and Play BIOS. This must be a *flash memory* because that's where the system configuration information is kept.

- A system with a Plug and Play motherboard. (Plug and Play supports the old ISA bus and the PCI bus mainly; running full Plug and Play compliancy on an EISA or Micro Channel machine may require an extra piece of software called an *EISA configuration manager* or a *Micro Channel configuration manager*. So far as I know, however, there is no EISA, MCA, or VESA Plug and Play specification; any cards in those buses will fall into the legacy category.)

- An operating system with Plug and Play support.

- Add-in cards that are Plug and Play-compliant.

So if you have an older computer that isn't Plug and Play compatible, then you can't, well, *play*. You'll need a new computer. Even if you *do* have a Plug and Play system, then you must also buy Plug and Play compatible add-in cards, and they're a mite scarce at this time.

Let's first define the parameters of Plug and Play. What is it, and what *isn't* it?

First of all, it does not unify existing software setup programs. If you have ISA boards in a Plug and Play system that have their own software setup routines (for example, most LAN or sound boards), then you'll still have to keep track of the disks containing those programs. Plug and Play can't help you there. It controls Plug and Play compatible boards only; the other guys are left out in the cold.

Why is this? I don't know. I once argued to a Plug and Play designer that Plug and Play should unify software setup, providing some way for all boards that are set up with programs to come under one roof. "It's a good idea," he conceded, "but it's not in the spec." Maybe next version.

Booting on Plug and Play Systems

What do you need to make a system Plug and Play *compatible*? First of all, a Plug and Play-compatible motherboard. These are motherboards with a BIOS that understands Plug and Play, and that also contain about 16K of *nonvolatile storage* (*NVS*). One easy way to implement this is by putting the NVS in amongst the BIOS code, which means using a *flash BIOS*; more and more systems do that these days.

You also must have add-in cards that are Plug and Play compatible. These cards are configured *every time you boot*, and that configuration is done by a routine called the *Configuration Manager* (*CM*). The CM can either be part of the BIOS, or a program loaded off disk. In order for maximum compatibility, however, the CM should be part of the BIOS.

In the ideal world (that is, everything is Plug and Play), the system powers up and the CM assumes control. It asks each board what resources it needs, and what is the range of resources that it will accept. (For example, a board might say, "I need an IRQ, and I'll take either 2, 3, 4, or 5," in the same way that the Microsoft ISA bus mouse interface does; even though there are other interrupts, its circuitry for some reason will only accept an IRQ in the range of 2 to 5.) The CM then assigns resources to cards, avoiding conflicts.

NOTE
> This means that potentially installing one new Plug and Play card to a Plug and Play system could cause all of the other cards to move their resources around. What does that mean for the network, SCSI, sound, and other board drivers, which must know which resources those boards use? Well, it implies that device drivers have to be a bit smarter than they are now.

For example, any client on a Windows NT network has a file called PRO-TOCOL.INI on its hard disk. In that file are often references like IRQ=10, IOBASE=300, and so on. On a Plug and Play system, the network software must take its cues from the CM.

Once all boards are taken care of, then the system boots in the usual way. The main difference of Plug and Play is that the whole process of hardware shuffling of resources (I/O addresses, DMA channels, RAM windows, and the like) happens every time you boot the system, and (one hopes) quickly and invisibly.

Oh, by the way, can you force a particular board to a particular resource? Yes—that's called *locking* the resource. The CM on your system should allow that, or your operating system might; Windows 95 lets you do it with the Device Manager, which is in the Control Panel.

How Plug and Play Handles Older Boards

This sounds good, but suppose there are non-Plug and Play boards in the system. (The term in the business is *legacy boards*, as if they were some kind of evil inheritance.) How does the CM know to avoid the resources that those boards have already taken up?

Well, the CM needs some help finding this out. For an ISA system, it gets help when you punch in the values into a program called the *ISA Configuration Utility*, or *ICU*.

More and more ISA boards ship with a helper file for EISA systems in the form of a `.CFG` file. Recall that `.CFG` files ship with EISA boards so that the EISA configuration program can set up the EISA board, but that it's a good idea to create `.CFG`s for ISA boards as well; some ISA boards ship with the files.

You'd think that Plug and Play would read EISA and Micro Channel configurations, but it doesn't. For an EISA system, you'll need a modified version of your EISA setup routine, an *EISA Configuration Utility* (*ECU*). Plug and Play even uses a superset of the EISA configuration storage format. Micro Channel machines, correspondingly, will have an *MCU*.

Plug and Play on Non-PCI Machines

All of this Plug and Play magic relies a lot on the PCI bus and the fact that PCI cards are extremely self-aware, knowing right in their hardware what resources they need. Does that mean that it's impossible to do Plug and Play on an ISA machine? No.

There is an ISA Plug and Play specification which provides for ISA-based motherboards that, again, only require a bit more hardware: a smarter BIOS and some NVS.

The way that Plug and Play ISA works is a kind of sneaky trick. The CM needs a way to get the Plug and Play ISA-aware cards to identify themselves. It does this by sending out a query on I/O address 279, which is normally part of LPT2. Now, address 279 is a printer status port address for LPT2, and is read-only within the LPT2 specification. The CM writes data to that location and waits for a response. If they're present, the Plug and Play ISA cards respond.

How Does a System Know If It Is Plug and Play Compatible?

I recently went a few rounds with a vendor who'd sold me a supposedly Plug and Play compatible system. The vendor claimed that its system was Plug and Play compatible. Windows 95 disagreed, as did Intel's Configuration Manager software. The vendor had inserted a line in the BIOS startup that said "Intel Plug and Play Extensions version 2.2," however, and felt that ended the argument. So I checked the specification. There are several things that identify a Plug and Play system:

- The string $PnP should appear somewhere between 960K and 1024K, F0000–FFFF.

- The string ACFG should appear somewhere in the 896–960K range, E0000–EFFFF.

- The NVS (non-volatile storage) is typically somewhere around the ED000 range. The NVS is preceded by the standard 55AA signature so memory managers will skip it.

The system had none of those, so I won the argument. Again, be careful when buying Plug and Play systems, at least for a few years.

Solving Hardware Installation Problems

What do you do if you've loaded some driver that the system absolutely relies upon—a video driver is an excellent example—and you loaded it wrong, or it's faulty? And you can't even get the system to boot?

In that case, remember safe mode. Just start up Windows 95, wait for the "Starting Windows 95..." message, and press F8. You'll see a menu with several options, including Safe Mode. Boot to that, access the Device Manager, and change back to the driver that you trust. Or boot to Safe Mode Command Prompt, and run the DOS-based diagnostic to be sure that the board works properly. Those are the keys to solving hardware problems under 95: Isolate the hardware, test it, try a more vanilla driver, and double-check that the resources are entered correctly.

Well, one day, you'll just buy a board, plug it into a system, and you *will* be able to play with it instantly. But that day's not here yet, at least not for most of us. For now, if you master the concepts in this chapter, then you'll be an expert Windows 95 hardware installer.

CHAPTER

11

Controlling Disks
with Windows 95

FOR those of you who have pre-Windows 95 experience with utilities such as partitioning, formatting, and defragging, this chapter will not reveal any startling new concepts. Basically, Windows 95 uses the same types of programs as under DOS. (But let me make clear that you cannot use the old DOS versions of these programs on Windows 95; only use the Windows 95 versions.) The only thing which has changed in terms of these programs is their interfaces: FDISK and FORMAT can be run from within Windows 95 and the other programs have a new look. But essentially, if you previously understood the concepts behind FDISK, FORMAT, defragmentation, and DriveSpace, this chapter will not throw you any curveballs.

That said, this chapter is not without new information. Under Windows 95, the disk cache and swap file are now dynamically managed. Those of you who enjoyed tweaking and fiddling with those settings may be disappointed with these changes. Also, there are two other new concepts: the Recycle Bin and long filename support. All of these features will be discussed in this chapter.

Before You Start

Before you jump into this chapter, keep a few things in mind. First, remember to use only Windows 95 compatible products (look for an explicit reference to Windows 95 compatibility). There are programs, for example some compression software, which, if not made specifically for Windows 95, can destroy all your long filenames. If this happens you'll have to repair all your shortcuts manually. I don't know about you, but I can think of better ways to spend hours and hours of my life...

Also, it is important to perform regular backups of your system. When playing with disk utilities, you could potentially damage your hard drive, so if you don't regularly back up your hard drive, at least do it before running any type of disk utility. If something goes drastically wrong on your system and you didn't back up your drive beforehand, …well, let's just say that you will be regretting the lack of a backup.

One last thing to keep in mind is that you should always have a Windows 95 startup disk nearby when performing invasive disk techniques on your drive. In an emergency, this disk will allow you to jump-start your computer and get to potentially vital programs. Making a startup disk is easy: Click on Add/Remove Programs within the Control Panel, choose the Startup Disk tab, then follow the directions from there.

Now, let's begin this chapter by taking a look at partitioning and formatting drives.

Disk Setup and Maintenance

In this section we'll take a look at several disk setup and maintenance issues: partitioning and formatting hard drives, undeleting files, and defragmenting your drive.

How to Partition and Format Hard Disks

You know the old saying, "The more things change the more they stay the same?" Well, this is an apt way to describe partitioning and formatting under Windows 95. Since Windows 95 still uses a FAT-based system, it relies on the old DOS programs FDISK and FORMAT to do its dirty work. So, if you understood how to partition and format drives under DOS, you'll have no problem doing it under Windows 95. However, one feature which sets Windows 95's partitioning and formatting apart from DOS is that you now can partition and format drives while still running Windows 95, as long as those drives are *non-boot drives*.

Information to Remember When Using FDISK and FORMAT

Before getting into the processes, here's some important information to keep in mind. First, you can only partition and format a drive within Windows 95 if there are no open files on the target hard drive; basically this eliminates boot drives. In the case where the drive you want to format *is* a boot drive, you must use the Windows 95 startup disk to partition and format; more on this coming up. Second, you can not repartition a disk with FDISK if the original partitions were created by Disk Manager, Storage Dimensions SpeedStor, Priam, or Everex partitioning programs. You must repartition the drive using the utility with which you originally partitioned it. Third, if you have compression software loaded on your drive, FDISK will show its *un*compressed size. In other cases, FDISK might not show information on drives compressed with other third-party software. Lastly, if you compressed your hard drive with DriveSpace, you must format the drive using DriveSpace.

That last point leads me to an example of what *not* to do when repartitioning your hard drive. Not too long ago I was experimenting with the DriveSpace compression software, and I had compressed my boot drive. I had finished for the day and decided to repartition, reformat, and restore my original data to the hard drive. I ran FDISK to repartition my drive, and was then ready to format when I saw a message which made my blood run cold. The message said that I had a compressed drive (I had forgotten to uncompress it before repartitioning) and that I needed to format it with DriveSpace. I started to panic when I thought, "Hey, DriveSpace *must* be on the Windows 95 startup disk." I looked, and there was only a file named drvspace.bin. Unfortunately, this file was no help at all. Luckily, I had a DOS 6.22 bootable floppy on hand, and I formatted the drive using the /u (unconditional) switch. Disaster averted. Morals of story:

- Don't forget to uncompress hard drives *before* repartitioning.

- Having a DOS bootable floppy on hand is a *good* thing.

Okay, end of digression. Before showing you how to partition and format, I will chance sounding repetitive and say: **Before running any disk utilities, *especially* fdisk and format, back up your hard drive! Fdisk and Format will destroy *all* the data on your hard drive. Period. If you do not back up your data, you will lose it *all*.**

In this section, we'll take a look at three possible scenarios for partitioning and formatting a hard drive:

- You want to partition and format free space on a drive.
- You just bought a new boot drive.
- You just bought an additional, non-boot hard drive.

So enough talking about it; let's go do it.

Partitioning and Formatting Extra Space on a Hard Drive

Partitioning and formatting a drive really isn't a painful process. When I originally partitioned and formatted my drive for this experiment, I left 118MB free. You may be asking yourself, "But didn't you do it while partitioning and formatting the rest of the drive?" The answer: I did it this way so I could show you how to do it from within Windows 95.

What I'll do here is show you how to create a logical drive in an extended DOS partition, then how to format the logical drive—all from within Windows 95.

Start off by opening the MS-DOS prompt and type **fdisk**. You'll see this in a screen like Figure 11.1.

Choose 1. Create DOS partition or Logical DOS drive and you'll see a screen like Figure 11.2.

Here, you want to choose 2. Create Extended DOS Partition, as you must first create an extended DOS partition before creating logical DOS drives. After typing 2, you will see a screen like Figure 11.3.

In addition to creating an extended DOS partition at this screen, you can see other partitions you have on your system. This screen shows that I have a primary DOS partition (401MB) with a volume label of LESLIE. Now to create an extended DOS partition, type in the size in megabytes (or percent of disk space, but be sure to type the number and a % sign) you wish to allocate to it. I typed in **118** and pressed Enter. This will bring you to a screen like Figure 11.4.

FIGURE 11.1

FDISK opening screen

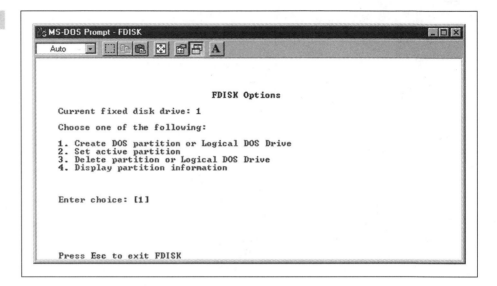

FIGURE 11.2

Create extended DOS
partition in FDISK

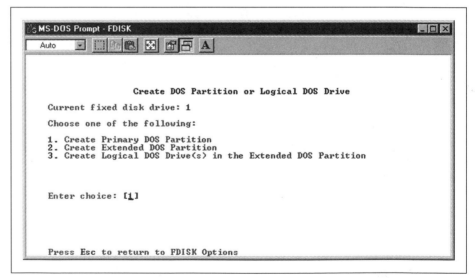

This is a sort of status screen. This informs you that FDISK created the
extended DOS partition, then gives you its statistics so far. You can see
that I now have a Drive C: with two partitions. The first partition is an
Active (thus the A under Status) primary DOS partition 401MB in size
with a volume label of LESLIE. (By the way, the Active status means that

FIGURE 11.3

FDISK Create
Extended DOS
Partition screen

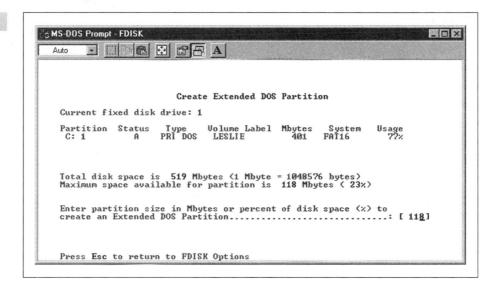

FIGURE 11.4

Extended DOS
partition created

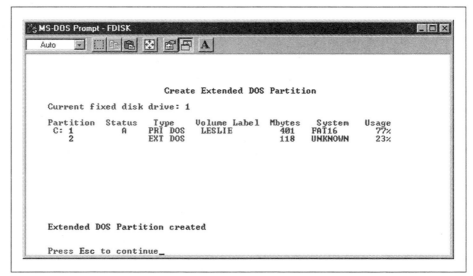

the C: drive is my boot drive.) I also have an extended DOS partition of
118MB, which is still without a volume label. Press Esc to continue and
you'll get a screen like Figure 11.5.

FIGURE 11.5

Create Logical DOS
Drive in the Extended
DOS Partition

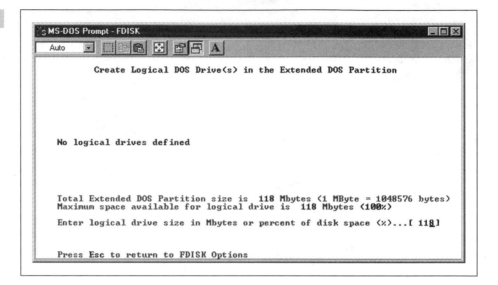

This screen prompts you to create logical drives. Here you need to decide how large of a logical drive you wish to create. I chose to create only one logical drive 118MB in size, so I typed **118** and pressed Enter. That brought me to a screen like Figure 11.6.

FIGURE 11.6

Logical drive created

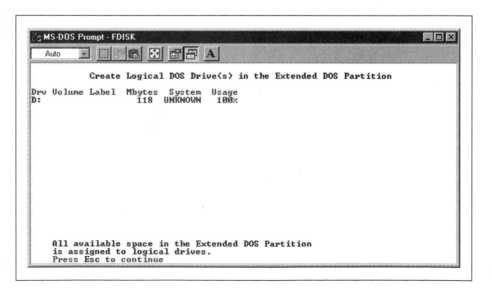

This screen tells me that I cannot create any more logical drives, as all the space in the extended DOS partition is allocated to one logical drive. Also notice that once I created a logical drive in the extended DOS partition, the logical drive received its own drive letter. Press Esc to get to the original opening FDISK screen, hit Esc again to exit FDISK, and type **exit** to end the MS-DOS prompt session. So far we're halfway done—now for formatting your drive.

You can format your disk from either the MS-DOS prompt or the Windows Explorer. Here we'll take a look at the Windows Explorer version of formatting your drive. If, however, you prefer the command prompt interface, you can format your disk from the MS-DOS prompt within Windows 95. The FORMAT command works the same as described in the section "Adding a New Boot Drive."

To format your drive, open up the Windows Explorer and right-click on the icon for your unformatted drive. You'll see the option Format; select this option and you'll see Figure 11.7.

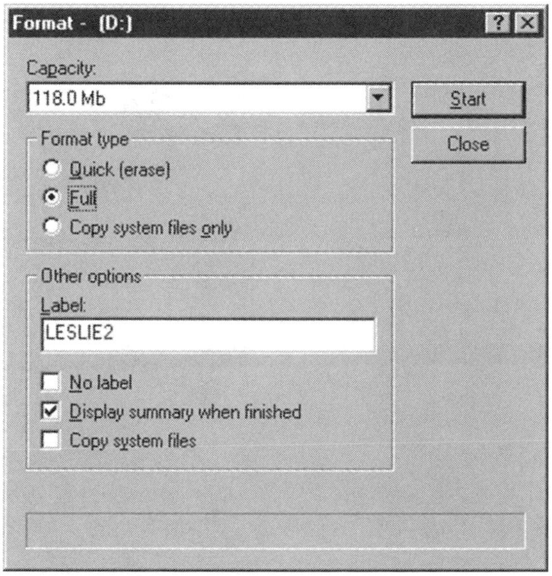

FIGURE 11.7

Formatting a drive with the Windows Explorer

As you can see I've already typed in my desired options. Under Format type, I've chosen Full. If your drive has been formatted previously, you can choose Quick (erase). In Other options, I chose to label my drive LESLIE2 (creative, huh?) and also chose to see a summary at the end of the format. When you click on Start, you'll receive a little warning, as in Figure 11.8.

Click OK and the formatting begins. During the format, you have a gauge at the bottom of the screen to see how far the format has progressed as in Figure 11.9.

When the format is finished, a summary dialog box pops up as in Figure 11.10.

FIGURE 11.8

Warning about formatting your drive

FIGURE 11.9

Meter: Format in process

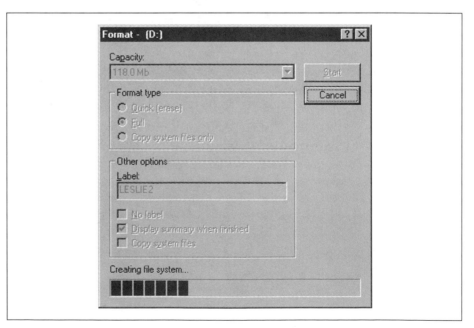

FIGURE 11.10

Summary of format

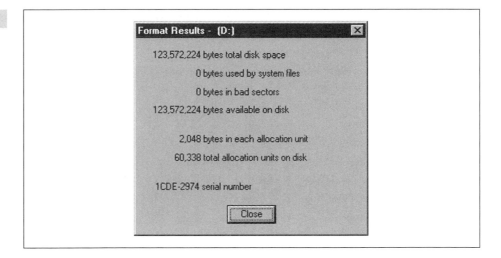

Windows 95 now takes this opportunity to advise me to run ScanDisk on my newly formatted hard drive. You can see how to run ScanDisk later in this chapter.

That wasn't too bad, was it? Now let's look at a slightly trickier situation—adding a new boot drive to your system.

Adding a New Boot Drive

Imagine this: you have Windows 95 on your system and then you decide to get a new hard drive. Before you can use this drive, you need to partition and format it. You will use the same programs as in the previous section, but you will be running FDISK and FORMAT from the Windows 95 startup disk rather than from the MS-DOS prompt.

Now, before we go on, a repeat of the warning: **Back up your files from your old hard drive!** Since you will be replacing the disk where the system files reside, you will need to reinstall Windows 95. If you have a CD-ROM copy of Windows 95, make sure you have some means of getting to your CD-ROM in order to reinstall Windows 95. In addition to backing up your data files, another good idea is to back up your Windows 95 configuration files. After you partition and format, you can perform a basic install of Windows 95, then you can restore all your Windows 95 files to recover your original settings.

Insert your Windows 95 startup disk in your floppy drive and type **fdisk**. You will go through the same type of process as described in the previous section, except you will be creating a primary DOS partition instead of an extended DOS partition. You will be asked the same type of questions; however, one thing which is different, and very important, is to set the primary DOS partition as active. (FDISK will remind you to do this.) Setting the primary DOS partition active allows the computer to boot from that hard drive.

After partitioning, you'll need to format your hard drive. With your Windows 95 startup disk in the A: drive, type **format /?** to see a list of the available FORMAT switches. (As you can see in Figure 11.11, I captured this screen from within Windows 95; however, the FORMAT switches will not change.)

The only switch necessary for our purposes here is /V. The /V switch allows you to name your hard drive. At this point, type **format c:**, add any switches you desire, then press Enter. At this point the formatting begins; typically this doesn't take very long (usually no longer than 15 minutes).

There you have it. Now your hard drive is ready for the Windows 95 installation process. For more on that, consult Chapter 4.

FIGURE 11.11

FORMAT options

```
Microsoft(R) Windows 95
    (C)Copyright Microsoft Corp 1981-1995.

C:\WINDOWS>format /?
Formats a disk for use with MS-DOS.

FORMAT drive: [/V[:label]] [/Q] [/F:size] [/B ¦ /S] [/C]
FORMAT drive: [/V[:label]] [/Q] [/T:tracks /N:sectors] [/B ¦ /S] [/C]
FORMAT drive: [/V[:label]] [/Q] [/1] [/4] [/B ¦ /S] [/C]
FORMAT drive: [/Q] [/1] [/4] [/8] [/B ¦ /S] [/C]

  /V[:label]   Specifies the volume label.
  /Q           Performs a quick format.
  /F:size      Specifies the size of the floppy disk to format (such
               as 160, 180, 320, 360, 720, 1.2, 1.44, 2.88).
  /B           Allocates space on the formatted disk for system files.
  /S           Copies system files to the formatted disk.
  /T:tracks    Specifies the number of tracks per disk side.
  /N:sectors   Specifies the number of sectors per track.
  /1           Formats a single side of a floppy disk.
  /4           Formats a 5.25-inch 360K floppy disk in a high-density drive.
  /8           Formats eight sectors per track.
  /C           Tests clusters that are currently marked "bad."

C:\WINDOWS>_
```

Adding an Additional Hard Drive

Let's now look at one last scenario: You just went out and bought an additional hard drive for your system (or maybe you were lucky enough to have a friend give you one) and you need to get the drive ready for Windows 95. To get the drive operational, you'll use the exact same programs described previously in the section "Partitioning and Formatting Extra Space on a Hard Drive." But keep in mind that you must be careful about two things: (a) which drive you are going to partition and format, and (b) exactly how you will go about deciding to partition this new drive. Read on for more details.

First, you must be sure to partition and format the correct drive. It would be a Very Bad Thing to accidentally partition and format the wrong drive. Open the MS-DOS prompt and type **fdisk**. You'll see a screen like Figure 11.12.

This screen is identical to the FDISK procedure described in the first section, except for one detail. You can see there is a new fifth option called Change current fixed disk drive. This is the option which allows you to select which drive to partition—and keeps you from partitioning the wrong drive. Choose 5 and you will see Figure 11.13.

FIGURE 11.12

Opening screen of FDISK when adding another drive

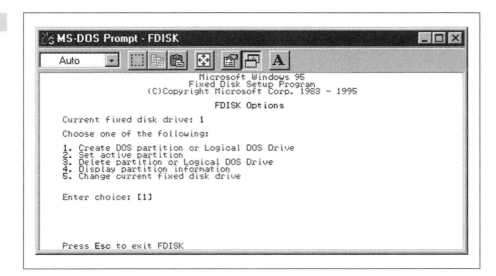

FIGURE 11.13

Change current fixed
disk drive screen in
FDISK

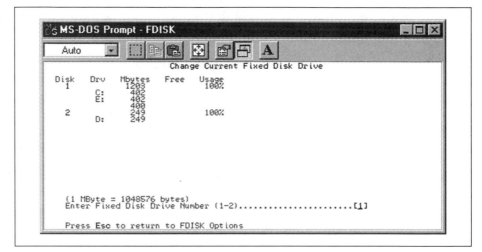

```
MS-DOS Prompt - FDISK                        [_][□][X]
 Auto        ▼   [] [▣][▣] [✛] [▣][▣] [A]
                       Change Current Fixed Disk Drive
  Disk   Drv   Mbytes   Free   Usage
   1            1203            100%
         C:      402
         E:      402
                 400
   2            249            100%
         D:      249




  (1 MByte = 1048576 bytes)
  Enter Fixed Disk Drive Number (1-2).......................[1]

  Press Esc to return to FDISK Options
```

As you can see, this computer already has two physical drives which have
been partitioned. To partition your newly added drive, press the appropriate disk drive number then press Enter. At this point, you would be
back at the original FDISK screen, but with one difference—look at Current Fixed Disk Drive (top of the screen) and you'll see that you have
changed drive numbers. Now you're ready to start, right? Well, there's one
more thing.

Before you can proceed, you need to decide whether to create a *primary*
DOS partition or an *extended* DOS partition. Choosing to add another
primary DOS partition will affect the names of all your other drives on
the system. By default, your first primary DOS partition is named drive
C:. When another primary DOS partition is added to the system, its default name is drive D:. Why might this be a problem? Take a look at Figure 11.14.

As you can imagine, having your drives renamed could lead to some headaches. How can you avoid this problem? Simply partition your new drive
as an extended DOS partition, not as a primary DOS partition. Figure 11.15 shows how your drive letters would be affected.

The rest is simple—just create an extended DOS partition with logical
DOS drives, then format. To refresh your memory on how to do this, just
turn back to the first section "Partitioning and Formatting Extra Space
on a Hard Drive."

FIGURE 11.14

Adding another
primary DOS partition
to the system

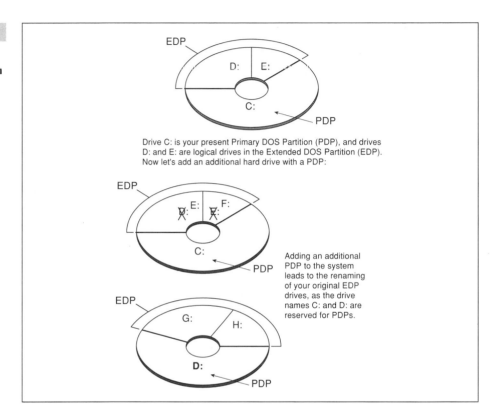

Drive C: is your present Primary DOS Partition (PDP), and drives
D: and E: are logical drives in the Extended DOS Partition (EDP).
Now let's add an additional hard drive with a PDP:

Adding an additional
PDP to the system
leads to the renaming
of your original EDP
drives, as the drive
names C: and D: are
reserved for PDPs.

Undeleting Files Under Windows 95

A handy feature which comes with Windows 95 is called the Recycle Bin.
Yes, now it seems that even computer software is politically correct and
environmentally conscious. How does the Recycle Bin work? Well, when
you delete a file from the Windows Explorer, the file isn't automatically
deleted. (This actually depends on your Recycle Bin settings, which we'll
discuss below.) In actuality, Windows 95 moves your deleted file to a
holding-space-type of directory on your hard drive.

Once a file is in the Recycle Bin, the user can undelete it by simply opening the Recycle Bin, clicking on the file, and choosing Restore from the
File menu. This restores the file to its directory at the time of its deletion.
Understand, though, that once a file is deleted from the Recycle Bin, it is
really deleted. How are files deleted from the Recycle Bin? This can occur

FIGURE 11.15

Adding an extended DOS partition to the system

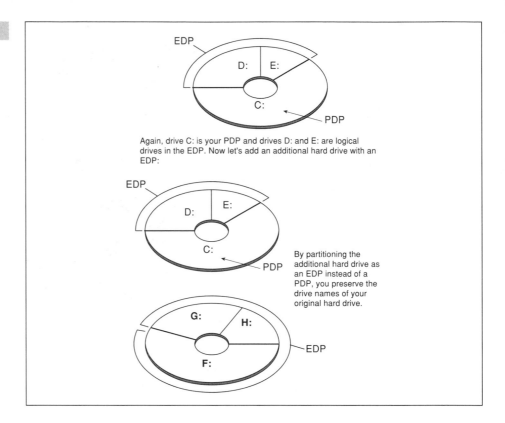

Again, drive C: is your PDP and drives D: and E: are logical drives in the EDP. Now let's add an additional hard drive with an EDP:

By partitioning the additional hard drive as an EDP instead of a PDP, you preserve the drive names of your original hard drive.

in two ways. Approach 1 is that the user can manually empty the Recycle Bin by right-clicking on the Recycle Bin icon and then selecting Empty Recycle Bin. Approach 2 is, when the Recycle Bin exceeds a certain size (set by you, but the default is 10 percent of your hard drive), the oldest files are deleted until the Recycle Bin comes under the maximum limit.

WARNING   If you choose to run the Windows 3.x File Manager instead of the Windows Explorer (to run the File Manager, click Run on the Start menu and type winfile), your deleted files are really deleted and *not* sent to the Recycle Bin.

To see how to configure the Recycle Bin, right-click on the Recycle Bin and select Properties. This will lead you to Figure 11.16.

FIGURE 11.16

Recycle Bin opening
screen

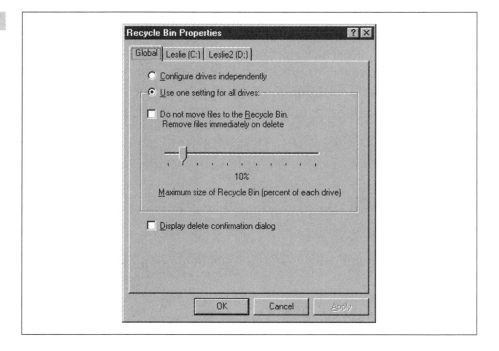

This screen shows the settings I've chosen, and all are the default values (except *Display delete confirmation dialog*—its default is that it is checked). Here you must make a choice concerning the configuration of your Recycle Bin: Use one setting for all drives or Configure drives independently.

- Use one setting for all drives: Just as it sounds, this allows you to have universal Recycle Bin settings for all drives on the system. If you choose this option, the options on other tabs, for example LESLIE2 (D:), will be grayed out.

- Configure drives independently: When you choose this option, you must determine settings for each drive on your system separately. If you select this, there will be a \recycled directory on each hard drive.

Whether you choose to use one setting or to configure each drive, both have three options in common: Do not move files to the Recycle Bin, Maximum size of the Recycle Bin, and Display delete confirmation dialog.

- If you choose *Do not move files to the Recycle Bin*, files will be automatically deleted and the Recycle Bin settings will be grayed out.

- If you choose to use the Recycle Bin, you can set its maximum size simply by moving the slider to the desired percentage of your disk space. (The default is 10 percent.) When the Recycle Bin exceeds its maximum size, the oldest files are deleted until the size of the Recycle Bin is less than the allotted space.

- The last option, *Display delete confirmation dialog*, lets you decide whether you want a warning when files are sent to the Recycle Bin.

That's really all there is to the Recycle Bin. Set the Recycle Bin options to suit your individual needs. If you feel you'll forget to clean out your Recycle Bin, allocate a smaller percentage of disk space. If you have a tendency to accidentally delete important files, perhaps setting a larger Recycle Bin would better fit your needs.

Optimizing Disk Speed with Defrag

Defragging your disk has traditionally been an important step in optimizing your disk speed. However, since installing Windows 95 on my system, my hard drive has been considerably less fragmented than it was with previous versions of Windows. (Why? It's discussed in an upcoming section.) That said, however, it is still important to defrag your disk on a regular basis.

Disk Defragmentation

In case you are wondering, defragmentation of drives places individual files contiguously at the beginning and free space at the end of the hard drive. As the hard drive doesn't have to access many different parts of the disk for one file, reads from and writes to the hard drive are faster and more efficient.

How often should you defragment your drive? I can say that just the other day I realized I hadn't defragmented my disk in 52 days. No, I don't have a notepad full of little tick-marks for each day that goes by without defragmenting—Windows 95 told me!

Open the My Computer group, right-click on your drive's icon, select Properties, then select the Tools tab. You'll see a screen like Figure 11.17.

This dialog box lets you see how long it has been since you last performed what typically should be routine disk maintenance procedures. Error-checking status shows how long it has been since I last checked my drive for errors with ScanDisk. Backup status tells us that Windows 95 does not know when I last backed up this drive. (This is because Windows 95's backup program is not installed, and, therefore, has not been run.) Finally, Defragmentation status shows how long it has been since I've run the Defrag on this disk.

Assuming that nearly two months worth of disk usage would result in quite a bit of file fragmentation, I clicked on the Defragment Now button to launch DEFRAG.EXE.

FIGURE 11.17

My Computer Tools tab

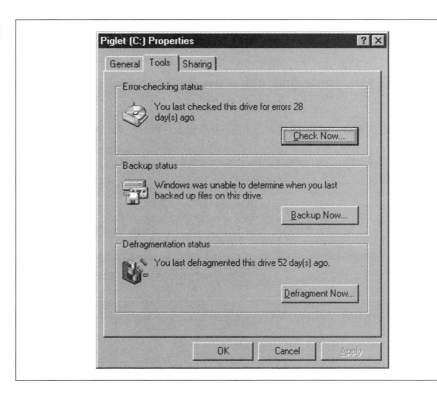

NOTE   You can also launch the defragmenter two other ways: one is by clicking the Run button from the Start menu and typing `defrag`. Another is by clicking the Start button, selecting Accessories, next choosing System Tools, and then (finally!) Disk Defragmenter. If you start defragmentation these ways, you will be prompted to specify which drive to defrag. Then the Defragmenter will proceed as described below.

Defragment Now presented me with some interesting information (see Figure 11.18).

Can this be right? Only 2% fragmented? I don't need to defragment the disk now? It is, believe it or not, true. After 52 days of daily usage there is almost no file fragmentation. This is due to new logic that Microsoft built into VFAT, Windows 95's file system.

Prior to Windows 95, saving a file was one of the worst things you could do to your disk. Over a period of time, this would cause your disk performance to degrade, sometimes noticeably (doesn't that sound like one of those motor oil ads on starting your car engine?). Under MS-DOS and Windows for Workgroups v3.11's VFAT, a great deal of file fragmentation occurred because the file system allocated the first available space found on the disk. The result was that most of your files were chopped up into tiny pieces and randomly spread across your disk.

Under Windows 95, VFAT uses a more intelligent method of allocating space when writing to the disk. By default, VFAT searches your disk for

FIGURE 11.18

Disk Defragmenter
advice dialog box

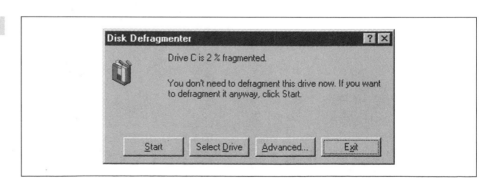

the first contiguous 0.5MB of free disk space before writing the file. This ensures that most, if not all, of your files can be written to the disk contiguously, which results in optimized performance. Unfortunately, VFAT will resort to the MS-DOS method if it cannot find at least that much free contiguous space.

Think of it this way: most of the wear on your car's engine comes from starting it. Upon startup, all of the protective oil is sitting in the oil pan; it is not coating and protecting any of the metal parts that will soon begin to rub against one another. Now imagine that you had a system in your engine that circulated the oil around all the necessary parts *before* you started it. The reduction in engine wear would be dramatic! Just as pre-lubricating your car's engine would dramatically reduce engine wear, pre-locating a large area of free space on your disk before writing the file dramatically reduces file fragmentation.

Now back to defragging my C: drive. Even though I don't need to defragment the disk I'll do it anyway. Before defragging, let's first take a look at what options are available to us, by clicking the Advanced button.

Advanced Options under Defragmentation

While our options are somewhat limited, we do have basic control over the defragmentation process. You can see the Advanced Options screen in Figure 11.19.

The first thing to do is choose the defragmentation method:

- **Full defragmentation (both files and free space).** Choosing this option causes DEFRAG.EXE to completely rearrange your disk—all of your files are placed at the beginning of the disk and the rest is left as a big chunk of free space. Any fragmented files will be written to their new location contiguously. This is the preferred method for defragmentation, but it also takes the longest to complete.

- **Defragment files only.** If you choose this option, DEFRAG.EXE will make sure that all the files on your disk are stored contiguously by rewriting any fragmented files to a location on the disk that is large enough to hold them contiguously. This method is faster than a full defragmentation, but it has a drawback: it does not consolidate the

FIGURE 11.19

Defragging Advanced
Options screen

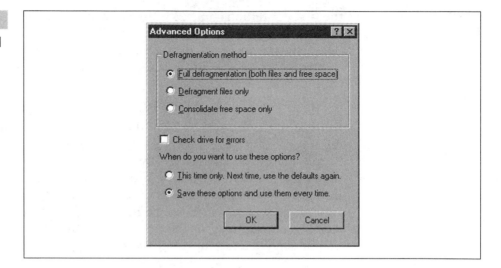

free space. The result: future files have a greater chance of becoming fragmented.

- **Consolidate free space only.** This option will cause DEFRAG.EXE to rearrange your disk so that all of the free space is in one large chunk. This option is interesting: Although it ensures that any files written to the disk in the future will not be fragmented, there is a high possibility that files already on the disk will become *more* fragmented! This happens because DEFRAG.EXE will find the largest area of free space, then move the smaller blocks of free spaces so they are contiguous with the largest one. This results in fragmentation because parts of existing files that border the large free block of space are moved into the smaller areas of free space. This may result in some non-fragmented files becoming fragmented.

The other two options are pretty simple. *Check drive for errors* simply says that the Defragmenter will check the drive for errors by running ScanDisk before performing defragmentation. The setting *When do you want to use these options* allows you to specify whether the settings you choose at this session are to be the default settings or a one-time deal.

Once you have chosen the desired options, click OK to return to the main defragging screen. Here you have the chance to change the target drive, if so desired. Click Start to begin defragmenting.

NOTE At this point, according to Microsoft, you should be able to go back to work on your computer while the Defragger runs in the background. However, the Defragger will reset itself every time there is a change in the target drive. Depending on your workload, you may wait quite some time for the Defragger to finish. So, if you work excessively from your local drive, you may want to start the defragger when you won't be using the computer very much—for example, run the program as you are leaving for lunch.

While the Defragmenter is working, you will see a defragging status bar on the screen. If you want to see each cluster during defragmentation, click on Show Details and you'll see something like Figure 11.20.

Clicking on Legend will explain the significance of the different colors on your screen while the Defragmenter is doing its job. This view of the

FIGURE 11.20

Show Details
dialog box during
defragmentation

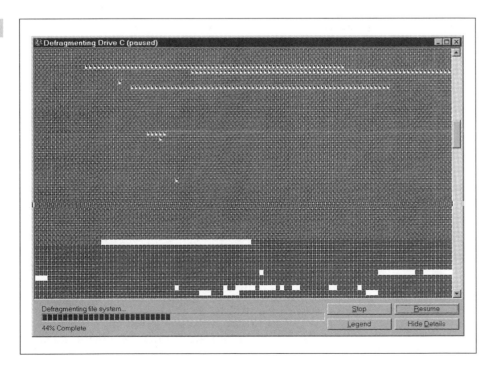

Defragmenter tends to slow it down, so when you're finished looking at this screen, select Hide Details to return to the small status screen. When the Defragmenter is finished, a dialog box will advise you to run ScanDisk to ensure the integrity of the disk. Keep on reading to learn more about ScanDisk.

Checking Disk Integrity with ScanDisk

ScanDisk is another disk utility included with Windows 95 that helps you to keep your disk in proper health. Depending on the options you choose, ScanDisk can search for and repair errors in your files, or physically on your hard drive. ScanDisk also checks for errors in the FAT, in long file-names, and with cross-linked or lost clusters.

You should run ScanDisk regularly to maintain your hard drive. In this section, we'll run ScanDisk on both an uncompressed and a compressed drive. (Information on how to compress drives is coming up in the next section.)

Running ScanDisk

To begin, click on My Computer and right-click on the appropriate drive. Next, click on Properties, then select the Tools tab. At the top of this screen you will see Error-checking status. Here you can see how long it has been since you last ran ScanDisk. Is it about time to run ScanDisk? If so, click Check Now, and you will see the screen shown in Figure 11.21.

This screen lets you choose which drive to test and gives you other options: Type of test, Automatically fix errors, and the Advanced button.

- **Type of test:** Here you can perform either a Standard or Thorough test.

    - **Standard:** As it says beneath its name, this test checks files and folders for errors. This is the faster test of the two, but it does not check the surface of the disk for errors. As seen in the previous figure, when this option is selected, the Options button is grayed out.

    - **Thorough:** This test checks everything that the Standard test checks; in addition it scans the surface of the hard drive for

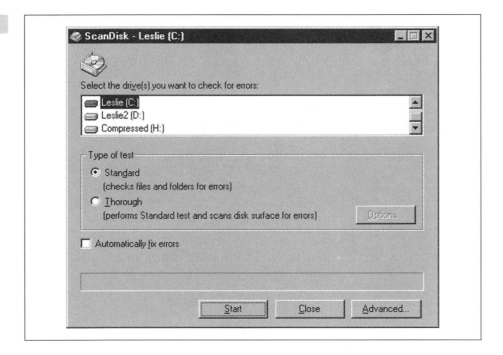

errors. When you choose a Thorough test, the Options button
can be selected. More on this screen coming up.

- **Automatically fix errors:** Do you want to be prompted to fix all
  errors which ScanDisk finds or would you rather let ScanDisk go
  and fix them itself? Your selection just depends on your personal
  preference.

If you decide that a Thorough test is the way to go, select it, then click on
Options; you'll see Figure 11.22.

Let's take a look at the options on this screen.

- **System and data areas:** This instructs ScanDisk to scan for errors
  in both the system and data areas of your drive. This type of test will
  usually take longer than the following two options.

- **System areas only:** With this option selected, ScanDisk will search
  for errors in the system area only, leaving the data area unscanned.
  Unfortunately, ScanDisk cannot repair errors in the system part of

FIGURE 11.22

ScanDisk's Thorough
Options screen

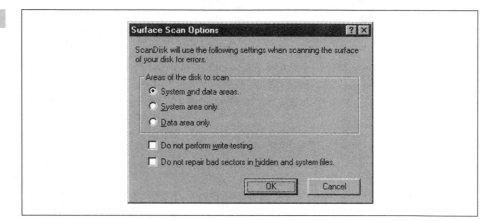

your drive. If errors are found, ScanDisk will alert you (depending on your Log settings, which is coming up).

- **Data areas only:** With this option, only the data areas, and not the system areas of the disk, are checked. Typically ScanDisk can repair errors in the data areas, and it does so by moving the data to another part of the disk. The bad area is then marked as unusable on the disk.

- **Do not perform write-testing:** Normally ScanDisk will check your disk by reading the data from your disk and then attempting to write the data back. If this box is checked, ScanDisk will read data but *not* attempt to write it back. This option is not necessary to perform on an IDE drive, because it does this kind of testing automatically.

- **Do not repair bad sectors in hidden and system files:** If this is *not* checked, ScanDisk will move any hidden or system files found to have bad sectors to other parts of the disk. This could cause programs that require system or hidden files to be in a specific place to work incorrectly. If this option is checked, ScanDisk will leave these files alone.

After selecting the desired options, click OK. This brings you back to the original screen of ScanDisk. But don't click Start just yet! There is still one other screen in which you must choose options: the Advanced Options screen. Click the Advanced button and you'll see Figure 11.23.

FIGURE 11.23

Advanced screen
in ScanDisk

The first two options are fairly self-explanatory and how you select these options, *Display summary* and *Log* file, depends entirely on your personal preferences. Do you want to see the summaries, including information on total and free disk space, bad sectors, folders, hidden, and user files? If so, click on *Always* or *Only if errors found*. Do you want to keep a log of every run of ScanDisk? If so, click on *Append to log*. The other options, however, could use a little bit of explaining.

- **Cross-linked files:** Cross-linked files are two files which both believe they have data written to a common cluster; actually, one file is mistaken. If your primary concern is to save data, *Make copies* would be the best option to choose. This copies both files elsewhere with their own copy of the cross-linked cluster. Unfortunately, there is no way to be sure that this will save the data; there is no guarantee that one or even both of the files will have all their data intact. However, choosing *Delete* will obviously not save the data.

- **Lost file fragments:** These are clusters which are marked as being used, but have no filename associated with them (kind of a file with no name). Choosing *Convert to files* will place all of the lost file fragments in your root directory into one file. At this point you can look through the files to see if there is any data you want to save. Choosing *Free* automatically deletes the lost file fragments.

- **Check files for:** This will check for corrupted long filenames and extended attributes such as creation date and time.

- **Check host drive first:** This is an option that should remain checked, but this will only show up if you have used disk compression. When ScanDisk checks a compressed drive, this option tells ScanDisk to check the host drive before the compressed drive. (If there is a problem with the host drive, it could affect the compressed drive, which is a very good reason to check the host first.)

That pretty much wraps up ScanDisk. When you've selected all the options, click on Start. ScanDisk will give you a status bar to let you know how far the program has gone, and, depending on your Summary selection, you may get a summary report when it is finished.

Advanced File System Settings

In addition to optimizing your system with the Recycle Bin, Defrag, and ScanDisk, you can also adjust your File System settings in the Control Panel to best suit your system's needs. To review these settings, click on the System icon in the Control Panel, and select the Performance tab. You'll see a screen like the one in Figure 11.24.

This screen gives you general information concerning your system, including memory, resources, and type of file system in use. Now click File System under the Advanced settings heading, and you will see a dialog box like the one in Figure 11.25.

The three tabs available from this screen allow you to adjust the properties of your hard disk and CD-ROM and let you try different settings to pinpoint bottlenecks and problems on your system. Let's first take a look at the Hard Disk tab.

Hard Disk Performance

The Hard Disk tab allows you to configure two settings: the role of your machine and its read-ahead optimization. You can choose one of three role settings: Desktop computer, Mobile or docking system, or Network

FIGURE 11.24

Performance tab in
the Control Panel

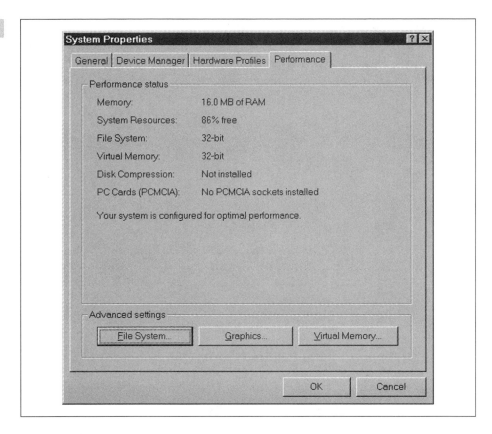

FIGURE 11.24

Performance tab in
the Control Panel

server. Although these settings are fairly cut and dried, here are a few guidelines on how to determine which is best for you:

- **Desktop computer:** This setting assumes that you are using a computer in the role of a network client (or even stand-alone) with more than the minimum amount of RAM, and not running on battery power.

- **Mobile or docking system:** This is the setting for laptop computers typically running on battery power which have a minimum amount of RAM. This setting will flush out the disk cache frequently.

- **Network server:** This is the setting for network servers which have enough RAM; this setting also assumes frequent disk activity and will optimize itself for that setting.

FIGURE 11.25

Optimizing your
hard disk

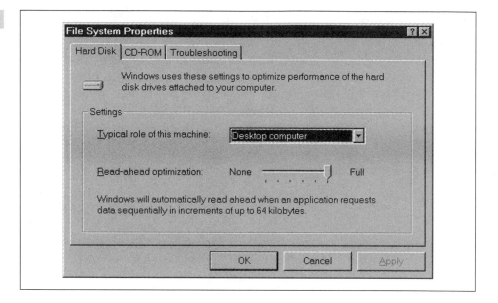

The second setting, Read-ahead optimization, lets you determine whether you want the hard drive to read ahead. Move the slider to the desired position.

CD-ROM Performance

Windows 95's new *CDFS*, or *CD File System*, offers 32-bit, protected-mode drivers, rather than Windows 3.x's real-mode MSCDEX drivers. CDFS does not use conventional memory. It allows for improved multi-tasking, and has a dynamically configured cache. However, you may configure a supplemental cache for improved CD-ROM performance. When you click on the CD-ROM tab, you will see the screen shown in Figure 11.26.

First, you can set *Supplemental cache size:* by moving its slider to the desired position. Keep in mind, though, that a large cache is only helpful if the cache is large enough to hold entire streams of multimedia; if not, sometimes a small to medium cache is sufficient.

Next, you must set the *Optimize access pattern for:* setting. Under CDFS, the CD-ROM reads ahead at the same rate as the application so that playback runs more smoothly. Therefore, you must base your determination

FIGURE 11.26

Optimizing CD-ROM
performance

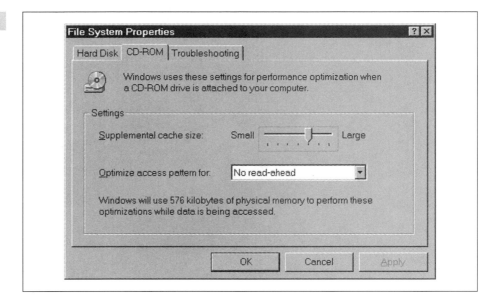

of this option on the amount of RAM on your system and the access
speed of your CD-ROM.:

- With 8MB or less of RAM and a single-speed CD-ROM, a 64K
  cache is created.

- With 8MB to 12MB of RAM and a double-speed drive, a 626K
  cache is created.

- With more than 12MB of RAM and a quad-speed (or higher) drive,
  a 1238K cache is created.

Keep in mind that, based on your choices, different size caches will be
created.

Troubleshooting Your System

The final tab in this section is the Troubleshooting tab; you can see it in
Figure 11.27.

FIGURE 11.27

Troubleshooting tab in
Advanced File System
settings

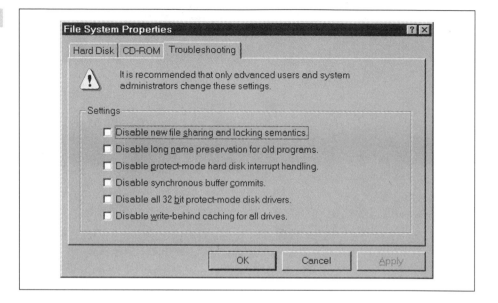

WARNING Changing the settings in the Troubleshooting tab is not
recommended, as it can lead to performance degradation.
Change them only for the purposes of troubleshooting problems.

In this screen, you can disable many different features of the operating
system in order to pinpoint problems on your system. Here's an explanation of these features:

- **Disable new file sharing and locking semantics**: You can disable
  this option when a DOS-based program is having trouble sharing
  under Windows 95. This changes the code which keeps open files
  from being shared and modified by other programs.

- **Disable long name preservation for old programs**: Choose this
  option when a legacy program cannot accept long filenames. This
  turns off tunneling, which preserves long filenames when used by
  programs which do not accept these filenames. (For more on long
  filenames, turn to the upcoming section, "Using Long Filename
  Support.")

- **Disable protect-mode hard disk interrupt handling**: When this is checked, it allows the ROM (instead of Windows 95) to handle hard disk interrupts; however, this can lead to a slowdown of your system. You may need to select this if your hard drive needs this type of interrupt handling. (By default, this is not selected; under Windows 3.x, however, the reverse was true.)

- **Disable all 32-bit protect-mode disk drivers**: As it says, this option disables all 32-bit, protected-mode drivers (except for the floppy drive); real-mode drivers are used instead.

- **Disable write-behind caching for all drives**: This entry basically disables write-caching for all drives.

That's all there is to these three Advanced File System settings. Adjusting these will help optimize performance on your system, as well as help you to troubleshoot problems when they arise.

Understanding the Disk Cache

Under Windows 3.x, if you were dissatisfied with the speed with which your hard drive accessed files, you could enable *disk caching*. You enabled software, in this case SMARTDrive, to set aside a certain amount of RAM to use as the disk cache. This allowed frequently accessed files to reside in RAM, and therefore they could be accessed faster when in RAM than when on the hard drive.

How Disk Cache Works

When you access a file from disk, the caching software makes a copy of this file and stores it in cache. The next time the user accesses the file, the software first looks for this file in the cache. If the file is in the cache, then the software does not need to look to the slow hard drive for the file, and accesses the file faster for the user. If the file is not in cache, however, it is necessary to go to the hard drive and retrieve the file. At this point, the caching software makes a copy of the file and stores it in cache again.

Disk Caching under Windows 95

The disk cache has undergone some changes from its Windows 3.x in-carnation. First, Windows 95 uses a 32-bit protected-mode driver, VCACHE, instead of the 16-bit real-mode disk cache software, SMART-Drive, used with Windows 3.x. Second, an improved algorithm used in VCACHE allows for greater speed and performance than was possible under SMARTDrive. Now here's what I consider to be the best new feature of the disk cache under Windows 95: The user no longer needs to specify settings for the disk cache, as it is dynamically configured. The system determines the size of the disk cache, as determined by the need of the system.

This means the Windows 95 user is not able to control any of the disk caching settings, which you might see as a mixed blessing. However, you can do one thing to see the best disk caching performance under Windows 95: Remove any SHARE or SMARTDRV settings from either your `autoexec.bat` or `config.sys` files. Also, if you notice that your system is paging a lot, don't fear, as the disk cache will automatically shrink to free up more memory for the system.

Should You Manage the Swap File or Allow Windows to Control It?

Under Windows 3.x, managing the swap file was an important part of performance tuning. You had to decide whether to have a temporary swap file (which did not require a contiguous block of disk space) or a permanent swap file (which did require a contiguous block of disk space, but in return gave improved system performance); you had to decide how much memory the swap file should have; and you had to decide whether or not to implement 32-bit disk access. Under Windows 95, these decisions and tweaking are really not necessary. First, though, let's look at how the swap file works.

How the Swap File Works

The swap file helps resolve out-of-memory problems. If your system needs another megabyte of RAM, but you are already using all your RAM, the system will just grab a megabyte of unused disk space and use it like RAM. There is a catch, though; since disks are slower than RAM, the swap file may have a tendency to slow your machine down a bit. But if the alternative is not running the program at all because you don't have the memory, it's not such a bad thing. Basically, the swap file allows you to run programs which require more from the system than the system could handle without the swap file.

Windows 95 and the Swap File

Under Windows 95, the virtual memory swap file can be dynamically managed by Windows 95 to best meet your system's changing needs. Unlike the disk cache, however, the user may choose to control the swap file settings. Windows 95's swap file can also take up fragmented parts of the drive with little performance degradation. Although this is true, it is still a good idea to defrag your drive before you set up a new swap file. If you are running a shared version of Windows 95 from a remote machine, your swap file resides on the remote machine's directory.

Now, should you control the swap file or allow Windows 95 to control it? Personally, I would recommend to allow Windows 95 to control it. Typically, dynamic control of the swap file will result in the most efficient use of your system resources.

Managing Your Swap File

If you decide that a dynamically controlled swap file is not for you, then here's how to change and control its size. In the Control Panel, click on System, then choose the Performance tab, and then click on Virtual Memory. You'll see a screen like in Figure 11.28.

Click on the radio button next to *Let me specify my own virtual memory settings*. This will highlight the three sections underneath. *Hard disk* tells you on which hard drive the swap file presently resides and how much free space is on that drive. Here you can change the swap file's location. Typically, to see the best swap file performance, place it on a fast hard drive,

FIGURE 11.28

Virtual Memory
screen in the
Control Panel

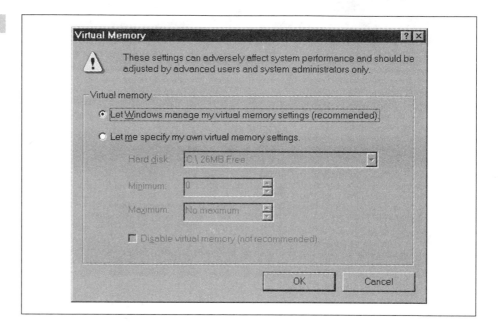

one with less user traffic, and/or one with adequate free space so it can
shrink and grow as needed. Then, with *Minimum* and *Maximum*, you can
specify the largest and smallest size of your swap file. If you set the value
of Maximum to equal the amount of free space on a hard drive, then additional free space becomes available on the drive, and the system will assume that it can increase the size of swap file by the amount of *new* free
space on the drive. The last option, *Disable virtual memory* is not recommended, as this can lead to system performance problems.

Using Long Filename Support

For years the DOS-based world has been constrained by the eight-dot-
three filename, which refers to the filenames with no more than 8 characters and file extensions no longer than 3 characters. Now with the
advent of long filename support, Windows 95 users are freed from these
constraints. Well, kind of.

How Windows 95 Implements Long Filenames

When a user creates a new long filename, Windows 95 automatically generates a second filename (known as an *alias*) conforming to the eight-dot-three standard, for the sake of backwards compatibility. The long filename is used in applications accepting long filenames, and the alias name is the filename Windows 95 uses to work with older programs.

The newly generated alias is composed of four different parts, in the following order: the first six letters in the long filename, a tilde (~), a unique number, and then an extension. The extension is created by taking the first three letters after the last period in the long filename. If there are no periods in the long filename, Windows 95 uses the default extension of the appropriate application. You may be thinking, "But what happens if two files have the same first six letters?" That's what the number after the tilde is for: Windows 95 generates different numbers so that the two filenames are unique. Another quality of the alias names is that they are all capital letters.

NOTE   Keep in mind that many non-Windows 95 programs will not accept long filenames, even though Windows 95 will.

Let's take a look at an example. I just created three documents in Windows 95's WordPad: the first document saved is named My project for September, the second file saved is named Another project for September.doc, and the third saved is My project for October. A unique alias is created for each long filename: the first file is now MYPROJ~1.DOC, the second is ANOTHE~1.DOC, and the third is MYPROJ~2.DOC. As you can see, these filenames conform to the eight-dot-three standard for compatibility. Also of note are the two MYPROJ~ files: Windows 95 simply generated a new unique number for the second filename in order to avoid having two files with the same name.

Tunneling and Network Support for Long Filenames

Tunneling is a process which allows applications not supporting long filenames to open and save these files (whether the files are local or on the network) without destroying the long filenames. Tunneling is supported with the VFAT, NTFS, and HPFS file systems.

N O T E Windows NT 3.1 does not accept long filenames on FAT volumes and will eliminate them. Windows NT 3.5 does not have a problem with them.

So What's the Catch?

All of this doesn't sound too bad, right? Well, before you jump in and begin to create long filenames, read the following list for the bad news.

- Unless you have applications written especially for Windows 95, you will not be able to have full support for long filenames. In the previous example, I created files with long filenames in Windows 95's WordPad; the version of Ami Pro that I use was written for Windows 3.x, and does not support long filenames. One possible way to get around this, though, is through some new products which claim to change your old apps to accept long filenames. (I haven't used any, so I can't say how they work.)

- Storing files with long filenames in the root directory can take up more than one entry; as the root directory can only store 512 entries, you must be careful with how many long filename files you store there.

- Many disk utilities not written specifically for Windows 95 will destroy long filenames. Take caution when choosing disk utilities not included with Windows 95. (This is not to say you shouldn't use non-Windows 95 disk utilities; just be careful!)

- A caution concerning alias names: Do not use the long filename of a file when issuing low-level commands (such as Copy or Rename) from a command line; use the alias. Otherwise, the operation will change the name to a different alias. For example, say you have a file with the name Letter to mom today.txt (alias LETTER~1.DOC). If you use the Copy command at the command prompt to copy it to another directory, your file Letter to mom today.txt will become LETTER~2.DOC. This changing of filenames could become extremely confusing.

DriveSpace under Windows 95

Included with Windows 95 is DriveSpace, a compression program which supports the VFAT file system and includes long filename support. Obviously, this disk compression routine is safe to use with Windows 95, but don't count on it being safe with other such programs. Be sure to check for the Windows 95 compatible sticker (or the like) on any new program you purchase. If the program isn't Windows 95 compatible, you will trash your long filenames. Two such programs are Stacker 4.0 and DriveSpace 6.x for MS-DOS; these programs will destroy long filenames on your disk.

How does compression work? Well, under Windows 95 a compressed drive really isn't a compressed drive—it's actually a *compressed volume file* (*CVF*). DriveSpace stores the new compressed drive as a CVF in the root directory of an uncompressed hard disk, which is known as the host drive. Even though the compressed drive is really only a compressed file residing on another hard disk, the compressed drive is assigned a letter and is accessed as if it is a separate hard drive. The CVF has read-only, hidden, and system attributes, and typically has a name such as DRVSPACE.000.

WARNING Don't mess with these files on your system. You could potentially lose the data on your compressed hard disk!

In the next few pages, we'll see:

- How to compress a new empty drive.
- How to compress a boot drive.
- How to uncompress a drive.

But first, let's take a look at the various options available within DriveSpace.

DriveSpace Options and What They Mean

Under the two main menu options in DriveSpace, Drive and Advanced, there are many different options which allow you to tailor your drives to suit your personal needs. Here we'll take a look at some of these options.

Under the Drive menu, users can choose from five options:

- The Compress and Uncompress options. I describe these in detail later in this section.

- The Properties option simply gives the user general information on the selected drive, such as whether the drive is compressed and a reading of free space versus used space on the drive.

- Format allows the user to format a compressed drive.

- The Adjust Free Space option allows the user to change the amount of free space between a compressed drive and its host drive. Take a look at Figure 11.29 to see the Adjust Free Space screen.

This screen would allow me to add more free space to Drive D: by taking space from Drive H:.

FIGURE 11.29

DriveSpace's Adjust
Free Space screen

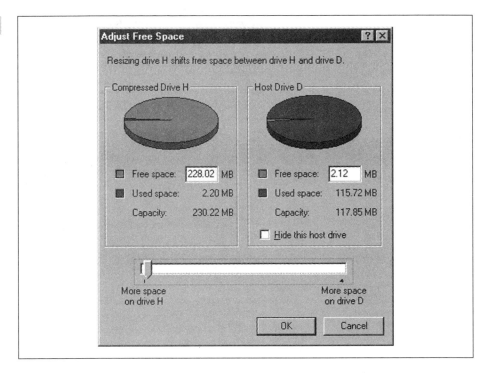

Under the Advanced menu there are eight possible options.

- The Mount and Unmount options only apply to compressed drives. To mount a compressed drive essentially means to assign it a drive letter. Unmounting, then, takes the drive letter away from a compressed drive. So for example, you could unmount a compressed drive from its host, perform Defragmentation or ScanDisk, then mount the compressed drive. This also allows a user to mount and unmount a compressed floppy disk.

- Create Empty is discussed in the following section.

- Delete deletes the selected compressed drive.

- Change Ratio allows the user to change the estimated compression ratio of future files. If you have an uncompressed drive, you know exactly how much free space you have on the drive. But when using a compressed drive, Windows 95 must estimate how much free space is available, as the amount of free space depends on the compressibility of files you will store on a drive in the future. Say that a drive is using a 2:1 ratio to estimate free space on a drive. If you store certain types of files which compress easily (bitmaps), the drive would be able to compress the bitmaps at a higher compression rate than other types of files which don't compress easily. Take a look at Figure 11.30 to see how to use this option.

What is the best ratio for you? Typically, a safe bet is to set the Estimated compression ratio at the same rate as the Actual ratio. If you know that you will be storing highly compressible files, you are safe setting the ratio higher. Remember that this doesn't change the compression rate of the files presently on your drive; this only affects how DriveSpace estimates the amount of free space on a compressed drive.

- Change Letter allows you to change the drive letter of the selected drive. Use this with caution, as changing the drive letter can affect other programs using the drive.

- Settings allows you to change the *automount* setting. The Windows 95 default is to have automount enabled. Automount means that upon startup, Windows 95 automatically mounts any unmounted compressed drive (for example, floppy drives).

- Refresh simply updates the window to reflect any recent changes to the drives.

FIGURE 11.30

Changing the
compression ratio
of future files

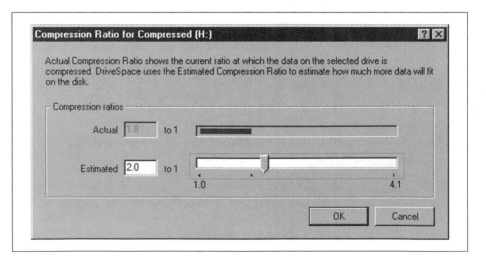

Up to this point, we've taken a look at the different options in the DriveSpace dialog box; now let's take a look at how to compress different types of drives.

Compressing a New Empty Drive

If you think back to the partitioning and formatting section, you'll remember that I had a 118MB logical DOS drive. Well, I decided to compress that whole 118MB drive to get more megabytes for my buck. Compressing this brand new empty drive was a snap; here's what you'd do.

First, click on the Start button and choose Run. Type **drvspace** and press Enter. Then you'll see a screen like the one in Figure 11.31.

As there is no data presently on Drive D:, I will be compressing an empty drive. Under Advanced, choose Create Empty and you'll see a screen like the one in Figure 11.32.

This screen lets you change two things: the default name of the new compressed drive and which drive will be the host. Here, you can also adjust the amount of free space between the two drives by simply typing in a

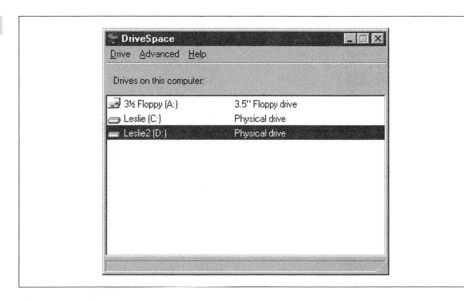

FIGURE 11.32

Creating a new empty
compressed drive

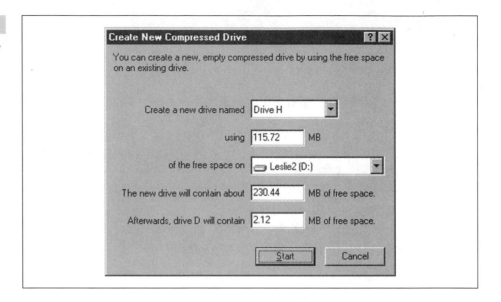

different value; the other value will automatically adjust to reflect the changes. I decided not to change anything, so I just clicked Start. A dialog box will appear on the screen and update you on the status of the compression. When completed, you'll see a screen like that in Figure 11.33.

This screen is simply a repeat of your original screen and doesn't really give any new information. It serves to let you know that the new compressed drive was created. After clicking Close, you will be prompted to restart the computer. Once you have rebooted the system, start DriveSpace again and you'll see the new compressed drive, as in Figure 11.34.

Now your new compressed drive is ready to be used.

Compressing a Boot Drive

Compressing a boot drive involves a slightly different process than compressing an empty drive, as you are compressing a drive with open files. Basically, the process is the same up to a certain point, when Windows 95 reboots in a special operating mode; this allows it to work with open files.

FIGURE 11.33

New Compressed
Drive statistics

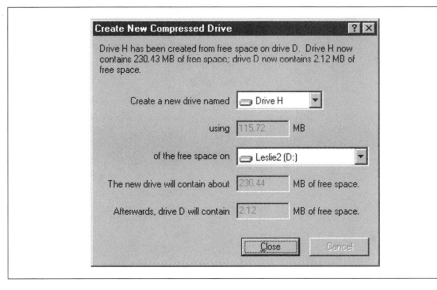

FIGURE 11.34

DriveSpace screen
with compressed drive

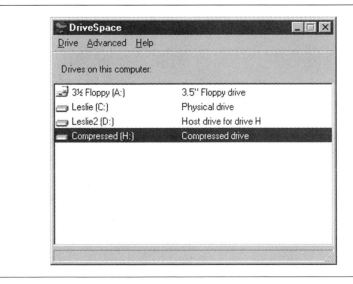

> **N O T E**
>
> Just in case you're wondering, the swap file can exist on a compressed boot drive if a protected mode driver (DRVSPACE .VXD) controls the drive. The swap file is marked as noncompressible and placed at the end of the drive, so that it can shrink and grow as needed.

To begin, run DriveSpace and select the boot drive. Next, under Drive, choose Compress. You will see Figure 11.35.

This screen tells me the statistics for Drive C: before and after compression, in terms of free and used space. Before you begin to compress, click the Options button. You'll see a screen like the screen in Figure 11.36.

This screen allows you to change the drive letter of the host drive and the amount of free space on it. If Hide host drive is checked, the host will not

FIGURE 11.35

Compress a Drive
dialog box

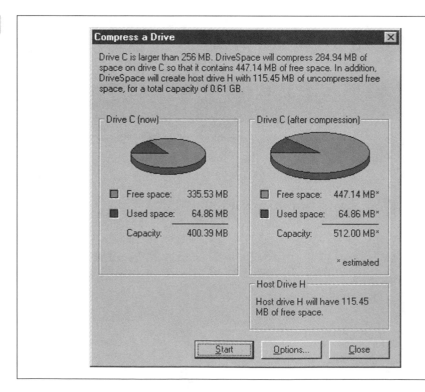

FIGURE 11.36

Compress a drive
Options screen

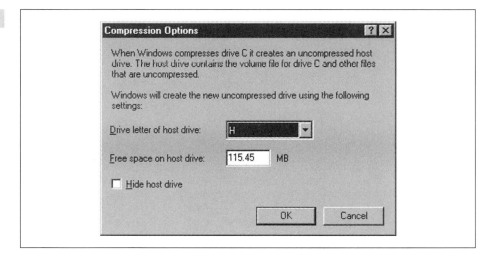

appear in My Computer, the Windows Explorer, and other browse lists. After setting the correct options, click Start, which will prompt you as in Figure 11.37.

If you haven't backed up your files at this point, do it before compressing the drive! Once your files are backed up, select Compress Now and the process begins. First, Windows 95 checks the drive for errors, then boots in a limited version of Windows. While in the limited version of Windows, you can watch the progress of the compression: Windows defrags and then compresses the drive. When finished, you will see a dialog box giving you statistics on the drive before and after compression. Upon clicking the

FIGURE 11.37

Are you sure?

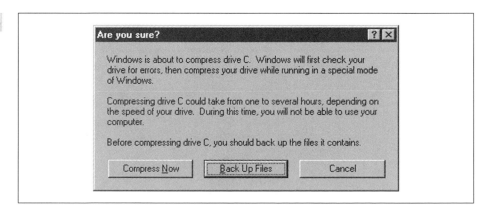

Close button, your computer will restart in Windows 95, and the compression of the boot drive is complete.

Uncompressing a Drive

You may remember from my story at the beginning of the chapter that you must uncompress a drive *before* you repartition and reformat it. Here, we'll go through the steps needed to uncompress a hard drive. Once again, start up DriveSpace and click on the compressed drive (not the host drive) you wish to uncompress. After selecting Uncompress from the Drive menu, you'll get a screen like the one in Figure 11.38.

After you select Start, you will see a series of dialog boxes:

- The first is an "Are you sure?" box, which confirms whether you really want to uncompress the drive.

- The next dialog box informs you that DriveSpace is checking for errors.

- A third asks you whether you want to remove the Recycle Bin on the host drive.

FIGURE 11.38

Uncompress a compressed drive

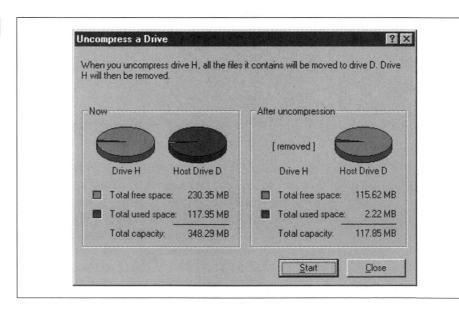

- The fourth dialog box asks you if you want to remove the compression driver from memory.

- Finally, Windows 95 gives you a status box, which tells you that uncompression is in progress.

Once DriveSpace is finished, you will see a dialog box like in Figure 11.39:

And there you have it. The decompression is complete, and, if you wish, you can safely repartition the hard drive!

FIGURE 11.39

Uncompress a Drive
final status

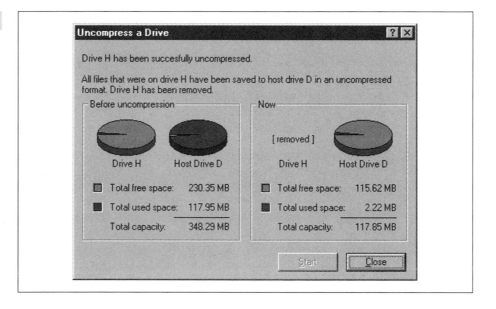

CHAPTER

12

Printing under 95

JUST how much better is printing under Windows 95 than printing under Windows 3.x? Well, I'd have to say that overall, it's not too bad. Printing under 95 has a few whistles and bells not previously found under older versions of Windows. You can see the differences between 95 printing and 3.x printing more clearly when you understand the details behind the printing process. Let's first take a look at Windows 3.x printing, then examine Windows 95 printing.

Here's how the process went under Windows 3.x:

1. First, the user began the print job from his or her Windows application.

2. Then, the print job was sent to the GDI (Graphical Device Interface).

3. Next, GDI sent the print job to the printer driver, as the printer couldn't understand the data in GDI's format. The printer driver was responsible for converting the print job into a language the printer could understand (typically, HPPCL).

4. When the driver finished converting, it sent the print job to the spool file.

5. At this point, the user regained control of his or her Windows application, and the following two steps were performed in the background.

6. The print job was spooled to the printer.

7. The printer then printed the document.

As you can see, the user had to wait through three stages: for the print job to pass through the GDI, then for the printer driver, then for the print job to be sent to the spool file. Once the print job was running in the background, typically the printing was slow and jerky. If you ever used

Windows 3.x, you know about all this. Under Windows 95, this process looks pretty similar, but has changes which improve the printing process, as illustrated in the following steps:

1. As above, the user initiates a print job.

2. Next, the GDI creates an EMF (Emergency Metafile). These files are typically smaller than HPPCL files, and they use less hard drive space.

3. At this point, the user regains control of the application, and the following steps occur in the background.

4. Then the GDI sends the print job to the spool file.

5. From the spool file, the job is sent to the printer.

6. The printer prints the file and the process is complete.

These improvements in printing are due to the new features under Windows 95. First, printing is controlled by a set of 32-bit virtual device drivers, as opposed to the Print Manager, which controlled Windows 3.x printing. This allows printing to run more smoothly. Also, EMF (Enhanced Metafile) spooling allows for a much faster return to application time for the user. Other improvements to Windows 95 printing include better support for DOS-based applications, built-in support for printers with bi-directional communications support, and deferred printing. This last feature allows people whose computers are not physically attached to printers to build a print queue by printing to a file.

Now that you have a feel for the improvements to the printing process, let's take a look at Windows 95's improvements to the process of adding a printer to your system.

Adding a New Printer

Under Windows 3.x and Windows NT Server 3.x, adding a printer was not completely straightforward. Users sometimes weren't sure whether to go to the Control Panel or the Print Manager... and once they did that, did they *create* a printer or *connect to* a printer? Under Windows 95, the user can always use the Add Printer Wizard to add and to connect to local and network printers. Having one central location where you can add a printer, local or network, to your system really cuts down on the confusion.

Another nice thing about the Add Printer Wizard is that if you incorrectly configure information on one screen, you can simply click the Back button and correct any errors. Just remember that you may need to re-enter some of the information on the following screens, as some settings will revert back to the defaults.

Adding a Local Printer to Your System

For this example, I'll add an HP DeskJet 550C printer to my local computer. To begin this process, go into your Printers folder and double-click on Add Printer. This will bring you to Figure 12.1.

Clicking on Next will bring you to Figure 12.2.

FIGURE 12.1

Add Printer Wizard
opening screen

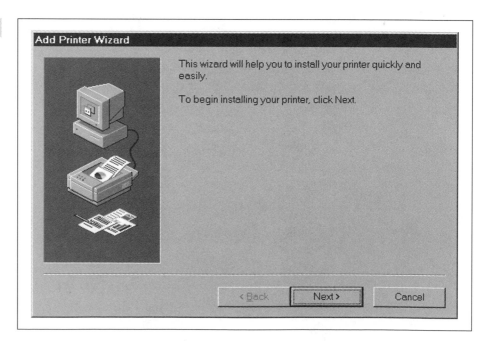

FIGURE 12.2

Add printer Wizard,
local or network
printer

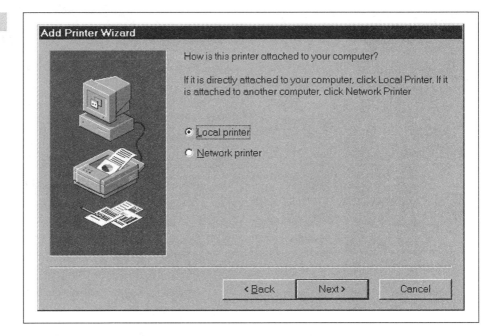

Here, you must choose whether to install a local or network printer. For this example, I will install a local printer, so I select Local printer and then click Next. This leads you to Figure 12.3.

On the left side of the screen, scroll down until you find the manufacturer of your printer, then scroll down on the right side to select the exact model of your printer. By clicking the Have Disk... button, you may choose to use the printer manufacturer's drivers.

This screen brings up the issue of whether you should use Windows 95 drivers or the manufacturer's drivers with your newly installed printer. I experimented with installing both drivers for an HP DeskJet 550C, and I found that both sets of drivers produce nearly the same print quality. (The Windows 95 drivers produced quality that was a tiny bit better than the manufacturer's drivers, but I had to look pretty hard to notice the difference.)

There is one deciding factor, however, with the printer driver issue: Just how old are your manufacturer's printer drivers? The drivers which came with the HP DeskJet 550C have dates of 1992 and 1993. Due to the fact

FIGURE 12.3

Add Printer Wizard, choose the manufacturer and model of your printer

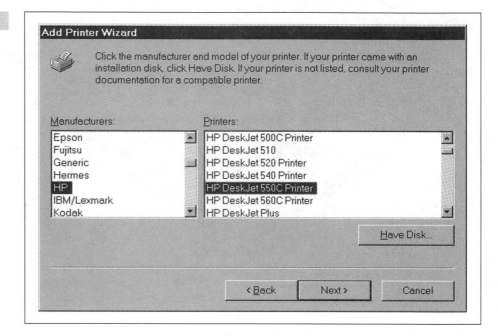

that these drivers are at a minimum 2 years old, they do not support EMF spooling for this printer. (As you learned earlier, EMF spooling can significantly decrease the time a user must wait to regain control of his or her program.) Before deciding whether to use Windows 95's or the manufacturer's drivers, think about the age of your printer's drivers. If you have a brand new printer, it is possible that the drivers were written for Windows 95. However, if you are like many other people and own an older printer, I would recommend using the Windows 95 printers.

Now, if you decide to use Windows 95 drivers, simply click Next. (You will not see the next two screens.) However, if you decide to go with your manufacturer's drivers, click on Have Disk... and you'll see a screen like Figure 12.4.

Pop your disk in Drive A: or browse as necessary, click OK, and you'll see Figure 12.5.

This screen can be a bit confusing. Once again select your printer, then click Next. You don't need to click Have Disk..., as it will simply ask you again for the disk. After clicking Next, you'll come to Figure 12.6.

FIGURE 12.4

Add Printer Wizard,
using the
manufacturer's drivers

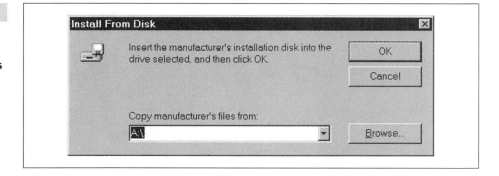

FIGURE 12.4

Add Printer Wizard,
using the
manufacturer's drivers

FIGURE 12.5

Add Printer Wizard,
using the
manufacturer's drivers
(part 2)

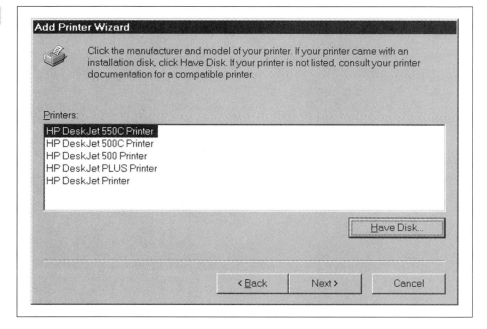

Here, you need to decide whether to use LPT1: or LPT2:. In my case, my printer is hooked up to LPT1:, so I highlighted LPT1:. Clicking on Configure Port... gives you Figure 12.7.

At this screen, decide whether you want to spool MS-DOS print jobs and whether you want to check the port state before printing. Click OK, then click Next to leave the port-choosing screen. The next screen asks you two

FIGURE 12.6

Add Printer Wizard, choose printer port

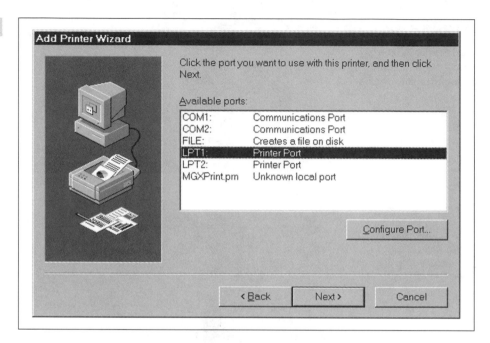

FIGURE 12.7

Add Printer Wizard, configuring your port

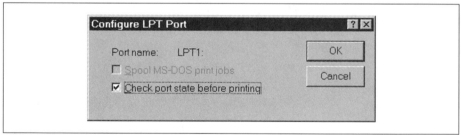

things: the printer's name and its status as the default printer. This screen looks like Figure 12.8.

I accepted the default name of the printer, then selected the radio button next to Yes to indicate that I wanted this printer to be the default printer. (No is the default.) Clicking Next will bring you to Figure 12.9.

It's not a bad idea to print out a test page—if nothing prints, you definitely know you have a problem. Another good reason to print a test page is because of the information it lists. The test page will give you statistics about

FIGURE 12.8

Add Printer Wizard, naming the printer

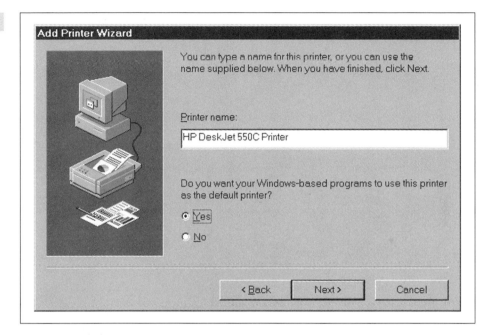

FIGURE 12.9

Add Printer Wizard, printing a test page

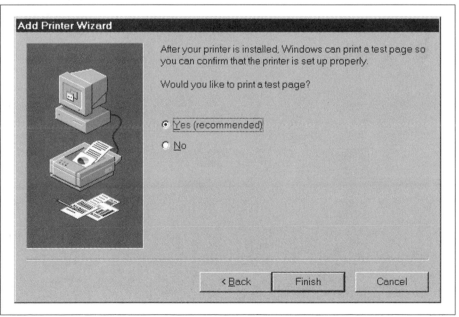

your printer, including the version of the drivers used, the port name, and the various files used by the printer. Make your selection, then click Finish. At this point, make sure you have the Windows 95 CD-ROM or disks on hand so the Add Printer Wizard can complete the process.

You will then see a status screen, which tells you which files are being copied. After the files are transferred, you will see a dialog box asking you whether your test page printed correctly. Clicking Yes brings you out to the desktop, and you will see the icon for your new printer in the Printers folder. Clicking No starts up Windows 95's help file for printing. It gives you examples of things to check to discover the problem with your printer.

Adding/Connecting to a Network Printer

The process of connecting to a network printer is fairly similar to that of adding a local printer, as you can add both local and network printers from the Add Printer Wizard. But when connecting to/adding a network printer, you have the option of beginning the process not only from the Add Printer Wizard, but also from the Network Neighborhood. Whether you begin in the Add Printer Wizard or the Network Neighborhood, the first step in getting to your printer will be browsing. Once you have found your network printer, both processes have identical screen prompts. So for the sake of doing something different, I'll begin this process from the Network Neighborhood.

First, double-click on the Network Neighborhood icon. In our network, Figure 12.10 is the screen you see.

Listed in this screen are all the available resources on our network. Select the computer which is connected to the desired printer and double-click on that computer's icon. If a printer does not show up on this list, make sure the machine is set to share its printers. (There's more on sharing printers later in the chapter.) You'll see a screen similar to Figure 12.11.

At this point you must know the share name of the printer to which you want to connect. (If you don't know, then go track down your network administrator.) In this case, I know that the printer's share name is hp550c, so I clicked once on its icon, then pulled down the File menu. From this

FIGURE 12.10

Network
Neighborhood,
connecting to a printer

FIGURE 12.11

Network
Neighborhood,
connecting to a printer

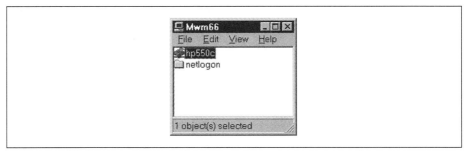

point, you can do two different things: You can choose Create a shortcut or Install the printer. What's the difference? Creating a shortcut places the printer's icon on your desktop; installing the printer places the printer's icon in your Printer folder. In both cases, you still must go through the following processes—you cannot place the icon on the desktop or in a folder without going through the installation process. For this example I've chosen Install; when you click it you'll see Figure 12.12.

The default here is No. If you will be printing from MS-DOS based programs, click the radio button for Yes and then click Next. If you chose No, then you will not see Figures 12.13 and 12.14.

As the dialog box says, in order to print from an MS-DOS-based program, the network printer must be associated with an LPT port. To do this, click on Capture Printer Port... and you'll see Figure 12.14.

FIGURE 12.12

Network
Neighborhood,
printing from DOS

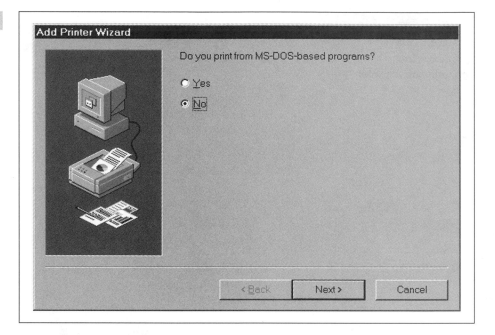

FIGURE 12.13

Network
Neighborhood,
capturing a
printer port

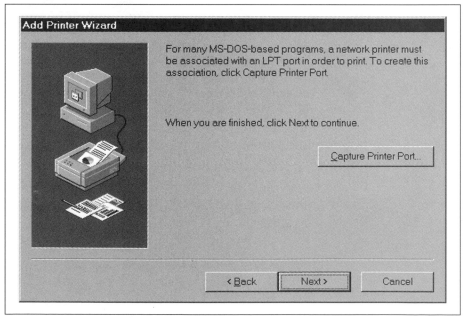

FIGURE 12.14

Network
Neighborhood,
capturing a printer
port (part 2)

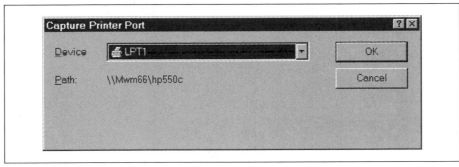

Why do this? So you can have a local printer on LPT2: and use LPT1: for a network printer. Keep in mind that LPT ports aren't important for Windows programs over a network, as everything is sent directly to the shared resource. Make sure the correct port is listed, then click OK. Now after this point, you will see the exact same screens as when you installed a local printer. You will be asked to:

- Choose the manufacturer and model of the printer (and at this point you need to decide whose drivers to use).

- Give a name to the printer and decide whether it will be the default printer.

- Decide whether to print a test page.

If you need to review these topics, consult with the previous section on adding a local printer. After you perform these steps, your network printer is ready for use.

Understanding the Printer Settings

Once you've installed your printer, there's still more to do in terms of printer setup. In the Printers folder, right-click on the newly installed printer and select Properties. This is the place where you select different settings for your printer's ports, graphics, fonts, and memory; this is what we'll discuss for the next few pages.

However, keep in mind that all printers have different capabilities, and therefore may require different settings. A setting that is best for one printer may not be the best for another. See these as suggestions and not concrete rules. Play around with the settings and find the ones that suit your printer the best.

Setting the Printer Details

Click on the second tab, Details, and you'll see a screen like Figure 12.15.

FIGURE 12.15

A network printer's
Details tab

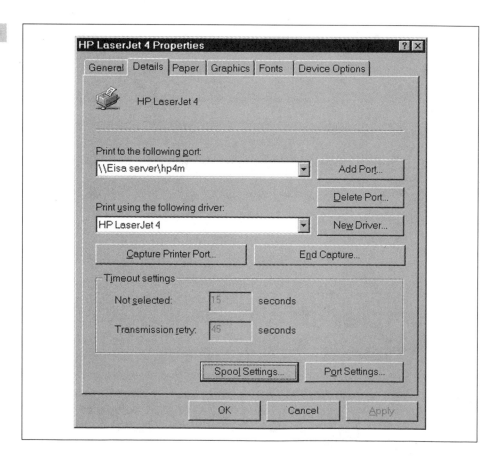

There are a few settings on this screen which require some clarification.

- **Print to the following port:** shows the port you chose during installation. It will show up as LPT*x* for a local printer and as *server* *printername* for a network printer. *Print using the following driver:* shows the driver you chose during installation.

- The **Add Port**... and **Delete Port**... buttons allow you to change the port settings for the printer. For example, if your network printer was moved to a different machine, you can click on Delete Port... and delete the present printer path. Then, you can select Add Port... and browse for the path on the network to which you want to print.

- You can select a new driver for your printer by clicking *New Driver....* A screen will warn you that changing a printer driver may affect the appearance of your documents. Click Yes and you'll see a screen nearly identical to the one you saw when originally selecting your driver in the Add Printer Wizard.

- The **Capture Printer Port**... button allows DOS programs to print to a network printer. DOS does not understand the network path to a printer and must print to a parallel port. Whereas the DOS app prints to LPT*x*, Windows 95's print system captures everything sent to the port and then redirects it to the share. This fools the DOS program into thinking it is printing to LPT*x* when, in actuality, the DOS program is printing to a network printer. By associating a parallel port with a network printer, DOS programs can print over the network.

- **End Capture**... simply disassociates a network port from a parallel port.

- **Timeout settings:** are the default for Windows. Basically, these settings specify that Windows 95 will wait for 45 seconds for the printer to come on line before reporting an error during printing.

- **Spool Settings**... lets you choose the method by which data is spooled to the printer; you can see this in Figure 12.16.

   For faster printing, choose *Spool print jobs so program finishes printing faster.* Under this, you may choose one of the two following options: *Start printing after last page is spooled* or *Start*

FIGURE 12.16

A network printer's
Details tab, spool
settings

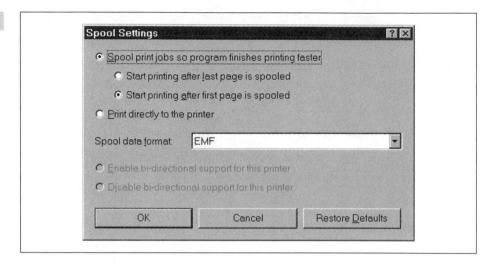

printing after first page is spooled. Your choice between the two is purely your own personal preference, but the second option typically will finish the print job faster than the first. If *Print directly to the printer* is chosen, the program cannot return control of the application until the entire document has been printed.

Spool data format: is an option available only when you choose to spool print jobs, so this is not available when you choose to print directly to the printer. This allows you to decide how the data is spooled to the printer: as raw data or as an *EMF* (*Enhanced Metafile*). When data is spooled as raw data, the printer drivers must interpret that raw data on the fly, and this results in the user waiting longer to regain control of the application. When data is spooled as an EMF, the printer does not have to interpret raw data; instead it interprets a file (EMF) created by the GDI. Interpreting the EMF is less taxing work, and can be done in the background by the printer driver, which allows the user to regain control of the application much faster.

- The two settings to Enable or Disable *bi-directional support* will only be highlighted if your printer has bi-directional support. If this is an option which your printer supports, you should take advantage of it. This enables the printer to let you know, for example, when there is a paper jam or when toner is low.

• **Port Settings**… allows you to configure the printer port; if this is not grayed out, you can decide whether to spool MS-DOS print jobs and whether to have the port checked.

Setting the Graphics Tab

This tab is quite important for the individual who needs to print high-quality graphics, as incorrect settings can lower the quality of the printed graphics. Let's take a look at the settings on this tab; you can see them in Figure 12.17.

FIGURE 12.17

A network printer's Graphics tab

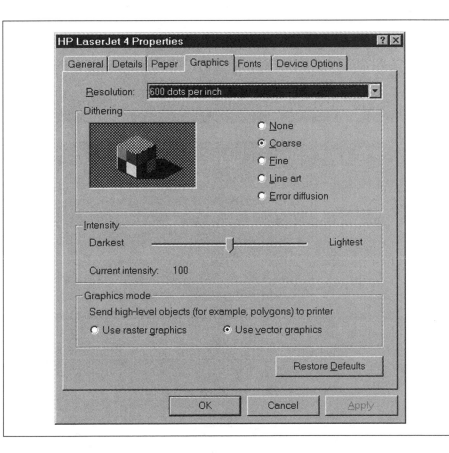

- **Resolution:** This allows you to control how finely detailed your printed graphic will appear. Resolution is the number of dots printed in one inch (measured in dots per inch, or dpi); obviously, the more dots in one inch, the more defined the picture will be. Check with your printer manual to find its highest resolution. Printing in a higher resolution can take more memory—so if you're simply printing a draft, you can change the resolution to a lower setting.

- **Dithering** is a process which produces shading in non-color printers and more realistic colors in color printers. This helps the printer know how to define a dark dot (black), a light dot (white), and all the settings in between (different shades of gray). The following are the guidelines recommended by Microsoft; however, all printers are different and you should test to see which setting gives you the best result.

  - **Fine** is typically the setting for printers capable of 200 dpi or less.
  - **Coarse** is the setting for printers capable of 300 dpi or higher.
  - **Line art** should be chosen if your graphics have sharp, well-defined borders between black, white, and gray.
  - **Error diffusion** is for printing graphics with ill-defined borders.

- **Intensity** tells you how dark your graphics will be printed. The default is 100; just move the slider to adjust this setting.

- **Graphics mode** tells the printer how to render the print jobs. Let's look at the differences between the two with an example of printing a circle. Under *Vector graphics*, the instructions, "Draw a circle" (with additional details about size, etc.) are sent to the printer. This is easier for the printer to render, but it is a greater stress on memory. With *Raster graphics*, the printer is instructed where to place every dot to form the circle. This is slower and creates more work for the CPU. So typically, vector graphics can speed up printing, but if you have problems, try switching to raster graphics.

Deciphering the Fonts and Device Options

These two tabs seem to have some of the most cryptic settings in all of the Printer Properties screens. Let's first take a look at the Fonts tab, as in Figure 12.18.

This screen is not very detailed, but is not immediately understandable. Cartridges shows you which cartridges are installed in your printer. Clicking Install Printer Fonts… allows you to install new cartridges.

FIGURE 12.18

A network printer's Fonts tab

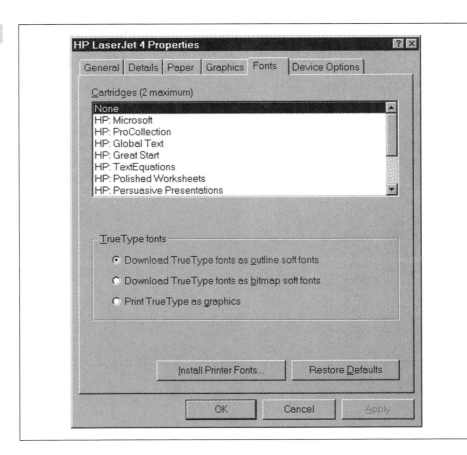

The True Type fonts section can lead to a little confusion. Let's take a look at each one of these options:

- **Download True Type fonts as bitmap soft fonts:** With this option, every different character is first downloaded to the printer's memory as a bitmap. This means that for each different type of font (different point sizes, bold, italic, etc.) there will be an individual bitmap sent to the printer. After these are downloaded, the application sends only text and not bitmaps. Generally printing with this option is faster than True Type as Graphics, especially when the same type of text is used on the majority of the page.

- **Download True Type fonts as outline soft fonts:** With this option, characters are seen as a collection of lines. These outlines are downloaded to the printer's memory with instructions on how to form them. Then the application will send the outline fonts to the printer; at this point the printer interprets the instructions and creates the different fonts. Just as above, this printing can be faster than True Type as Graphics.

- **Print True Type as graphics:** In essence, each page from the application is sent to the printer as one large bitmap and printed this way. Printing True Type as graphics uses more memory, but in cases where graphics or many different types of fonts are used, it can be faster than the two above options.

Now let's discuss the Device Options tab under printer Properties. Take a look at Figure 12.19.

The settings on this screen are actually pretty straightforward.

- **Print quality:** This allows you to choose which type of text quality you want for your documents. These settings will differ from printer to printer.

- **Printer memory:** This is the amount of memory in your printer. The default is the amount of memory that the printer has at purchase. If you have increased your printer's memory, you must manually select the correct amount of memory. It is important that this setting is correct, as overestimating or underestimating the amount of memory may result in an Out of memory error.

FIGURE 12.19

A network printer's
Device Options tab

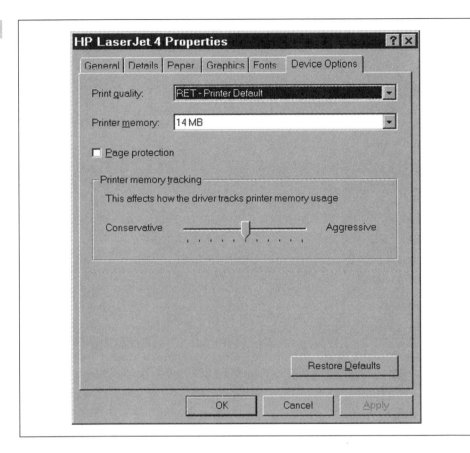

- **Printer memory tracking:** This controls how the printer driver
  estimates the amount of memory needed to print a page and com-
  pares it to the available memory. If this is set at Conservative, the
  printer driver will not try to overextend its memory capabilities, but
  at some points it may not print a document for which there is sufficient memory. If this is set at Aggressive, the printer driver may over-
  estimate its memory and attempt to print documents for which there
  is insufficient memory.

Configuring the Sharing Tab of a Local Printer

When you install a local printer, you will see a tab that does not appear with a network printer: the Sharing tab. The reason for this is that when you install a local printer, it is directly attached to your machine; therefore you have control over which individuals can access the printer. (Sharing for network printers is performed at the server by the administrator.) So how do you share a printer attached to your own machine? Take a look at the Sharing tab for an HP DeskJet 550C printer as seen in Figure 12.20.

FIGURE 12.20

A local printer's
Sharing tab

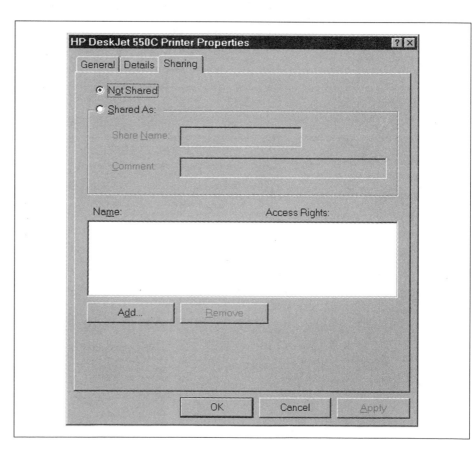

By default, the printer is not shared; it is up to you to decide if you want others to use it. Click on the radio button next to Shared As:, and the two boxes beneath will be accessible. In these two boxes, give the printer a Share Name and a Comment. Share Name is where you give the printer its name as you want it to appear on the network. (Typically, names which detail the type of printer are quite helpful.) If you add a $ to the end of the share name, it won't show up in browse lists; however, it will be available to those who know about it. Under Comment, you can type any other helpful information to help identify the printer. One useful comment would detail the location of the printer (especially if you have a large network). Figure 12.21 shows how I filled out these two boxes.

FIGURE 12.21

Sharing your
local printer

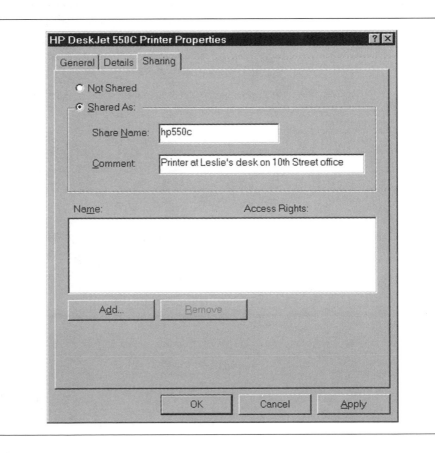

The next step in sharing is deciding which individuals have what type of access on your printer. Click Add... and you'll see Figure 12.22.

FIGURE 12.22

Adding users to
a local printer

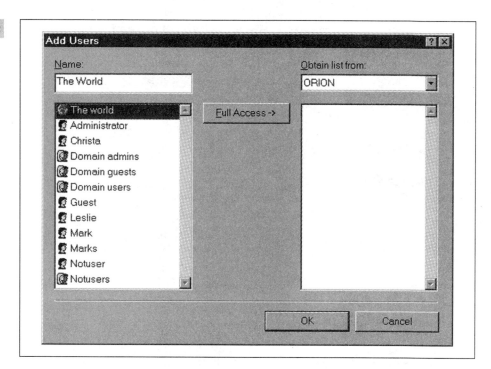

To add users, simply click on their name then click on Full Access. Under Obtain list from:, you can choose to add users from another domain if you wish. (By the way, your list of users won't appear like this unless you're connected to a Windows NT domain.) After you have added users, you should have a screen similar to Figure 12.23.

FIGURE 12.23

Completed list
of added users

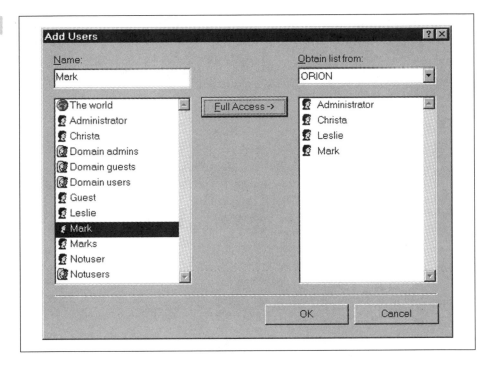

Click OK and you will return to Figure 12.24, the original sharing screen,
now with the list of users.

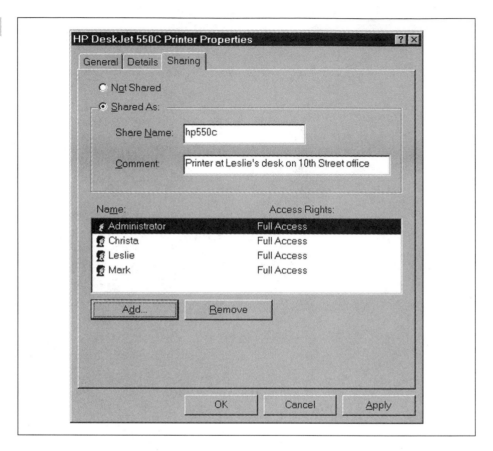

What do you do when you need to delete a user from your shared list? It's simple; just click on the individual's name and then click Remove. This gives you a screen like Figure 12.25.

Once you are finished, click OK. The red × will remain on the screen until you exit out of the printer's Properties box. When you re-enter the Properties box, the user will be deleted from the box.

FIGURE 12.25

Sharing tab after
removing a user

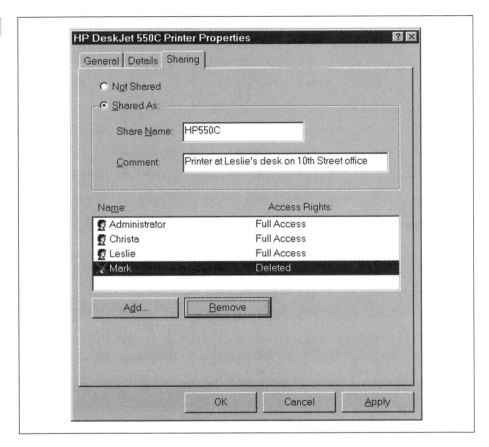

Troubleshooting Common Printer Problems

After a printer is installed, there are a myriad of things which can go wrong. In the following sections, we'll discuss how to tackle various printing problems. But before going into specific problems relating to either a local or network printer, let's simply review a few questions you can ask yourself to eliminate potential problems.

- Is the printer plugged in? If it is plugged into a strip outlet, do the other appliances plugged in work?

- Is the printer turned on? Is it on line?

- Is there paper in the printer? Is the paper jammed? Has the printer run out of toner?

- Are any of the cables loose?

- Do you have share permissions to use the printer?

- Are you connected to the correct printer?

It is usually best to make sure that all the little things are in place before looking for a high-level solution. Now let's go over some of your printer's symptoms and possible solutions.

- Symptom: Your graphics print lighter or darker than they should.

    I experienced this problem after installing Windows 95. I first thought that perhaps Windows 95 had problems with my graphics program, but I found the problem existed when I printed from several other programs. When I originally set up my Graphics tab in the printer Properties, I had set my Dithering to Fine. By playing around with the Dithering option, I found that the setting Coarse printed my graphics correctly. The reason that the Fine setting didn't fare well for me was that I typically use an HP LaserJet 4 with a resolution of 600 dpi—and the Fine setting is for printers with resolutions of 200 dpi or less. One other possible solution is to check that the Intensity setting on the Graphics page is not pointing too far towards either the right or left.

- Symptom: Printing is slow.

    First check your Spool Settings on the Details tab. Do you have it set to print directly to the printer? The fastest setting on the Details tab is *Spool jobs so program finishes printing faster*, with a sub-setting of *Start printing after first page is spooled*. Another possibility to consider is this: Are you printing documents laden with graphics? If you have your Fonts tab configured to *Download True Type fonts as bitmap or outline soft fonts*, consider changing to *Print True Type as graphics*. The latter setting uses more memory but handles graphics better than the previous two.

- Symptom: It takes too long to regain control of the application after starting a print job.

  Try setting your Spool data format box in the Details tab to EMF, rather than RAW. The EMF spooling cuts down on the return-to-application time.

- Symptom: The printer prints text or graphics which is unreadable.

  Check to make sure you have the correct driver installed for your printer.

- Symptom: You keep seeing the error "Print Overrun."

  First, check on the Device Options tab that you have the correct amount of memory installed for your printer. Remember that you must manually change the settings to reflect any memory added past the default. If you don't know how much memory your printer has, consult the printer's manual for help. You can also enable *Page protection*, which creates an output buffer.

- Symptom: Pages are only partially printed.

  Your printer may not have sufficient memory; see the previous solution.

Now that you're well-versed with Windows 95 printing, look to the next chapter to learn about DOS apps and Windows 95.

CHAPTER

13

Running Legacy
Applications under Win95

WINDOWS 95 applications began hitting the shelves not long after the release of the operating system itself. The problem is, if you're a a typical user, you already have a massive investment in existing DOS and Windows apps. Unless you're prepared to replace all of your applications, you'll need to know how to keep those legacy applications up and running on Windows 95.

Windows applications under 95 require about the same fine-tuning that they did under Windows 3.x: not much. DOS applications, on the other hand, have special needs arising from their position in an alien environment. Therefore, in this chapter we'll talk about getting both DOS and Windows apps to work under Win95, focusing more on DOS applications.

How Win95 Supports
Older Applications

As you read in Chapter 2, the Windows 95 kernel is 32-bit, rather than 16-bit—although 386+ computers have been around for years, only now does Windows fully support the 32-bit architecture of the 386+ family of machines. (For backward compatibility with the 286, previous versions of Windows are 16-bit. Windows 95 won't run on a 286.) Being a 32-bit operating system means that everything should happen twice as fast as it did with 16-bit Windows.

Except for one problem.

DOS and Windows 3.x applications aren't 32-bit programs. How are they supposed to use Windows 95's 32-bit API for communicating with the system hardware?

The answer, as you may remember from Chapter 2, is that they don't. Instead, Windows 95 has a 16-bit API that DOS and Windows applications can use for an operating system. That's important: The Windows 95 that, say, Excel 5.0 sees is *not* the same Windows 95 that Excel 7.0 (the 95 version) sees.

The importance of this goes beyond the fact that Windows 3.x applications and Windows 95 applications see different coding. Since all Windows applications use the same virtual machine (that is, they're not isolated from each other), that means that one Win16 application drags down the entire operating system to being 16-bit, rather than 32-bit. Through no fault of their own, applications designed for Windows 95 are reduced to a 16-bit operating system, kind of like members of a platoon who have to do pushups when one person screws up. The bottom line is that you won't get full 32-bit performance from Windows 95 unless you're only running Windows 95-optimized applications. The good news is that, once you close the last 16-bit program (*close*, not minimize), the operating system reverts to 32-bit. ("Awright, you, g'wan out—you're slowing up the rest of us.")

That's the bottom line on how Windows 95 supports Win16 applications. Running DOS applications affects Windows 95 applications less because each DOS app runs in its own virtual machine (thinking that it's the only program running on the machine).

Setting the Properties of DOS Apps

Win95 can run your DOS applications, and in many cases can run them better than DOS can. You can multitask, context-switch, and (sometimes) run them in windows. Additionally, you can load and unload TSRs without having to reboot—just close the window, and the TSR leaves memory.

A nice feature for those terribly useful DOS TSRs that you've been using forever and don't want to give up, but don't want hanging around in memory either.

Windows 3.x required a certain amount of hand-tuning to get these DOS applications to work, using a tool called the *PIF Editor*. The PIF Editor, or Program Information File Editor, is where you'd set environment variables like the amount and kind of memory the application received, whether it ran in a window or full-screen, and what fonts it used.

Windows 95 does not have a PIF editor. Instead, the job of the PIF editor is handled by the Properties dialog boxes associated with every DOS application. Properties is a little simpler to use than the PIF editor because it's broken down into smaller chunks and doesn't provide some of the options that the PIF editor does. Generally speaking, however, the two programs have the same function: fine-tuning DOS applications.

To open the Properties dialog box, right-click on an application's object (in the figure below, I've chosen Lotus 1-2-3 version 3.1), and choose Properties from the pop-up menu. You'll see a screen like the one in Figure 13.1.

Please note that only DOS applications will have such detailed Properties dialog boxes; Windows applications will only have the General tab and, if you've created a shortcut, a Shortcut tab.

WARNING Be careful when editing the contents of a program's Properties dialog. There's no Restore Defaults button.

To illustrate the function of each of these tabs, let's go through them one by one with a sample program—Lotus 1-2-3 version 3.1.

FIGURE 13.1

Opening screen of
Properties dialog

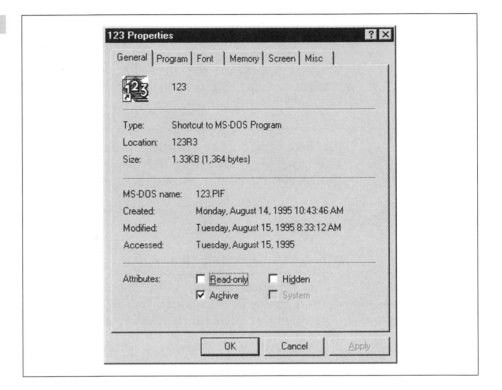

General

The opening screen in the Properties dialog (shown in Figure 13.1) gives
you some general information about the application, including:

- The file name and type
- Which folder the file is located in
- The size of the file on the hard disk
- The dates and times the file was created (if you installed the program
  after installing Windows 95), last modified, and last accessed
- The attributes associated with the file

When you install a DOS application, Win95 does a lot of the preliminary
work, so when you open this screen the file and folder information will

already be in place and uneditable. There's not much for you to do here except perhaps note the file size (remembering that this number is the space that the file requires on disk, not the amount of memory it needs to run) and adjust the attributes as necessary. For example, if you wanted to make sure that the program file gets backed up the next time you back up your disk, you could set the archive bit.

The Win95 Resource Kit warns you in rather dire terms not to adjust the file attributes, but the only thing that you really need to worry about is hiding the file (setting the hidden bit) and then not being able to find it. Otherwise, there's not much damage to be done here.

Program

The next tab has more for you to do, as you can see in Figure 13.2.

At the top is the full name of the application and its version number. This doesn't appear in the folder or at the top of the application screen when it's running, so there's little point in adjusting it.

The next entries, however, are worth exploring.

- **Cmd line** is the name of the executable file for the program. Don't change this entry, or else you won't be able to run the program. Win95 will automatically update this entry if you move a file, but be aware that not all programs will run from just any folder—homebodies, like 1-2-3, insist on their program directory.

- **Working** is the place that the application will go first to load and save data files. If you don't enter anything here, the application will look first in its program directory. You can enter any drive or directory here, so if you store all of your files in your home directory on the server, you can enter the directory information here.

  When specifying a working directory, make sure that that directory will be available. If you specify a network directory (for example) and the network is not active, you'll slow up your application as it tries to connect to the unavailable directory.

- **Batch File** allows you to specify a batch file to be run each time you start up the application. For example, there is a shareware program called Dcopy that won't work unless you specify a source drive in the

FIGURE 13.2

Program tab of
Properties dialog box

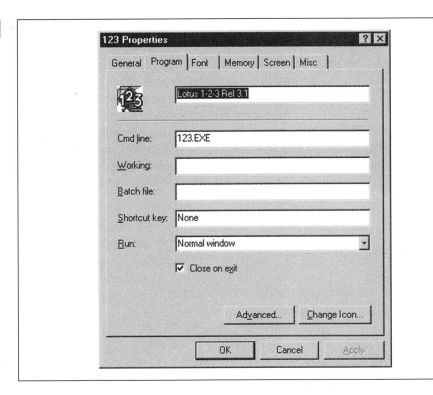

startup command. Double-click the icon, and all you'll get is instructions telling you how to start the program, and the help file. Therefore, to make this program work in Windows 95, I must type **DCOPY A** in the Batch File box. Then the program works as though I'd typed DCOPY A from the command line.

Make sure that you include the full path information if the batch file is not in the same directory as the program file.

- The **Shortcut Key** is a hotkey combination that allows you to start up an application without having to pull it from its folder or the Toolbar. Shortcut keys must include Ctrl or Alt (like Ctrl+J) and cannot conflict with any other shortcut keys, including Win95 combinations, or they won't work.

You cannot use the Tab, Escape, Enter, Spacebar, Backspace, or the Print Screen key in a shortcut key.

- **Run** specifies how the program should run: as a window, full-screen (maximized), or minimized on the desktop. Not all programs can run as a full screen, so the default Normal Window option may be your best bet.

- **Close on Exit**. In previous versions of Windows, deselecting this option meant that when you shut down an application, its DOS window would remain open. I'm not sure why this remains an option in Win95, however, as shutting down a program (windowed or not) shuts down the window with it, whether or not this box is checked.

- In addition to the main screen, the Program tab is the starting point for a couple of what Win95 calls advanced program settings: changing the program icon and adjusting the CONFIG.SYS and AUTO-EXEC.BAT settings discussed in the Registry chapter.

N O T E The CONFIG.SYS and AUTOEXEC.BAT files in the Advanced Program Settings only apply to the program when it's running in MS-DOS mode.

Advanced Program Settings

Clicking on the Advanced button allows you to adjust the CONFIG.SYS and AUTOEXEC.BAT which that particular DOS program uses *when it's running in MS-DOS mode*. The mechanics and effects of changing these files is covered in the Registry chapter, so we don't need to go into much more detail. Just remember that there's no Restore Defaults button to revert back to the original configuration files, so be careful about what you change here. Also, you can't edit either file until you select MS-DOS mode—until then, the file information is grayed out.

Running Programs in MS-DOS Mode

In the Advanced Program Settings dialog, notice the check box that lets you prevent DOS programs from detecting Windows 95. Some DOS applications just don't like multitasking operating systems, so they'll balk if you try to run them under Win95. To get around this, try checking this option and seeing if the program will run. If it still won't, you may have to switch the computer to DOS mode. To do so, click Shut Down on the Start menu. You'll see a dialog box that looks like Figure 13.3.

Choose *Restart the computer in MS-DOS mode*, and see if the program will run like that.

> **WARNING** Make sure that you save files in all active programs before attempting to restart the computer in MS-DOS mode.

Please note that you shouldn't run programs in MS-DOS mode unless they won't run any other way. If you can run a program in a DOS session within Windows, then your application can still use the protected mode drivers and other advantages of the Windows 95 architecture. Run an application in MS-DOS mode, though, and not only will you have to use real-mode (slower) drivers, but you'll have to load them into memory, which takes up part of that precious 640K.

Changing the Icon

When you first install any DOS application, it gets the default MS-DOS icon, even if an icon file is included in the program directory. Boring, right? (Not to mention confusing, if all your DOS apps look alike.) To

FIGURE 13.3

Shut Down menu

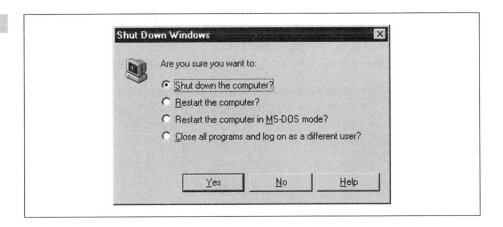

change the icon, click on the Change Icon button in the Program tab, and you'll see a dialog box that looks like Figure 13.4.

A veritable cornucopia of icons! As it happens, I know that 1-2-3 version 3.1 comes with its own icon (I can see the 123.ICO object in the 123R3 folder) so I'll browse for it instead of using one of the generic Win95 icons. I click on the Browse button, and see a dialog box like the one in Figure 13.5.

FIGURE 13.4

Change icon
dialog box

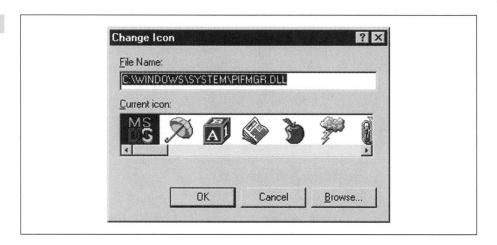

FIGURE 13.5

Browsing for the
1-2-3 icon

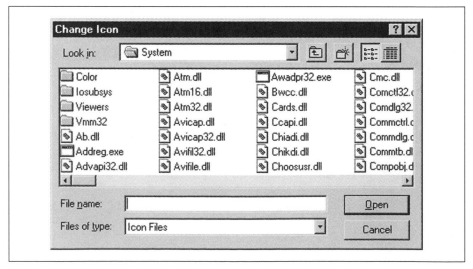

From here, I move to the 123R3 directory and choose the 1-2-3 icon (123.ICO). When I click OK, I'm back in the previous screen, as you can see in Figure 13.6.

There's only one icon in this directory, so it's selected. I choose OK to associate this icon with 123.exe, and I'm done. Now, when I open the 123R3 folder, I'll see this icon rather than the MS-DOS one.

Fonts

Click on the next tab. You'll see a screen like the one in Figure 13.7.

From this screen, you can select the font that the DOS *window* will use, choosing from either bitmapped fonts or True Type. I personally don't like the True Type fonts for DOS windows, as they're very finely drawn and thus difficult to read, but you can see how a given font will look in the Font Preview window and decide for yourself. Choosing Auto will make the font size correspond to the size of the window—if you make the window bigger or smaller, the font size will adjust accordingly. If you select a specific font size, you won't be able to resize the window. Notice how, as you select different fonts, the image in the Window Preview box changes.

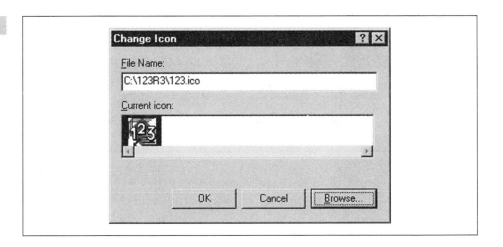

FIGURE 13.6

Choose Icon dialog box with 1-2-3 icon loaded

FIGURE 13.7

Font tab in the
Properties dialog box

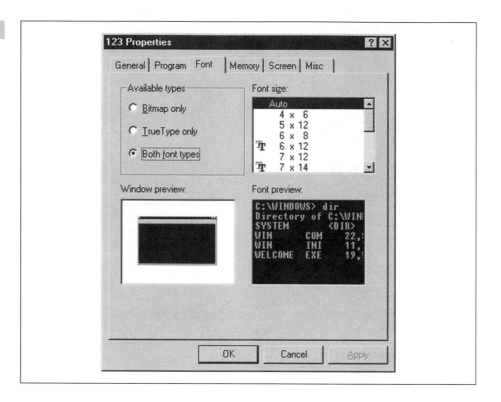

NOTE   Changing the font size here doesn't affect the font that the
application uses, if there is one—whether you choose Auto or
16×12, a Lotus 1-2-3 spreadsheet (for example) will use the
same font. Changing the font only makes a difference if the
application uses the DOS command line.

For the record, you can also set the font used by the command line from
the DOS window itself. On the toolbar (shown in Figure 13.8) either select a new font size from the drop-down list on the left end of the tool bar
or click the A button to return to the Font tab of the Properties dialog box.
Any changes to the font settings will take place immediately.

FIGURE 13.8

Toolbar for a DOS window

Memory

The Memory tab and Program tab contain the most important settings for making sure that your DOS application is working properly. The Program tab controls how your application runs, while the Memory tab determines the amount and kind of memory that your application gets. You can see 1-2-3's Memory tab in Figure 13.9.

This is a fairly complex dialog box, so let's look at each entry in turn.

FIGURE 13.9

Memory tab in 1-2-3's Properties dialog box

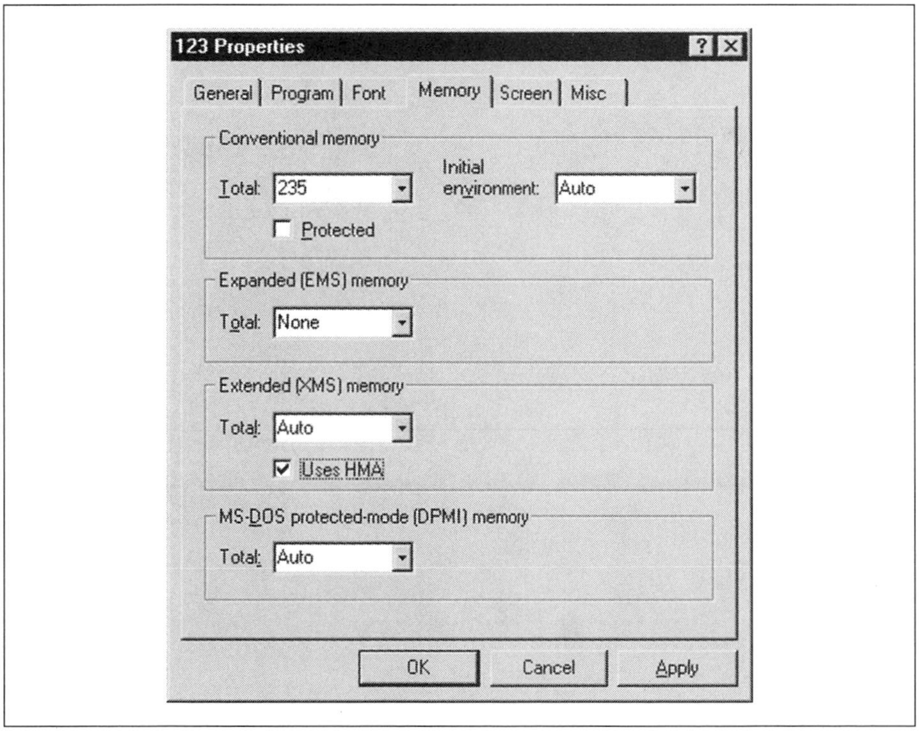

Conventional Memory

The Conventional Memory setting contains two parts: Total Memory and Initial Environment.

- **Total Memory** is the amount (in kilobytes) that 1-2-3 needs to work at all. Win95 allocated 235 bytes without me having to do anything about it, and that amount seems to work pretty well. If you're trying to reduce the amount of memory that a program uses, you can tweak this amount to see the point at which the application no longer runs. To let the application take as much conventional memory as it needs, select Auto from the drop-down list.

- **Initial Environment** sets the number of bytes (not kilobytes) reserved for COMMAND.COM, the part of DOS that understands what to do when you type a command. Win95's Help says that if this amount is set to Auto, then this parameter is set by your SHELL= statement, but *I* don't have one in my CONFIG.SYS and 1-2-3 still works fine.

WARNING Be careful when adjusting the Initial Environment setting! Sometimes, if you set this amount too low, all of Windows will crash and you'll have to reboot to get the system back.

In addition to the two drop-down list boxes, there's a small check box below the Total text box. Checking this box (Protected) keeps the application from affecting other programs if it crashes. As you probably know, one downed application in Windows often starts a domino effect of crashing applications, so although this setting may slow down your program a little it might not be a bad idea if you *know* that an application is buggy and liable to go down in flames. The difference in speed is not always noticeable.

Expanded Memory

The Expanded Memory setting specifies the amount of paged memory available to 1-2-3. Win95 set this number to Auto, but since Lotus 1-2-3 versions 3.x and later use extended memory, rather than expanded, this setting doesn't mean much for this particular application. Check your application's documentation to see if it can use expanded memory—if not, then you can select None from the list box.

In previous versions of Windows, the expanded memory manager included the bottom 640K in the expanded memory pool, so if I allocated, say, 1024K to Lotus 1-2-3 v2.2, the program would only see about 350K. That seems to be fixed in Win95—if you allocate 1024K of expanded memory to a DOS application, it gets the full amount.

Extended Memory

The Extended Memory setting determines how much memory above 1024K is available to the application. Many recent applications (including 1-2-3 version 3.1) support extended memory, but check the documentation to be sure. Do *not* set the amount of XMS memory to an amount greater than the memory physically *in* the machine, or the program won't run.

Although there's a check box in this section permitting a program to use the High Memory Area (HMA), most of the time there's no point in enabling this option. The default CONFIG.SYS specifies that DOS is loaded high, and there's only room for one program in the HMA. Unless you remove the DOS=HIGH line from CONFIG.SYS, then nothing else can use the HMA, even if you give the program permission.

DPMI Memory

The DPMI Memory setting describes the amount of *managed* extended memory that you allocate to the application. The difference between normal extended memory and DPMI memory is this: In normal extended memory, there's nothing preventing one application from attempting to access the extended memory that another application is using—with predictable results. Unless you know the specific amount of extended memory that the application will need, just leave this set at Auto, and the application will take what it needs.

Interestingly, although allocating more extended memory than physically exists on the machine will prevent the application from running, allocating more *DPMI* memory than exists on the machine doesn't seem to affect the application.

Troubleshooting Memory Settings

To a significant extent, memory settings determine how a DOS app will run or whether it will run at all. Generally speaking, 95 handles your program's memory requirements without requiring too much guidance. If your programs aren't working right, however, here are some things to check.

- **Is enough conventional memory allocated to the application?** If you play around with the conventional memory settings and set them lower than the amount of memory required, the program won't run. There's no warning system in place, so if you change the settings in the Properties box, you won't know that anything's wrong until you try to start up the application and you see an error message like the one in Figure 13.10. If the program settings allocate enough memory (or are set on Auto) but you're still getting this message, see if the program will run if you unload some programs from memory.

- **Is more expanded memory allocated than exists on the computer?** Expanded memory won't hurt programs not equipped to use it (although it wastes memory). However, if you allocate more memory than exists on the machine (for example, telling an 8MB machine that Lotus gets 16MB of expanded memory) then the program won't run. Unless you watch *very* carefully, it's not easy to tell what's going on, but in between the "welcome" screen for your application and being ignominiously dumped back in Windows 95, a brief message flashes that not enough memory is available.

If your DOS program seems to start up and then fail, check the settings for expanded memory. Set them to None if the program can't use the memory (check the documentation), or Auto if it can.

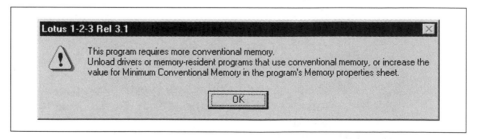

Lotus 1-2-3 Rel 3.1

⚠ This program requires more conventional memory.
Unload drivers or memory-resident programs that use conventional memory, or increase the value for Minimum Conventional Memory in the program's Memory properties sheet.

OK

- **Have you allocated more extended memory than exists on the computer?** The Extended Memory setting on the dialog box determines the maximum amount of memory above 1024K that the program can use. If you specify a number greater than the amount in your PC, then your program will start up and then fail, with the message "Cannot initialize memory manager." If you see this, press Esc to clear the screen and then adjust the extended memory settings to Auto or a lower number.

  Some programs don't cope well with having an unlimited amount of memory available, so if your programs don't work, try designating a specific extended memory quota.

- **Is there sufficient memory for the operating environment?** I recommend that you leave the settings for the initial environment alone. Auto, the default setting, ensures that the application can take up as many bytes in memory as it needs for its operating environment (COMMAND.COM). COMMAND.COM doesn't require a whole lot of memory; however, if you set this value too low, the application may run normally but crash when you attempt to exit. When I set the initial environment to 0, for example, Lotus 1-2-3 started fine and worked normally, but when I exited the program the display became unreadable and I had to reboot to restore my system.

Screen

The application's screen settings determine how it will look while running and how memory is allocated to drawing the screens used. Look at Figure 13.11 to see how Windows 95 set up Lotus 1-2-3's appearance on one machine.

Full-Screen or Window?

First, there's the decision of whether to run the application as a full screen or a window. Depending on the application, you may not have a choice about this, as some applications, especially very graphically oriented ones using EGA or VGA, insist on their full screen. 1-2-3, for example, will let you *set* it to run in a window, but as soon as the program begins it will revert to a full screen.

FIGURE 13.11

Screen settings for
Lotus 1-2-3

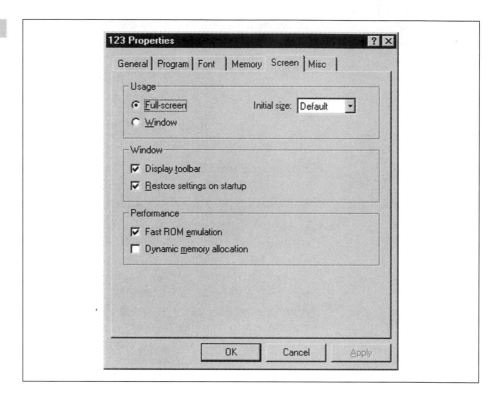

If you run the program in a window, you can set its size beforehand. If you preset the window size, you can't resize it while the DOS session is running.

Window Appearance

If the program will run in a window, you can specify whether to show the DOS toolbar at the top of the window or leave it blank. Unless you prefer the streamlined look of no toolbar, there's really no reason to remove it, as it doesn't seem to affect program performance. By default, it's displayed. In this same section, you can use the Restore Settings parameter to determine whether all the appearance parameters that you've set—the font, window size, and window position—will be used the next time that you start up the program.

Oddly enough, although these two settings only apply if you're running the program in a window, they're not grayed out even if Full Screen is selected.

Performance

There are two options that you can set to fine-tune the performance of your application: ROM emulation and Dynamic Memory Allocation.

Windows 95 contains some programs that perform the function of some of the BIOS routines found in your system ROM (like display or keyboard controls). These programs often work better than the hardwired BIOS, but unless you tell DOS programs to use them they'll consult the instructions found in the BIOS. Enabling ROM emulation causes the program to write to the screen faster, since the system will use the more efficient video-display routines in Windows 95 rather than the ones in your system's BIOS. For most applications, you won't see a noticeable difference between enabling and disabling this option, but Win95 does suggest that you leave it enabled unless your application uses nonstandard ROM functions or you're having problems getting the application to write to the screen. For most applications, however, ROM emulation should present no problems.

Some DOS applications have both text and graphic modes; one example is WordPerfect 5.0, which runs in text mode until you preview a print job, and then it switches to graphic mode. Graphic mode requires more video memory than text mode. To allocate video memory to an application only as it's needed, click Dynamic Memory Allocation, and Windows 95 will supply the program with only as much video memory as it needs, leaving the extra left over for other programs. If you select this option, then when an application switches from text mode to graphic mode Win95 will attempt to allocate more video memory to the application. If not enough video memory is available, then Win95 won't be able to run the program in graphic mode, and you may not be able to see your print preview (for example). Therefore, if you want to be sure that your program will work no matter what mode it's in, make sure that this box is *not* checked.

> **N O T E**   Unchecking Dynamic Memory Allocation does the same thing as *checking* Retain Video Memory under Windows 3.x.

Miscellaneous Settings

To finish, click on the Misc tab. It will look something like the dialog box shown in Figure 13.12.

Foreground

If you enable Allow Screen Saver (active by default), then the screen saver you chose in the Display section of the Control Panel will come up if you

FIGURE 13.12

Miscellaneous tab in the Properties dialog box

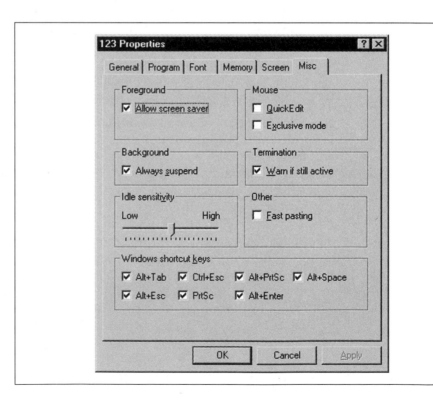

haven't input anything to the system for the predetermined amount of time.

Windowed and full-screen DOS applications recover from the screen saver somewhat differently. When you return to the screen by moving the mouse, a windowed application will be in the place you left it. If a full-screen application was active when the screen saver came up, however, then when you move the mouse to retire the screen saver you'll be back at the Win95 desktop, with the application minimized in the Toolbar. Click it to return to the application.

Background

If you click Always Suspend, Win95 will cease the operation of the DOS application when it's in the background. For example, if you're calculating a spreadsheet in 1-2-3 and then fire up a DOS game like Warlords to while away the weary hours while the spreadsheet's assembling, then the spreadsheet will stop while you're playing Warlords.

This may seem like a bad thing, but the fact of the matter is that an awful lot of programs don't do anything when they're in the background anyway; they sit, waiting for some input from you. For example, if you're working in a word processor, most of the time the system's waiting for you, even if you're a fast typist. (The only computer that I've ever seen that couldn't keep up with a fairly speedy typist was an old computerized engraver that was something of a relic even in 1988, and comparing it to modern computers is like comparing a moped to the Concorde.) Even if a program isn't doing anything except waiting, however, it's still using up CPU cycles.

To get the most out of your CPU's time, therefore, Win95 can keep them in a state of suspended animation until you express an interest in seeing them again. If you don't want Win95 to do this with one of your programs (such as that spreadsheet), then make sure that Always Suspend is not selected. This setting will only affect the program whose Properties you are adjusting.

Note that the Exclusive setting included in the Windows 3.x PIF Editor is not part of Windows 95. If you want a DOS program to get all the resources allocated to DOS programs when it's in the foreground, you'll have to check the Always Suspend option for every other windowed program at the same time.

WARNING If you're accustomed to working with 3.x's PIF Editor, be careful with this setting. Under previous versions of Windows, selecting Background meant that the program *would* run in the background; under 95, it means that it *won't*.

Idle Sensitivity

This setting affects the amount of time that a DOS application must be idle before some of its CPU cycles are allocated elsewhere. The higher the setting, the sooner an application will lose CPU cycles, although it will not lose all of them unless Always Suspend is checked.

Adjusting this setting can make DOS multitasking smoother. A simple multitasking system would perform basic *time slicing*, a process whereby X percent of the time goes to program 1, Y percent to program 2, and so on. But we can do better than that. It turns out that DOS programs tend to have one thing in common: they're interactive. As I said just a minute ago, an application spends a lot of time waiting for input.

So if there are three programs running, and two are basically waiting for input, then Win95 should give all of the CPU time to the one program that *isn't* waiting for input. The only problem is figuring out which programs are waiting for keyboard input. It's not an exact science, so Win95 has some rules of thumb that it uses to guess which programs are waiting for input and which aren't. Try fiddling with these settings to help Win95 use those rules of thumb. Depending on where you set the slider, Win95 will temporarily shut down any program needing input, automatically reactivating that program when you next give it a keystroke.

The down side (you knew there'd be one) is that it takes some time for Win95 to monitor a program for inactivity, and that time may really slow down a program. So adjust each program's PIF to the amount of idle time that you're willing to allow, but if the system seems slow, move the slider down so that more idle time is permitted. (This seems counterintuitive, to move a slider *down* to get *more* of something, but then I've always been unsure whether you turn air conditioning up or down to get colder air.) It's just one of a number of PIF options that really require some experimentation to get just right.

Here are some programs that you should probably set the idle sensitivity as low as possible for:

- Background communications
- Background printing
- 3270 emulation

Once again, if you find that an application is not getting enough resources to work in the background, adjust the setting downward.

Mouse

You can adjust how the mouse works with DOS applications in two ways:

- Permitting the user to select text for copying and cutting without using the Mark tool in the DOS toolbar.
- Restricting the mouse to just the active DOS application.

Activating QuickEdit means that you can select data within the DOS window without needing to mark it. From there, you can copy the data to another application or to Notepad. You can still copy data from an application without QuickEdit activated, but to do so, you must first click the Mark button (a rectangle with a dotted border) so you can select the data to be copied. QuickEdit just saves you a step.

If you set the mouse to Exclusive Mode, you can get the mouse back for Win95 use by pressing Alt+Tab or Alt+Esc to cycle to another application. For as long as that application is active, however, you can only use the mouse while in that application. Move the mouse from the window, and the cursor will disappear.

Termination

Warn if Still Active alerts you that a DOS program is still running if you attempt to close a DOS window without first exiting the program running in that window. Try it, and you'll see a warning like the one in Figure 13.13.

FIGURE 13.13

DOS application
still active

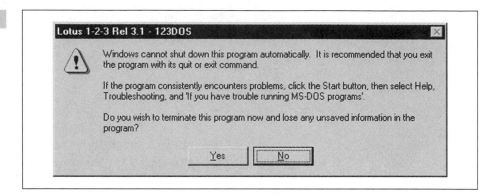

You might as well keep this option enabled (it is by default) as Win95 won't prevent you from closing the window without exiting first, but only warns you that doing so could cause problems.

Other

You know that Microsoft didn't know how to categorize something when you see it in the Other box in the Miscellaneous tab. Fast Pasting refers to how data can be pasted from the Clipboard. With this option enabled, if you have data in the Clipboard, you can actually paste it into your application just as if it were a Windows app—maybe.

If you select this check box, the application will paste information as quickly as Win95 can transfer the data. Because some applications cannot paste properly using this method, test it before relying on it—try to paste information from the Clipboard back to the application. If the paste is successful, you can use the option.

Windows Shortcut Keys

If you uncheck any of these key combinations, then you're telling Win95 to ignore them and reserve them for the use of that particular DOS application. You can't use this setting to assign shortcut keys to an application that it didn't already have—this is just for letting you get full functionality from applications designed before Windows took over some key combinations.

Defining Multitasking

Now that you're familiar with the DOS Properties dialog box, we can talk about how to optimize DOS multitasking under Win95. For this discussion to make sense, however, there's some terminology that you must know. Many of the concepts of multitasking are familiar to those who've worked with previous versions of Windows. Since, however, multitasking is one of those words that means different things to different people, let's take a minute to define a few terms you'll see in this chapter.

Multitasking, at least as I'll use it here, means being able to load more than one program into a computer. The programs may or may not all run—i.e., receive CPU time—at the same time. There are two kinds of multitasking: *context switching* and *concurrency* (also known as *concurrent multitasking*). We'll discuss the differences a little later in this chapter.

Focus refers to the particular window which is currently positioned to receive any user keystrokes or mouse clicks. The window with the focus is also known as the *active* window. If you press a key, the kernel delivers that key to that window, even if there are other windows on the screen. You can identify the focus window because it sits in front of other windows, and its title bar is a different color from the non-active windows (unless your color settings don't distinguish between active and inactive windows, of course). In Figure 13.14, Lotus has the focus; Word for Windows does not.

Note that the focus window is *not* the same as the *foreground program*, a term that you may have heard. Foreground is not meaningful when discussing Windows programs running under Win95, but it *is* meaningful when discussing Win95 while it multitasks DOS programs, as you'll see in the following two definitions.

Session refers to a group of programs that share the video screen. When you start Win95, you start a series of programs that control the Win95 screen, or desktop. Together, these programs are called the *Windows session*. Any Windows program that's running is part of the Windows session.

FIGURE 13.14

Active and inactive windows

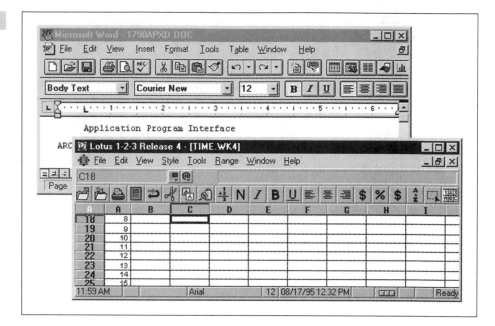

N O T E Regardless of whether a DOS program runs in a window or a full screen, it's running in a separate DOS session, not the Windows session that all Windows apps share.

If, however, you're running a DOS program, the story's a little different. Since the inception of Windows, all DOS programs running in Windows have run in their own session, unable to see the Windows session or other DOS sessions. DOS programs get their own sessions whether they're windowed or full-screen. These DOS sessions are called *virtual machines*, or *VM*s. A session is called a virtual machine because as far as the programs running in that session are concerned, there are no other sessions. A good DOS multitasker must provide the illusion that each session has an entire computer all to itself, hence the name virtual machine. We'll look at virtual machines a little later in this chapter, in the section on DOS multitasking.

Foreground refers to the session that is currently on-screen. If you see the Win95 desktop at the moment, then the Win95 session is the foreground session. If, on the other hand, you're running Lotus 1-2-3 3.1 in a DOS session, and that session is visible on-screen, then that session is the foreground session. Note that when Win95 is the foreground session, then a particular Windows program has the focus within that foreground session.

Context switching or *task switching* refers to loading two or more applications programs into a PC's memory, then switching from one to the other with some series of keystrokes. Context switching is relevant to how Win95 processes share time among themselves and also to how the 386-enhanced mode shares time between Windows programs as a whole and whatever DOS programs are running. Note that in context switching, only the active or foreground program is getting CPU time. A communications program that was downloading data would stop when shifted to the background; a word processor printing a document would suspend printing when put in the background.

That doesn't sound good, but context switching has two main benefits. First, if you spend much of your day shifting from one program to another, perhaps a word processor to a personal organizer to an electronic mail program, then context switching removes the need to constantly exit one program, load another, and then soon exit *that* program and reload the first program. Second, context switchers usually include some kind of cut-and-paste capability, providing an easy method of data integration. Context switching is simple, but it's quite enough for most of us, most of the time. One example of a pure context switcher is the DOS shell that comes with MS-DOS 5 and PC-DOS 5; it allows you to load multiple DOS programs into memory, then switch from one to the other by pressing Alt+Esc.

Concurrent multitasking is like context switching, but with the addition that the background programs continue to receive CPU time and run, even when not visible.

While concurrency sounds more complete and powerful than context switching, it's not always the preferable alternative of the two. Giving CPU time to a background process denies that CPU time to the foreground process, slowing it down—and remember, the foreground process is the one that you're directly interacting with, the one that you want to be quick and snappy in responding to your commands.

Suppose you had a spreadsheet, word processor, and graphics program loaded into Windows. You probably *wouldn't* want concurrency there, as all three are interactive programs—they basically don't do anything unless you're typing or clicking-and-dragging at them. There's no point in wasting CPU time letting the spreadsheet check the keyboard over and over again in anticipation of your next keystroke when the spreadsheet's in the background, and so couldn't *possibly* receive a keystroke.

When, then, does full multitasking make sense? Here are a few examples.

- Communications: When transferring data in the background, or even just to keep a connection open in the background, a communications program must continue to get CPU time when not in the foreground. (Again, for the purposes of these examples, "background" refers to a Windows program that does not have the focus.)

- Along the same lines, some communications programs must "wake up" periodically to poll your electronic mail, or might have to monitor the serial port so as to be able to answer the phone in the background, as is the case when you're using your PC as a fax machine.

- Printing, saving and reading files, or recalculating very large spreadsheets—all are improved by being able to do them in the background.

- Timer and alarm programs must be able to run in the background.

While the uses for concurrency aren't nearly as numerous as they are for context switching, concurrency has enough uses to make it *de rigueur* for any modern PC environment.

Background refers to any program that is not the one that the user is currently interacting with. A background window is an inactive window, and a background session is any session not currently being used. (Remembering how DOS windows get their own session, sometimes a background window and a background session can be the same thing.)

Multitasking DOS Programs Under Win95

The whole point of running DOS programs in a multitasking operating system is to let you use more than one application at a time. Here, we'll talk about how to juggle your DOS apps without dropping them.

Who Handles Multitasking?

There are actually two levels of multitasking in Win95: the Windows Kernel and the Virtual Machine Manager (VMM32.VXD). The kernel handles Windows applications. The VMM has two functions: providing a stepladder that allows DOS programs to use XMS memory and managing the DOS sessions, or virtual machines, that you run.

> **N O T E** VMM32 replaces WIN.386 that appeared in previous versions of Windows.

VMM32.VXD multitasks by dividing the computer into *virtual machines*. The idea with a virtual machine is that the operating system takes the computer's time and memory and divides them up, treating the system as not one computer but several computers, each a virtual machine (VM). The virtual machines are all largely unaware of one another, a very positive feature for any program that's trying to multitask DOS programs; DOS programs don't know how to share a 386, so the virtual machine manager (VMM) just carves up the PC into multiple virtual machines, and drops a copy of DOS into each machine. Each machine thinks that it has its own video board, floppy and hard disks, keyboard, and so on.

All Windows programs live in a single VM, but each DOS program is its own virtual machine. That's worth stressing—to VMM32.VXD, there *is* no such thing as a Windows program, just a big system called Windows. If you're running the Windows programs Excel, Designer, and Ami Pro, and the DOS programs 1-2-3 v3.1, dBase III+, and WordPerfect 5.1, then the VMM only sees four VMs—the Windows VM (which, unknown to the VMM, contains Excel, Designer, and Ami Pro), the 1-2-3 VM, the dBase III+ VM, and the WordPerfect VM. Remember that, as the upcoming discussion on virtual machines and priorities will seem to contradict what I said in the previous section. *The VMM can only assign a priority and control multitasking to the entire Windows VM*; it cannot reach inside and control how the kernel gives CPU time to Windows apps.

This two-layered approach to multitasking was made necessary by the nature of DOS, as I mentioned before.

Activating DOS Multitasking

In previous versions of Windows, the Windows VM was by default the only one that ran in the background. DOS VMs simply froze in place, receiving no CPU time and performing no tasks. In Win95, however, it's the other way around: By default, DOS VMs run in the background. You can demonstrate this with a simple DOS batch file. Open a DOS session and type the following at the DOS prompt:

```
copy con annoy.bat
:top
echo ^G
goto top
^Z
```

Note that you don't type the **^** symbol and a **G** in the second line of the batch file; you press Ctrl+G to make the **^G** appear on the screen. The same for the **^Z**—it appears when you press Ctrl+Z. You will then see a message like "1 file(s) copied," followed by the DOS prompt. Now type **annoy**.

This will cause the PC to beep repeatedly. Now try to switch away from the DOS session with the Alt+Esc or Ctrl+Esc key—it will keep beeping, as the program is still receiving CPU time. The only way that you can get it to quit is to either close the window or press Ctrl+C to interrupt the batch file. (Do it now, before the person in the next cubicle clubs you.)

NOTE   When you're pressing Ctrl+C to stop the ANNOY batch file, make sure that the DOS window has the focus!

To keep a DOS session from operating in the background, open its Properties dialog box and turn to the Misc tab. Check the box that says Always Suspend, and that program will no longer run in the background.

Inside 386 Multitasking

As I've said, DOS programs don't share the CPU and are designed to assume that they pretty much own the CPU and anything attached to it. How, then, does the 386 mode make all of these spoiled children live together?

Well, as was suggested before, the Virtual Machine Manager first creates a virtual machine for each DOS program—an imaginary PC with a specified set of memory, I/O devices, and so on. The programs that enable the VMM to present this panoply of imaginary I/O devices are the virtual device drivers, introduced earlier in this guide as VxD's, for Virtual your device here Drivers.

Once the virtual machines are in place, the VMM must give all of them some CPU time so that they can get their programs executed. The VMM uses a *timeslicing* system whereby each program gets a certain amount of CPU time. At regular intervals, the virtual machine is interrupted by the VMM, which then hands control of the CPU over to the next program for a time, and then on to the next VM, and so on, 'round and 'round. The basic unit of measure is called a *timeslice*. Some VMs may get more timeslices than others, but they all use the same unit.

Under timeslicing, the VM Manager sets a timer programmed to "tick" every, say, 1/20th of a second. Once the timer is programmed, the VM Manager hands control of the CPU over to one of the VMs; then, 1/20th of a second later, the timer ticks—and here's the interesting part. The timer is actually able to interrupt the VM that is currently active and give control back to the VM Manager! That means there's no need for cooperative multitasking. That's why this is sometimes called *preemptive multitasking*.

So you see that the VM Manager divides up CPU time into timeslices. Each non-Windows application gets its own timeslice, and Windows gets a timeslice. That's important: all Windows apps share a single timeslice. Open up a bunch of DOS applications, and Windows will slow to a crawl. (A particularly good example is the Print Manager—slow at best, but crippled when a DOS app or two are loaded.)

N O T E Every DOS program gets its own timeslice, but all Windows apps share a single timeslice.

You can control how DOS programs (but not Windows programs) run from their Properties dialog boxes. As we discussed earlier in this chapter, turn to the Misc tab and establish whether programs should run in the background and how sensitive to idle time Win95 should be.

Tuning Tips for Better DOS Multitasking

Now that you understand how Windows doles out the CPU's attention between the programs that you run, you can tune your system for better overall multitasking. Here are some other specific suggestions.

Microsoft built into WIN386.EXE a lot of adjustment features: knobs, levers, and gears that you can often use to solve a multitasking problem. Most of these tips involve changing or adding a line in the [386enh] section of SYSTEM.INI. Why SYSTEM.INI rather than the Registry? Because DOS programs can't access the Registry, so they're dependent on old Windows settings.

Change the Order in Which You Load Programs

One tip doesn't involve SYSTEM.INI: Load your DOS applications before the Windows applications. The Windows apps will hog memory and other system resources if you load them first. Load the DOS machines first, or you may not have any memory left over.

Tweak the Minimum Timeslice

Open SYSTEM.INI and adjust the setting for MinTimeSlice (in the [386Enh] section). A smaller timeslice will make the system less efficient, because it will have to spend more time flipping between VMs, but it will ensure that your application gets the CPU's attention more often. Try 5 milliseconds (the default is 20). On a 486, you can even set it to 1. Test it out by running a DOS program in the background. For example, communications is the most demanding user of background CPU time, so if you have a DOS communications program, then try downloading a large file in the background several times, each time with a different minimum timeslice. You may find significant differences between the amount of time needed to do a large download.

Some authors recommend very simple programs that just count to themselves in the background; these are usually QBASIC programs that just count to themselves until stopped. The idea is that the multitasking setting that allows more counts while the program is in the background is the right one. The problem with this approach is that it's not realistic; it does not model the very real problem of servicing input/output devices like the serial ports. Use the download benchmark from the precedign paragraph, therefore, to find your best minimum timeslice.

Why does a smaller timeslice make the system less efficient if it means that programs get the CPU more often? The answer is *switching time*. Just as you can't switch from one work task to another without a little setup time (opening a file, or pulling out some paperwork, for example), there's some prep time involved with switching between VMs.

Let Your Programs Access Your PC's Timer Ports Directly

There's a SYSTEM.INI command called TrapTimerPorts; in a word, it can be used to make some timer-dependent programs work more smoothly and reliably. Timer-dependent programs (mainly communications programs, games, and screen blankers) need to directly reprogram the PC's timer, something that they can do without trouble under DOS. A program would use a timer to allow it to track the passage of external time. For example, if your program receives data at 9600 bps, it must know how long 1/9600 of a second is.

With this option enabled, Windows intercepts attempts to reprogram the timer, and instead simulates a timer for the application. That's a nice capability, but it just isn't as consistent as letting the program do the timing itself, and the result can be that you have programs that are too slow, too fast (in the case of games), or jerky. Set this parameter to OFF, and Windows will allow direct access to the timer hardware. For example, you'd add this line to your [386enh] section of SYSTEM.INI:

TrapTimerPorts=OFF

You'll have to add this line, as currently there is no TrapTimerPorts=ON setting—the ON condition is the default. Whichever way it's set, this is a system-wide parameter, so you can't choose which programs get the real timer and which don't—either they all do or they all don't. As there are only two settings for TrapTimerPorts—ON or OFF—it's simple to experiment to find out which setting is right for your problem software.

Turning off this option may cause the side effect that the system time maintained by Windows gets behind the time of day in the real world. If that happens, you can tell Windows to periodically resynchronize its time with the time in your CMOS (setup) clock/calendar by adding the line **SyncTime=True** just below the TrapTimerPorts line in SYSTEM.INI.

Raise Your Program's Priority When It Does I/O

There's plenty of CPU horsepower to hand around in most PCs, even in comparatively slower systems. Most of it's wasted, unfortunately, and that hurts when you're trying to get your computer to respond quickly to communication information and/or keystrokes. That's why there are two SYSTEM.INI commands, ComBoostTime and KeyBoostTime, that allow you to momentarily increase the percentage of CPU time that a program gets after it's received some communications or keyboard input. Both commands are in the [386enh] section. If you enter either one, you'll probably have to add a whole new line to SYSTEM.INI—neither appear in SYSTEM.INI by default, even though they both have default values.

- **ComBoostTime=(milliseconds):** ComBoostTime=*n* tells Windows to temporarily increase the priority of any program for *n* milliseconds after each byte was received from the communications port. The default is 2 milliseconds, a pitifully small value. I've been able to improve background downloading times by 30 percent by increasing it to 150. Just as I suggested earlier in the minimum timeslice discussion, use a DOS communications program running in the background to find the best value for ComBoostTime. Do several downloads with values of 2, 20, 200, and 2000, and see how long a download takes in each case. This will be particularly helpful for slower machines.

- **KeyBoostTime=(seconds):** similar to ComBoostTime, KeyBoostTime increases a program's priority for a short time after it receives each keystroke. *Unlike* ComBoostTime, the value is specified in seconds, so a one-millisecond boost is not specified as 1, it's specified as 0.001. Set it higher for slower machines. When running other applications in the background, increase the key boost time.

  By default, Windows gives extra priority to an app for only 0.001 seconds (a millisecond) after each keystroke. Increase that value to 0.01, ten times longer. Use the download-in-the-background test with a word processor in the foreground, and try out values of 0.001, 0.01, 0.1, and 1.0. As you raise the values, the foreground program will get smoother in feel—but the download in the background will take longer. Raise the number until you can't detect the difference between its effect and that of the next *largest* number, then stick with that next-to-last number.

Make Video Faster

Here are a couple of tips for getting faster video response on your system:

1. Include the line **local=EGA$** in SYSTEM.INI. This command forces Windows to treat the video board as a local resource for each DOS machine. It costs a little memory, but it'll speed up video on some applications. Try it. It goes in the [386enh] section of your SYSTEM.INI file. You will already have a local=CON$ line in SYSTEM.INI—*do not erase it*! These lines can coexist without trouble.

2. Change the WindowUpdateTime=(milliseconds) setting. When Windows runs a DOS application in full-screen mode, it must *virtualize* the display. That means that it must take the graphical or textual output of the program and put it in a window. That's not

straightforward, because the window may not be full-screen, meaning that Windows must clip the output of the DOS program that doesn't fit in the screen. Windows does this by basically "sweeping" across the screen, scanning to see what data sits where on the display.

Once a DOS screen has been placed in a window, Windows doesn't want to have to rebuild the screen over and over again, as that takes time. Ideally, Windows would only redisplay the DOS screen when the screen changed or when the user resized the window. Unfortunately, there's no way for Windows to know when the DOS screen has been modified. So Windows just sweeps the screen every so often. Exactly *how* often is determined by the WindowUpdateTime parameter. Furthermore, DOS programs don't inform Windows of when they've modified the screen, so Windows doesn't know how often it needs to update that screen. By default, Windows updates every 200 milliseconds, whether a DOS application needs it or not. (This applies more to graphical screens than textual screens, by the way.) You can change that value with this SYSTEM.INI parameter, again in the [386enh] section.

The bigger this number is, the choppier the video seems, but then Windows doesn't waste a pile of time modifying DOS screens. Reduce the number, and screen scrolling and updates will be smoother, but at the cost of slower Windows overall. Try out different numbers and find the one that suits you best. On faster PCs, you can get away with using smaller numbers without a speed penalty; on slower PCs, it may be best to settle for some choppiness and get some more CPU speed in return.

Switching Windows

Moving from application to application is easy if you're running them in windowed sessions: just click the icon on the Taskbar that corresponds to the program you want, or click on its window. If one or more of your apps operate only in full-screen mode, however, that won't work—'cause there's no Taskbar visible. To remove the focus from a full-screen DOS application while keeping it open, you must press either Alt+Tab or Alt+Esc to return to the GUI. Your application will appear as an icon on the Taskbar.

If you've used Windows NT, you may wonder if pressing Ctrl+Alt+Del will get you a Task List from which you can select the application that you want. Nope. In Win95, if you press Ctrl+Alt+Del, the system assumes that you want to shut down a program, and it doesn't offer any mechanism for just moving to another one. You can shut down an erring application, but you can't change the focus from one open program to another.

DOS Memory Management under Windows 95

DOS memory management under Windows 95 isn't all that different from DOS memory management under DOS. Keep the number of programs loaded in conventional memory to a minimum, load DOS high, and that should prevent many memory problems.

Maximizing Conventional Memory

DOS can only see the lowest 640 kilobytes of memory, so if you're running a DOS program you're going to want to squeeze all the good from that 640K that you can. And that means that you want as much of that memory free as possible.

Load Fewer Programs (TSRs and Device Drivers)

The first step to maximizing conventional memory has already been taken for you in Windows 95. Rather than relying on external device drivers (like the one controlling your mouse) that must use part of the lowest 640K, Windows 95 includes 32-bit device drivers in the operating system that can reside in memory above 640K, thus freeing up conventional memory. You can follow in that tradition by not loading TSRs unless you really need them.

Load DOS High

By default, this step has been done for you as well. If you turn to the Program tab in a DOS program's Properties dialog, you'll notice that, by default, DOS is loaded high so that most of it isn't cluttering up conventional memory.

32-Bit Device Drivers and DOS Programs

Windows 95 is composed mostly of 32-bit (read: "faster than 16-bit") code. Part of that code includes its device drivers, which control how applications access the PC's hardware by way of the operating system. The fact that Windows 95 is its own operating system, independent of DOS, means that it doesn't have to switch back to real mode to access hardware devices—a good thing. Even better is that your DOS sessions within Windows can use these 32-bit drivers as well, since they're not running DOS as such, but emulating DOS.

If, however, you run a DOS program in exclusive MS-DOS mode, the application can't use any of the Windows 32-bit protected-mode drivers. That presents two consequences: First, the drivers are slower because they're 16-bit instead of 32-bit. Second, drivers must be loaded in memory for the application to use them. The bottom line here is that, if you can run a DOS program in Windows 95, do so—you'll probably get better performance.

Expanded Memory

Expanded memory is a classic example of how something originally intended to be a short-term solution can outlast its supposed lifespan. It came to be like this: After Lotus Corporation had captured a lot of market share and spreadsheets with 1-2-3 version 1A, it released version 2.0 with much fanfare. Unfortunately, there was a teensy problem with version 2.0: it used more conventional memory (the bottom 640K in your machine) than version 1A did. Any spreadsheets written under version 1A that used up all available conventional memory—and there were plenty— would not run under version 2.0. So Lotus, in conjunction with Intel and

Microsoft, designed a kind of workaround memory that would permit the spreadsheets to load even without sufficient conventional memory. That workaround, which still haunts us today in a few programs, is called *expanded memory*.

That's where expanded memory came from, but what is it? In a nutshell, it's non-conventional memory (either add-in boards, or in 386 machines and later, *extended* memory) that an expanded memory manager divides up into *pages* which the application can use like conventional memory. Early expanded memory required add-in expanded memory boards, but today programs that require expanded memory can use the *extended* memory (memory above the first 1024K) that's on your motherboard.

Windows 95 will automatically supply extended memory to DOS programs that can use it (unless you deselect that option from the Advanced screen of the Program tab). If you edit the expanded memory statement, do *not* use the **noems** parameter, or else Win95 won't be able to provide the memory. If you exclude any memory from potential expanded memory, use the x=*mmmm-nnnn* syntax to do so.

DPMI Support under Windows 95

Extended memory, as you probably know, is memory above the top 1024K. Under normal circumstances, DOS apps can't use extended memory—they require some special software called a *DOS extender* to boost them up to where they can see and access memory above 1024K.

Windows contains a DOS extender that allows DOS programs to use memory beyond 1024K, so long as they don't know that they're doing it. Windows maps conventional memory to one megabyte of extended memory, and then tells the DOS session, "Look! I found you this lovely computer memory that you can have for your *very own*." DOS takes the bait and accepts the extended memory as conventional memory. Any time that the application tries to access memory, it looks for an address in conventional memory, but Windows intercepts the memory access and forwards it to the address in the extended memory which that DOS application has been allotted. A nice system, as it allows DOS programs to run with what they think is conventional memory, when in reality the conventional memory is shared among a number of virtual machines.

Some DOS programs have their own DOS extenders built into them. If you need to make them work with Windows, you'll find that some do... but some don't. Is there some kind of overall rule?

Back in the days when OS/2 was still under development, and Windows was just a curiosity that no one used for anything serious, a number of companies started writing DOS programs that could access extended memory on 286 and later computers. Accessing extended memory requires installing a *supervisor* program, a program that makes sure that no program treads upon another program's territory. OS/2, Windows, and Windows NT are all examples of supervisor programs. Given that these DOS programs didn't want to multitask, however—they only wanted to support themselves in extended memory, and no other programs—they didn't need a very big supervisor program. Examples of early programs that used extended memory were Oracle, Informix, and VDISK.SYS, the "RAM disk" program that came with DOS 3.0 and later versions of DOS up to DOS 5.0, and the IBMCACHE.SYS disk cache program that IBM shipped with the PS/2. These simple supervisors were called *DOS extenders*.

All went well until someone tried to run a DOS extender program in a computer at the same time another supervisor was running—for example, running a DOS extender program in a DOS box under Windows 3.0. That led to Windows and the DOS extender fighting over who got to be the supervisor, as there's only supposed to be one supervisor program active in a PC at a time. The two supervisors slugged it out, and the PC lost. To make matters worse, memory managers must *all* be supervisors, so the simple act of running, say, the 1988 vintage of Oracle (a database) on a system that uses 386 To The Max (a memory manager) would result in a lockup.

As a result, the makers of DOS extender products got together and developed a method whereby DOS extenders could peacefully coexist. The Virtual Control Program Interface, or VCPI to us acronym-lovers, provided an agreement whereby two or more DOS extenders could coexist by defining an organized, agreed-upon method whereby one DOS extender would make a note about how it had memory organized, save that note somewhere, and then hand control over to the second DOS extender, which would then reorganize memory the way it wanted it. When it was time for DOS extender number two to hand control back to DOS extender number one, it did so by restoring things the way it had found it, and then passing the baton back to DOS extender number one.

A lot of a DOS extender's job involves keeping track of which section of memory is being used by each part of the program that it is extending. That's kept with some data structure in memory called *page tables*. Pretty much every DOS extender uses page tables (they *must*, for reasons relating to how the 286 and later chips dole out extended memory; the technical terms for these tables are the LDT, or Local Descriptor Table, and the GDT, or Global Descriptor Table), but they all organize them differently. And that's the big problem: Two programs keeping GDTs that are organized differently are bound to step on one another at some point. But that doesn't happen if we only run one program at a time, and switch the entire memory image when moving from one program to another. This is pretty much what happens with VCPI-compliant programs. They can't multitask with each other, as they each see the GDT in different ways. But they *can* share the GDT in the sense that they can unload their own GDT, and reload another VCPI program's GDT before passing control to that program.

If that isn't clear, consider the following analogy. An assembly plant runs 24 hours/day in three shifts. There's a day manager, an evening manager, and a night manager. Each are totally different in the way that they do their jobs, but they must each use the desk that sits at a good observation point above the assembly line floor. So they've made an agreement: No matter what happens on any manager's shift, that manager's got to leave their desktop clean when he leaves, the way he found it. There's no way that two of these managers could work at the desk at the same time, but they can share it in an eight-hours-at-a-time way. So it is with VCPI-compliant programs: they *context-switch* well, but do not multitask well.

For that reason, VCPI applications cannot work reliably in the multitasking framework of Windows 95. They will probably work in MS-DOS mode, however, for the simple reason that standard mode uses context-switching rather than multitasking—when you activate a DOS program under standard mode, the memory image of standard mode gets swapped out to disk, clearing the desk for the next VCPI program. Examples of programs that follow the VCPI standard are 1-2-3 version 3.0, Paradox 3.5, AutoCAD, FoxPro, and Interleaf Publisher.

One problem you may find with VCPI programs is that there are two ways for VCPI programs to access extended memory. A few use an old method of extended memory access called INT 15 access. Most, however, use a newer method whereby memory is allocated via XMS, the extended memory specification. XMS-type VCPI programs will probably run fine as DOS applications under standard mode. INT 15-type VCPI programs require that you preallocate memory for them with a parameter on your HIMEM.SYS invocation, using the /INT15=*nnnn* switch. For example, if you were planning on running a INT 15-type VCPI app that needed a megabyte of extended memory, then your HIMEM.SYS invocation in the DOS program's CONFIG.SYS would look like this:

```
device=c:\windows\himem.sys /int15=1024
```

But, to continue with the VCPI-versus-DPMI explanation: As you'd expect, the next step was to teach all of these managers how to share a desk—that is, to get all DOS extender programs to agree on how to address the GDT and LDT page tables, so that they could all have page tables in memory at the same time, allowing smooth multitasking of DOS extender applications and Windows. That standard is called the DOS Protected Mode Interface, or DPMI. That's basically the difference between Lotus 1-2-3 version 3.0 and 3.1—3.1 is DPMI compliant, 3.0 is VCPI compliant. DPMI applications should run without trouble in a DOS box under Windows, just so long as you give them XMS memory in the PIF for the DPMI-compliant application, and the vendor has implemented DPMI correctly. Not all software vendors implement DPMI completely correctly, and Lotus is one example. Although 1-2-3 version 3.1 is DPMI compliant, and as such uses extended memory, it still requires that you create an expanded memory page frame in order to run properly. Look for DOS extender applications to be DPMI compliant.

As time progresses, more and more DOS programs that use memory managers will switch to DPMI compliance, and so will run much more easily under Windows. One example is Paradox; version 3.5 was VCPI, and version 4.0 is DPMI.

Multitasking Windows 3.x Applications

Multitasking Windows 3.x programs under Windows 95 shouldn't pose any problems to experienced users of Windows 3.x once you've figured out how to use the different interface. Actually, multitasking Windows 3.x applications carries some pleasant surprises compared to using the same applications under previous versions of Windows:

- Better resource sharing, so that more programs can be open at once without hurting system performance

- Preemptive multitasking with Windows 95 actions, like printing (although not with other Win16 applications)

- Improved resource tracking, so that when you close an application its resources return to the system for use by another application

Better Resource Sharing

The biggest problem with the way that Windows 95 multitasks Win16 programs comes when you move from a machine running Windows 95 to one running Windows 3.x. Since Win95 handles resource sharing so well, you get accustomed to loading cc:Mail, loading the word processor, the spreadsheet, the other word processor, Solitaire, etc., and minimizing them on the desktop rather than closing them.

Now, if you've been using Windows 3.x, you know that loading a bunch of programs and minimizing them on the desktop is one of the fastest and most efficient ways in which you can crash your system. As a matter of fact, you don't even have to load a whole bunch of programs; just load a couple of exceptionally huge spreadsheets or documents, and your system resources will drop dramatically. I found this out the hard way some years ago as a new Windows user. As I watched the words in my document turn to gray blocks, the person looking over my shoulder commented, "Well, I'll be. I didn't know that Windows would *run* with only 3 percent resources." As a matter of fact, it wouldn't—the system crashed shortly after.

In Windows 95, you can load more programs simultaneously than will fit on the Taskbar and the system will keep running. Admittedly, it runs *better* with fewer programs open (you'll get faster response and screen redraws), but you can keep the spreadsheet, document, graphics program, e-mail program, and Solitaire minimized on your desktop and the system should function without any problems—even with only 8MB of RAM.

NOTE Windows 95 does better resource handling with 8MB of RAM than Windows 3.x does with 16MB.

Some Preemptive Multitasking

Recall from earlier in this chapter that when the Virtual Machine Manager interrupts a process when its timeslice is up to pass control to the next process, that's called *preemptive multitasking*. The idea is that, even if a program is in the middle of something, once its timeslice is up, it's *up*—the VMM wrests control of the system from that program and passes it to the next one. Thus, an operating system that supports preemptive multitasking won't make you wait while a multitasking program does any of the following:

- Saves a file
- Prints a document
- Renders a drawing
- Calculates a spreadsheet

The only catch is that Win16 applications don't support preemptive multitasking with each other. Therefore, if you're running Excel 5.0 under Windows 95 and the hourglass comes up, you're stuck until it's done. On the other hand, if you were running Excel for Windows 95 (7.0), then you could do other things while the spreadsheet was calculating, because it would only have control of the system during its timeslice.

Although you don't get full preemptive multitasking until you get Win32 applications, Windows 95 allows for preemptive multitasking between Win16 applications and Windows 95 functions like printing. Therefore, although Win16 applications won't share with each other, they'll share with Windows 95.

Improved Resource Tracking

Every time that you open an application, you use Windows resources— that's the way Windows works. Unfortunately, all too often with previous versions of Windows it *also* worked that the applications wouldn't relinquish their share of the resources once they were done with them; use Designer once in a Windows 3.x session, for example, and your resources are depleted until you restart Windows.

Windows 95 not only makes applications, including Win16 applications, use resources better, it makes the applications return most of the resources when they're through. Thus, if you open all your applications, enough to slow down the system from depleted resources, once you close the applications you get almost all the resources *back* without having to reboot or restart Windows.

On my system, for example, there's 98 percent free resources when I first log on to the system. I open AmiPro and the count goes to 93 percent. Logging onto cc:Mail doesn't take much out of the system; the count remains at 93 percent. Opening Lotus 1-2-3 v. 4 demands more—the count drops to 85 percent. Loading Designer 3.11 drops the count to 81 percent. From there, I load Word 6.0 for Windows (75 percent), an undemanding PaintShop Pro (75 percent), another copy of Designer so I can compare pictures easily (one of the few drawbacks of that version is that it doesn't have a Window feature to let you flip between files) that puts me down to 70 percent, and so on. The system, by the way, is working just fine—not even slow screens.

The good part is what happens when I start *closing* all these applications. Close the second copy of Designer—back to 74 percent. Closing PaintShop Pro doesn't increase the count, but then it didn't decrease it either in the first place. When I shut down Word 6.0, the count's up to 79 percent. When I close the first copy of Designer, the count goes back to 83 percent, and after closing Lotus we're back to 88 percent... After closing everything down I can get system resources back to 93 percent. I've lost 5 percent from when I started, but that's better than older versions of Windows can do.

Why Do I Still Have .INI Files?

The Registry (discussed earlier in this book) takes over the job of containing the user and system configuration information from the .INI files that you came to know and love in previous versions of Windows. The only trouble is, those .INI files are still there—as are all the .INI files belonging to each Win16 program (AMIPRO.INI, PSP.INI, etc.). If Windows 95 has the Registry, why do you still have .INI files?

The answer is backward compatibility. Win16 programs don't know how to access the Registry, so they must get their system and user information from WIN.INI and SYSTEM.INI, as well as their specific program information from their own .INI file. Win16 applications don't know or care that the Registry exists, except as something that gives them an operating system to work in.

Editing a Program .INI File

Since Win16 files can't see the Registry, to configure a Win16 application, you'll need to edit its .INI file in Notepad (if the configuration you want is not available from the application itself). For example, I use a graphics program called PaintShop Pro to edit screen captures. PSP remembers where you pulled your last file from and returns to that directory to open files. Most of the time, this is a convenience, but when at one point our ISDN connection was having a bad hair day and the last drive I'd accessed was across the connection, it meant that, for all practical purposes, the program was unusable. I could start it up, but when I tried to open a file it went looking for the inaccessible networked drive, and looking, and looking... the program never admitted that it couldn't find the drive but kept searching until I shut the program down.

To get around this, I needed to change the default open drive, but there was no way to do this from within the program without opening a file—which I couldn't do. So, I opened up the Notepad (type **notepad** in the Run... dialog box accessible from the Start menu) to edit the file.

Now, .INI files are usually in the program directory (or, if not there, the Windows directory). I found it where I expected, and when I opened PSP.INI I saw the following:

```
[Paint Shop Pro]
OpenDir=H:\WINDOW~1\PICS
FileData=0,17
Gamma=1.25
Undo=1
SaveDir=H:\WINDOW~1\PICS
```

Many program's .INI files are pretty straightforward, as you can see here, and it was pretty easy to see where the change should be made. I edited the OpenDir entry so that it read from the local C: drive, and saved the file. The next time I opened the application, it was able to open files without any problem because it was no longer looking for an inaccessible drive.

Running DOS Diagnostic Programs

Thus far in this chapter, we've talked about memory management and how to set up DOS and Windows 3.x programs for best use under Windows 95. To finish, we'll discuss how to use an unusual class of DOS programs—diagnostics—under Windows 95.

Why Use DOS Diagnostics?

Windows 95 comes with some disk maintenance software. Why use anything else? The best reason is that diagnostics may be more accurate (not necessarily, but it's possible) when they're written by someone other than the company who designed the operating system. Just as the person proofing text shouldn't be the person who wrote it, machine diagnostics may perform a harder test when written by a third-party vendor than one written by the author of the operating system.

In addition, the maintenance tools that come with 95 are limited. You have a defragger, a disk scanner, and compression software, and, so far as hard disk maintenance goes, that's it. There's no memory testing, and no slow disk testing. Therefore, to do serious testing of your hardware, you need third-party diagnostics.

Tips for Running Diagnostics

The first consideration about running diagnostic software—programs that are intended to isolate hardware problems on your PC—is to make sure that there's as little going on in the PC as possible. To that end, don't try to run diagnostics from a DOS prompt in Windows, because at the very least you have all the graphical software loaded, probably network drivers, and so forth. Instead, before running diagnostics, I'd recommend booting the disk to Safe Mode command prompt only (press F8 when you see the "Starting Windows 95..." message during the boot process, and choose that option from the startup menu). That way, you'll have about as vanilla a configuration as you can get: no network, no GUI, no other programs running in the background.

Second, as always, if you're going to run diagnostics, make them a serious test. Most diagnostic tests of disks or memory have a slow mode and a fast mode. To do a real exhaustive test of your PC's hardware, choose the slow mode and be prepared for it to take a while. ("A while" can mean all night for a good memory test to see if your SIMMs are working properly, or even a couple of days to test a 1GB+ hard disk.)

That's about it for running legacy applications under Windows 95. Now go grab that software and get to it!

INDEX

Note to the Reader: Throughout this index **boldfaced** page numbers indicate the primary discussion of a topic. *Italicized* page numbers indicate illustrations.

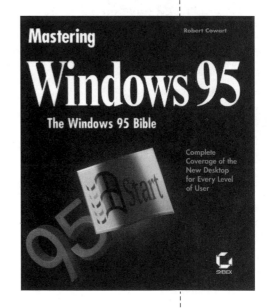

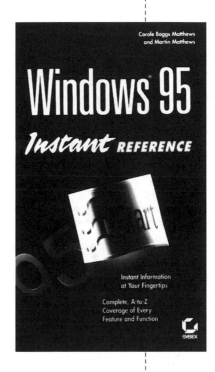

AllMicro

ANTI-VIRUS SURVIVAL KIT ™

With dozens of new and deadly viruses being unleashed weekly, the most effective way to keep your computer protected is to be armed with a powerful arsenal of virus-fighting weapons. That's why the AllMicro Anti-Virus Survival Kit has **FOUR LEVELS OF DEFENSE** to help keep your PC virus-free and your data safe.

> *"I found the product better than F-PROT, MACAFEE, VSD, Norton, Central Point and even Anyware AntiVirus.*
>
> *It detects thousands more viruses than the competitors. And it eliminates the virus without wiping out half of your file!"*
>
> **Chuck Gallagher**
> **Johns Hopkins Hospital**

LEVEL 1 - SOFTWARE
- Protects DOS, Windows & Windows 95 Systems
- Fast Detection & Elimination of over 8,200 viruses
- Protection Against As-Yet-Unknown Viruses
- Scans Compressed/Zipped Files

LEVEL 2 - UPDATES
- Available with optional 1-year subscription service

LEVEL 3 - EMERGENCY TEAM
- Customized cures for new viruses made available as quickly as within 48 hours at no charge

LEVEL 4 - DATA RECOVERY
- AllMicro's Anti-Virus Survival Kit is equipped with **RESCUE**, the foremost data recovery utility available. It's your *ultimate* defense against data loss.

FIX YOUR WINDOWS ...FAST!

If you use Windows 95, you need Skylight™!

Skylight is the #1 rated Windows diagnostic that tunes, optimizes and troubleshoots Windows for maximum speed and performance. Edits all .INI files safely. Graphically displays how Windows 95 is actually using memory, system metrics, GDI heap usage, and what programs are using which system resources… plus much more, with hundreds of reports!

Features

- Editing and Context Sensitive Help for Word Perfect, Windows for WorkGroups & Norton Desktop .INI Files. No other program has this complete support!
- Windows System Interrogator troubleshoots System .INI and WIN .INI files.
- Diagnose Windows from the DOS prompt even if Windows won't load.
- Displays memory usage as Windows sees and uses it.
- Graphical display of memory shows you where programs are loaded.

PC MAGAZINE
Editor's Choice July 1993

"SKYLIGHT the Windows Program, is a model of elegance and clarity… Among the Windows based reporting tools, the Editors' Choice is … SKYLIGHT."

Call Today for More Information and Special Discounts for Sybex Customers

1-800-653-4933

AllMicro

18820 US Hwy 19 N #215
Clearwater, FL 34624
International: (813) 539-7283
FAX: (813) 531-0200

SYX

To Use This CD

The enclosed CD works best from within Windows 95. To see and hear the author's video instruction files (the .AVI files), we recommend that you have at least a double-speed CD-ROM player and a 486 66-MHz machine with a sound card.

Load the CD into your computer's CD player, go to My Computer on your Windows 95 desktop, and click on your CD drive (drive D in most cases). To use the utility programs from AllMicro, go to the AV folder (for the AntiVirus program) or the Skylight folder (for the Skylight diagnostic program) and double-click on Setup to install the program. Refer to the program's help files or documentation files for instructions on using the program. To view one of the author's .AVI files (instructional videos), go to the Videos folder and double-click on the filename you want. You must be running Windows 95 or Video for Windows to view the .AVI files.

Descriptions of the videos and programs can be found on the inside front cover of this book.

Warranty

SYBEX warrants the enclosed CD-ROM to be free of physical defects for a period of ninety (90) days after purchase. If you discover a defect in the CD during this warranty period, you can obtain a replacement CD at no charge by sending the defective CD, postage prepaid, with proof of purchase to:

SYBEX Inc.
Customer Service Department
2021 Challenger Drive
Alameda, CA 94501
phone: (800)227-2346
fax: (510) 523-2373

After the 90-day period, you can obtain a replacement CD by sending us the defective CD, proof of purchase, and a check or money order for $10, payable to SYBEX.

Disclaimer

SYBEX makes no warranty or representation, either express or implied, with respect to this medium or its contents, its quality, performance, merchantability, or fitness for a particular purpose. In no event will SYBEX, its distributors, or dealers be liable for direct, indirect, special, incidental, or consequential damages arising out of the use of or inability to use the software even if advised of the possibility of such damage.

The exclusion of implied warranties is not permitted by some states. Therefore, the above exclusion may not apply to you. This warranty provides you with specific legal rights; there may be other rights that you may have that vary from state to state.